AN

ELEMENTARY TREATISE

ON

LOGIC;

INCLUDING

PART I. ANALYSIS OF FORMULÆ.—PART II. METHOD.

WITH AN

APPENDIX OF EXAMPLES

FOR ANALYSIS AND CRITICISM.

AND

A COPIOUS INDEX OF TERMS AND SUBJECTS.

DESIGNED FOR THE USE OF SCHOOLS AND COLLEGES AS WELL AS FOR PRIVATE STUDY AND USE.

BY

W. D. WILSON, D. D.,

TRINITY PROFESSOR OF CHRISTIAN ETHICS, AND PROFESSOR OF LOGIC, OF INTELLECTUAL PHILOSOPHY, AND OF HISTORY IN HOBART FREE COLLEGE, AT GENEVA, WESTERN NEW YORK.

"Logic—the Mathematics of Thought."—Cousin.

NEW YORK:
D. APPLETON AND COMPANY,
346 & 348 BROADWAY.
LONDON: 16 LITTLE BRITAIN.
M.DCCC.LVI.

PREFACE.

The following work has grown out of my necessities and my experience as a teacher. When, several years ago, I accepted a professorship, the duties of which required me to teach Logic, I could nowhere find a text-book that seemed to me to satisfy the demands of the science.

Nor was this feeling peculiar to myself. Mr. Thompson, in his excellent work on "*The Necessary Laws of Thought*," begins his preface with saying: "The system of pure Logic, or analytic that has been universally accepted for centuries past, is very defective as an instrument for the analysis of natural reasoning. Arguments that commend themselves to any untaught mind as valid and practically important, have no place in a system that professedly includes all reasoning whatever; and an attempt to reduce to its technical forms the first few pages of any scientific work, has generally ended in failure and disgust."

It would not be difficult to produce almost any amount of testimony to the prevalence of a similar feeling with regard to the present state of literature in this department of science and instruction.

Of all the efforts which have recently been made to remedy this deficiency, two can be considered as requiring notice in this place: that of Prof. De Morgan, and that of Sir Wil-

LIAM HAMILTON. The work of Mr. Thompson just referred to, is, in its essential features, little, if any thing, more than an exposition of Sir William's theory.

Prof. De Morgan has earned a name in his own department (mathematics), which scholars hereafter will be pleased to remember and contemplate. But philosophy, in any of its departments, is not his calling. His theory is essentially numerical. He measures every thing by numerical quantity rather than logical. For the purposes of calculation, 2 X, X, and X^2 are truly different terms, and can no more be substituted for each other than X, Y and Z. In this case, X, Y and Z, 2 X and X^2, are assumed as representing simply number; that is, a number of units. Now, units have no individual properties—nothing to distinguish one from another. Much less have they any separable accidents; and the only difference, therefore, between the sums for which X, Y, Z, &c., stand, is in the number of units comprehended in each sum, and, consequently, 2 X and X—the one being twice as much as the other—are no more the same than X and Y, when they represent those different quantities.

But the words or symbols used in Logic represent the conceptions that we form of objects of thought, which are not units merely, but individuals also, having each of them inseparable and peculiar properties of their own, upon which not only their adequate conception, but any use which we can make of that conception in the Formula, whether of mediate or of immediate deduction, depends. This fact has been overlooked in Prof. De Morgan's Formal Logic, to an extent which deprives it of any great value as a system.

Perhaps the best test of any theory, is a comparison of its deductions with the obvious facts and first principles of knowledge. De Morgan refers to an anecdote told of Zerah Colburn, which relates, that having been asked how many black beans would make ten white ones, he replied—"*ten if you skin 'em!*" "But," adds De Morgan, "the ten skinned beans would not be the *same beans* as before—except, indeed, to those to whom black is white."—(p. 54 Formal Logic.]

In the common sense of mankind, the beans *are the same* after being skinned. Philosophy may undertake to correct the common sense notions of mankind, but Logic cannot. And with how much success philosophy can pursue such an attempt we will not now undertake to decide. But in this case it cannot succeed. The conclusion, if established, would be generalized at once—as in fact it ought to be—and we should have the doctrine that identity depends upon the separable accidents; and then all science, all knowledge, ethics, and religion, too, will be afloat and dissolved into fragments. A man's separable accidents change from day to day; consequently his identity changes. He is not the same man to-day that he was yesterday —is not bound to fulfil the contracts of yesterday, or to suffer the penalty due to its transgression.

A theory that not only gives such results, but openly avows them, may be safely considered *ab absurdo.*

I cannot but regard Sir William Hamilton's theory as equally unfounded.

Sir William's name is one of the greatest of the present century of great names in philosophy. His rank will undoubtedly be in the first class—with Aristotle, Plato, Descartes, Locke, and Cousin—the few great names that stud the galaxy of history. For an acquaintance with the learning and works of others in the department of speculative philosophy, he stands unrivalled, and probably will never be surpassed. But I have not been able to form any such high estimate of his attempts at originality.

He assumes that there may be affirmative judgments with distributed predicates. This is so. But, as I have shown (Part I, chap. II, sec. 3.—See also p. 65, § 244), this is never done by the mere force of the affirmative copula. The fact, if fact it be, in any case, must always be indicated by something not essential to the judgment, and I have provided for all such cases—(p. 124, § 498—see 456).

But, again, he assumes that there may be negative judgments with undistributed predicates. To this I have given what I think will be found a sufficient answer in p. 67 § 254 and the *note*. A subject is excluded from a Predicate only because it has not the Essentia of the class-conception denoted by that predicate. But the Essentia of one part of the individuals contained in it, can never be different from that of another. Hence, whatever would exclude a subject from a part of the predicate—that is, the predicate as an undistributed term—would exclude it for the whole of the predicate as a distributed term.

If Sir William's theories were correct on these points, doubtless we should be obliged to abandon the old nomenclature altogether and begin anew; as, indeed, Sir William proposes to do. But believing as I do, and for the reasons given, that his theory of quantification is fundamentally wrong, I have adhered to the old doctrine, so modifying the statement and exposition of it as to provide for the cases which he had regarded as demanding the new theory.

It will also be observed, that in the following treatise I have made more account of Method than recent writers have been generally inclined to do. Many of them, in fact, have omitted it entirely. Perhaps the manner in which it had been treated by the scholastic writers, may serve, in some measure, as a justification for the estimate in which the modern authors have held that part of Logical Science. But not only is it of the utmost importance in itself; there is, moreover, as I conceive, no way of obviating the objection to devoting so much time as is requisite to the mastery of what Whately and others with him who omit method altogether, have included in their treatises, without revising that part of Logic which is properly denoted by the word Method, and in thus giving a practical direction and applicability to the whole study. This is what I have attempted to do in the part on Method, and I hope that scholars and teachers will agree with me in the esti mate I have placed upon the subject.

If Logic is as COUSIN has remarked, "the Mathematics of thought," it must comprehend not only an analysis of the Formula which we use in thinking, but also the methods of the successful application of these Formulæ, and the discussion of Methods will require some consideration of the Matter to which they are to be applied, and the faculties by which we apply them.

As the Analytic of Formulæ may be compared to Geometry, so Method may with equal propriety be compared to Arithmetic, Algebra, and the Calculus in pure Mathematics—the former treats of Form in Space, considered simply as continuous quantity; the latter of methods of finding results in discrete quantity. Such Methods are not only Addition, Subtraction, Multiplication and Division, Involution and Evolution, but also the Binomial Theorem, the system of Indeterminate Coëfficients, and all the Methods, in short, of Differentiation and Integration. Every mathematician knows that the truth of the result depends upon two conditions, (1.) that the Method be applied to proper matter; and (2.) that the Methods themselves are legitimate.

I have also provided in the Appendix a liberal supply of examples for Praxis. These examples may not be sufficient to illustrate every principle and formula, as, from the necessities of the case, they are for the most part ultimate parts in themselves, and do not admit of the application of some of those principles which relate to the construction of more comprehensive wholes. Our limits will not allow of the insertion of examples illustrative of some of the principles of Method which we have described. Such examples can be found only in the books and treatises which are altogether too long to be reprinted here. Nor can they be represented in any brief or abstract, in such a way as to test the principle or be of use in criticising the examples themselves.

I have also divided these examples into classes, so that, if thought best, they may be used as the student progresses in the Analysis of Formulæ—the first four sections being arranged with a view to corresponding divisions of Part I. of this work.

Among the many analogies between Logic and Grammar, no one is more important and striking than that property in common from which it results; that as in the one case, so in the other, there is scarcely the possibility of getting a thorough knowledge of principles and formula without much experience in what in Grammar we call *parsing*. This practice in Logic has come to be called *Praxis*. It consists in a careful analysis of all argumentative sentences with reference to the logical connection and sequence of the judgments which they express, the methods of argumentation, and the adaptation of the Methods to the matter.

But the very process by which we thus perfect our knowledge of the Principles and Formulæ into familiarity with their use, is precisely that which we are obliged to practise in all cases where we apply our Logic at all in the purposes and uses of life. Praxis only makes perfect in the art of using our faculties and our knowledge in the wider and more important spheres for which our studies are designed to fit us.

It is, I believe, owing to the neglect of Praxis, together with the practical difficulty (which nothing but much practice can remove) of putting propositions into a Formal shape, that the impression that a large part of the arguments in every book to which the mind assents, cannot, nevertheless, be put into any one of the known and recognized Formulæ, has become so general.

Language seldom expresses all that is in the thoughts, and

still more seldom all that is implied in what is actually said. Rules of rhetoric and taste would forbid such prolixity, even if it were possible. But Logic *supposes* nothing. It demands that all that is in the thought should be fully and explicitly stated. And one who has given a thorough logical analysis to any production, must of necessity understand it as well as he who wrote it, and probably, in nine cases out of ten at least, he would really understand it much better. He must understand it *thoroughly*, which is certainly more than can in all cases with propriety be said of the author himself. How many Enthymemes are uttered, the suppressed premises of which are wholly unknown and unsuspected to him who expresses the Enthymeme? How many conditionals, the sequences of which are unknown to the writer or speaker himself? But all the latent elements of these imperfect arguments must have been brought out, stated, and examined by him who has gone through with a thorough logical criticism of the production.

The student and the teacher likewise will probably find the chapter on Methods of instruction the least full and satisfactory of any. The reason for this is assigned in the chapter itself. I could not make it full and satisfactory without going further than unity of plan would permit into the department of Rhetoric, nor (waiving that objection), could I go into the subject so fully as such a modification of my general subject would require, without expanding the volume beyond all reasonable bounds. And, after much deliberation, I have decided to send it out as it is, regarding it as the best that I can make of the matter now and under the present circumstances. Such as it is, however, I trust that it will not be found unworthy of attention and diligent study.

In conclusion, I wish to express my decided conviction not only of the usefulness of Logic as an instrument, but also that it needs more attention and more time than any work on the subject hitherto given to the public, has seemed to me to deserve. It is to all the speculative sciences, every branch of knowledge except mathematics, what arithmetic and algebra are to the Mathematics themselves—as an instrument in constructing those sciences—and it is as necessary as grammar itself to rhetoric, and all the departments of literary criticism, dialectics, and oratory.

In speaking thus of the importance of the science, and of a thorough education in it, I am not of course advocating the introduction of its technicalities and Formulæ into public speaking and writing; the analogy of grammar and rhetoric holds here also. No one, in speaking or writing, stops to parse his words, or to name every figure of speech which he uses, or every rule of rhetoric which he may have had in mind when he wrote or spoke. No more is it expected that the same thing should be done in regard to Logic. Here, as elsewhere, it may be said, the greatest art is to conceal art—to write with a perfect knowledge of all the terms and principles of the science of writing, and yet never thrust them forward in such a way as to be offensive to good taste, or vexatious to the reader.

To reason *logically* is not the same as to reason *formally*. All good reasoning is of necessity logical, just as all good writing must fulfil the rules and requirements of grammar and rhetoric. But it is not expected that the arguments will always be stated in the precise forms that are given in this book; nor that all that is requisite to their completion shall be expressly given. Logic *supposes* nothing. It allows of no omissions—no ellipses. On the contrary, rhetoric, good taste, brevity, and more than all, the scantiness of thought in the mind of the speaker, make this necessary. Logic teaches what these omissions are, how they are to be restored or produced to fill up the vacancies. And thus the reasoning fulfils the Formula—becomes formal—or, as it is commonly but very improperly called, logical. But nothing can be more idle than the objection to the study of Logic, based upon the fact that its

Formulæ and technicalities do not appear, and are not expected to appear, in the written or published discourse of ordinary life. One might with as much propriety object to the study of the Binomial Theorem, on the ground that in equations of the second degree, we seldom or never find the square of the Binomial complete. Without these Formulæ and technicalities, what *is* written and said can never be comprehended or intelligibly discussed.

But, after all, it must be distinctly considered that Logic, like the pure Mathematics, is only a means and not an end. The pursuit of the study may be valuable as a discipline. Its results will be of great service to any one who has thoroughly comprehended them. But if one looks to its Formulæ as a substitute for common sense in the common affairs of life, or of investigation in the higher pursuits of literature and science, or of patient and laborious thought anywhere, he will be sadly disappointed.

W. D. WILSON.

GENEVA, Dec., 1855.

CONTENTS.

PART I.

ANALYSIS OF FORMULÆ.

CHAPTER I.

OF TERMS.

CHAPTER II.

OF PROPOSITIONS.

CHAPTER III.

OF SYLLOGISMS.

CHAPTER IV.

OF FALLACIES.

PART II.

LOGICAL METHODS.

CHAPTER I.

OF THE ELEMENTS OF METHOD.

CHAPTER II.

METHODS OF INVESTIGATION.

CHAPTER III.

METHODS OF PROOF AND REFUTATON.

CHAPTER IV.

METHODS OF INSTRUCTION AND CRITICISM.

APPENDIX OF EXAMPLES FOR CRITICISM.

LOGIC.

INTRODUCTION.

1. The word Logic has been used in many different senses, and most treatises on the subject have included matter belonging to widely different spheres of thought and inquiry. It sometimes denotes the science which explains the laws of thought merely. It is sometimes used to denote the art of convincing and persuading. It has been thought to imply the consideration of the means of discovering truth, and also the general principles of Method.

Logic variously defined.

2. Philosophy was in existence and cultivated some time before Logic appeared as a distinct Science or Art. The reason is obvious. Men do not seek a Canon of Truth until they feel the danger of error, and have reaped the bitter fruits of its experience. The earliest schools of Greek Philosophy (and of the Hindoo Philosophy we cannot now speak, for want of chronological data)—the Ionian and the Pythagorean—argued and dogmatized without fear or expectation of contradiction; they were too sanguine and confident to feel the need of Logic.

Philosophy before Logic.

3. But as soon as the doctrines of these two schools came into conflict, some Canon, or test, of truth was found to be necessary. Not only terms in which to discuss the points at issue, but an inspection of first principles, and of the processes of deduction from them, came to be regarded as indispensable to the discovery of truth, and the proper testing of the means by which it may be proved to be true.

The origin of Logic.

4. No system of Logic, however, was formally developed and digested until Aristotle. Aristotle* himself, however, says Zeno the Eleatic, was the inventor of Logic, or rather Dialectics, Διαλεκτική.

Aristotle the Author of the first system.

5. As soon, however, as Philosophy had sufficiently explored the field which it had to occupy, to form any definite idea of what is contained in it, we find Plato dividing it into three cöordinate branches:—Physic, Ethic, and Logic;†—the former including all of the Natural Sciences; the second, all that concern the relations and duties of man; and the latter, Logic, the science of mind, and the rules by which its activity is to be guided to the proper results.

Threefold division of Philosophy.

6. Logic is derived from the Greek Λόγος, and in the sense used by Plato, it means whatever pertains to the Mind, the Reason, the immaterial power or faculty which is manifested in the words and speech of men. Logic was used to denote the whole of what, in modern times, has been called Intellectual Philosophy, or Metaphysics.

Logic, how used by Plato.

7. But Intellectual Philosophy or Metaphysics, in this broad extent of meaning, includes at least three distinct departments of science.

(1.) *Psychology*, as it is called, describing the facts of the mind, of which we are immediately conscious;

* Sext. Empir. adv. Math. B. vii. c. 1.
† Diog. Laert., Procem. seg. 18.

such as Sensation, Perception, Abstraction, Conception, Association, Imagination, Memory, Intuition, Judgment, Inference, &c. Psychology.

(2.) *Metaphysics* proper, which investigates the necessary *a priori* conditions and laws of thought, and the ideas which determine cognition and judgment, and those necessary axioms, or first principles, which are assumed in all sciences, and underlie them, as the ground of their possibility and reality. Metaphysics.

And (3.) *Logic;* which treats of the relations of conceptions to one another; the deduction of secondary from primary and intuitive judgments, and the laws of Synthesis, by which truths are constructed into systems. Logic in this narrower sense.

8. The last element of this definition is what has usually been called METHOD; and latterly there has been a tendency to regard it as a science by itself. Excluding Method, therefore, from our definition, Logic may be defined as the *Science of Deductive Thinking.* Method not included latterly.

9. As there may be true and legitimate deductions as well as such as are false and delusive, there must be a *Science* of deduction, by which the true may be distinguished from the false; and the laws and formulas of deduction itself so explained and developed, as to enable one to select and pursue those methods which lead to right conclusions, and avoid those that are fallacious. Logic a *Science.*

10. But it is necessary for the practical benefits of the science, to take some note of language, or the words and signs by which thinking is expressed; of the matter of which we think and reason; and especially of the various ways in which the Formulæ may be used in the construction of what, in popular language, are called Arguments; these form the transition from Logic, as a Science, to Logic as an Art. Logic, as an Art, is more properly called *Dialectics* or *Rhetoric.* It is, of course, with Its relation to the *Art* of Dialectics or Rhetoric.

Logic as a Science, that we have chiefly to do in this volume.

11. The purpose which we have now before us does not lead us to regard Logic as a means of discovery, or of so constructing such methods of argumentation, as are used in speeches and books, as to be most successful in a dialectic point of view; not, in short, to teach directly *how to reason well*, but rather what is good reasoning, and why it is so.

The Science teaches what is good reasoning.

12. In this view, Logic sustains about the same relation to public writing and speaking that Grammar does, or that Moral Science sustains to good morals; the Science of Music to good singing; or anatomy and physiology to the principles of health and the practice of Medicine and Surgery.*

Logic analogous to Grammar, &c., as a Science.

13. As in Grammar, for example, we need some terms and names, by which to represent the parts of speech, and the rules determining the inflection and relation of each part to others, and to the whole sentence; so in Logic we need names for each part of a process of thought, and rules and laws determining their relation, both for the purpose of discussing and analyzing the thoughts of others, and to assist in the due expression of our own. Without such aids it is impossible to study Rhetoric and Oratory, or Psychology and Metaphysics with much success; and they are of the greatest importance in all departments of study and instruction.

Logic as an instrument of criticism.

14. There is obviously a distinction between a process of thought and the matter about which the thoughts are occupied; the order, arrangement, and dependence of the thoughts upon one another

Form and Matter of thinking.

* Of course one may speak without knowing Grammar, or sing without a knowledge of the scientific principles of harmony and melody. But he could speak and sing much better with such knowledge, and he could hardly teach or compose without it.

may remain the same, and the matter be different; and *vice versa*, the matter may remain the same, and the order and sequence of the thoughts be different. Hence the distinction between the *Form* of an argument, or processes of thought, and the *Matter;* the Form denotes merely the order, dependence, and arrangement of the thoughts. Thus, if I say, "men are mortal, and therefore they should prepare for death;" and "men should prepare for death because they are mortal;" the Matter would be the same in each case, but the form would be different. But if I should say, "men are mortal, therefore they should prepare for death;" and "spring is coming, therefore we should prepare for summer;" the Form would be the same in both instances, but they would differ in matter.

15. But again, in any continuous process of argumentation, as in a Speech, an Essay, or a Book, these Forms or Formulæ may be combined and used in different relations, and follow each other in different order. Hence, besides the Matter and Form of an argument, we have to consider also the *Method;* that is, the way in which the Forms are used. Thus, if I wish to prove that four times twenty-five is one hundred, I may do it by writing twenty-five four times, each directly under the other, and then *add them up;* or, by writing it once with a four under it, and then *multiply*, the result will be the same in each case, but the Method will be different; the former is the Method of Addition, the latter of Multiplication. **Method.**

16. Logic is called *Formal*, and sometimes *Analytic*, when it investigates the varieties and laws of the Formulæ. When it goes farther and inquires into the grounds of the validity of these Formulæ, it is called *Rational;* and when it goes one step farther, and takes into consideration the diversities of the various kinds of matter, and the peculiarities in the forms of expression by which that matter is repre- **Formal Logic.** **Rational.**

sented, and the application of Formulæ as modified by the matter, it becomes what we call *Applied* Logic.

Applied.

17. Logic always presupposes, or takes for granted, certain premises or starting-points; the truth or falsehood of which it belongs to other branches of science to determine. It is concerned with the truth of Propositions, only so far as they are given as resulting from certain others. But the first elements of reasoning, the primary facts, it takes from other branches of knowledge, as they have been ascertained and established in those branches representing them. It does not undertake to prove the self-evident axioms or the primary facts of science in any department; but with those axioms and facts, given in philosophy and experience, it directs and guides the mind at every step, to its most remote results, to the highest generalizations, and to the most comprehensive truths; as well as in every application of those truths to the practical purposes of life.

Logic presupposes some truths.

How far concerned with the truth of Propositions.

Logic therefore does not supersede, but rather presupposes, a knowledge (derived from other sources) of the subject matter with which our minds may be occupied. It simply explains the laws by which the mind is guided in arranging and combining that matter into scientific systems, and in its application to the various purposes and uses of life.

It explains laws and processes.

18. Nor, again, does Logic propose a new way for doing what we have been accustomed to do in another. From the earliest development of intellect, and the very commencement of intellectual activity, the mind has been accustomed to think and to draw inferences, or think deductively; so that we have all been long in the practice of Logic, before we begin the study of its science.

Logic not a new way of reasoning.

19. Those forms and processes in which we proceed

from one thought to another, which depends upon the preceding, are called in the popular language Arguments. How long soever or how complicated soever they may be, Formulæ and Method are thus undistinguished from each other. The Formulæ, or separate processes, each of which has one subject and but one, are called in Logical language, *Syllogisms;* the word is of Greek origin, and signifies a putting together for the sake of a Conclusion.

Syllogisms

20. A Syllogism, therefore, first presents itself to our reflective thought as a completed thing; having already all of its parts, and most of them in their legitimate places, and connected with the other parts. Each argument consists of several *Propositions;* one of which we call a *Conclusion*, and the others the *Premises;* these Propositions consist most of them of two *terms* and a *Copula*. One term, called the *Subject*, denotes that about which we are speaking; the other, called the *Predicate*, denotes what we say of it; and the *Copula* is the verb affirming or denying the agreement between the Subject and Predicate: as A is B, or A is not B. Here "*A*" is the Subject, "*B*" is the Predicate, and "*is*" and "*is not*" the Copula; the former of which is called the *Affirmative* and the latter the *Negative* Copula.

The parts of a Syllogism.

The parts of a Proposition.

Subject—Predicate.

Copula; Affirmative and Negative.

21. That act of the mind by which the Copula is affirmed or denied, is called a *Judgment*, or when expressed in words, a *Proposition*. "A" and "B" are called Terms, and that in the mind which they represent, is called a *Cognition*, or a *Conception*.

A Judgment.

Terms, Conceptions or Cognitions.

We come therefore to *Conceptions* or *Cognitions*, as the simplest element with which Logic, in our use of the word is concerned, and the point of departure with which we must commence in the methodical construction of the Science.

Conceptions the starting-point.

Logic presupposes Psychology.

22. Logic, however, presupposes some knowledge of Psychology, and we must look to that for the explanation of some of the facts and terms which it assumes as already known. These, however, for the sake of completeness, we will run over in a very cursory manner.

PART I.

ANALYSIS OF FORMULA.

CHAPTER I.

OF TERMS.

23. TERMS are the words or signs by which any conception or cognition is expressed, for the purpose of conveying it from one mind to another. Terms defined.

SECTION I.

Of Conceptions.

24. When we look at any object an act of the mind ensues, which in psychology is called *perceiving*—and the result of that act is called a PERCEPTION. But the mind retains the result of that act after the object has been removed from any physical connection with us, and the mind can recall it at pleasure. In this view of it, that result is called a CONCEPTION or a COGNITION. Perceptions.

25. Perception is an instantaneous act, and on each occasion, when the same object is presented anew to the senses, we perceive it anew, and form anew, or again, a cognition of it. We have thus at the second time a new or second per- An instantaneous act

ception, which the mind compares with the first, and gives the judgment of identity in regard to the object which occasioned them.

Identity and diversity of objects perceived.

26. But if the perceptions differ so much or in such ways as to imply a difference in any of the inseparable properties of the object perceived, the mind conceives the objects as diverse from each other.

Different cognitions of the same object.

27. In Logic we regard the different cognitions of the same object as one and the same cognition, except when we wish to take into consideration the changes which the object itself may undergo, by a change of those separable accidents and modes of existence, which may be changed without changing the identity of the object itself.

Distinction between cognition and conception.

28. A distinction is sometimes made in the use of the words "*cognition*" and "*conception*," by which the former is used to denote the idea of one individual object only: as "*a man*," "*a pen*," &c.; and conception, the idea of a class: as "*mankind*," "*villages*," "*pens*," &c. I shall not take pains to adhere to this distinction very closely; although I shall never employ the word "cognition" to denote the idea of a class. I shall, however, very often use the word "conception" when I mean to refer to the idea or cognition of an individual thing only.

Conceptions adequate and inadequate.

29. A *conception* or a *cognition* may be *adequate* or *inadequate*. It is adequate only when it includes, so that we may be said to know, all the properties, uses, purposes, and the history of the object; otherwise it is, strictly speaking, inadequate.

Diverse sensations requisite to an adequate conception.

30. No one of the senses by itself and alone can ever enable us to form an adequate conception of any object. We *see* its color; we *smell* its odor; we *taste* its flavor; we *feel* its density and its smoothness, &c. Nor can we ever know,

or form an adequate conception, of any considerable proportion of the objects with which human knowledge is occupied, by any contact of those objects with our own senses. Hence we have to rely upon the testimony of others, historians, travellers, and observers in every department of science, for by far the largest part of what we know.

31. Moreover, there are many objects of thought of which we have conceptions, which however never have and never can have any connection with the external senses, as means of cognition; such as truth, justice, virtue, eternity, &c. These objects of thought are sometimes called IDEAS, and are said to be furnished by the Reason itself.

Conceptions of Ideas.

32. It would appear that man can have but very few, if any, conceptions or cognitions that are strictly and absolutely adequate; and hence we are accustomed to call those "*inadequate*" only, which are not sufficient for the purpose for which the conception itself is used. Thus, if one were writing a treatise upon iron, and did not know, or have as a part of his conception of iron, its property of becoming magnetized, his conception would be inadequate. But if his object was merely to describe its adaptedness to some particular purpose, not at all affected by its magnetic properties, his conception might be adequate for that purpose; without including a knowledge of its susceptibility to magnetic influences.

Few conceptions *absolutely* adequate.

33. Logic requires, and always presupposes, that all conceptions which are introduced as elements of its Formulæ, are adequate in this secondary and limited sense. And if any conception is not adequate, it must be rendered so by further acquaintance with the object of thought which it represents to the mind, and the conception can be conveyed adequately to the minds of others by means of definitions, description, &c.

Conceptions, how made adequate.

34. The objects of which our cognitions are formed,

are distinguished as *possible*, *impossible*, and *real*. An object is said to be real when it has an actual existence. It is said to be possible when it is not known to have any existence, but is nevertheless supposed to have the possibility of existing; thus all realities were merely possible before they were brought into actual existence. But an object of thought which can never exist, is called impossible, as a triangle with only two sides.

Objects of thought *possible*, *impossible*, and *real*.

35. Realities, or things real, have also been distinguished into two classes: *the Realities of Being* and *the Realities of Truth*. Mind, and all the forms of material existence, are considered as Realities of Being or Existence. But, besides justice, virtue, &c., which exist only as properties of some intelligent being; there are also certain objects of thought, as time, space, the point, the line, &c., and the first axioms of all knowledge, as the whole is equal to the sum of its parts, &c., which have no *substantial* existence, and from their very nature they can have none. Nor yet are they considered as merely the properties of any substance, whether material or immaterial. Their reality would remain unchanged even if there were no mind in existence to comprehend them. They are called *Realities of Truth*.

Realities of Being and of Truth.

36. It has sometimes been said, that we can have no conception of the impossible. But we must make a distinction between a conception and the construction of an image of the object in the mind. An image of the impossible we cannot have, but a conception we may have; for we use the word conception to denote any thing of which we can speak. If, therefore, we can speak of that which is impossible, we can have a conception of it, which comprehends all the properties that can be predicated of it—a conception therefore adequate to all the purposes for which a conception can be needed or used.

Conceptions of the Impossible.

37. The objects of thought, of which we form conceptions or cognitions, are considered as sustaining several different relations to each other, upon which deduction depends in several ways; such as Substance and Property, Whole and its Parts, Cause and Effect, Identity, Difference, Resemblance or Similarity, Contrariety and Analogy.

Relations of Conceptions.

SECTION II.

Of Substance and Properties.

38. By SUBSTANCE, we mean, that which can be conceived of as existing by itself (*quod substat per se*). By a PROPERTY, an object of thought which cannot be conceived to exist, except as inhering in some Substance; thus iron is a substance; hardness is a property of it.

Substance.

Property.

39. Each Substance must have several properties, and may have many. Consequently, any subject may have many predicates; thus, "*Matter* is extended," "*Matter* is divisible," "*Matter* is inert," &c.;—"*Iron* is hard," "*Iron* is malleable," "*Iron* is ductile," "*Iron* is useful," &c. &c.

Each substance has several Properties.

40. Each predicate also may be predicated of more than one subject; thus, not only is "Iron *hard*," but "Lead is *hard*," "Diamond is *hard*," "Oak is *hard*," &c.

Each property may belong to several substances.

41. When a term is thus used as a predicate, it is said to be *predicated* of its subject; and the subject is said to be in the *category* denoted by the predicate; thus, "man is *mortal*." Here "mortal" or "mortality" is said to be predicated of "man," and "man" is said to be in the category "mortal."

Predicated.

Category.

42. Words or terms which may thus be predicated of several subjects, are called *Predicables* or *Categorematic*; those which cannot be predicated of more than one subject are called

Predicables.

Categorematic and Acategorematic.

Acategorematic. Such are all words standing for individual objects, proper names, &c.

43. Any word which expresses an object, or the property as belonging to or inhering in its substance, is called a *concrete* term: as "*white*," "*long*," &c. But a word that expresses the property considered by itself as an object of thought, is called an *abstract* term; as "*whiteness*," "*length*," &c.

Concrete terms.

Abstract terms.

44. But such terms as "white," "long," &c., while they *de*note the abstract property, also imply something that is "*white*," "*long*," &c. Hence such terms are called CONNOTATIVES, and are said to *de*note the property of "*length*," for instance, and to *connote* the body or substance that is long.

Denotatives and Connotatives.

45. Every conception is considered as having two elements, a SPHERE and MATTER; or, as it is sometimes designated, a *Comprehension* and an *Intension*.

Sphere and Matter of a Conception.

46. The *Sphere* or *Comprehension* is the number of individuals included in the conception for which a word stands. Thus, take the word "hard," or "hardness," the sphere of the conception includes every object of which we can say "it it is hard."

Sphere.

47. The *Matter* or *Intension* of a conception is the number of properties which may be ascribed to the subject or substance of which we have a conception. Thus with the subject "Iron," the matter of the conception is "*hardness*," "*ductility*," "*malleability*," &c., including whatever may be predicated of iron.

Matter.

48. Or to take the conception "man," the *sphere* includes Cæsar, Cicero, Washington, &c., &c., every individual of whom we can say that "he is [or was] a man;" the *matter* of the conception is "*bimanous*," "*biped*," "*rational*," "*religious*," "*accountable*," &c., including every thing that can be predicated of man, whether as a physical, or an intellectual, or a moral being.

49. A distinction is sometimes made in speaking of conceptions between being contained *in* a conception and being contained *under* it. The Matter is said to be contained in the conception; thus *rational* is contained in the conception "man." But Cæsar, Washington, Bonaparte, Franklin, &c., are said to be contained *under* the conception "man."

Contained *in* and contained *under* a Conception.

50. The Matter of a conception limits and determines the sphere; thus we include in the conception or class "man," every individual who has the properties of a man.

The Matter limits the sphere.

51. Conceptions of the same object formed from different points of view, are called *Alternate Conceptions*. Hence Alternate Conceptions each denote the same sphere by different matter, and constitute different names for the same object. Thus "height" and "depth" are Alternate Conceptions of distance, perpendicular to the horizon, viewed from different points. Almost every object in Nature has several names, according as it is viewed in one or another of the relations which it sustains. Thus a Naturalist would speak of certain animals as "*sheep*" simply; the Farmer, with reference to his farm, would call them "*stock*;" and the Commissary, with reference to their use as a supply for the army, would call them "*provisions*."

Alternate Conceptions.

52. The cognition of the sphere and the matter of a conception are not usually simultaneous acts. In the first perception of a single object, we get the sphere of its conception, by means of some of its most obvious properties; we acquire the others, one after another. In the question, "*what is that?*" "*that*" refers to the sphere of the conception which we already have in our minds; and "*what*" to the matter which we have not and wish to acquire. The same thing occurs in efforts at recollection. We remember that something happened, was said or done, without remembering *what* it was; we have the sphere

The Matter acquired before the Sphere.

of its conception in our memory, but the matter has for the most part escaped us.

53. The questions "who" and "what," are answered by the matter of a conception, which enables us to determine the sphere. But the question "which," is answered by the sphere of the conception,—which enables us to study out the matter for ourselves.

Questions who? what? and which?

54. But in regard to the conception of a class, we get the matter of the conception before the sphere, since it is the matter which determines and limits the sphere.

55. Among the properties or attributes of an object of thought, we distinguish some that are inseparable from it, as extension and divisibility from matter; and in a man his complexion, his features, his stature, &c.; and other properties which are separable or different, at different times and in different places, as sickness and health; his posture, as sitting, standing, or walking, &c. Properties of the former kind are said to constitute the *Essence** of an object of thought; the latter its *modes* of existence; thus the name of any object always implies all the essence of its reality. But if we wish to express its modes we must add something to the name, expressive of that mode; thus "George Washington" denotes the man, but does not imply any thing of his modes, as sickness or health, eating or sleeping, commanding an army, presiding in his cabinet, or delivering his farewell address.

Essence and Modes.

56. Most terms, however, denote a substance as existing in some particular mode; and substance and

* We use the word "*Essence*" in its Logical sense and not its Ontological, as denoting that which it is in itself, aside from all the changes it may undergo, without becoming a different object; and not that which is necessary to its existence as an object in reality. Without its Essence, in its ontological sense, an object could not exist at all; but in the Logical sense it might exist as an individual in another genus.

mode, in Logic, is somewhat an arbitrary distinction. Strictly speaking, in the ontological sense there are but two substances, matter and spirit; and most other words denote one or the other of these substances existing in some particular mode; thus take the word "*air*," it denotes matter existing in a certain mode. Again, considering "air" to be a substance, and "*wind*" is a modal term, denoting the existence of "air" in a particular state; or if we take "wind" for one substantive word, then "gale" will be a modal denoting the existence of wind in some one of its modes.

Terms denoting a substance *in* a mode.

57. When any property, or a number of them, are considered as constituting several objects of thought, to which they belong, a class, these properties are called ESSENTIA; thus "man" denotes a class; and those properties, without which one would not be called a man, are the Essentia of the class; and the class, with reference to these Essentia, is called a GENUS. Essentia is the matter of the conception, and the Genus is its sphere.*

Essentia.

Genus.

58. A word denoting a Genus is called a *General* term. But if the word denote a number of individuals, not by essential marks belonging to each of the individuals separately, but rather by some mark which belongs to them only as a whole, or a body, the word is called a COLLECTIVE term; as "congress," "church," "army."

General and Collective Terms.

59. From the nature of a general term, whatever may be predicated of the term, may be predicated of any individual object included under it; thus if we say, "man is a two-footed being,"

Difference in their predicates.

* I do not think so much has been made of the distinction between the terms which denote the matter, and those which denote the spheres of conceptions, as might with profit, in explaining what has been called the Predicables. Of these, Porphyry, and after him the Scholastics generally, have reckoned five: Genus, Species, Differentia, Property and Accident; the two first, Genus and Species, denote spheres, and the other three matter of conceptions.

we may say of each man, "he has two feet." But this is not true of the collective term; thus we can say of the church, "it is a divine institution," but we cannot say of its members, "they are a divine institution."

60. Some words are used only as collective terms, as those just mentioned; while others are sometimes used as collective, and at other times as general. Thus if we say, "the Romans conquered Carthage," we cannot say that "Cicero conquered Carthage," although he was a Roman. "Romans" is here used as a collective term. But if we say, the Romans spoke the Latin language, we may say of Cicero, he spoke the Latin, for we then use "Romans" as a general term.

Some words used in both ways.

61. When we consider any of the properties of an object as distinguishing it from a class to which it does not belong, those properties are called DIFFERENTIA, or distinguishing marks. And all the individuals which have these marks or properties, are called a SPECIES. Thus woolly hair, black skin, &c., if considered as distinguishing those who have them from other men, are the Differentia; and "Negro" is the term denoting the species thus distinguished.

Differentia.

Species.

62. Hence the same property may be either Essentia or Differentia, just according to the point of view from which it is regarded. If we regard black skin, woolly hair, &c., as constituting a class, then Negro is a Genus, and these properties are Essentia. But if we have in mind at the same time "man," as a higher and more comprehensive class, including those who have black skins, woolly hair, &c., as well as others which have them not, "man" is the genus, and "Negro" is the species.

Essentia and Differentia; their relation to each other.

63. Hence those properties which are the Differentia of a class, considered as a species, become Essentia when the same class is regarded as a genus, including species under it, and *vice versa*.

64. Properties, when regarded as Essentia or Differentia, are considered *Essential;* but when not so regarded, are usually spoken of as *Accidental.**

Properties Essential or Accidental.

65. When any property is considered as distinguishing one individual from another, it has been called INSEPARABLE ACCIDENT, INDIVIDUAL MARK or PECULIARITY; and the object thus denoted, is called an INDIVIDUAL.†

Inseparable Accident.

Individual.

66. Hence Individuals are included under Species, Species under Genera, and so on; Genus being considered the higher and comprehending sphere, and Species and Individuals, each in order, lower and comprehended spheres.

Individuals, Species, and Genera.

67. Spheres are said to *coincide* or be *coincident*, when they contain some individuals common to both; as for instance, "Christian" and "man;" since all who are included in the sphere

Spheres Coincident and Opposite.

* Properties that belong to an individual, or to the individuals of a class only, are said to be *peculiar* to that individual or class. If a property belongs to *all* the individuals of the class, it is *general* in respect to the class, or universal. If it belongs to several classes, it is said to be *common; a common property.*

Properties, when considered in reference to some end or object, for which the thing to which they belong is designed or desired, are also called *Qualities*, or that which *qualifies* a thing for its use or end.

† It will appear from the above, that of the five Predicables of Porphyry, two, Genus and Species, must be nouns, as denoting classes; and the other three, Differentia, Property, and Accident, will be adjectives; thus, of John Smith, we predicate, as they say, *Genus*, "man;" *Species*, "Caucasian;" *Differentia*, "white;" *Property*, "civilized;" *Accident*, "very short," or "sitting in a chair."

Genus and Species are said to predicate "*in Quid;*" Differentia, "*in Qualequid;*" Property and Accident, "*in Quale.*"

"Genus," says Aldrich, "is that which is predicated of many, as their *material* or common part, as "animal."—Differentia, that which is their *formal* part, as "rational."—Property, that which is joined with the essence, as "risible;"—and Accident, that which is *contingently* joined to the essence, as "white," "black," "to sit." But in this account of terms, he regards Essentia and Differentia as one, or the Differentia as the Essentia (see Aldrich, Oxford ed. 1849, p. 20, and the notes).

denoted by "Christian," are in the sphere "man" also; since "Christians are men."

68. But if two spheres have no individual common to both, they are called *contrary* or *opposite* spheres; as "dog" and "man," "Christian" and "Mahometan."

Contrary or opposite spheres, however, although they may have no individual contained under them common to both, may, nevertheless, have matter contained in them in common. **Analogous Spheres.** Thus any two species comprehended under the same genus, must be contrary spheres; as black or white, as properties of men, so that no object can be in both at the same time; yet black and white may be both species of men, in which the essentia of humanity is common to all the individuals in both species. Such spheres are called *Analogous.*

69. That genus which can never be comprehended under a higher genus, is called the *summum* or *maximum* genus. **Summum Genus.** That species which can never comprehend one below it, is called the *infima* species. **Infima Species.** All others are called subalternate species and genera. The genus, however, which is next above any two or more cöordinate species is called, in reference to those species, the *proximate genus;* **Proximate Genus.** as "man" is the proximate genus to "Negro" and "Mongol."

70. Those properties which indicate only the different modes of the same individual, are called SEPARABLE ACCIDENTS; **Separable Accidents.** as sickness or health in man, sharp or dull in a knife.

71. When attributes are common to all the individuals of two or more species, they are called INDIFFERENTIA, **Indifferentia.** or *points of indifference;* or even sometimes "common properties," as to have hoofs is common to the horse, the ox, the goat, the sheep, &c. Hence the having hoofs is the point of indifference to those several species, and may become the Essentia of a

proximate genus, under which all hoofed animals shall be comprehended.

72. Hence the Differentia is essential to the species, and the peculiarities or inseparable accidents are essential to the individual.

73. The matter of a term, used as a general term, is the Essentia of the Genus; the matter of a term, used as a specific term, or to denote a species, is the Essentia of the Proximate Genus (and of course, therefore, of all higher and comprehending genera), plus the Differentia of that species. And the matter of an individual term is the Essentia, plus the Differentia, plus the Inseparable Accidents or individual properties.

The Matter of General Terms.

Of Specific Terms.

Of Individual Terms.

74. Besides this matter, however, every class must have some properties which are not considered as either Essentia or Differentia, and each individual must have some separable accidents, which are not necessarily included in the conception of the individual. Thus, in forming a conception of a man, it is not necessary that we should include in the conception any particular posture, style of dress, state of health, &c., although he cannot exist except in some posture, state of health, &c.

Accidental Matter of Terms.

SECTION III.

Of the Whole and its Parts.

75. The sphere of any conception is regarded as a whole. But there are three ways of considering wholes; that is, there may be three alternate conceptions of the same whole, which we call *Logical*, *Continuous*, and *Collective* wholes. The estimate of a whole is called QUANTITY; the process of resolving the whole into parts, is called DIVISION.

Wholes, of three kinds.

1. Of Quantity.

76. As there are three alternate conceptions of any whole, so there are three ways of estimating the amount of that whole, or three kinds of Quantity; *Logical*, *Continuous*, and *Discrete*.

Quantity, of three kinds.

77. Logical Quantity is that which estimates the comparative size of the sphere of conceptions, as measured by the individuals included under them; thus a species is always less than its proximate genus, and so on.

Logical Quantity.

78. In Continuous Quantity the object of thought is always considered simply as a reality; thus a point, a line, a surface, a triangle, a circle, &c., are considered as continuous quantity. Theorems which are demonstrated concerning them in Geometry and Trigonometry, have no connection with the *length* of the lines, or the amount of the area that may be inclosed by them.

Continuous Quantity.

79. So also the properties which may be predicated of substances in different degrees of intensity, are considered as continuous quantity.

80. Discrete Quantity contemplates a whole as a union or accumulation of parts. These parts may be unequal, and each have a differentia of its own. Or they may be equal and have no distinguishing marks. In that case they are merely units, and quantity is mere number;—the science of this kind of quantity is Arithmetic.

Discrete Quantity.

81. In Continuous Quantity, the whole is not conceived as made up of parts, or divisible into parts; though of course it may be so made up, and consequently divisible.

Continuous wholes not made up of parts.

82. In Discrete Quantity we have such terms as the cardinal numbers, fractional expressions. Nothing, or zero, denotes not any quantity, but the absence of quantity or quantification; and the last expression, in discrete quantity, is the *indefinite;*

Terms and Limits in Discrete Quantity.

a sum so large that it cannot be expressed, the limit cannot be pointed out, but not so large that it may not be increased by addition and diminished by subtraction.

83. In Continuous Quantity we have such terms as denote indivisible objects of thought; any object in fact whose conception does not imply a union of parts. And besides names denoting such objects of thought, we have also the positive, the comparative, and the superlative forms of adjectives denoting degrees of intensity; and the last expression of continuous quantity is "*infinite*," and it implies that of which extension cannot be predicated.*

Limits in Continuous Quantity.

84. Logical Quantity begins with the individual, and takes note of the higher classifications, up to its last term, *the Absolute*,—that which includes all being, which is genus without ever being species, the summum genus.

Limits in Logical Quantity.

85. Discrete Quantity is applied to the objects which are included in the terms of the other kinds of quantity; thus a line, or angle, are continuous quantities. But when we say the line has so many feet, or the angle is of so many degrees, we apply discrete quantity to the measurement

Application of Discrete Quantity to Logical and Continuous.

* Even space and time form no exceptions to this remark: for neither time nor space, strictly speaking, are extended. We have simply a conception of extension, as applied to something in space or in time, but not to space and time themselves.

Among the many classifications of properties, we have one that is useful for many purposes—into primary and secondary; of which the primary can be predicated of substances only,—the secondary not of substances at all, but only of their primary properties; thus, extension is a primary property of matter, length is a secondary property—a property of the extension of a body. When we say a body is so long, we mean that its extension or extent is so long. "Thinking" is a primary property of mind; "intense," "close," &c., are properties of "thinking."

Now, "infinite" and "extension," are incompatible properties; both primary; and can neither of them be predicated of the other, nor in fact of the same substances. We say space is infinite, and we have extension *in space*. We say GOD is infinite, but we never speak of His extension.

of objects of continuous quantity. In like manner, when we attempt to number the individuals comprehended in the sphere of any logical whole, whether species or genus, it must be done in terms of discrete quantity; thus the discrete quantity of the sphere "man" is 800,000,000; that is the whole number of men on the earth.

Not all objects in Continuous Quantity can be so measured.

86. But by far the greatest part of the properties of substances, considered as continuous quantity, cannot be measured by discrete quantity; thus we cannot measure in any such way the intensity of color, of taste, of smell, of density, &c., among the properties of material substances; nor that of virtue, wisdom, courage, &c., among the properties or attributes of mind. We may be able to distinguish a greater or a less intensity—that is, a more and a less—but *how* much greater or less is what we have no means of measuring or expressing.

2. Of Division.

Division of three kinds.

87. That process by which a Whole is resolved into its Parts is called Division; and, as there are three kinds of Quantity, so there are three kinds of Division: *Physical*, *Mathematical* or *Numerical*, and *Logical*.

Physical.

88. *Physical Division* divides continuous quantity; thus we divide a loaf of bread into pieces. Now these parts are *bread*—that is, have the essentia of the whole, but they have no proper differentia of their own constituting them different species of bread—as "wheaten bread," "barley bread," &c., but they are considered still as parts, and are conceived of in relation to the whole.

Numerical.

89. *Numerical Division* divides a discrete quantity or number into parts, each of which is considered as a unit or factor in reference to that whole. Thus we divide a foot into twelve inches, a yard into

three feet, &c., and the collective whole with reference to Mathematical Division is called DIVIDEND.

Dividend.

90. *Logical Division* divides the sphere of the Genus or Logical Whole into species, each having the Essentia of the whole and a Differentia of its own, belonging to each individual contained under it; and into individuals, each having individual marks or inseparable accidents of its own. Logical Division is called Classification.

Logical.

Classification.

91. Thus *physically* we should divide a man into head, trunk, and extremities—or into bones, muscles, tendons, membranes, fluids, &c. *Mathematically* we should divide the race into companies of tens, or fifties, or thousands, as the case might be. *Logically* we should divide them into Mongol, Caucasian, and Negroes; or into Pagans, Mahometans, Jews, and Christians; or into civilized, barbarous, and savage, &c.

Illustration of Division.

92. The number of individuals included in any conception or logical whole may be divided in several different ways. Thus the inhabitants of the Earth may be divided ethically into Caucasians, Mongols, Negroes; or politically into English, French, Spanish, Russians, Chinese, &c.; or in reference to their religion into Christians, Jews, Mahometans, Buddhists, &c.

Several Divisions of the same kind.

93. That which determines us to any one of these several divisions of which any logical whole is susceptible, is called the *Divisive Principle* or the *Principle* of *Division*. As in the example just given, Race, Polity, and Religion are the Divisive Principles by means of which the divisions are effected. In mathematical division the divisive principle is called the *Divisor*.

Divisive Principle.

94. The divisions of the same whole effected by the different Principles are called the COÖRDINATE Divisions.

Coördinate Divisions.

95. The several parts into which any whole may be divided by means of the same Principle of division

are called COÖRDINATE PARTS, and the terms denoting them are COÖRDINATE TERMS, as Christians, Jews, and Mahometans, &c.

Coördinate Parts.

96. The Coördinate parts of a numerical Division are called *Factors*—with reference to the divided whole, or *Dividend*. In Logical Division, the Whole is called a Genus, and the Coördinate parts are *Species*.

Factors, Species.

97. But the parts of two coördinate divisions of the same whole are called DISPARATE parts; and the terms denoting them *Disparate* terms in reference to each other—as Caucasians, Russians, and Mahometans.

Disparate parts.

98. Any one of these parts however may be assumed as a whole, and divided as though it were not included in a higher and more comprehensive whole, and so on, until the sphere of the conception comes to be an individual.

Parts assumed as wholes.

99. But when any whole is divided into coördinate parts, and these coördinate parts are again subdivided, these divisions with reference to the first division are called SUBORDINATE, and the parts of these subordinate divisions are called SUBORDINATE parts.

Subordinate Divisions.

Thus let X be divided by coördinate divisions, and on different principles of division, as follows:

Illustrations.

1st.	2d.	3d.
X into	X into	X into
A, B and C,	D, E and F,	G, H and I,

X 1st. X 2d. X 3d. are coördinate divisions.

A, B and C are coördinate parts in relation to each other, so also are D, E and F, and likewise G, H and I. But A, D and G, or B and F, or E and G, &c., are disparate to each other.

Let now A, B and C be subdivided,

A into	B into	and C into
a, *b*, and *c*,	*d*, *e*, *f*,	*g*, *h*, *i*.

These are subordinate divisions.

a, *b*, *c*, *d*, *e*, *f*, *g*, *h* and *i* are all subordinate parts to $X^{1st.}$

But *a*, *b* and *c*, &c., are coördinate to each other, and *a*, *d*, *g*, &c., are disparate to each other, as in the first division the parts occupying similar places were disparate.

Any conception may be a whole.

100. Any conception including in its sphere more than one individual, though it may denote but a coördinate or a subordinate part in reference to another and more comprehensive whole, may become nevertheless a logical whole or unity itself with coördinates and subordinates under it. And each term or conception, whether whole, coordinate or subordinate, and in whatever degree of subordination, until we come to a term that denotes but one individual, will have a sphere and a matter of its own, and so be capable of a logical division.

Alternate parts or Species.

101. As we have said, the parts in any Logical Division are called *Species*. And besides the Coördinate, Disparate, and Subordinate Species just described, we have in Logical Division *Alternate* Species also. These are species the Differentia of which is a part of the matter of *Alternate* conceptions of the same object. Thus statesman and philosopher may be Alternate conceptions of the same individuals, so that the same men may be both statesmen and philosophers, though of course an individual may be one without being the other. In this view of the matter statesmen and philosophers are said to be Alternate Species.

Absolute Individuals.

102. The last element of a Logical Division is called individual. But the individual may be either *Absolute* or *Relative*. It is absolute when it can be divided no farther. Thus the mind is an absolute individual; the chemical simples such as iron, sulphur, sodium, &c., are also absolute individuals, because they cannot be resolved or analyzed into any component elements.

103. On the other hand, most of the objects of

thought are merely relative or assumed individuals; that is, they are individual only in reference to the purposes for which they are at the time before the mind. In this view "man" is an individual, in reference to any classification of the animal kingdom. But in reference to a classification of substances as spiritual and material, man is not an individual—his mind belongs to one class and his body to another. So with reference to a Treatise on Materia Medica, carbonate of soda, for instance, is an individual; but in reference to chemical analysis it is a compound, resolvable into carbonic acid and sodium.

Relative Individuals.

104. The following are regarded as the fundamental Canons of Division.

Canons of Division.

(1.) The coördinate parts must contain all that was contained in the whole, and nothing that was not contained in it.

(2.) Each coördinate part must have a narrower sphere or be smaller than the divided whole.

(3.) No unit or individual can be contained in more than one coördinate part.

Thus if one should divide his library into the coördinate division, folios, quartos, octavos, &c., and Greek, Latin, English, French, German, &c., and into philosophy, history, physics, mathematics, poetry, &c., each division would be good. But if he should divide into folios, octavos, Greek, history, philosophy, &c., the division would be faulty. It would not be made on any one principle of division, and the same book might be included in several of the parts.

Examples.

105. The division of a Logical Whole into Alternate Species is only an imperfect division, and does not fulfil the conditions as above specified. It results from the very nature of Alternate conceptions, that they may be all of them predicated of the same object; since they are but Alternate conceptions or different views of that object. Hence if they are taken as the Differentia of Species, the same individual may be in more than one of them

Alternate Species violate these Canons.

at once; thus a man may be a Christian, a gentleman, and a scholar, all at the same time. Still, however, the Alternate Species must include all the individuals comprehended under the Logical Whole or Proximate Genus. If we divide the writers of a nation, for instance, into poets and prose writers, the same writer may belong to both species; but there must be no one who does not belong to one or the other of them.

Must contain all the Individuals.

SECTION IV.

The relation of Cause and Effect.

106. When any object of thought is considered in relation to that which brought it into existence, or as having had a beginning, it is conceived of as an EFFECT; and when an object is conceived in reference to what it may bring into existence, it is conceived of as a CAUSE.

Cause and Effect.

107. Nearly every object of thought is conceived as both Cause and Effect;—Effect in reference to something which has preceded it as a condition of its existence; and as Cause in reference to something which follows it or whose existence is either occasioned or conditioned by it.

Every object conceived either as Cause or Effect.

108. Thus starting from any object of thought conceived as effect, we may direct our thoughts to its cause, and from that cause conceived as effect, to its cause, and so on until we come to the First Cause or Cause Absolute. So it is that whatever we know by its own properties directly we always know and conceive of as effect; and the mind of necessity refers to something else as the ground and cause of its being. But when we come at last to that Being whom no man hath seen or can see, and whom we know only through the manifestation of His wisdom, and power, and goodness—through the effects of these transcendent attributes, Him we know only as CAUSE. He is not only the Cause and Creator of all things

Cause Absolute.

visible and invisible, but He is also the Cause as Author of the Revelation which He has made. Hence we know Him only through His works and His Word, and the mind refuses to conceive of Him as an Effect.

Cause and Effect Alternate Conceptions.

109. But with this only Exception, cause and effect are but alternate conceptions of the same object of thought. Each object of thought is susceptible of both conceptions, and each in turn demands both. In this view all objects of thought, considered as causes, are distinguished into *Absolute* and *Relative*—the ONE only being Absolute, all others being relative.

Cause Primary and Secondary.

110. Again we conceive of Mind as a cause in a different sense from what matter can be. Motion, in matter, always refers the mind to something out of the moving mass, as its cause—this cause we call a Force. But if we see a being possessing mind, in motion, we are content to consider himself as the cause of his own motion; and reason is satisfied when we refer to his will as the cause of the movement. Hence we distinguish between *Primary* and *Second* causes, and call those Primary which are sufficient causes—and those Secondary which only refer us to something else as the cause of its acting, as cause; and so on until we come to intelligent moral Agency, as the only Primary Causes.

111. Besides the above distinctions there are several other senses in which the word Cause is used, or in which the object of one conception may be regarded as the cause of the object of another.

Efficient Cause.

(1.) The *Efficient* Cause is that from which emanates the force that produces the Effect.

Occasional.

(2.) The *Occasional* or *Exciting* Cause is that which puts the Efficient Cause in operation, as the spark in the explosion of gunpowder.

Material.

(3.) The *Material* Cause is the matter or Essentia of which any thing consists.*

* As the Essentia of any class considered as a Genus is the Material of that Genus, the Essentia may be called with reference to this fact the *Material* Properties.

(4.) The *Formal* Cause is that which determines the specific mode of the existence.* Formal.

(5.) The *Final* Cause is that for which any thing exists or is done; and, Final.

(6.) We have also what are called *Negative* Causes, as when we say "the want of rain caused a severe drought,"—"the absence of heat," or which is the same thing, "cold congeals the river." Negative.

112. Of the six kinds of Cause just enumerated, the 1st and 2d, the Efficient and Occasional, are usually spoken of as Causes; and much confusion often arises from not distinguishing between them. The Material Cause is usually spoken of not as a cause but as "the nature of the thing;" the Formal Cause as its "characteristic;" and the Final Cause as its "design" or "object." Common Names of them.

113. Thus if we take an act of virtue, the person who performed it is the Efficient Cause; the motion which induced him to do it is the Occasional Cause; the fact of its being a free act and not one of necessity, or even instinct, is the Material Cause; the nature of the act, its conformity to right rules of action is its Formal Cause or characteristic, and makes it a virtue and not a vice; and the object for which it was done is its Final Cause. Illustrations.

114. Causes are sometimes considered as *Transient*, *Permanent*, or *Immanent*.

A Transient Cause is one which passes away after its efficiency has been exerted. Thus occasional causes are for the most part transient, as the spark that ignites the powder. A Permanent Cause is one that remains, and from which the effect is continually flowing—as the sun and the lamp are permanent causes of light. An Immanent Cause is one that remains *in* its effect; the Material and Formal Causes are always Immanent. Transient Cause. Permanent Cause. Immanent Cause.

* As the Differentia of Species are the Formal Cause of the Species, with reference to this fact they may be called for the sake of convenience the *Formal* Properties.

115. *Causes* with reference to the fact that they always exist before the Effect, are sometimes called Antecedents merely. So also Effects for the same reason are sometimes called *Consequents* or *Consequences* merely.

Called Antecedents and Consequents.

116. *Effects* are either *Immediate* or *Remote*. The *Immediate* effect is that which follows at once; the *Remote* effects or consequences are those which appear afterwards, but not until after an interval in which they are not seen.

Immediate Effects. Remote.

117. Again, Effects or Consequences are *Direct* and *Accidental*. *Direct* when necessarily following from the activity of the Cause, and always implied in the conception of its agency. But those effects which are not invariable attendants upon the activity of the Cause, and are not considered as necessarily implied in it, or as necessary to its adequate conception as a cause, are called *Accidental*; and in reference to an intelligent cause they are called *Undesigned*.

Direct. Accidental. Undesigned.

SECTION V.

Of Difference, Identity, Resemblance and Analogy.

Difference is of two kinds—(1) in kind, and (2) in degree.

Difference of two kinds.

118. Although any common name may be used as genus, yet there are certain obvious and natural properties of all objects of cognition, by which they are referred to natural classes. In this classification these more obvious properties are assumed as the basis of the classification. When therefore two objects do not agree in possessing each the same property in this natural classification, they are said to differ in kind.

Difference in kind.

119. But when two objects of cognition are conceived as belonging to the same natural genus, and are compared only with reference to some one property or class of properties which they have in

In Degree.

common, they are said to differ *in degree* only. In this case the objects possess—the one more and the other less of—the property or properties which are made the basis of the comparison. They differ only in the degree or intensity in which they possess the property common to both, and in reference to which they are compared.

120. When the difference is only in *separable* accidents then it is said to be "*identity*." It is the same individual under different circumstances or at different times; thus "sick" or "well," "sitting" or "walking," "sleeping" or "waking," with regard to a man; "hot" or "cold," "round" or "irregular," "bright" or "rusty," &c., of a piece of metal, are mere separable accidents denoting different states or modes of the same individual substance. Identity.

121. The properties common to any two or more individuals conceived as belonging to the same species, constitute what is called *Similarity* or *Resemblance*. And the properties which are different in any two or more individuals conceived as belonging to the same species, constitute *Contrariety*. Similarity and Contrariety.

122. Hence similarity and contrariety are between individuals conceived as belonging to the same species. Or these terms may be applied in the same way to species conceived as comprehended within the same proximate genus.

123. The properties in common between individuals conceived as belonging to opposite or different species constitute what is called *Analogy*. Analogy.

SECTION VI.

Of Definition and Description.

Before proceeding to explain more fully the terms which will be of frequent use throughout this Treatise, it may be well to say what we mean by a Definition, and what by a Description; reserving the fuller discussion of the subject to the chapter on Method.

124. A *Definition* is any Proposition in which the Definition. word or thing defined is the subject, and the predicate gives us the matter of its conception.

125. A *Description* is any Proposition which indi- Description. cates the sphere of a conception, either by enumerating its parts or pointing to the place in which or the time where it may be found.

SECTION VII.

Of the Quality of Terms.

126. The Quality of a Term indicates the manner Quality of Terms. in which it represents the conception or cognition for which it stands.*

* Aristotle divided the categories into ten: Substance, Quantity, Quality, Relation, Place, Time, Position, Possession, Action, Passion, (Organ. c. iv.) And he adds (Top. I. c. ix.), "for accident, and genus, and property, and definition, [I am not responsible for his division,] will always be in one of these categories, since all propositions *through them* signify either what a thing is, or its quality, or quantity, or some other category." Aristotle's illustration is, Substance "*man*," Quantity "*one*," Quality "*white*," Relation "*greater*," where "*in the Forum*," when "*yesterday*," Position "*sitting*," Action "*whatever he may be doing*," Passion "*whatever may be being done to him*."

Now it is very possible that every thing that can be said of any subject may be included in one or another of these categories. The list seems to be very complete. But I have been unable to see its utility, and therefore I have omitted it. And in that respect it is like much else in the writings of this Father of Logical Science.

At a later period Kant gave another list of the categories. Aristotle had classified them from the outward properties of things. Kant classified them from the ideas determining their cognition—into four, each of which contains under it three varieties or dimensions.

I. Quantity { One. Some. All.

II. Quality { Real. Limited. Non-Real.

III. Relation { Substance, or Property. Cause, or Effect. Action, or Reaction.

IV. Modality { Possible, or Impossible. Existence, or Non-Existence. Necessary, or Contingent.

This list of categories is important rather to Metaphysics than to Logic, as determining the conditions and possibility of knowledge rather

127. We have already had occasion to explain what we mean by concrete and abstract terms (see 43), by denotative and connotative (see 44), by substantive and modal (see 55) terms.

Concrete and Absract.

Denotative and Connotative.

Substantive and Modal.

128. A term denoting a class is called *general* with reference to its including more than one individual, and *specific* with reference to its distinguishing them from all others.

General Terms.

Specific Terms.

We will now proceed to notice a few more of the differences in the Quality of a Term.

129. Terms denoting the same conception are called *Synonymous*.

Synonymous.

130. Terms denoting Analogous Spheres are called *Analogous* Terms.

131. Terms having the same logical force, though not analogous or synonymous, are called *Equipollent*.

Equipollent.

132. Terms which denote sometimes one conception and sometimes another are called *Ambiguous*.

Ambiguous.

133. Terms which cannot be predicated of the same subject at the same time and in the same respect, are called *Incompatible*. Thus "*sitting*" and "*standing*" cannot be predicated of the same man at the same time. "*Master*" and "*servant*" can be predicated of the same subject at the same time, but *not in the same respect*. Thus one may be the servant of his superior and master of his dog; but he is not master and servant in respect to the same thing or in the same respect.

Incompatible.

134. A POSITIVE Term is one which implies the reality of that which it denotes. All terms therefore denoting genus, species, or individuals, or the properties of them, are Positive.

Positive.

than the deduction of one thought from another, and the systematic construction of those thoughts into knowledge and science.

In the following Sections, therefore, I have confined myself to such classifications of terms as seemed to be useful for the purposes of deduction, and omitted all others on the ground that the inclusion of whatever is not useful is a hinderance.

135. But the sphere of a positive term is a limited sphere,* and excludes all that has not the Essentia of the conception denoted by the Positive; thus the conception circle excludes from its sphere all figures that are not circles.

The Sphere of Positive Terms limited.

136. A Positive sphere therefore necessarily implies another, in which are included all objects that do not possess the attributes contained in the matter of that conception. The term that denotes this sphere is called a NEGATIVE Term.

Implies a Negative Sphere.

137. The sphere of the Negative Term is the complement of that of its Positive in the summum genus, or absolute totality of things.

Negative a complement of the Positive.

138. A PRIVATIVE Term is one which denotes an object or class of objects in which there is an absence of some property, usually considered as belonging to the conception of its proximate genus or species.

Privative.

139. When we speak of the Essentia as that without which an individual cannot belong to a genus in natural classification, we refer rather to the conception than to the actuality of the individual. Thus one would say that reason is of the Essentia of man, and yet we would not say that an idiot was not a man. We recognize the idiot as one who is accidentally deprived of that which belongs to the idea or conception of his species. He is no less a monster, a *lusus naturæ*, than a horse with reason or a dog that could talk.

Illustrations.

* This is so, or *Pantheism* is inevitable. *Infinite* is not so much without limits as out of limits; as red is not so much a long color as a color out of length; that is, not included in any Genus of which any of the terms denoting extension can be predicated. But if the term GOD does not denote a limited sphere, then of course there is nothing which is not God—God is all—or Pantheism. But it is one thing to say, the term "God" denotes a limited sphere; and to say, that God is limited, or not infinite. "Limited" and "infinite" are not antithetic or opposites in the same kind, like "*long*" and "*short*," "*red*" and "*yellow*," but disparates rather, like "*long*" and "*red*," or "*short*" and "*yellow*."

140. Thus "*idiotic*" when predicated of man, or "*blind*" when predicated of an animal, are Privative terms. We do not speak of "*dumb*" as predicable of a triangle, although it implies the presence of no property, but only the absence of one which never belongs to a triangle. So with "*idiotic*" in reference to a mountain or a brute even; Privative though it be, it denotes the absence of a Differentia or Property which can never be predicated upon the Essentia of "angles," of "mountains," or of "brutes."

Privatives complements of the Positive in the Proximate Genus.

141. The Negative, as we have said, is the complement of the Positive in the Summum Genus or absolute totality of things. But the Privative is the complement of the Positive in the Proximate Genus only; as "wise" and "idiotic" in reference to men—"blind" and "seeing" in reference to "animals," which thus become *pro hac vice* a proximate genus.

But few Negative Terms.

142. Hence it is obvious that Privative terms are vastly more frequent than Negatives. In fact there are but few really Negative terms in use. Which they are can be determined only by the *usus loquendi* of each language, and the peculiarities of localities and of the authors who use them; thus A and non-A are a Positive and its Negative.

Importance of the distinction between Negatives and Privatives not great.

143. The distinction between them however is less necessary to be made on account of the following facts with regard to their use. If the term occurs as a subject, it is of no importance whether it be Negative or Privative; though not the same they are equipollent in that position. But if the term occur as a Predicate it is of no importance for the most part, since the subject itself is the sphere of the Proximate Genus, and thus limits the individuals which are taken into the scope of the judgment, and all individuals comprehended in the sphere of the subject and not included in any position used as a Predicate, must be included in its Privative as well as its Negative. Thus let "wise" be a positive

Predicate, and we say "some men are wise, and some men are foolish." It is of no importance whether foolish is a Negative or a Privative term, since in either case and alike, it includes all men who are not "wise;" since some men are "wise" and the rest are "otherwise."

SECTION VIII.

Of the Quantity of Terms.

Numerals and Ordinals.

144. Terms expressive of Discrete Quantity are either *Numerals* or *Ordinals.* The Numerals denote the number of units, as "*three,*" "*four,*" "*five;*" and the Ordinals the order in which any particular unit stands with reference to the other units in any given series, as "*third,*" "*fourth,* "*sixth.*"

Units, Tens, and Hundreds.

145. Terms expressive of Discrete Quantity are also divided into such as express units merely, as "*one,*" "*two,*" "*three,*" &c.; such as express tens of units, as "*ten,*" "*twenty,*" "*thirty,*" &c.; and such as express hundreds, as "*one hundred,*" "*two hundred,*" &c. This classification of the terms in Discrete Quantity is of great service in discussing the elementary Methods of the science of Numbers.

Odd, Even, Roots, Powers, Surds, &c.

146. We have also other classifications, as "*odd*" and "*even,*" "*roots,*" "*squares,*" "*cubes,*" "*surds,*" "*rationals,*" &c. But as we shall not go into the discussion of the Logic of Discrete Quantity—far enough to require the use of these terms—it will be unnecessary to discuss them at length.

Positive and Negative in Discrete Quantity.

147. Then we have such terms as "*Positive*" and "*Negative,*" which have been already considered in the preceding sections. As expressions of Discrete Quantity they have relation to "zero" or "*nothing.*" They indicate the distance above and below that starting point—the one showing the number of units above or more than nothing, and the other the number below or less.

148. The word "*infinite*" when used in discussions of Discrete Quantity, indicates either the absence of Quantity altogether, or that the object of thought is out of the sphere of Discrete Quantity altogether. That which is *infinitely small* is Nothing; and that which is *infinitely large* is something with which the terms of Discrete Quantity are incompatible. Thus if we divide nothing by two $\frac{0}{2}$, the answer or quotient is said to be infinitely small; that is, there is none. If we divide two by nothing $\frac{2}{0}$, the quotient is said to be infinitely large or infinite. But there is no quotient at all. There is no division in either of the above cases, for the obvious reason that we cannot divide without both a divisor and something to be divided. In each case therefore we perform no operation and get no results in Discrete Quantity. "*Small*" and "*large*" imply Continuous Quantity; but when they become infinite, they are beyond the reach of Discrete Quantity. This is shown also by the fact that they never occur in the process of a calculation, but only are results at the close of the process.

No Infinite in Discrete Quantity.

149. In Continuous Quantity "*Positive*" is a term which denotes the reality of Quantity, and "*Negative*" is a term which denotes its absence; the same in relation to Continuous Quantity, as "Infinite" does in relation to Discrete Quantity.

Positive and Negative in Continuous Quantity.

150. Then we have "*Comparatives*" and "*Superlatives*, and these too in opposite directions from the Positive; thus let us take "wise" as a positive term, and we have "*more* wise," and "*less* wise," as Comparatives of opposite intensity; and "*most* wise," and "*least* wise," as Superlatives of opposite intensities.

Positive, Comparatives, and Superlatives.

Opposite Intensity.

151. In Logical Quantity we have but two varieties of terms to be noticed.

152. Any term denoting a Logical Whole, whether

Individual, Species, or Genus, is called a DISTRIBUTED term. And any term denoting any undetermined part of such a whole is called an UNDISTRIBUTED term.

Distributed and Undistributed.

153. All individual terms are therefore always and necessarily Distributed. Any term denoting genus or species, standing alone and singly, or used as the subject of a Proposition, is always taken as Distributed, or in its broadest sense, unless the contrary is indicated by some word or words limiting its comprehension, as "*some* men," "*many* books," "*few* wise men."

Terms without a sign are Distributed.

154. We are to notice, however, that any words which give the Differentia of an included species, constitute thereby a *specific* and not an undistributed term. As in the cases just given, "*some* men" does not indicate what part or how many of the race of men we intend to speak of. "Many" implies a larger part than "few" ordinarily, but neither of them enable us to distinguish the individuals intended, from the others included in the same general term. But if we say "*wise* men," "*religious* books," the adjectives "*wise*" and "*religious*" give differentia of species, comprehended under the genera "*man*" and "*books;*" and the specific term "wise men" is as completely a distributed term as the generic "men" itself—"some wise men" would be undistributed of the specific term.

Specific terms are distributed.

SECTION IX.

Of the Opposition of Terms.

155. Among the properties of substances we perceive some which always imply others. Thus length as a property of matter always implies breadth, so that whatever has the one must have the other. (A line can hardly be said to *have* length; it rather *is* length.) A beginning always implies an end, extension always implies divisibility, &c.

Opposition of Terms.

156. The relation of such properties is called a *Relative Opposition*, and may be of two kinds.

Relative Opposition.

(1.) Where the correlative properties inhere in the same substance, as "length" and "breadth," "beginning" and "end," "extension" and "divisibility," &c.

In the same substance.

(2.) Where they necessarily imply different substances, as "parent" and "child," "subject" and "ruler;" and the two terms taken together are called *Correlates*.

In different substances.

157. Again there are certain properties which imply the absence of certain others; this relation constitutes *Contrary* Opposition, as "vice" and "virtue," "white" and "black," "hot" and "cold." In fact the differentia of coördinate species are always contraries to each other. Contrary terms are called *Antithetic* in relation to each other.

Contrary Terms.

Antithetic

158. There are properties also which may coëxist in the same substance, yet in such a way that the more of the one the less of the other—these are called *Sub-contraries*. Thus "bitter" and "sweet" are words which denote two sub-contrary spheres, since whatever object is the one is capable of being the other. The same object may be both at the same time, that is "bitter-sweet," and the more of the one the less of the other. Beauty and Utility are two more such sub-contrary spheres, since the same object may be both beautiful and useful, and for the most part that which is the most of the one is the least of the other.

Sub-contraries.

159. In the case of both Correlative and Antithetic terms the one always implies the other, though in different ways, and in both cases also one of the pair can never be fully understood without the other.

160. When terms are opposite, both in Quality and Quantity, they are said to be in a CONTRADICTORY OPPOSITION. Thus any Positive term

Contradictory Terms.

and its undistributed Negative have a Contradictory Opposition, as "men," and "some not-men;" or "some men," and "all not-men."

161. From the foregoing discussions the following inferences may be drawn, which it will be useful to remember.

(1.) Of any term as subject the specific term next above it, as animal to man, or its matter, may be predicated, and so on through the subaltern genera and species up to the summum genus.

(2.) Of *correlative* terms:

(*a*) If they are correlated in the same subject, if one is predicated of a subject the other must be also.

(*b*) If they are correlatives in opposition subjects, the other cannot be.

(3.) Of *sub-contraries*, both may be predicated of the same subject.

(4.) Of *contraries*, both cannot be predicated of the same subject.

(5.) Of *contradictories*, if one is not predicable of a subject the other must be.

CHAPTER II.

OF PROPOSITIONS.

SECTION I.

Of Judgments.

162. A judgment is an act of the mind affirming a relation between two objects of thought by means of their conceptions. Hence in every judgment there must be metaphysically two conceptions and the act affirming the relation. The conceptions are represented physically by the terms Subject and Predicate, and the act affirming the relation by the Copula, and the judgment thus expressed is a Proposition.

Judgments.

163. It will be observed that this definition distinguishes the judgment from the command, the question, and the exclamation; inasmuch as no one of them affirms a relation of agreement or disagreement between the terms or conceptions which are included in them. With these forms of speech Logic has nothing to do, except as we shall see by and by the question is sometimes to be regarded as furnishing the matter upon which a judgment is sought. Thus we say "A is B;" this is a judgment. But in the question "is A, B?" we furnish the matter A and B, and ask for the copula; or in the other form "what is A?" we furnish the subject and copula, and ask for the Predicate.

Distinguished from Questions, Exclamations, &c.

Question and Judgment.

164. The terms of a Proposition are regarded as

Matter and Form of Judgments.

constituting its matter. Hence judgments may be in the same matter though differing in form, as A is B, and B is A; and A is not B, or B is not A; are all in the same matter. But A is B, and A is C, and B is C, &c., are the same in form though differing in matter.

Scope of Judgments.

165. By the *scope* of a judgment we mean its comprehensiveness in either continuous or discrete quantity. Thus "*one* man is walking," and "*two* men are walking," differ in scope; the latter being twice as large as the former. Again, "men catch at straws," and "men catch at straws *when they are drowning*," differ in scope also; the former being more comprehensive, since the latter limits "the catching at straws" to some particular time or condition.

Species of Judgments.

166. Judgments have been divided into three classes in reference to the Relation which they affirm to exist between the parts of the Judgment—CATEGORIC, CONDITIONAL, and DISJUNCTIVE.

167. This Division corresponds with the three great fundamental relations of conceptions to one another—namely, the Substance to its Attributes or Properties, the Cause and its Effects, and the Whole and its Parts, which have been discussed in the preceding chapter.

Categorical.

168. If the judgment simply affirms or denies an agreement between a Subject and a Predicate it is called *Categorical*, as A is B, or A is not B.

Conditional.

169. If the judgment affirms the reality of a Predicate on the ground of the reality of the Subject, the judgment is called *Conditional*, thus, If A is, B is.

Disjunctive.

170. But if the judgment affirms the reality of one of two terms, on the ground that the other is *not* real, the judgment is called *Disjunctive;* thus, Either A or B is. If A is not B is.

Conditional and Disjunctives imply more than two terms.

171. But in both the Conditional and the Disjunctive the terms instead of being single cognitions or conceptions are always categorical judgments. Thus If A is, B is,—is the same

as if A is *existing* or is *real*, B is *existing* or *real*. And so with the Disjunctives, Either A or B is *existing* or *real*.

172. Now as the Conditional affirms its Predicate on condition that the subject is real, and the Disjunctive on the condition that it is *not* real; the two judgments unite in the point of indifference that they both affirm under a condition (*sub conditione*, ἐξ ὑποθέσεως). They are sometimes considered as two species of *Hypothetical* judgments. Hypothetical judgments.

173. But as the members of both the Conditional and the Disjunctive jugments are, by themselves considered, Categorical Judgments; these judgments are never primary. The judgment itself, that is the subjective act, is as simple as in the Categoric Judgments; but there must always have been a Categorical Judgment before either form of the Hypothetical. Presuppose Categorical Judgments.

174. We will therefore postpone the consideration of the Conditional and Disjunctive, until after we have examined the Categorical Judgments.

175. Categorical Judgments are of three kinds: Categoricals of three kinds.

(1.) In the first place they simply affirm or deny the Predicate of the Subject, as A is B, or A is not B; or

(2.) They compare the Subject with the Predicate, as A is greater than B, or A is equal to B.

(3.) They represent the Subject and the Predicate as sustaining some numerical relation to each other, as A is one-half of B, or A is three times as much as B.

176. The first of these are Categoricals in Logical Quantity, which we will call *Pure Categoricals;* the second class are Categoricals in Continuous Quantity, and are called *Comparative* or *Relative* Judgments; and the third are in Discrete Quantity, and in one of their forms of expression constitute what are called *Probable* Judgments. Pure Categoricals. Comparative. Probable.

177. We will therefore consider these Judgments

and the Propositions in which they are expressed in the following order.—(1) Categoricals in Logical Quantity: (a) simple, (b) complex, (c) compound.—(2) Comparative Judgments.—(3) Probable Judgments.—(4) Conditional;—and (5) Disjunctive Judgments.

SECTION II.

Of the Terms in a Proposition.

178. Categorical Judgments have been defined as those which affirm or deny simply an agreement between the Subject and Predicate.

179. Since a judgment necessarily implies two cognitions, two terms must be contained expressly or implicitly in every Proposition. In some cases there is no difficulty in finding them at once, as "*man* is *mortal*." But in other cases it is not obvious to the inexperienced at first glance what the terms really are. A little consideration however will always bring them to light. Thus if we say "John loves," we have for subject obviously "John;" we predicate of him "*loving*," and the proposition is the same as "*John* is *loving*." "God exists."—Here existence is what we predicate of God, and we may say "God is existing." It is the same if we say "there is a God;" "*God*" is still the subject though coming after the copula, and "existence" the predicate implied in the copula itself. Or again if we say "it rains,"—"rain" is the subject, and that which we predicate of it is that it is falling, "rain is falling."

Two Terms.

180. In English the subject is placed before the copula for the most part, yet not always or necessarily. And it is often necessary to know something of the connection of a proposition with others, or of the circumstances under which it was uttered, in order to decide which is the Subject and which the Predicate. But that is always Subject of which we are speaking, and that is Predicate which is affirmed of it.

Subject placed before the Copula.

181. We use the Subject chiefly with reference to the sphere of its conception, and the Predicate with reference to its matter; that is, in the subject we are thinking of the thing itself in its substance, and in the predicate of its properties or what may be said of it. Subject used with reference to its sphere. Predicate with reference to its matter.

182. The Subject may be either a noun or a verb in the infinitive mood, as "man is mortal," "to err is human." But for the most part when the subject is a verb in the infinitive mood, it is placed after the copula in English, as "It is hard to deny oneself." Here "to deny oneself" is manifestly the subject, and that which is said of it is that "it is hard." What may be Subject.

183. The Predicate of a Proposition may be either a noun denotative, or an adjective connotative, or a verb in the infinitive mood;—as "man is an animal," "man is mortal," "to be good is to be great." What Predicate.

184. In perceiving an object we perceive it as a whole—substance and properties all combined in one objective reality. But by a subsequent process of reflection and analysis we come to separate it in our thoughts into substance and properties, and each of these properties may be predicated of the object. We see the snow, we analyze it into substance and properties, we think of whiteness and say the snow is white; because that property is one of those which was contained in our very perception of the snow. Objects perceived as wholes.

185. Any property which belongs thus to a logical whole, whether it be individual or universal, may be predicated of that whole. The formation of Judgments.

186. When a property is ascribed to a subject in any judgment, the subject being taken as a distributed term, the judgment may be resolved into a cognition, as "the snow is white," into "white snow." Propositions resolvable into terms.

187. But when the property is ascribed to an un-

determined part, the subject being undistributed, we may resolve the judgment into a term, making the Predicate an adjective, as "some trees are deciduous," becomes "deciduous trees." By this process that which in the judgment was the property of a genus, becomes now the differentia of the species included in the genus, or next higher and comprehending conception. Thus by every change in our form of expression, and by every assertion we make, we change our classification. We have all noticed such expressions as "horse-chestnut" and "chestnut-horse," "brandy-peach" and "peach-brandy," "sand paper" and "paper sand." They illustrate the point under consideration—they invert the order of classification; the noun, here as in all cases, denoting the genus, and the adjective, when not a mere explicative, the differentia of the intended species, which is really the subject of the predication.

Into Terms with Modals.

Examples.

188. Logically, therefore, the use of an adjective before a noun is indicative of a contained species, as in the cases just given, "sand paper" and "paper sand" for instance—the former denoting a kind of paper as distinguished from other kinds, and the latter denoting a kind of sand distinguished from other kinds of sand.

The Logical force of Adjectives.

SECTION III.

Of the Copula.

189. The Copula is the formal Cause or constitutive of the Judgment. The effect of the Copula in pure categorical judgments in Logical Quantity, is that it includes the subject in the sphere of the Predicate; that is, supposing the Copula to be affirmative—and of affirmative Copulas only will we speak at the present.

Copula.

190. Some *Categoricals* affirm an identity between the Subject and the Predicate. These are called *Identical Judgments.* As "Victoria

In Identical Judgments.

is the Queen of England," "common salt is chloride of sodium," "a triangle is a figure with three sides," &c.

191. But in all other cases the Copula in pure Categoricals includes the Subject within the sphere of the Predicate; and of course shows a coincidence of sphere to the extent of the comprehensiveness of the sphere of the Subject, and an analogy between the spheres so far at least as the matter of the conception of the Predicate extends—which is of course the Essentia of the Genus denoted by the Predicate.

In pure Categoricals the Subject there is coincidence of Spheres and analogy of Matter.

The simplest form of the Copula is—"*is*," or "*are*." As "A *is* B." "All men *are*," &c. &c.

Forms of the Copula.

192. But we sometimes have the verb "to be" in past or future tenses. "Alexander *was* King of Macedon,"—"To-morrow *will* be Tuesday." For the most part there is no necessity of being more precise in expressing or analyzing the Copula. But if there is, the thing is easily done. "*Alexander* is *that which was King of Macedon*,"—"*To-morrow* is *that which will be Tuesday*." This destroys indeed the rhetorical beauty or structure of the sentence. But Logic takes no note of such things.

Copula in intransitive Verbs.

193. Again and more frequently still the Copula is merged in a transitive verb. As "Fortune favors the brave," "*Fortune* is *that which favors the brave*."—"A wise King makes happy subjects," "*A wise King* is *that which makes happy subjects*."

Copula in transitive Verbs.

194. Mistakes are often made in attempting to decide what is Copula and what belongs to the terms in a Proposition. Thus if we say that "heat is the cause of fluidity," we must not suppose that "heat" and "fluidity" are the terms, all the rest being copula. The predicate in this case is not "fluidity," but the cognition expressed by the words "the cause of fluidity." Again, "animal includes man." Here it has been supposed that the predicate is included in the sphere of the subject. But the predicate

Mistakes to be avoided.

is not "man" merely, but "that which includes man;" that is, "animal" is the genus which includes "man."

The Real and the Designed Effect of the Copula.

195. In saying that the effect of the Copula in categorical Propositions in Logical Quantity, is to include the subject in the sphere of the Predicate, I do not mean to say that such is the intended effect; or that in forming the judgment the *sphere* of the Predicate is at all before the mind, or consciously in the thoughts. Thus when I say that "man is an animal," I am not thinking of *animals;* that is, I am not thinking of the class of objects to which I refer man. On the contrary, I use the predicate as a general term—with reference to its Essentia and not its sphere; not the individuals contained in it are the objects of thought, but simply and only the necessary matter of the general conception.

Predicate used only for the Essentia of the Genus.

196. Now this necessary matter of the general conception, as we have seen, is only the Essentia of the genus to which the subject is referred. It does not include the Differentia of any comprehended species, still less of course the individual properties which distinguish one individual from another, and without which no conception of any one of the individuals included in the genus can be formed.

The Subject most conspicuous in the thoughts.

197. In the act of judging the Subject is distinctly and conspicuously before the mind as a sphere, and the sphere of the Predicate is only indirectly and remotely before the mind. Hence it is the sphere of the subject and the matter of the predicate between which the mind consciously and intentionally affirms the agreement. The effect, however, is that the subject is of necessity thereby included in the sphere of the predicate as a proximate genus.

Pure Categoricals make a classification.

198. Since the copula in pure categorical judgments includes the subject within a higher sphere, or refers it to a comprehending class, the

principles of classification are necessarily implied in the investigation of categorical Propositions.

As we have already defined the principal terms used in Classification, we shall need to resume the subject only for the purpose of stating its general principles, so far as they are implied in or requisite for the purposes of Logic.

Principle of Classification extends to more than three grades.

199. When there are more than the three grades, Genus, Species, and Individual, the same principle holds in the subordination of classes. Thus the matter contained in the conception of the Genus = Essentia,

" Species = Ess. + 1st Differentia.
1st Sub-species = Ess. + 1st Diff. + 2d Differentia.
2d Sub-species = Ess. + 1st + 2d + 3d Differentia.
" Individual = Ess. + 1st + 2d + 3d Dif. + Peculiarities.

Necessary and contingent Matter in Conceptions.

200. But besides this, each class will have properties, and each individual accidents, which are not included in the above analysis of the matter of the conceptions; what is named above is *necessarily* included in the conception. All else is merely contingent and accidental.

Comprehensiveness of Principles and exclusiveness of Matter.

201. It will appear from the above statement of subordinate spheres and their matter, that the more comprehensive of individuals the les comprehensive of matter any conception will be; and *vice versa*, the more comprehensive of matter the less comprehensive of individuals.

Relation of Differentia to Essentia.

202. As the principles of classification are founded in the nature and truth of things, the Differentia of a species must therefore always sustain a certain relation to the Essentia of any genus under which it can be included. Thus the Differentia of "wise" and "foolish," of "pious," of "humane," &c., can be predicated only upon the Essentia of "man," as a genus. We can predicate "right" and "wrong" in a moral sense only of the acts that proceed from freedom of choice, and having

this [freedom] as an essentia. We can predicate "hard," "soft," "heavy," "light," &c., &c., only of material things.

203. When a word is used to denote a class, we use it without the article in English, as "man," &c. We do not say that "*an animal*" denotes merely the essentia—that which is essential to all animals. For when the word is thus used with the article it denotes some existing animal without denoting precisely which perhaps, and consequently implies the differentia and accidents of an individual also. But the word "animal" when used simply and without the article, whether definite or indefinite, implies merely that which is essential to the animal nature, and by no means all that is found in any existing animal. We can form no image in our minds representing merely "*animal;*" the image must be of *an* animal—some animal already existing, or which might possibly exist—and consequently the image must contain in it more than is represented by the generic term.

Words denoting class used without the article.

204. The words "the animal" always refer to some individual animal before the mind, and consequently imply the individual properties necessary to the conception of the individual referred to. "*An animal*," used as a subject, as also "*animals*" in the plural, always implies something more than the mere essentia of the genus "animal," since all animals and each animal must have some system of nutrition for instance; and the essentia of such a system is always implied when we speak of "an animal," or of "all animals." But yet as all animals have not the same systems, no one individual system can be included in the conception. But when we use the word "an animal" as a Predicate, the matter of the conception is precisely the same as if we had used "*animal*" without the article, as "man is an animal" is merely ascribing to man the essentia of animal nature, just as when we say "man is animal."

The Effect of articles "*the*" and "*a*" when used with the Subject.

With the Predicate.

205. We have thus far been speaking of the classifications that are based upon those inseparable properties of objects which are the most conspicuous. But such properties are not always or the only ground of classifications. In classifications, for the purposes of the Natural Sciences, a very different principle is often found the most conducive to the end in view.

Conspicuous Properties not the only basis of Classification.

206. The classifications of the Natural Sciences or Natural Genera or Species, are for the most part based on properties which are not only inseparable, but also incapable of different degrees of intensity—of a more and a less—thus "man is biped." We have no such expressions as "more biped," "less biped," &c. So it is also with such words as "quadruped," "winged," "dogtoothed," "hoofed,"—and the words "mental," "material," "eternal," "infinite," &c. They have no comparatives. It is the same with the mathematical differentia, "triangular," "quadrilateral," "circular," "elliptical," "conical," &c.

Basis of Natural Classifications.

207. But besides this it is obvious that any mode or separable accident whatever, may be the ground or principle of a mere transient classification. Thus we may classify the inhabitants of a city into sick and well—those in a room as those that are sitting, and those that are standing, &c. The mode or accident which serves as differentia to these transient classifications must, however, be such that the terms denoting its presence and absence cannot be *both* predicated of any one individual at the same moment of time and in the same respect.

Logical Classifications.

208. It will follow from what has been said, that if any individual contains the Differentia of any species, it must be included in that species; and if either individual or species contains the Essentia of any genus, it must be contained in that genus. The Differentia are essential to the species, and the Peculiarities to the individual. The

Individuals necessarily included in Species.

peculiarities also are the differentia of the individual.

209. Hence every assertion we make by the necessary laws of thought or of affirmation, makes a classification. It refers the subject to a class whose essentia or differentia, as we may regard the class, a genus, or a species, is denoted by the predicate. We say that "this man is a farmer;" we refer him to the class of farmers. We say "the snow is falling;" we refer it to a class of things whose differentia or essentia is denoted by the state expressed by the predicate "falling." We say "God is good;" we refer Him to the class of objects which are characterized by the attribute or property of goodness. We say "the wicked will be punished;" we refer them to a class, whose only point or property in common it may be, is the doom that is declared by the predicate to await them; and yet this point or property is made, *pro hac vice*, the ground or basis of a classification.

All assertions classify their subject.

210. But by the very nature of the case we cannot make an assertion without referring the subject of which we speak to a class; and every time we speak of it in a different connection, to a new class—the differentia of which is expressed by the predicate we use. If we call a man, brave or a coward, honest or a knave, wise or ignorant, good or bad, polite or rude;—if we say of him, he is standing or walking, sitting or sleeping, all these classes are called up before the mind, and every new assertion concerning any subject of which we are speaking, like a fresh turn of the kaleidescope, groups and classifies all things anew. And upon this classification depends alike the cogency of an argument, the merriment of humor, and the keen relish of wit. Even a jest is but a ludicrous classification. A sarcasm does no more than to class one with persons and things that are contemptible, and a bad name, a disgraceful epithet, a conviction of wrong, brings

Every judgment classifies anew.

A jest is a ludicrous classification.

upon one only the differentia of the species to which he is thus referred.

SECTION IV.

Of the Adequacy of Propositions.

211. Let us now consider some of the principles and laws of predication with reference to the adequacy of Propositions, as expressions of the judgments which they represent.

212. A Proposition for the purposes of Logic should be like the testimony given under the Common Law oath in civil suits, "*the truth, the whole truth, and nothing but the truth.*" Adequacy of Propositions.

(1.) Of any object or class of objects, its name and its definition may of course be predicated. Name and Definition Predicated.

(2.) Synonymous terms may also always be predicated of each other. But any two or more names, which are not mere individual names, and which may be predicated of the same object of thought, must denote Alternate Conceptions of that object, and are not likely to be predicable of each other. Synonymous Terms.

(3.) Of any general term, that is, a term denoting a genus, we may predicate any term denoting the essentia of the genus, or any one of the essentia in an abstract term, or by a connotative adjective. Of a Genus.

(4.) Of the Species we may in the same way predicate not only the Essentia of any higher and comprehending genus, but also its own Differentia. Essentia of Species.

(5.) Of any individual we may also in the like way predicate the Essentia of any genus in which it is included, the differentia of the species to which it belongs, and the peculiarities of the individual (inseparable accidents). Of the Individual.

(6.) Whatever may be predicated of each individual

Of Individuals as a Class. in a class, may be predicated of the class as a whole. Thus if each individual man has two feet, then "man is a two-footed order of beings."

213. Besides the above there are always properties which are not regarded as either Essentia or Differentia, as well as separable accidents which constitute the various modes or conditions of being, that may be predicated of any subject whenever we have any sufficient reason to affirm them of it.

Accidental Properties predicable.

214. If the subject denotes any real or possible thing, then the Predicate may be a positive term and denotes some property that is predicated of it. For if it be a possible or a real thing, we can say "it is possible," "it is real." But if it be an impossible thing its predicate must be a negative term, since no property or mode can exist without its substance; thus if the conception denoted by the subject A be an impossibility, we can say that "it is impossible."

Predicates of real and possible Subjects.

215. Whenever a given predicate is to be used that Alternate Conception of the subject should be used, which represents it by the matter on account of which it is contained in the genus denoted by the Predicate.

Alternate Conceptions as subjects.

216. Alternate Conceptions represent the same object by different matter. But the subject is included in the sphere of the Predicate, only because it has the properties which constitute the Essentia of the genus denoted by the Predicate. Thus, Washington *as General* commanded the American Army; gave Commissions to the Officers in the Army and Navy, &c. But *as President* he presided over his Cabinet, nominated Civil Officers, sent Messages to Congress, possessed the Veto Power. But it would be logically faulty to say, "the *American Commander* ate his breakfast," for instance; for *as* Commander he did not eat, but it was simply as George Washington that he ate. So it should not be said of an act in his military

Examples.

command,—the *President* did it; for as President he did not do it, but only as Commander did he do it. Nor should we say George Washington vetoed this bill, for not as George Washington but as *President* Washington did he possess the veto power, or exercise it.

217. Words denoting titles and ranks are however but Alternate Conceptions of the individuals to whom they are given, and custom has so far not only sanctioned, but required the use of a man's title even when we are speaking of his personal acts and properties, that a disregard of the usage would be regarded as discourteous if not as intended for an insult. Titles.

218. The subject of any proposition should always be so comprehensive as to include all the individuals to which the predicate used in the proposition is applicable. Comprehensiveness of the Subject.

219. This condition is often violated for rhetorical purposes; nor does its violation necessarily involve an error in the conclusion, though it renders us liable to fall into one. Thus we say "the Papists hold to the supremacy of the Pope," which is correct. But if we say "the Papists believe in the Divinity of Christ," we say what is indeed true; but as other Christians believe in that dogma also, our subject is of too narrow a comprehension, and suggests the inference that a belief in the Divinity of Christ is one of the differentia of the Papists. Although therefore there may be cases in which the violation of this rule does no harm, yet unless there is something in the context or in the circumstances under which the rule is violated to guard against the error, the rule must be strictly adhered to, or our proposition does not state "the whole truth." * Rhetorical violations.

* I have before me a case in point. In an infidel author, whom I need not name, there is an accumulation of statements designed to show that the Scriptures, as *we now have them*, cannot be relied upon as inspired. He says of the Scriptures (his subject), "the oldest manuscript does not reach back to within centuries of the origin which the Scriptures claim for themselves.

220. When the Predicate is a general term and not a mere connotative of some accident of the subject, the accidents of the subject are not included by means of the proposition in the matter of the Predicate. Thus when we say, "the rich are anxious," we take no notice of the color, size, or any other accident of the persons included in the word "rich." If we say "John is sick," this implies nothing concerning his accidents, and no connection of the Predicate with them; the Predicate is affirmed of what is essential to the subject *as such* and not of any of its accidents—that is, what is essential to it as a subject, and not what is necessary to its reality.*

Properties of the Subject included in the scope of the Judgment.

Separable Accidents of the Subject not included in the Judgment.

221. But whatever term is predicable at all of either individual species or genus, must be predicable of the individual or individuals (if the subject be either a specific or generic term), as containing in this conception whatever is necessary to their existence as individuals, species, or genus as the case may be.

The Predicate must include the necessary matter of the Subject.

222. Thus if we say "This mountain has existed since the creation of the world," we are understood to say not merely that the matter of which it is composed has existed so long, but that that matter has existed not

It is written in a letter entirely different, now divided into words, surrounded by points indicative of the meaning and punctuation of words, divided up into chapters and verses, and the manuscripts abounding in various readings, interpretations, omissions, and corruptions." But the author does not state, and the unlearned reader does not know, that precisely the same thing could be predicated of the text of Herodotus, Thucydides, Livy, Tacitus, and in fact of every ancient author, and yet no one ever doubted the genuineness of the works which are received under those names on that account. If he had made his subject as comprehensive as the Predicate would allow, and included these works with the Scriptures in his Proposition, it would have destroyed the effect which he designed to produce.

* The scholastic writers expressed this distinction by the use of the ablative pronoun *qua*. The subject *qua* subject—this expression is also used to distinguish between the different predicates which any object of thought may have when represented by its Alternate conceptions. Thus Washington *qua* President possessed the Veto Power, *qua* Commander-in-Chief gave Commissions to the Officers of the Army and Navy.

only as *mountain* [the species], but also as *this* individual mountain with its inseparable accidents. So when we say "men are immortal," we mean not only that what is essential to humanity, but also whatever is distinctive of each individual as an inseparable accident is included in the immortality; so that men will exist there individually, distinct and distinguished by the same inseparable accidents of personality as here.

223. For rhetorical purposes this rule also is often violated. In all those figures of speech called Metaphor, Trope, &c., these rules of Logic are departed from for rhetorical purposes. It becomes necessary therefore to consider in all cases whether the word used is the real subject, or merely some figure of speech used in its stead. Rhetorical violations.

SECTION V.

Of the Quantity of Propositions.

224. The scope of the judgment is not important to its deductive force or position in a syllogism, since whether it includes much or little in a numerical estimate it goes in for what it is.

225. But the Logical Quantity is of the utmost importance, since that indicates its relative amount and determines the laws of predication and deduction. Importance of Quantity of the Terms.

226. Logical Quantity in its broadest sense is of three varieties,—(1) comprehensive; (2) intensive; and (3) protensive. Three Dimensions of Logical Quantity.

(1.) Comprehensive, or Extensive Quantity, is the comprehensiveness of the sphere of the conception. Comprehensive.

(2.) Intensive Quantity is measured by the amount of matter in the conception. Intensive.

(3.) But we have also a Protensive Quantity brought in by the consideration that the facts included Protensive.

in the sphere of any conception are not always actual facts at the same moment of time. If we say "all men are mortal," we mean to include in our category not only all men *now living*, but all who have lived in time past or will live in time to come—all beings that are men. But a predicate may be ascribed to a subject at one time, or as true of it at some times, which could not be ascribed to it with truth at others.

After having thus named this variety of Quantity, we shall leave it out of consideration for the present, and proceed to consider Comprehensive or Extensive Quantity in reference to judgments.

Intensive Quantity determined by the Comprehensive.

Protensive assumed as absolute.

227. In reference to the object now before us Intensive quantity is unimportant in itself, and is always determined by the Comprehensive quantity being always in the inverse ratio to it. The Protensive quantity is assumed to be absolute; that is, to include all time—and the same as if it were expressed by the word "*always*," as "All A is always B;" "Men are always mortal."

Three Dimensions of Comprehensive Quantity.

228. There are three dimensions of Comprehensive Quantity, according as the subject of a judgment may be;—(1) an individual; (2) several individuals considered as a part of a class, not denoted by any term which constitutes them a species within that class; or (3) several individuals considered as constituting a class, species, or genus.

229. The first class are called *Individual* judgments; the second *Particular* judgments; and the third are called *Universal.*

230. It is obvious that on these principles of division, and in reference to Quantity, there can be but three Species; for a judgment must be either of *one*, of *some*, or of *all*. If we say that, "some" may include many or only a few; nearly all or only two; we do not thereby constitute a Logical whole.

SECTION VI.

Of the Quality of Judgments.

231. The Copula of a Judgment may be either (1) affirmative, or (2) negative; that is, we may say A (*is*) B, or A (*is not*) B. The first A is B, includes A in the sphere of B, and is an *Affirmative* judgment; the second A is not B, excludes A from the sphere of B, and is a *Negative* judgment. But B and not-B are antithetic terms. They denote spheres which are the complements of each other. Hence if A is not in the sphere of B, it is in the sphere of non-B; and we may say that A is non-B. This is called (3) an *Indefinite* judgment. Hence three varieties in reference to Quality—1st, includes the subject in the sphere of the Predicate; 2d, excludes the subject from the sphere of the Predicate; the 3d, includes the subject in the Negative sphere connoted by the Predicate of the Affirmative.

Three Qualities of Propositions.

It is obvious that in reference to Quality there can be no other species of judgments than these three.

SECTION VII.

Of the Modality of Judgments.

232. In reference to the certainty of the Judgment, we may have three kinds of judgments;—*Problematical*, *Assertive*, and *Necessary*, or *Apodictical*. This is called the MODALITY of Judgments.

Three Modes of Propositions.

(1.) The Differentia of the Problematical is that they merely affirm that the subject *may* be in the category of the Predicate, or the possibility of the Proposition being true.

Problematical.

(2.) The second is called ASSERTIVE;—they affirm the truth of the judgment as a matter of fact and reality.

Assertive.

(3.) The third are called NECESSARY or APODICTICAL; they affirm that the truth could not be otherwise—as when we say "two and two make four."

Necessary.

SECTION VIII.

Of the Four Cardinal Propositions.

233. Combining Quantity, Quality, and Modality, we have the following table of Categoric Judgments.

Twenty-seven Categorical Judgments.

Categoric	Individual	Affirmative	Problematic.
			Assertive.
			Apodictic.
		Negative	Problematic.
			Assertive.
			Apodictic.
		Indefinite	Problematic.
			Assertive.
			Apodictic.
	Particular	Affirmative	Problematic.
			Assertive.
			Apodictic.
		Negative	Problematic.
			Assertive.
			Apodictic.
		Indefinite	Problematic
			Assertive.
			Apodictic.
	Universal	Affirmative	Problematic.
			Assertive.
			Apodictic.
		Negative	Problematic.
			Assertive.
			Apodictic.
		Indefinite	Problematic.
			Assertive.
			Apodictic.

234. But as Problematical judgments never enter as Premises into any Argument merely as Problematical, we may omit them from any further consideration at present.

235. Again the difference between the Assertive and the Apodictic or Necessary has no effect upon the general principles of deduction. If a Proposition be true, that is all that is required, the modality of its truth being wholly unimportant. We may take the Assertive therefore for all our purposes, neglecting the difference between that and the Necessary.

The three Modals reduced to one.

236. But again, the Negative and the Indefinite sub-species are the same so far as all the laws and purposes of deduction are concerned. For since the Positive and the Negative Spheres are complements of each other, to *exclude* from the Positive (which is the differentia of the Negative) is the same as the *inclusion* in the Negative sphere (which is the differentia of the Indefinite).

The three Qualities reduced to two.

237. Again in respect to Quantity the Individual and the Universal are alike, in that the subject (in which alone is found the differentia of Quantity) is in both of them a logical whole. Whether an individual or a class, it is immaterial for all the purposes of deduction, so long as it is a logical whole. Hence we consider Individual judgments the same as Universal for all the purposes of deduction.

The three Quantities reduced to two.

238. But a Universal Judgment may be either Negative or Affirmative, and so likewise may a Particular judgment. We have only four cardinal judgments which we need consider. These are UNIVERSAL AFFIRMATIVE, UNIVERSAL NEGATIVE, PARTICULAR AFFIRMATIVE, and PARTICULAR NEGATIVE. These may be considered the four cardinal Propositions in Logical Quantity.

Quantity and Quality combined.

239. As these occur so often, writers on Logic have

generally designated them by the first four vowels of the Alphabet. Thus

U. A.	All A is B, is represented by	A
U. N.	No A is B " " "	E
P. A.	Some A is B is " "	I
P. N.	Some A is not B is " "	O

These are all Categorical, all Assertive, and differ only in Quantity and Quality.

SECTION IX.

Of the Distribution of Terms.

240. When a term is taken into the scope of a judgment as a logical whole, it is said to be *distributed* in the judgment; but if it does not enter in as a logical whole, it is said to be *undistributed* in the judgment.

241. It is immaterial whether the part of the whole be a large or small part, "many" or "few;" and these words therefore indicate an undistributed term as well as "some."

Undistributed Subjects.

242. So also we may say "some," when we mean "some at least and possibly all;" or when we mean "some but not the whole." But the undistributed term as such indicates nothing of the kind, and if any such modification of the term is intended, the Proposition expressing it becomes a compound one [either copulative or discretive], expressing two judgments in fact and not one merely.

243. The conception represented by an undistributed term is not a logical whole, and the term itself must necessarily be a general one. But if the term denotes a part of the whole, *conceived as a species*, it is no longer undistributed; for the part conceived as a species becomes by the very fact of its being so conceived a logical whole.

Not Logical Wholes.

244. Hence the word "*some*," though generally

used to denote an undistributed term in the subject, is not an infallible indication that the term is undistributed. Thus in the illustration given by Sir William Hamilton, "*some* stars are all planets" (all the planets are stars). But one must have a conception of those stars as a class, which are planets, and *as distinguished by the differentia* of planets, or he could not say that they were all the planets that there are among the stars. If therefore there ever was, or ever should be such a Proposition, except when got up for the purpose of seeing what one can do, the subject must be regarded as distributed, notwithstanding the usual signs of an undistributed term.

Mistake of the force of "some."

245. There are three ways of ascertaining whether a term is distributed or used distributively in any proposition or not.—(1) By the nature of the term; (2) by a modal sign; and (3) by its position.

Three ways of distribution of terms.

446. A term is distributed by its nature when it is used to denote any individual object, such as proper names of persons, places, &c.

By the nature of the term.

Terms are distributed by signs in three ways.

By signs.

247. (1.) The particles "*the*," "*this*," "*that*," by pointing out a particular individual in a class, of which the predicate is affirmed, make the term distributed; since the force of these particles is to include only the one of the individuals comprehended within the genus thus pointed out in the scope of the judgment.

"The," "this," and "that."

248. (2.) Such words as "*all*," "*every*," &c., distribute the terms; in fact they are the most usual signs of a distributed term used in the subject of a Proposition.

"All," "every," &c.

249. "All" of course clearly and expressly includes all of the individuals included in any genus within the scope of the judgment.

250. As "all," so also "*every*" indicates a distributed term, since it necessarily includes all the indi-

viduals of the logical whole within the scope of the judgment. *All* is indeed sometimes a *collective* rather than a *distributive* sign. Thus if we say "all these trees make a fine shade," it is most likely that we mean to take "trees" as a collective term rather than as a general term; that we have predicated of them taken together as a collective whole, what could not be predicated of each of them individually. This difference is unimportant to the purposes now before us, but it will be seen by and by that it lies at the bottom of a most serious fallacy.

Difference between "All," and "Every."

Two Pronouns distribute the Subject.

251. (3.) Two pronouns, as "he who," and "they that," are clearly indicative of a distributed subject, as "*he who* transgresses the law commits a sin,"—"*who so* transgresses the law commits sin;" these forms of Propositions clearly include the whole class denoted by the specific term, whose differentia is given in the words "transgresses the law," in the scope of the judgment.

"Each" and "Any."

252. (4.) Again, we have another class of signs, which, although they do not cause the general term to be included as a whole in the scope of the judgment, constitute it what is called a distributed term. These terms are such as "*each*," "*any*;" for while by their force they apply the predicate of the proposition to one individual of a class only, and sometimes in such a way as that it can be applied to one only at the same time, yet they imply that before any actual predication it is applicable to them all and every one of them taken individually, although it may cease to be so the moment it has been predicated of one. Thus if we say of a young lady, "any man would marry her;"—"*man*" must be taken as a distributed term, though it is not supposed that more than one man will actually marry her.

The Indefinite "a."

253. (5.) The indefinite article "*a*" also sometimes distributes the subject in the same way, thus "a poison destroys life;" that is, "any poison," or "all poisons destroy life."

254. In all Negative Propositions the Predicate is taken as a Whole.* The differentia [characteristic] of Negatives is that they exclude the subject from the sphere of the Predicate. They do not merely partly exclude it, they may exclude merely a part of the subject, but they must exclude the subject whether as a whole or as a part from the whole of the Predicate, "No vice is commendable." If now among all the things that are commendable one vice can be found, the Proposition is not true. Hence it distributes the Predicate or speaks of it as a whole. Or if we say "some men are not brave," which is a Proposition in O, the same is found to be the case with the Predicate. We here mean that among all the things that are "brave," the "some men," are not included.

By position the Predicates of Negative Judgments.

255. But the Affirmatives do not necessarily distribute the Predicate. If I say that A is B, all that is affirmed thereby is that A is in B, or A is some part of B. A is included in the sphere of B. But B may include much besides A. "Men are mortal;" but men are not the only things that are mortal. The sphere of "*mortal*" is not coincident and identical with that of "man,"—it is much more comprehensive. Hence in A we do not speak

Affirmatives do not distribute the Predicate.

* Sir William Hamilton in his new method of Notation, insists that there may be Negative Judgments with undistributed Predicates.

But besides the proof given in the text of the position there taken, we may say further that his doctrine directly contradicts the old axiom, "it is impossible for a thing to be and not to be at the same time." For suppose S is not P and P not taken as a whole, the sphere of P as of any term is determined by its matter; and the subject S is included in it if it possesses the matter of P and excluded from it if it does not. Now suppose that S has not the matter of that part of P which we take into the scope of our judgment, when we say S is not P, and the judgment S is not P is true. But suppose it has the matter of the part of P, not taken into the scope of the Negative judgment, and then we have S is P;—

that is, S is not P,
S is P,
and P is P,
and P is not P.

of the predicate as a whole. The predicate is undistributed.

256. For the same reason we do not speak of the Predicate as a whole in I. "Some men are black;" we do not speak of "black things" as an entire class, comprehending no more than the "some men" of whom we were speaking.

Rules. 257. Hence the following Rules for the Distribution of Terms by position.

1. All universal Propositions distribute the *Subject.*

2. All negative Propositions distribute the *Predicate.*

Or more definitely:

A distributes the subject.
E " both the subject and predicate.
I " neither.
O " the predicate only.

Illustrations. 258. Various devices have been resorted to, to represent by some diagram these various Judgments or Propositions. Many of them are ingenious and useful, but all are liable to misapprehension, arising from the nature of the case and the difficulty of representing any mere conception by actual forms.

The following is perhaps as good as any that can be given. It is substantially Euler's:—

A.—All S is P, in which case one circle S is included wholly in the other as P, but does not occupy the whole of its sphere.

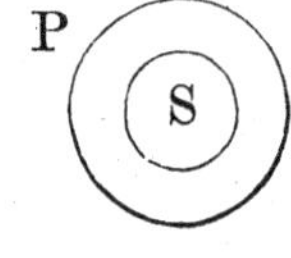

E.—No S is P, in which case one circle S is wholly excluded from the whole of the other P.

I.—Some S is P, in which case we have two incomplete circles S and P, cutting each other so as to have a part x common to both.

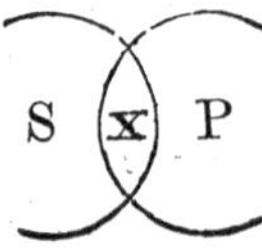

O.—Some S is not P, in which we have an incomplete circle, S not included in any part of the complete circle P.

259. One difficulty attending the above diagrams is, that they represent in A and I the subject as constituting a definite part of the Predicate, or occupying an ascertained portion of its sphere, whereas the judgment does not so represent the spheres.

Danger of using them.

260. It will be noticed that in A when the sphere of S becomes so large as to fill up and occupy the whole of P, the Predicate has become distributed and is taken as a whole. The spheres are then coincident and identical.

The Predicate in Affirmatives distributed.

SECTION X.

Of Immediate Inference.

The form Judgments expressed by the Propositions A, E, I and O, which we have just examined, have certain relations to each other which it is important to examine.

261. Such is the relation of judgments to each other, that no judgment can be true without implying the truth of some other judgment, either in the same or in the opposite Quality.

Every Judgment implies another.

262. These judgments which are thus inferred from others, as from All A is B, we infer that some A is B, and that "some A is not B" is not true, are called by KANT "Syllogisms of the Understanding." I shall prefer, however, to adopt the more English name of *Immediate Inference.*

Immediate Inference.

263. I call it "*immediate*" because the inference or conclusion is drawn without the intervention of that medium or middle term, which is always necessary in the complete Syllogism, as will be seen hereafter.

Why so called.

264. By Immediate Inferences then I mean all those inferences or conclusions that can be drawn from any Proposition without the intervention of any other matter or term than was given in the Proposition itself. And as it will be the most convenient to point out these Inferences as we examine the Opposition, Permutation, and Conversion of Propositions (since it is by these means that the Inference is made), I will keep them in mind as a subordinate object while discussing these topics.

I. Of the Opposition of Judgments.

265. (1.) A and E being Universals, I and O are called in reference to A and E their *Subalterns*. I being subaltern to A and O to E.

Subalterns.

(2.) A and E in relation to each other are *Contraries*.

Contraries.

Sub-contraries. (3.) I and O are *Sub-contraries*.

266. (4.) E and I as likewise A and O are *Contradictories* to each other.

Contradictories.

267. If now a Universal be true its *Subaltern* must be true also. If All A is B, Some A is B, is true as an Immediate Inference, and if the Subaltern be true the Universal as a Problematical Judgment is true also, as an Immediate Inference; that is, If Some A is B, all A *may be* B.

Inference from Subalterns.

268. Of the *Contraries* only one can be true in the same matter, though both may be false. Hence If A is true E is false as an Immediate Inference, and *vice versa;* that is, No A is B, then All A is B is untrue, although of course *Some* A may be B.

From Contraries.

269. Of *Contradictories* both cannot be true or false in the same matter. Hence If E is false I must be true, and *vice versa.* If A be false O must be true, and if I be false E must be true, and if O be false A must be true as Immediate Inference.

From Contradictories.

270. The *Sub-contraries* may both be true in the same matter. If some A is B, some A is not B, may also be true.

Sub-contraries cannot both be false.

271. But the Sub-contraries cannot both be false in the same matter.

272. We may represent the relation of these four Judgments by the following diagram, in which it will appear that the sub-contrary of any subaltern is the contradictory of its Universal; and if therefore two contradictories cannot be false at the same time, then *a fortiori* the two sub-contraries cannot.

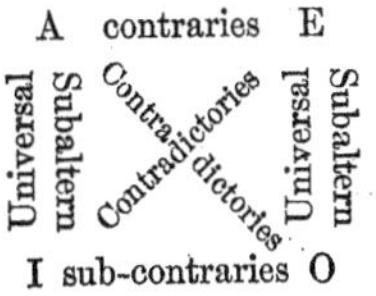

A contraries E
Universal Subaltern Contradictories Contradictories Universal Subaltern
I sub-contraries O

273. The subject in each of the sub-contraries is undistributed, and the more nearly it approaches to the Universal in one quality in any case, so much the more nearly does it approach it in the other. Thus the more nearly Some A is B is to All A is B, so the more nearly is Some A is not B to No A is B.

Ratio of Quality.

II. Of Contra-Position or Permutation of Quality.

274. The same judgment may be stated in either quality, Affirmative or Negative as we choose, by means of Negative terms and copulas.

275. In reference to this fact we will call the first form in which a judgment is stated, or rather that form which states the judgment in the Proposition of the same quality as the judgment itself, the *Exposita;* and that form of the Proposition which states it in the other quality, the *Contra-posita;* and the change itself we call *Contra-position* or *Permutation.*

Exposita and Contra-posita Permutation.

276. Thus let us suppose in the first place that we have the Negative Proposition "A is not B," or "No A is B." In this case we have simply excluded A from the sphere of B, and thus denied of it the matter of the conception B. But since the Negative

Illustration.

of B or non-B is the complementary sphere of B, whatever is not in B is in non-B, and consequently whatever has not the Essentia of B must have that (if there is any) of non-B. Hence "A is not B" is equivalent to "A is non-B,"—"non-B" being a Negative term; and But A is non-B is an Affirmative Proposition with a Negative Predicate.

277. Hence from a Negative Exposita with an Affirmative Predicate we may always permute into Contra-posita, by substituting for the Positive Predicate its Privative or Negative, and dropping the Negative from the Copula. Thus "if man is not wise," he is "*un*wise;" if he is "not free" he is a "slave."

278. But if the Predicate is a Negative or a Privative term in the Exposita, we have to substitute for it its Affirmative, and drop the Negative from the Copula also. Thus we may say that "Centaurs are not impossible," then "Centaurs are possible."

Negative or Privative Predicate

279. The same holds true of the subject when the Predicate denotes a reality and not a possible only. We may substitute for the subject its antithetic in the opposite Quality by dropping the negative from the copula, always remembering that the term substituted is an undistributed term.

When true of the Subject.

280. But since no property or mode can exist or be real without its substance, the Predicate may denote a property which has no existence. In that case there can be no Contra-posita by means of the negative subject; thus if one should say "horses are not Centaurs," we could not therefore say "some not-horses are Centaurs," for this would imply the reality of "Centaurs."

281. But if the Predicate be a reality at all we may always say, if A is not B some non-A is B.

Let "holy" be the Predicate and "man" the Subject, "no man is holy," or in the other form "all men are not holy."

Illustration.

If now we connect the negative with the subject "no-man," this is no longer the same term taken in a different sense, but it is a totally distinct term. It includes nothing that was included in the first term "*man*," and precisely all that was not included in it. It includes whatever is not "man." Of these things manifestly not all are holy, although if there be such a thing as holiness, and if it do not belong to man, it must belong to something that is not man. Hence we may say "some not-man is holy."

282. If, however, we connect the negative with "holy," and say "All men are not-holy or *un*holy," the term represents an entirely different cognition from the term "holy." But the new term must be regarded as undistributed, for we do not mean to say that man is all that is "not holy," or that whatever is "not holy" is "man." And yet if our first Proposition is true "some thing not holy" is "man."

Privative used for the Negative in the Predicate.

283. In the use of intelligible signs we may use the Privative instead of the Negative in the Predicate, since the nature of the subject limits the range of the thought or judgment to the proximate genus. Thus for "man is not holy," we may substitute the privative Predicate, and say "man is *un*holy;" the subject "man" limiting the scope of the judgment to the proximate genus to which the capacity for holiness is an essentia, and also a differentia in the next higher subaltern genus.

But not in the Subject.

284. But when we change the Quality by changing the subject we may not use the Privative, since there can be no *a priori* necessity that the Predicate should be predicable of some one individual in the proximate genus to the subject, or in any genus below the summum or absolute whole of realities.

Permutation of Affirmatives.

285. If the Exposita be Affirmative we change the quality by means of two negatives—two negatives in English making an affirmative.

286. This change of the quality of Affirmatives by means of two negatives may be effected in three ways.

1st case. (1.) With two negative copulas, as "there is no A that is not B," consequently All A is B. Thus "there is *no* man without [that has *not*] sin," or "all men are sinners."

2d case. (2.) The second form is with a negative copula and a negative Predicate. "All A is not non-B," or "No A is non-B;" as "No earthly creature is immortal."

287. In this case the whole of the subject is excluded from the Negative sphere, and must therefore be included in the Positive which connotes the Negative. A Privative term will answer just as well as the Negative, since the subject always confines the judgment to objects included within its own sphere, which becomes for this purpose a proximate genus, of which the Positive Predicate and its Privative are the coördinate parts.

Privative for Negative sphere.

3d case. (3.) By a negative copula and a negative subject used distributively, we have I by contraposition. As "No one who has not enough is rich." Here "one who has *not* enough," or "all who have *not* enough," is a negative term, and the judgment is the same as "some [perhaps all] who have enough are rich" (see 277).

288. This form however states something more than I, since it would never appear from the fact that "some who have enough are rich," that "no one who has not enough is rich."

289. The course of this investigation shows that we may always have from any Exposita its contra-posita by Immediate Inference.

III. Of the Conversion of Propositions.

Conversion. 290. By the Conversion of Propositions we change the relative place of Subject and Predicate, as from A is B to B is A.

Exposita and Converse. 291. In the Conversion of Propositions, the first form we call *Exposita*, and the second the *Converse*.

292. The fundamental canon which governs the Conversion of Propositions is this: Fundamental Canon.

No term may be distributed in the Converse which was not distributed in the Exposita.

293. As E and I are alike in reference to the distribution of their terms, one distributing both and the other distributing neither—their conversion takes place in the same way; that is, simply, No A is B, therefore No B is A. Some A is B, therefore Some B is A. Conversion of E and I.

Exposita, No quadrupeds have wings, therefore
Converse, No winged animals are quadrupeds.
Exposita, Some Poets are Americans, therefore
Converse, Some Americans are Poets.

294. This is called *Simple Conversion*, and hence the Rule, when both Subject and Predicate are distributed, and when neither are distributed the Proposition may be converted simply. Simple Conversion.

295. But in A the Subject and not the Predicate is distributed. Hence we cannot convert simply if we say, "all American citizens are free," we cannot say that therefore "all freemen are American citizens." We must limit the subject and say, therefore "*some* freemen are American citizens." Conversion by limitation.

296. This is called *conversion by limitation* or *per accidens.*

297. A, however, when stated by contra-position, may be converted simply. Thus All A is B, No A is non-B, therefore No non-B is A. If the whole of A is in the sphere of B, nothing which is not in B can *a fortiori* be in the sphere of A. A by contra-position may be converted simply.

298. O, cannot be converted except by first changing its quality. This we may do by connecting the Negative with the Predicate by which we permute it into I. And then of course it may be converted simply. Thus "Some A is not B, therefore Some Not-B is A." Conversion of O.

Exposita, Some brave men are not soldiers,
Converse, Some not-soldiers are brave men.

299. Hence we may convert E and I simply. A by limitation, or *per accidens*, or *particularly*, and O by permutation into I and then simply.

300. In consequence of the laws of Conversion we have from any Exposita, its converse as an Immediate Inference.

Immediate Inference by Conversion.

IV. Of the Substitution of Terms.

301. In every categorical Affirmative Proposition we may always substitute for the Predicate any term which denotes a wider and comprehending sphere and the Proposition will remain true, but it will cease to be the whole truth. In the same way we may substitute for the subject any term which denotes a narrower and comprehended sphere, and with the same effect upon the Proposition it will still be true, but not the whole truth that was contained in the Proposition before the change was made. Thus, if A B is "a negro," he is "a man," "an animal," "a created being," &c. Or if we say, "men are mortal," we may say "Caucasians are mortal," "Americans are mortal," "Yankees are mortal," "Bostonians are mortal," &c.

Substitution of Predicates in Affirmatives.

Substitution of the Subject.

302. By such change Propositions are said to become more general or more indefinite; they are true but not the whole truth.

303. In Negative Propositions, in consequence of the fact that the Predicate is distributed, we may substitute in the Predicate terms in the inverse order; that is, for any comprehensive term we may substitute any one of its included spheres. Thus A B is not a man, therefore he is not a Negro. If Victoria is not a sovereign she is not Queen of England.

Substitution of Predicates in Negatives.

304. But we may not substitute Predicates in the

inverse order in either case; that is, not a narrower for a more comprehensive in Affirmatives, nor a more comprehensive for a narrower in Negatives. This would be in either case asserting something more than the truth.*

No substitutes in the inverse order.

305. By these substitutions new Propositions are made, the truth of which depends upon that of the Propositions for whose terms the new ones are introduced. Hence the new Propositions must be true (though inadequate), by Immediate Inference.

Immediate Inferences by substitution.

SECTION XI.

Of Complex Propositions.

306. A Categorical Proposition is called *simple* when its two terms are expressed by single words. But when several words are required to express the cognition the term is called *Complex.*

Simple and Complex Propositions.

307. It is evident that any substantive, or other word which is the name of a thing, a property, an action, or a series of actions, may be a term, as "man," "whiteness," a "step," "walking," "to err." And if any language were copious enough to afford a name for every possible conception which we might ever wish to express, as either the subject or the predicate in our judgments, we should

Necessity for Complex terms.

* It may be well to give a diagram illustrating the preceding paragraph.

Thus let S and P be any two circles or spheres. S included in P—this represents the affirmative Proposition S is P. It is manifest that any sphere comprehending P must comprehend S also. Let S be Negro, P be Man, and we have "Negroes are Men." But let a circle drawn around P denote "animal," so that all men are animals, then will it include S also, and we shall have "Negroes are animals."

But in case of the Negative Proposition the Subject is not included in the Predicate, and we have two circles S and P, having no point in common. S is not P, consequently S cannot be in any narrower sphere which is included in P, or any part of it.

never need to use any other words to express our meaning than these simple terms. But such is not the case and never can be the case with any human language.

308. In most cases also when the predicate denotes a property which is not one of the differentia of a species, we wish to use in the subject not merely the specific term but also the term denoting the genus under which the species is included. Thus if we say, "Men who walk by faith place a light estimate upon the mere vanities of worldly splendor," we give first in the subject the genus "men," and then the species "who walk by faith." It is obvious that we do not intend to affirm the predicate of the whole genus denoted by the term "man," but only of one species of men, whose differentia is that they "walk by faith."

Modals.

309. A simple term, as "man," thus limited becomes a *complex* term; and the words limiting or qualifying its meaning or its sphere, are called MODALS.

310. Modals are either *Explicative*, *Differential*, *Exceptional*, *Exclusive*, *Conditional* or *Protensive*.

Explicatives.

311. *Explicative* Modals are merely rhetorical. They amplify the meaning of the term itself, as when we say "*mortal man*." Since all men are mortal the adjective adds nothing either to the matter or the sphere of the conception for which the term "man" stands, however much it may add to the rhetorical effect of its utterance.

Differential.

312. *Differential* Modals limit the sphere of the conception denoted by the absolute or simple term. In that case the term is really the species, as the Differential Modal furnishes the Differentia of the contained species. Thus "white men,"—here "*men*" is the simple term, "*white*" the modal; and "white men," the complex term, is but a species of the genus "man" denoted by the differential "white."

313. While Differential Modals indicate the part of the Proximate Genus, which is included in the scope

of the judgment, we have another class of modals called *Exceptionals*, which indicate the part which is not included in the scope of the judgment. As "all *except the Apostles* were scattered abroad." Instead of giving the differentia of that portion of the Proximate genus which is included in the Predicate, it gives the differentia of the part which is not included. Hence the Differential and the Exceptional modals are in a sense counterparts and complements of each other. Exceptionals.

314. The *Exclusive* Modals are those which show that the predicate can have no other subject than that of which it is predicated in the judgment. As "Virtue *is the only* thing worth living for." Here virtue is declared to be worth living for. But by the modal every thing except virtue is excluded from the sphere of the conception denoted by the matter "worth living for." Hence of necessity Exclusive modals distribute the Predicate. Exclusive.

315. *Conditional* Modals express some separable mode or condition of the object represented by the term, so that the object is included in the scope of the judgment only while it is subject to that condition. Thus "*drowning* men catch at straws;" that is, "men in the condition of drowning." It does not apply the predicate to any species of men at all times and under all conditions as the Differential modal does, but it makes it applicable to all men when they are in the specified condition. Conditional.

316. *Protensive* Modals limit the inclusion of the term within the scope of the judgment *in reference to time.* Thus "the weather is excessively cold *in winter*,"—"our plans will *sometimes* fail,"—"testimony *sometimes* deceives us." Protensive.

117. The Protensive Modal neither makes nor implies any change in the properties of the term, but only refers to the time when the object denoted by the term is included in the scope of the judgment. This it may do *definitely*, as "in winter;" or *indefinitely*, as "some-

times;" *instantly*, as "now;" or *absolutely*, as "always."

318. There is another kind of adjective phrase that has sometimes been regarded as a modal, which however I have preferred to regard as constituting a compound Copulative Categoric Proposition (see 322),—as "*Hamilton, the greatest statesman of his age*," or "*who was the greatest statesman*," &c., "*was a Federalist*." But the words marked in italics do not constitute a modal of "Hamilton," they are the Predicate of a judgment to which "Hamilton" is subject, and the Proposition expresses the two entirely distinct and independent judgments, that "Hamilton *was* the greatest statesman," &c., and that "he *was* a Federalist."

SECTION XII.

Of Compound Propositions.

319. Any Proposition which has more than two distinct terms is called a *Compound* Proposition, and contains either expressly or impliedly more than one judgment. If it has but two terms, whether simple or complex, the Proposition is *simple*.

Compound Propositions.

320. Compound Propositions are usually divided into *Express* and *Implied*. They are called Express when two or more judgments are expressed in the same Proposition, and Implied when one only is expressed and the other is implied.

Express and Implied.

The Compound Express Propositions are either *Copulative*, *Causal*, *Discretive*, *Conditional*, or *Disjunctive*.

321. In the Copulative Propositions either the Subject or the Predicate, or both, consist of two or more terms connected by a conjunction. Thus A and B are C; A is B and C; A and B are C and D. "Life and Death are both before us;"—"Bacon was both a philosopher and a statesman."

Copulative.

322. Sometimes the conjunction is omitted entirely, as "Hamilton *the greatest statesman of his age* was a

Federalist." And again its place is supplied by the relative pronoun and the verb, as "Hamilton who was the greatest statesman, &c., was a Federalist."

323. Copulative Propositions can be resolved into simple ones according to the number of simple judgments contained in them. Thus in the example, "Bacon was a philosopher and statesman," we have—Bacon was a philosopher, *Resolved in simple Propositions.*

" " a statesman;

or in the other example given, we have the following:

Life is before us,
Death " " "

324. Or the connective may be a disjunctive conjunction, as "Neither wealth nor friends can free the body from its pains, nor the mind from its fears;"—and we have, *Disjunctively connected.*

Wealth cannot free { the body from pain, / the mind from fears.
Friends cannot free { the body from pain, / the mind from fears.

325. It is of course quite possible that one of the judgments in a compound copulative will be true, and the other or others be untrue. And advantage is often taken of this fact for the purpose of introducing and gaining assent to a judgment which is untrue, by ascribing to a subject two predicates, one true and the other false. *Pure and false Judgments combined.*

326. Compound Propositions are called *Causal* when one of the judgments assigns the cause or sign of the truth of the other. "Christians are happy *because they have obtained the favor of God;*"—"The evil are exalted *that they may fall;*"—"Christ came *to save the world;*" that is, "Christ came [first judgment] that he might save the world," [the final cause or object for which He came into the world.] *Causal.*

327. Compound Propositions are called *Discretives* when they contain two judgments in opposite qualities. Thus "A is B, but it is not D. "A and not B is C." "A is B but C is not D." "Fortune *Discretives.*

may take from us our friends but it cannot take our honor." "But few men succeed in enrolling their names on the list of those who are never to be forgotten;" that is, "some men do and some do not succeed," &c.

328. We have already seen that Conditional and Disjunctive Propositions are compounded, implying first categorical judgments and then a hypothetical relation between those judgments. Hence in one point of view they are to be regarded as compounds of categorical judgments.

329. In the compound of the categorical with the conditional, the conditional clause is to be regarded as a modal. Thus if A is B, C is D; that is, C is D (*sub modo*) A is B. "If the Scriptures come from God they are entitled to the highest respect."—"The Scriptures are entitled to the highest respect *on condition* [conditional modal] that they come from God."

Conditional.

330. So with the Disjunctive, A is either B or C. A is B on condition that it is not C, or either A or B is C; that is, A is C on condition that B is not. "The author of this statement is either a fool or a knave." He is a knave *on condition* he is not fool enough not to know better.

Disjunctive.

331. The more usual form, however, of the compound categorical with one disjunctive term, is that in which one term denotes a logical whole, and the other the parts; as "All men are either Caucasian, Mongol, or Negro."

We shall of course reserve the consideration of the judgments which connect the Conditional and Disjunctive members of these compounds until a subsequent place in our treatise.

332. Of the Compound Implied Propositions two only need to be mentioned, the *Exceptives* and the *Exclusives*. They each imply a judgment different in quality from the one expressed—this is done by a modal.

333. Thus *Exceptives* while including the expressed subject in the sphere of the predicate, make an exception of some of the individuals included in the implied subject, which consequently are excluded from it. Thus "*All but the Apostles fled*," implies that there were some who were not Apostles that did flee.

Exceptives.

334. In this case the expressed judgment is affirmative and the implied is negative. But if we say, "*None but the Apostles remained*," we have the negative judgment expressed, "*None*;" that is, "no Christians remained,"—and the implied affirmative judgment, "the Apostles did remain."

335. The *Exclusive* Propositions, while including a subject in any predicate, exclude by an implied negative judgment all other subjects from that predicate, as "Virtue is the only thing worth living for." This is precisely the same as the Exceptive in which the negative judgment is expressed, as "Nothing but virtue is worth living for."

Exclusives.

336. The article "*the*" before the Predicate of an Affirmative judgment constitutes it an Exclusive, by making the Predicate a definite and distributed term. Thus "Christ is *the* Saviour of the world;" this implies that He is the only Saviour.

337. In the conversion of complex and compound Propositions they must, as a general thing, be first resolved into simple incomplex propositions, and permuted and converted according to the rules already laid down. In one or two cases, however, there are facts in regard to their conversion worth noticing.

338. Exceptionals and Exclusives are easily converted into each other. "All but the Apostles fled;" becomes by substituting the exclusive instead of the exceptional modal, and changing the quality of the Proposition, "The Apostles alone did not flee." The same thing would be accomplished with the antithetic Predicate without changing the quality of the copula, as the Apostles alone re-

Exceptionals and Exclusives convertible.

mained, i. e., did not flee. "Virtue is the only thing worth living for," is converted into an exceptional by substituting for the subject "nothing," and the exceptional modal before the subject, as "Nothing except virtue is worth living for."

339. Any Compound Proposition, whether Express or Implied, may always be regarded for the purposes of Deduction as a simple Complex Proposition. Thus the Copulative "A and B are C." A (*sub modo*, that is, on condition it is joined to B) is C. For the Causal take "A is B because it is C." A (*sub modo*, that is, because it is C) is B. For the Discretive "A is B but not C." A (*sub modo*, that is, on condition it is not C) is B. The same is obvious, too, with regard to the Exclusives and Exceptionals; the exclusive and exceptional phrases may be made or regarded as merely a modal of one of the terms.

Compound Propositions reducible to Complex.

340. But we may carry this matter one step further, and regard the Complex as a Simple Categorical so far as the purposes of deduction are concerned. It depends very much upon the fulness of a language, whether a conception shall be expressed by a single term or not. If we have no single term for it, we must use several, and give either its description or its definition instead of the term itself. And all the words which Logic requires in the expression of judgments, are either the copula or the terms; or instead of terms, their definitions or descriptions. Hence whatever words are necessary to express any cognition, become but a complex term for that cognition, and it is merely accidental for all logical purposes, whether a term be expressed by one word or by many.

Complex to Simple.

SECTION XIII.

Of Comparative Judgments.

341. Comparative Judgments do not include the subject in the sphere of the Predicate.

342. In Comparisons there are three terms and two implied categorical judgments; as "A is wiser than B." Here we manifestly have the two judgments, A is wise and B is wiser. And we have three terms, A the Subject, B the Predicate, and the Comparative term, which in this case is "*wise*." The Predicate is assumed as the *Standard* or *Positive* term, and the Subject is compared with it and is the *Compared* term.

Three Terms in Comparative Judgments.

The Positive and the Compared Terms.

343. Of Comparative Judgments there may be reckoned seven kinds: 1. *Comparatives of simple Intensity.* 2. *Comparatives of Intensity considered as a Cause.* 3. *Comparatives of Time.* 4. *Of Place.* 5. *Of Manner.* 6. *Of Means* or *Method.* 7. *Of Ratio* or *Relation.*

Different kinds of Comparatives

344. We may have comparisons in Intensity of three varieties: (1) of Equality; (2) the Indefinite; (3) Comparisons of Inequality.

(1.) In Comparisons of Equality the Positive and Compared terms are affirmed to be equal in the intensity of the term of Comparison; as A is equal to B, in which it is also implied that B is equal to A, or that A and B are equal in the intensity of that in respect to which they are compared.

Comparisons of Equality.

(2.) In the Indefinite we have the Compared term declared to be of as great an intensity as the Positive; as "A is as great as B," or "A is as wise as B." In these judgments it does not appear that B is not wiser than A, &c.

Indefinite.

(3.) In Comparatives of Inequality the term of comparison is used in the comparative degree, and a difference in degree of intensity is declared to exist between the Positive and the Compared terms; thus A is greater than B, or A is less than B.

Inequality.

345. Comparatives of Inequality differ in their intensity, by being on the different sides of the positive degree, and are accordingly called comparisons of *greater* or of *less intensity.*

Difference of Intensity.

346. Comparisons are said to be of greater intensity when the Term of Comparison is affirmed to belong to the Compared in greater intensity than to the Positive, and Comparisons of less intensity when the Term of Comparison is affirmed of the Compared in a less intensity. Thus A is greater than B, is a comparison of greater intensity—A is less than B, is one of less intensity.

Greater Intensity.

Less Intensity.

347. We may have Comparatives in which the intensity of the comparative term is considered as a Cause. Thus, "The weather is so cold that the water freezes."

Intensity as a Cause.

348. For a comparison of Time we say that "A occurs when B occurs;" as "It lightens when it thunders."

Of Time.

349. For a comparison in Place we say, "A is where B is."—"Where two or three are gathered together in My name, there am I in their midst."

Of Place.

350. For a comparison of Manner we say, "A is like B."—"The Boy walks like his Father."

Of Manner.

351. We have also a comparative of Method or Means, as "He came *as* he went;" in which case the "as" comparative may refer to either the means used or to the way by which the act was performed.

Of Method and Means.

352. Then we have Ratios, or comparisons of value, in which one term varies as the other. Thus "A is to B as C is to D.—"The Mercury in the Thermometer rises and falls as the weather grows warmer or colder."

Of Ratio.

353. In comparisons of Inequality conversion may be effected by change of the intensity to its opposite. Thus "A is *greater* than B,"—"B is *less* than A."

Conversion of Comparatives.

354. But in the Indefinite no conversion can be effected; we say, "A is as great as B." But the judgment leaves it possible for A to be greater than B, and the mind is uncertain whether it is or not. Hence B may be either equal to A, or less

Indefinites cannot be converted.

than A; and the judgment does not furnish the means for determining which it is.

355. Comparatives in which the Intensity is regarded as a Cause, are converted into Causal Categoric Propositions. "It is so cold that the water freezes," becomes "the water *freezes* because it [the weather] is so cold." Comparatives converted into Causal.

356. All the other forms may be regarded as Comparatives of Equality so far as conversion is concerned, and as such may be converted simply, A is equal to B, therefore B is equal to A.

SECTION XIV.

Of Probable Judgments.

357. A Problematical Judgment is one in which it is affirmed that the Copula may be affirmative. But a Probable Judgment is one in which there is given an estimate of the reasons for affirming the Copula. Probable Judgments.

358. The value of the Probability is always estimated (if at all) in a fraction of unity or in a ratio; unity being assumed as the same as a certainty. Their value.

359. The value is ascertained by a calculation of chances. One reason for believing any Proposition which comes into the present class to be true, is because we have known it, or something like it to hold true. Thus of any given side of a die there is a probability that it will fall uppermost at any given throw. If a man commits a crime there is a probability that he will be detected, based indeed upon the means used for his detection; but estimated by the proportion which the times in which similar means have been successful in similar cases bear to the times in which they have failed. How ascertained.

360. All the known cases are considered as so many *Chances*, which are divided into two classes—the favorable and the unfavorable; Chances favorable and unfavorable.

and the probability of any affirmative judgment having an individual case for its subject, and the term including the favorable cases for its Predicate being true, is determined by the proportion which the favorable chances bear to the unfavorable. Thus a die has six sides—at one throw therefore one of the six sides must come up: call that the favorable chance, and as there are five other sides, no one of which will be up when that specific one is uppermost, we may call the unfavorable chances five. The probability, therefore, of any particular side, say the *ace*, being up, is one to five, or one-sixth of the whole number.

361. In order to estimate the probability of any judgment therefore, we must have a totality of cases. This may be the absolute totality including all actual and all possible cases of the same kind, or it may be any part of that totality which has fallen under our observation, assumed as the representative of the whole. For the estimation of the probability, it makes no difference which is assumed, provided the part taken be an exact representative of the whole. Thus suppose the whole to be one thousand, out of which one hundred have been favorable and nine hundred unfavorable, the chances are one to nine. Now if we take any part of this totality, say one hundred, if it be an exact representative of the totality, the chances will be ten to ninety—that is, one to nine; or if we take ten, they will be one to nine still as before.

Absolute and assumed totality.

362. The improbability, which is the probability that the individual will be included among the *unfavorable* chances, is of course the complement of the probability in the unity of the whole, whether absolute or assumed. Thus if the Probability is *three-fourths*, the Improbability is *one-fourth*.

Improbability.

363. The balance of Probabilities is the difference between the two fractions, and is in favor of the probability or the improbability, as the one or the other happens to be the largest.

Balance of Probalities.

364. The Improbability is not however the same as the Probability of the opposite. Thus, in throwing a penny, the probability of the head side falling up is ½, the probability of its falling up in two throws is, say ¾, consequently the improbability is ¼. But the probability that the head will fall down, or the tail fall up, one in two, is also ¾ instead of ¼.

Improbability not the same as Probablity of the opposite result.

365. Both the Probability and the Improbability are sometimes called *Antecedent* Probability and *Antecedent* Improbability, with reference to the fact that they are estimated before or *antecedent to* the special reasons for affirming the judgment in any given case. Thus the antecedent improbability of a miracle is based upon the uniformity of nature; that is, the numberless instances in which no miracle has been wrought. On the other hand, it has been claimed that when we consider the *special occasion* on which it is claimed that miracles have been wrought, there is an antecedent *probability* in their favor; the difference in the estimates arises from the assumption of different totalities of cases or chances. In the one case, forgetting the special occasion or purpose,* the absolute totality of historic events and of occurrences in nature is assumed. In the other it is assumed that the object for which the miracle is alleged to have been wrought, is to constitute the basis of an entirely different totality, is the Differentia of a much narrower sphere, within which the chances are not only much fewer, but are such as to turn the balance of the probabilities on to the other side.

Antecedent Probability.

Effect of different totalities.

366. In many cases this value can be expressed with as much certainty as any categorical judgment whatever. But there are also some objects both in logical and in comparative quantity, whose quantity cannot be expressed in terms of discrete quantity at all.

Exact estimate of value.

* *Nodus deo dignus.*

367. In most cases, however, our estimate of the value of a probability can be only approximate. We judge as nearly as we can from what has fallen under our experience, assumed as a representative of the whole, the proportion of the favorable cases to the unfavorable in the absolute whole.

Approximate estimate.

368. The probability against any judgment or Proposition is called its *im*probability; and the probability and the improbability together make up a unit or certainty.

Probability and Improbability make unity.

369. Hence if we have either the Probability or the Improbability given in a fraction or a ratio, we can find the other by subtracting the fraction from unity, or by converting the ratio.

370. But while the improbability can never be more than the complement of the probability in the unity of the logical whole, it may often be less.

Improbability may be less than the complement of the Probability.

371. It will happen in many cases that we know of many reasons for believing a proposition, and none for disbelieving; that is, we may know many favorable chances and be entirely ignorant whether there are really any unfavorable ones or not. Thus in the moral government of God, it is perfectly certain that in many cases sins are punished in this world, and perhaps it is not certain that there is any case in which they are not punished in this world. Hence there is on the supposition a strong probability in favor of the opinion, that any particular sin will be punished in this world and none whatever against it.

Illustration.

372. Improbability, therefore, is not the mere want or absence of probability or grounds for believing. But it is something positive. It is based upon and therefore implies positive ground for *dis*believing, or believing the contradictory of a proposition.

Improbability not mere want of Probability.

373. There may also be an improbability against a proposition, when there is no probability or nothing in its favor; and for the same reasons as we have just

given for there being in some cases a probability without any counter improbability.

374. There may be many cases in which the general probability of which we have just been speaking, may be increased or diminished by special grounds. Thus, in a community where one in ten die of any special disease, the probability that any particular individual would die with that disease is increased or diminished by the peculiarities of his constitution, mode of life, &c. The rates of life insurance are fixed upon the general probability of the duration of life. But this probability becomes so much diminished by one's being sick or constitutionally diseased, that Life Insurance Societies refuse insurance in such cases. In Marine and Fire Insurances also, the rate of insurance is increased above the general rates by considerations affecting the probability of loss, arising from the special circumstances of the property insured.

General and special Probabilities.

SECTION XV.

Of Conditional Judgments.

375. Conditional Judgments affirm the reality of the Predicate, on the ground of the reality of the Subject. But as the Subject and Predicate are not cognitions merely but rather judgments, of which the copula of the second is affirmed on the ground of the copula of the first, the first judgment is called the *Antecedent*, and the second the *Consequent*; thus "If A is B, C is D." Here "A is B" is Antecedent—"C is D" is Consequent.

Conditional Judgments.

Antecedent and Consequent.

376. The Antecedent and Consequent taken together are called the Members of the Conditional; they are also its Matter.

Members or Matter of the Conditional.

377. In all Conditional Judgments there must be at least three terms and two copulas, as in the case just given. There may also be four terms, as "If A is B, C is D." "If each man may

Three Terms at least.

hold what opinion he chooses without blame, atheism itself will be innocent." Here we have the four distinct terms, "each man," "hold what opinion he chooses," "atheism," and "innocent."

Sequence. 378. The ground of affirmation in Conditional Judgments is called the *Sequence*. Thus if we have, "If A is B, C is D," we may ask why? On what grounds can we affirm the judgment, "C is D," as a consequent of the judgment that "A is B?"—the answer to this question is what is called the Sequence.

Not always self-evident. 379. For the most part the sequence or ground of affirmation is self-evident; and for this reason it has seldom received much attention. But we may have a conditional judgment when there is really no sequence; thus the gardener says, that "If he plants any onions in the new of the moon, they will fail to have large bottoms;" the judgment is *in form* a conditional. But still one may fail to see any connection between its members.

Sequence can always be stated as a Categorical Judgment. 380. It becomes necessary, therefore, to consider the grounds of affirmation in the Sequence. This can of course always be stated as a Categorical Proposition. If one says, "If John has a fever he is sick," and we ask why?—the appropriate answer is, "Because all who have fevers are sick."

Immediate Inference. 381. Any Proposition may be an Antecedent upon which any Immediate Inference—whether by (1) Opposition of Judgments, or (2) by Contraposition, or (3) Conversion, or (4) Substitution—may be affirmed as a Consequent, in accordance with laws and principles of Immediate Inference already explained.

Identity of Antecedents. 382. If the unlike terms are mere synonymes or even equipollent, there can hardly be said to be any sequence, and yet the Conditional is good. Thus "If common salt is good for seasoning food, chloride of sodium is good for seasoning food;" the sequence in this case is identity of Antecedents.

383. If the Subject is the same in both Members, the Predicate of the Consequent may be a superior sphere, comprehending the Predicate of the Antecedent; and for the same reason, if the Predicate is the same in both Members, the Subject of the Consequent may be any inferior sphere comprehended in the sphere of the Subject of Antecedent. Thus as an example of the first case, "If the English are Anglo-Saxons, they are Caucasians." Here "Anglo-Saxons" are assumed as but a species of "Caucasians." As an example of the second take the following: "If virtue is expedient, temperance is expedient;"—"temperance" being one species of "virtue," or one of the virtues. But in the first case, if the Antecedent is negative, the Predicate of the Consequent may be any narrower sphere predicated negatively;—"If the English are not Caucasians they are not Anglo-Saxons."

Predicate of the Consequent comprehending that of the Antecedent.

Subject of the Consequent comprehended in that of the Antecedent.

384. If the Predicate of the Antecedent be one of two or more Correlatives inhering in the same subject, the Predicate of the Consequent may be any other of these Correlatives. Thus, "If an ultimate particle of matter has extension, it has divisibility." But if the Correlatives do not inhere in the same object, they must be predicated negatively in one of the members; thus "If the man is the master he is not the servant." Or in general, if one of any two Antithetic terms be predicated of any subject in the Antecedent, the other may be predicated of it negatively in the Consequent, and *vice versa*.

When the Predicates are Correlatives in the same object.

Correlatives in opposite objects must be predicated negatively in one Member.

385. The Cause of any thing is always in some sense the ground of its reality. Under this general principle we may have the following classes of Conditional Judgments with Antecedents expressive of the Cause of the Consequent.

386. Hence if of several contrary terms, having analogous spheres, some property be predicated in the

Antecedent, which is of the essence of the proximate genus—that is, the Material Cause—the same term may be predicated of any contrary term in the Consequent, whether that term be a coördinate or the subordinate of any coördinate to the subject of the Antecedent. Thus, "*If vice is voluntary, virtue is voluntary;*"—here voluntariness of action is assumed as the Essentia or Material Cause of *Moral* actions, and vice and virtue are two coördinate species of Moral actions, each having a Differentia or Formal Cause of its own. And we may also have, "If vice is voluntary, temperance [one of the virtues] is voluntary."

Of opposite Subjects the Material Cause may be predicated in both Members.

387. If the Antecedent affirms the conjunction of the Efficient and Occasional Causes, the reality of the Effect may be affirmed in the Consequent; thus, "If the spark falls upon the powder it will explode, or an explosion will ensue."—"If the boy takes cold he will be sick."

Of the conjunction of the Efficient and Occasional Causes in the Antecedent, the Effect may be affirmed in the Consequent.

388. If the Material Cause is affirmed in the Antecedent, the substance or genus may be affirmed in the Consequent. Thus, "If extension exists matter exists."—"If the moderate indulgence of pleasures is right, the temperate use of alcoholic drinks is right."

Of the Material Cause in the Antecedent the Effect or Consequent may be affirmed.

389. If a Formal Cause be affirmed in the Antecedent the Consequent may affirm the species. Thus, "If the temperate use of alcoholic stimulants be in accordance with the law of temperance and self-denial, it is right."

Of the Formal Cause in the Antecedent, the species may be affirmed in the Consequent.

390. In cases where the Conditional has four distinct terms, the sequence becomes complex or double. In this case we may have several grounds of affirming the Consequent.

Complex sequence.

391. When the Subject of the Antecedent is regarded as the Cause of the Subject of the Consequent, and the Predicate of the Antecedent affirms of its Subject some mode which

Substance and Mode in the Antecedent causes of Substance and Mode in the Consequent.

is regarded as the Cause of the mode of the Subject of the Consequent, it may be predicated of that Subject in the Consequent. Thus, "If the Moon is full the tides will be high." Here the Moon is regarded as the cause of the tides, and the "fulness" of the Moon as the cause of the "highness" of the tides.

Subject of Antecedent comprehending that of the Consequent, and the Predicate of the Conseq'nt comprehending that of the Antecedent.

392. Again the Subject of the Antecedent may include the Subject of the Consequent, and the Predicate of the Consequent include that of the Antecedent. Thus, "If the English belong to the Teutonic branch of the human family, the Puritans must be Caucasians." Here "Puritans," Subject of the Consequent, are regarded as part of "the English," the Subject of the Antecedent—and "Teutons," the Predicate of the Antecedent is included in Caucasians, the Predicate of the Consequent.

Subjects in both Members contraries as Formal Causes.

393. Or again we may have the Subjects of both Members contraries to each other regarded as Formal Causes, and in that case the Predicates will be contraries to each other also; "If vice produces misery, virtue may be expected to produce happiness."

And the reverse.

394. Or we may invert the order and say, "If happiness results from virtue, misery will result from vice."

Of the Effect as an Antecedent the reality of the Cause as Conseq'nt may be affirmed.

395. But besides this the Effect though in no sense the ground of the reality of the Cause, is often the sign or ground of our knowledge of the reality of the Cause, and for that reason becomes an Antecedent, upon which we may always affirm the reality of the Cause. If the Cause be Immanent or Permanent the Antecedent may be affirmed in the present tense or without regard to protension. But if it be only a Transient Cause, as most occasional causes are, its reality can be affirmed in the Consequent only in the past tense. Thus, "If there is daylight we may say that the sun shines;"—but "If there

Immanent and Permanent Causes affirmed in the Present Tense.

Transient only in the past.

is an explosion, we may say that there *has been* powder and fire."—"If there is small pox, we may say that the infecting virus *has been* communicated to the system."

Quantity and Quality of Members.

396. I have said nothing thus far of the Quantity of the Members of the Conditional. But as the Antecedent is the ground on which we affirm the Consequent, it is evident that no term which has not been used as a distributed term in the Antecedent, may be used as a distributed term in the Consequent. But for the most part terms are regarded as Continuous Wholes in Conditional Judgments.

Complex and Compound Members in Conditionals.

397. We have also spoken only of simple Categoricals as Members of the Conditional. But these Members may be either Complex or Compound Categoricals; and as we have before seen the Compound may be regarded as Complex, and the Complex as simple Categoricals—only taking care not to separate or omit any of the parts of the Complex term.

Besides the above modes of compounding the Conditional, there are two others which deserve a mention.

Compound Conditionals.

398. If we have two or more Antecedents, the Copulas of which are each independent of the Copulas of the others respectively, and one Consequent, the Copula of which is affirmed on condition of the truth of all the Antecedents, we shall have what may be called a *Compound Conditional;* thus,

$$\left.\begin{array}{r}\text{If A is B}\\ \text{and If A is C}\end{array}\right\}\text{ A is D;}$$

"If the Departed are cognizant of what takes place on earth, and if they retain the same feelings towards us as they had while they were here, they must sometimes be intensely pained by what they see in the course of life which we are now pursuing."

Continuous Conditionals.

399. Again we may have what is called a *Continuous* Conditional in which the Consequent of the first becomes the Antecedent to the

second, and so on. Thus, "If A is B, A is C. If A is C, A is D," &c.—"If God is just He will punish the wicked. And if He punishes the wicked, surely they that blaspheme His Name will be signally confounded."

SECTION XVI.

Of the Disjunctive Judgments.

Disjunctive Judgments have been defined to be those in which one of two Categorical Judgments is affirmed to be true, on the ground that the other is not true. Disjunctive Judgments.

400. This is called the Principle of *Excluded Middle.* It supposes two judgments so related as that there is no other judgment in the same matter, differing only in quantity and quality, or both, and being in a sense between them. Excluded Middle.

401. Thus if we take A and E, we have the subalterns between them; thus, None between Contraries.

All A is B,
No A is B;

Now "Some A is B," is less than "All A is B" (in affirmative quantity), and more than "No A is B;" since the latter has no affirmative quantity. In the same way "Some A is not B" stands between "No A is B," and "All A is B."

402. Hence either of these Subalterns may be true while both the Universals in the same quantity are false.

403. But if we take the Contradictories there is no such Middle Proposition;—"Either All A is B," or "Some A is not B,"—and "Either No A is B," or "Some A is B." There is no Middle Proposition—no other Proposition in the same matter which can be true and both of these be false. Between Contradictories.

404. The same will hold true of the Sub-contraries also. "Some A is B, and Some A is not B." Now both may be true—but there is no Between Sub-contraries.

Middle Proposition between them; so that if one be false, the other must be true.

405. Hence in the first place if we have two Propositions in the same matter, being either Contradictories or Sub-contraries, we may affirm that one or the other of them is true, and consequently we may affirm one of them to be true on condition the other is not.

Inference from the foregoing.

406. But we may have Disjunctives in matter either partly or wholly different; they all come back, however, as we shall see, to the case just stated, of either Contradictories or Sub-contraries. It will be necessary to investigate this relation a little further.

407. Since in nearly all cases of Disjunctive Judgments there is one term common to the members, we may call those terms, which are different in each, for the sake of convenience, *Coördinate* Terms.

Coördinate Terms.

408. Any term and its privative being complements of each other in the proximate genus, must be contradictories to each other in reference to any individual contained in that genus. If then we have "A" and "non-A,"—as the two coördinate parts of a whole,—as X, and Z as an individual contained in that whole; then "Z must be either A or non-A;" that is, it must be included in one of the parts. But of course the part "non-A" may be denoted by a positive term representing a coördinate species of X, just as well as by the privative "non-A." Hence making this substitution, we may have "Z is either A or B."

Positive and its Privative in the Proximate Genus give an Excluded Middle.

409. But again, if instead of Z denoting an individual, we have any term denoting a class comprehended also under X, then in one of the members of the Disjunctive it must be used as an undistributed term. Thus let "man" be a whole, and "free" and "slave" the coördinate species;—let "Negro" be also a class comprehended in "man," and we may say either "all

If the common subject be a general term, it must be undistributed in one member.

Negroes are free," or "some Negroes are slaves;" or either "some Negroes are free;" or "all Negroes are slaves."

410. In the second case we may have a logical whole, with a property common to some of the parts or individuals contained in that whole. This property we may constitute the Differentia of a species, and then divide the whole into parts in such a way that this property will be predicable of some one part or of some thing contained in the whole which is not that part. Thus let "vegetables" be such a whole, and "poisonous" such a property, and "cereals" a class of vegetables, then we may say, "Either cereals are poisonous, or some [vegetables] not cereals are poisonous." Or again, let "substance" be any logical whole, and "matter" one kind of substance, and we may say "either matter, or something which is not matter, is eternal." Now suppose that substance which is not matter is "spirit," and we may say, "either matter or spirit is eternal."

The two Members with Coördinate Subjects.

411. In this case, as in the preceding, one of the coördinate terms must be undistributed in case they do not stand for individuals.

One of the coördinate terms must be undistributed if they are general terms.

412. If there are more than two coördinate terms, they must be positive terms, and each denote its part by differentia of its own. These parts, how many of them soever there may be, may always be reduced to two, by taking any one as positive, merging the Differentia of the others, and including them in the privative of the one assumed as positive. Thus the coördinate parts, A, B and C, may be reduced to two, as "A" and "non-A,"—or "B" and "non-B," in which case "non-A" includes "B and C,"—and "non-B," "A" and "C."

More than two coördinates.

413. The Divided Whole may be regarded as a logical, or a continuous, or a collective whole, and it may be the absolute whole, or only

The Divided Whole.

some assumed relative whole. When, however, it is but a relative whole, some means must be given in the Proposition stating the Disjunctive, to fix the mind upon the limits of the sphere of the assumed whole. Thus, "A wise lawgiver must either recognize the rewards and punishments of a future state, or appeal to a Providence administering them in this." Here the assumed whole is "*wise lawgivers*," and it is divided into two classes,—(1) those who appeal to rewards, &c., in the future life; and (2) those who refer to a Providence administering such rewards and punishments in this state of being.

Coördinate and Subordinates of its Coördinate.

414. Instead of coördinate terms we may have one coördinate and the subordinates of the other, as in the following case: "The earth is either eternal, the work of chance, or the work of an intelligent Author."

Here "the origin of things" is the logical whole. The first division, all things either had an origin or had none, i. e., "*are eternal*." But things that had an origin (the positive part, with reference to the whole) are divisible into two classes;—(1) those that came by chance, and (2) those that had an intelligent Author. Hence the Formula above given: "The earth is either eternal (had no beginning), or (its beginning) is from chance, or from an intelligent Author."

The Coördinate terms may not be Disparate in the same whole.

Alternate Species may constitute Coördinate Terms in a Disjunctive Judgment.

415. But it is not necessary that the coördinate terms should denote coördinate parts of any division. They cannot indeed be disparate parts, since there is no necessity that any number of disparate parts should include all that was comprehended in the Divided whole. Privatives, as well as Negatives, are always and only coördinates of their Positive. But while disparate parts do not necessarily include all the individuals of a Divided whole, Alternate Species do include them all; and more than that, they include some of them twice at least. Every individual must be contained in one of a set of coördinate

species, and can be contained in no more than one. In Disparate Species or Parts the same individual may be contained indeed in several, but many may not be contained in any enumeration of Disparate Parts. But in Alternate Species, while no one may be omitted, many may be contained in several of the species.

416. But although the sphere of two Alternate Conceptions is the same, the matter is not. Hence the Differentia of several Alternate Species is likely to have many points in common, and must have some that are not so. Now suppose an individual to have a property which we know to be a part of the Differentia of one or two Alternate Species, we can predicate these species of that individual disjunctively. Suppose we have a collection, consisting of portraits of poets and philosophers alone, this collection being one whole—poets and philosophers would be the Alternate Species, including all the individuals in that whole. But they are not Coördinate Species, since the same man may be both a poet and a philosopher, conceived of from different points of view. Hence of any one whose portrait we know to be in that collection, suppose it to be Coleridge, we may say, "Coleridge was either a poet or a philosopher."

The Matter of Alternate Species not the same.

417. But finally there may be Disjunctives with no term common to the members, as, "Either A is B, or C is D, or E is F," &c. It is hardly possible to enumerate the particular forms and relations which the terms may assume; since these judgments, as in all preceding cases, must be parts of a whole, and reducible to an Excluded Middle. We must be able to show that there is no judgment except one of those enumerated, that will contain the truth which the Disjunctive is designed to affirm.

Disjunctives with four terms.

418. Thus if I wish to account for the diversities in the human race, I may say, "Either they sprang from different origins," or "the diversities have been produced by the influence of climate, mode of life," &c.,—

or "God must have interposed to produce the variety miraculously." Here the divided whole is "the origin of the diversities in the human family;" and if the members of the disjunctive enumerate all the parts and species to which it can be referred, whether Coördinate or Alternate, one of them must be true. If not, there must be some other and Middle Judgment which may be true.

419. The Conditionals and the Disjunctives are compounded in two ways:

Compound of Conditionals & Disjunctives.

(1.) A Conditional Antecedent with a Disjunctive Consequent, as, "If A is B, A is either C or D."—"If the world had a beginning, it is either the work of an intelligent Author or the product of chance."

Dilemma.

(2.) We may have a Disjunctive Antecedent, thus, "If either A is B, or A is C, A is D." This constitutes what is called the DILEMMA—"If the patient either eats or abstains from food, he will die" (in the one case from the effects of the food, in the other from want of food).

420. In stating Dilemmas it is not uncommon to omit the Consequent to the Disjunctive Antecedent, as being too obvious to need explicit mention.

Disjunctive Judgments converted into Conditional.

421. Since Disjunctive Judgments always affirm one of the Members to be true, on condition that no one of the others is false, we may always convert the Disjunctive into a Conditional by contra-position of one Member for an Antecedent, and using the other or others, if there be more than one, as Consequent; thus, "Either A or B is C," therefore "If A is not C, B is C."

SECTION XVII.

Of the Grounds of Affirmation.

Grounds of Affirmation.

422. The grounds upon which judgments are affirmed are reducible to three:—(1) the Prin-

ciple of Identity and Contradiction; (2) Sufficient Reason, and (3) Excluded Middle.

(1.) The first Principle is sometimes spoken of as two, as in fact it is.

(*a*) Where the terms are synonymous, or the judgment affirms the identity of the Subject and the Predicate. Such is the case in all Definitions; thus, a triangle is "a figure with three angles,"—"a quadruped is an animal with four feet." Principle of Identity.

(*b*) But there are some terms the relation between which is so founded in the nature of the objects for which they stand, that the relation cannot be denied without destroying the conception of one or the other of these objects. Thus if we say, "every effect must have a cause;" this is not a judgment of identity, for "effect" and "cause" are not the same. But the affirmation depends upon the principle of contradiction; that is, if we say "here is an effect without a cause," we at the same time deny that it is an effect. If we say that "this triangle has but two sides," we deny that it is "a triangle." Principle of Contradiction.

423. The force of this ground of affirmation is well exhibited and tested by resolving the judgment into a cognition with its modal. Illustration.

Thus in the Principle of Identity, we have "Victoria is Queen of England," resolved into a cognition or term, it is "Victoria Queen of England." Again, a "triangle has three sides,"—a "three-sided triangle."

424. Or to try the principle of contradiction, "this effect has no cause," becomes "a causeless effect;"—"this triangle has two sides only," becomes "a two-sided triangle." In each of these cases the term and its modal are incompatible, and taken together constitute an impossibility.

425. (2.) The second ground of affirmation is called *sufficient cause* or *sufficient reason*. Sufficient reason.

(*a*) This ground assumes that there is no sufficient ground or reason in the nature of the matter itself.

If we say, "the Earth exists," the will of the Creator is considered as the ground of the reality of its being. If we say, "all bodies gravitate," the will of the Creator is again considered the ground of the reality of the truth which we affirm. Or if we speak of the acts of man, whether past, present, or future, his will is considered the sufficient ground of the reality of these acts, the *ratio essendi*.

Reason of being.

(*b*) The means by which we know the reality, the *ratio cognoscendi*, may and generally are in fact quite different from the ground of the reality itself. Take the reality of gravitation, for instance, the ground of the reality is the will of God; but our means of knowing the reality are experience and observation. The reality of the Positive Institutions of Christianity depends upon the will of God for its ground, but one means of knowing that reality is Revelation.

Reason of knowing.

426. (3.) The third ground of Affirmation is called the Excluded Middle.

Excluded Middle.

Between any Judgment and its Contradictory there is no Middle or Third Judgment.

Hence in any case if we prove the falsity of one judgment, this becomes the ground for affirming its contradictory.

427. But there is especially one class of Judgments which can be affirmed on no other ground than that of Excluded Middle.

428. Such is the case with all affirmative Propositions with negative Predicates, and all in which the Predicate denotes infinity.

Affirmatives with Negative Predicates.

429. In proving a Proposition with an affirmative Copula, we include the Subject in the sphere of the Predicate, and this we do by showing that the Subject has the Essentia denoted by the Predicate. But if the Predicate be negative, it is denoted by no matter of its own; and we can include the Subject in the sphere of a negative Predicate only, by showing that it does not contain the Essentia of its

Proof of Negatives.

Positive. That is, we disprove the Proposition with the positive Predicate (A is B), and infer by Excluded Middle its contradictory that "A is non-B," which is at once resolved into "A is not B."

430. So also if the Predicate is infinite, as "space is infinite;" we can affirm or prove our own judgment only on the ground of the falsity of the contradictory, and by the principle of Excluded Middle.* God, Eternity, and Space can have no bounds, therefore they are infinite.

Proof of Infinites.

* I do not propose here to touch the question between Sir William Hamilton and Schelling and Cousin, with regard to our direct cognition of the infinite and unconditioned. I am not speaking of cognition but of proof; the former in their phrase is the function of the Reason, the latter of the Understanding.

CHAPTER III.

OF SYLLOGISMS.

SECTION I.

Classification of Syllogisms.

431. A Judgment is called *Intuitive* when the mind perceives and affirms the relation between two cognitions when they are brought together in consciousness, without the intervention or aid of any other cognition.

Intuitive Judgments.

432. But it is not always the case that when two cognitions are thus brought together in the consciousness, the mind affirms or denies any kind of agreement intuitively. It may be at a loss or in doubt. This doubt or inability to see the relation must be the result of the limited nature of our faculties. No such doubt or hesitation can be felt by an *omniscient* mind.

Limits to Intuition.

433. If now we have two cognitions, A and B, and cannot see the relation between them, so as to constitute them into a judgment intuitively, we may see the relation between each one of them, and a third term, as C for instance. We may see that "A" is C, and that C is "B," and from these two intuitive judgments we may have the judgment A is B, which in that case is called a *Deductive* Judgment.

Deductive Judgments.

434. Thus all deductive judgments, which in fact make up the great mass of human knowledge and science, are based upon intuitive judgments as their premises, and may be resolved back into such intuitive judgments.

Deductive Judgments based upon Intuitive.

435. The term which is thus brought in as the means of forming the two judgments is called the MIDDLE TERM. And when there is but one Middle term, the conclusion A is B is a Deductive judgment of the first degree, or but one step removed from the Intuitive. If, however, two such Deductive judgments become Premises to a Conclusion still further removed, there will have been more than one Middle term and more than two Intuitive judgments. The Deductive judgments, however, differ from each other only in the degree of remoteness from the primary Intuitive judgments, which constituted the first elements in their deduction.

Middle Terms.

436. The Deductive Judgment or Conclusion is never contained in or derived from *one* of the Premises alone by any process of Immediate Inference. But it is deduced from the two Premises by means of the Middle term, and is therefore a Mediate Inference.

Mediate Inference.

437. By SYLLOGISM we mean any combination of two judgments as Premises in such a way as that a third, different in matter from either of them taken separately, results. The judgment so resulting is called the *Conclusion*.

Syllogism defined.

438. Syllogisms are of three kinds; CATEGORICAL, CONDITIONAL, and DISJUNCTIVE. They are *Categorical* when all the Premises are Categorical; *Conditional* when one Premise is Conditional; and if one Premise is *Disjunctive*, we call the syllogisms *Disjunctive*.

Syllogisms divided into classes.

439. But Categorical Syllogisms are still further susceptible of division, according as the Premises may be either purely Categoric, Comparative, or Probable Judgments.

Categorical Syllogisms divided into varieties.

440. In the pure Categorical Syllogism there are three Propositions, two Premises, and a Conclusion, and three distinct Terms.

Pure Categoric Syllogisms.

441. Of these Terms in the simplest and most natural Formula (Barbara), one, as individual or sub-species, is included in the second as a species, and then this second is included in the third as the Genus—in the Premises; and thus in the Conclusion the first is included in the third.

Relation of Terms in the Premises and in the Conclusion.

442. Hence the first, as its sphere is the narrowest, is called the MINOR term; and the third, as its sphere is the largest or most comprehensive, is called the MAJOR term; the other is called the MIDDLE term. The Minor and the Major terms together are called the EXTREMES.

Names of the Terms.

443. But this order is not always observed; and as in some syllogisms it is impossible to determine which term has the widest sphere, a more artificial denomination is given to the terms for ordinary purposes, by which the *Predicate* of the Conclusion is called the *Major* term, and the *Subject* of the Conclusion the *Minor* term.

Local, Minor, Middle, and Major Terms.

444. Hence the *Nominal* Minor Term, whether the real minor or not, is the real subject of the Syllogism; and the Nominal Major is the real Predicate of the Syllogism, and the Syllogism is made for the purpose of proving the Major term as Predicate of the Minor as its subject.

445. From this denomination of the Terms in a Syllogism the names of the Premises are derived. As each term must appear in two Propositions, and as the Minor and the Major appear in the Conclusion, the Middle term must be found in each of the Premises. The other term in each Premise must therefore be either the Minor or the Major, and hence the Premise is called the Minor or Major Premise, according as it contains the one or the other of the extremes.

Names of the Premises.

Thus S is M,
" M is P,
" S is P.

Here "S is M" is the Minor Premise, "M is P" is the Major Premise, and "S" and "M" are the Extremes.

446. It is usual in stating Formula to state the Major Premise first. In popular language, when we are speaking of an argument, it is usual to call the Major Premise "*the Principle*" upon which one argues; and the Minor Term "*the Case*," or "*the Instance*," or "*the Example*," coming under it. "Principle" & "Instance."

447. The Conclusion until it is considered as proved, that is until satisfactory Premises have been assigned, is called "*the Question*," and is considered as yet *sub questione*, or under inquiry. Question.

448. As a Question it may be stated in two forms, *What is S? And is S, P?*

449. In the former case we are supposed not to know what is the Major term; or in other words, we do not know the proximate genus to which it belongs, and consequently we are said to be in doubt about the Predicate, and the Question is concerning the Predicate. Question as to the Major Term.

450. When the Question is in the other form, "Is S, P?" we have both terms given, and are said to be in doubt about the Copula—or the question is said to be concerning the Copula—not what is the Predicate, but whether it may be affirmed of the Subject or not. Question of the Copula.

451. If the Question be concerning the Copula it is answered by some one of the Formula, which we are about analyzing. But if it be concerning the Major term, it can be answered only by means of some one or other of the Methods of Investigation, treated of below, (Part II. Chap. II.) Questions of the Copula settled by Formula. Questions of the Major Term answered by Investigation.

452. In Categoric Formula the question concerning

the Copula is determined by means of the Middle term, which for this purpose is used in four different ways:—(1) When the Copula is expressive of the identity of the terms in either or both the Premises; (2) when it expresses a relation in Logical Quantity; (3) when one or both Premises are Comparative; (4) when one or both are Probable judgments.

Office of the Middle Term.

Four ways.

SECTION II.

Of Pure Categorical Syllogisms.

I. OF THE FIGURE OF THE SYLLOGISM.

453. We have already remarked that the Middle term by position is not always the Middle in Logical Quantity between the two extremes, and its office and effect depends very much upon its position. These different positions which it may occupy are four in number, and are called the Four FIGURES, as follows:

Figures.

1st.	2d.	3d.	4th.
M is P.	P is M.	M is P.	P is M.
S is M.	S is M.	M is S.	M is S.
S is P.	S is P.	S is P.	S is P.

454. The Differentia of these Figures may be thus stated:

In the First Figure the Middle term is Subject of the Major Premise, and Predicate of the Minor.

Differentia of the Figures.

In the Second, it is Predicate in both Premises.

" Third, it is Subject in both.

" Fourth, it is Predicate of the Major and Subject of the Minor.

455. From this it appears that the Fourth Figure is only the inverse of the First.

456. This Fourth Figure has been objected to on the ground that it is unnatural, and one against which the mind rebels. On the

Fourth Figure objected to.

other hand Professor De Morgan thinks it the most natural of any.

457. But such considerations or arguments are of no force. The question is not what is pleasing, but what is possible. The Subject or Minor term of an argument is generally fixed or determined beyond our control by the circumstances and necessities of the case, and we are obliged to take the arguments as we find them.

Answers.

458. It has been claimed also that there is an "Unfigured Syllogism" by Mr. Thompson.* Thus "Copperas and sulphate of iron are identical—sulphate of iron and sulphate of copper are not identical, therefore copperas and sulphate of copper are not identical." This he argues is *unfigured*, because neither term in any one of the Propositions can be called either Subject or Predicate. But if a man speaks, he must speak of *something*, and that is "the Subject;" he must say *something of it*, and that is "the Predicate." Thus the Proposition, "Copperas and sulphate of iron are identical," is precisely tantamount to either "copperas is sulphate of iron," or "sulphate of iron is copperas;" and either term would become Subject or Predicate, just according as the one or the other object was the subject of the conversation.

No unfigured Syllogisms.

459. It will be remembered that the Comprehending Sphere is always to be predicated of the Comprehended Sphere in an Affirmative Proposition. Thus, If A is comprehended in the sphere of B, we have A is B. Consequently "A" and "B" have spheres that are coincident to the extent of "A's" comprehensiveness; and all the matter included in the conception "B," is ascribed to every individual included in the sphere of "A."

Comprehending and Comprehended Spheres.

460. Nor do we need to make any exception in favor of those Propositions in which the Subject and

* "Outline of the Laws of Thought," p. 253. Thompson, however, is but following Sir William Hamilton.

the Predicate are Identical, or Alternate Conceptions of the same object; as "common salt is chloride of sodium;"—"Victoria is the Queen of England." In this case the spheres of the Subject and Predicate are identical, indeed, but still the Subject is included in the sphere of the Predicate as truly as a man is included in his own skin.

Identical Spheres.

461. If, however, one sphere is excluded from another, as "A" from "B," then "B" is the predicate of "A" in a negative Proposition, and we have "A is not B;" and the spheres "A" and "B" have no individual common to both.

One Negative Sphere.

462. And if both Premises are Negative they will give us the three spheres, possibly exclusive of each other, though by no means certainly so. Hence we shall have no conclusion.

Both Spheres Negative no conclusion.

463. This may be constructed thus:—Two circles, S and P, exclusive of each other; this is read, "S is not P." Now suppose we have another sphere M, and we read, "M is not P," or conversely, "P is not M." We know from this that P is not in M, nor M in P, but whether M is included in S or not, we do not know. It may be or it may not for aught that appears.

464. The First and Fourth Figures being but the converse of each other, we may construct the Principle upon which their validity depends, thus three circles as follows:—If S is in M it must be in P, and some of P must be in S.

The Principle of the First and Fourth Figures.

(1.) If now the Middle term is a species comprehending another, as S, and wholly comprehended in another, as P, then S is comprehended in P, and conversely some part of P must be comprehended in S; that is, "All S is P," and "Some P is S."

Affirmative Conclusions.

(2.) But if the Middle term comprehends one Extreme, and is not comprehended in the other, then we can have only a Negative Conclusion; that is, the Extremes have no part of their spheres coincident.

Negative Conclusions in First and Fourth Figures.

(3.) Or suppose that the Middle term is in the larger circle and the smaller one is not in the Middle, then some part of the larger one must be out of the smaller one.

465. But in the Second Figure the Middle term is Predicate in both Premises.

Principle of the Second Figure.

This we may construct as follows:—By one large circle M, comprehending two smaller ones S and P;—S and P need not cut each other, although they may do so. They may also both be in M without being at all coincident with each other. But the fact of their being both in M proves nothing with regard to their being coincident. Hence we can have no Affirmative Conclusion by necessity.

No Affirmative Conclusion in Second Figure.

466. If, however, either S or P is made coincident with M, then of course the other Extreme cannot be included in M without being in the other, and we may have an Affirmative Conclusion.

If the Middle be distributed we may have a Conclusion.

467. But if either S or P be in M, and the other be not in it—that is, if one Premise be negative, S and P cannot be coincident, and we shall have a Negative Conclusion.

468. If the Middle term, whether species or individual, is contained in two others, they must be coincident in part.

We may construct this by three circles drawn as follows:—If the small circle M be in both the others, they must be coincident in part, and have enough in common to include M at least.

This explains the validity of the Affirmative Syllogisms in the Third Figure. But if the Middle term be wholly excluded from one of the circles, that part of the other in which it is contained

Principle of the Third Figure.

must be excluded from it also. But the Middle term must be excluded as a whole from one of the circles, or else they may be entirely coincident, and a part of M be excluded from both. Hence we have only *Particular* Conclusions in the Third Figure.

No Universal Conclusion in the Third Figure.

469. It is also necessary that the Middle term be once distributed in the Premises. For

(1.) In the First and Third Figures, when it is Subject in the Major Premise, if it be not included as a whole in the Major term, or excluded as a whole, the Minor term may be included in the Middle without being included in the Major term, if the Premise is affirmative, or being excluded from it if it be negative.

(2.) In the Second Figure, as we have seen, one Premise must be negative, and consequently the Middle term will be distributed as Predicate of a Negative Premise. Or if either S or P become coincident with M, and we have an Affirmative Conclusion, it is because in that case M or the Middle term becomes distributed; and in the Fourth Figure the same reasoning applies as to the First, only taken in the inverse order.

470. It appears from the foregoing demonstrations, that the Middle term must be once distributed; that is, taken as a whole in one of the Premises. Otherwise we have the fallacy in Form which is called *Undistributed Middle.*

Undistributed Middle.

As an illustration of this Fallacy take the following:

"Moral virtues are habits.
Skill in the mechanic arts is a habit.
∴ Skill in the mechanic arts is a virtue."

Both Premises in this Syllogism are true. But there are "*habits*" of at least two different kinds—moral virtues being habits of one kind, and skill in the mechanic arts habits of another kind. And since the term "*habits*," being the Middle term, is not distributed, the Major term is compared with one part of what is included in the Middle term—that is, one kind of habits—and found to agree with it; and the Minor term is compared with the other part.

II. Of the Moods of Syllogisms.

471. The Mood of a Syllogism is that which indicates the nature and order of the Propositions which constitute it. As any one of the Four Judgments may be the Major Premise, Minor Premise, or Conclusion, it is seen by permutation and combination that there may be sixty-four Moods.

The Mood of Syllogisms.

472. But by no means all of the sixty-four Moods are valid in any Figure, and of those that are valid, not all are valid in all four of the Figures. Hence we must effect what is called an *abscissio infiniti*—that is, a continued cutting off of the several classes of invalid Moods, until we get them reduced so as to include none that are not valid.

Not all Moods valid.

473. From the Diagrams and remarks upon them just given, it will appear with regard to the *Quality* of the Conclusion, that

(1.) If both Premises are Affirmative, and the Middle term be once distributed, the spheres of the Extremes must be in part at least coincident; that is, the Conclusion must be Affirmative also.

Quality of the Conclusion.

(2.) If either Premise be negative, and the other affirmative, and the Middle distributed, then the Extremes must represent contrary spheres; that is, the Conclusion will be negative.

474. In regard to the *Quantity* of the Conclusion, the Rule is that "No term may be distributed in the Conclusion, which was not distributed in the Premises." Any violation of this Rule is a Fallacy in Form, and is called *Illicit Process*. It may be of two kinds, *Illicit Process of the Minor*, and *Illicit Process of the Major*.

Quantity of the Conclusion.

Illicit Process.

We have two cases in which the Minor term may be illicit in the Conclusion.

(1.) When the Minor term is Subject: No more of the Minor term can be either included in or excluded from the Major by means of the Middle than is included in the Middle itself.

Of the Minor first case.

(2.) When the Minor term is Predicate only that part of it which is coincident with the Middle, can be included in or excluded from the Major by means of the Middle; or if the Minor term is excluded from the Middle, then no more of it is excluded from the Major by means of the Middle than is excluded from the Middle itself—this will be seen from the preceding Diagrams.

Second case.

475. As Affirmatives do not distribute the Predicate, there can be no Illicit Process of the Major, except when there is a Negative Conclusion.

No Illicit of the Major in Aff've Conclusions.

Illicit of the Major.

476. We may have two cases:

(1.) When the Major term is Predicate. If the Premise is Negative the Major term is of course distributed. But if the Premise is Affirmative, then the Major term as Predicate must be taken as a whole; and as such it can comprehend nothing which is not in the Middle term. But if it be not taken as a whole, the Minor term may be in that part of the Major which is not occupied by the Middle term.

First case.

Thus let us have a large circle P, including M and something more. Thus S may be in the part of P, not occupied by M, without being in M, thus we may have:

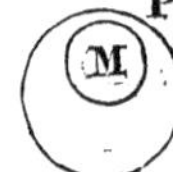

M is P,

S is not M, and S may or may not be P.

(2.) But in the second case if the Major term is subject in the Premise, it must be wholly included in M, or S may be in that part of it which is not included in M.

Second case.

Thus let us have a large circle M, and another P only part included in it. Then S may be in the part of M which is not included in P.

Then we have Some P is not M,
S is M,
and S may or may not be P;

Or suppose some in P only is in M and the rest not, and then we may have—Some P is M,
S is not M,
in this case too, S may be or may not be P.

477. From what has been said, it will appear,

1. That if both Premises are negative, we can have no Conclusion. Five Canons of validity.

2. If one Premise is negative the Conclusion must be negative.

3. If both Premises are affirmative the Conclusion must be affirmative.

4. The Middle Term must be distributed in one of the Premises; and

5. No Term may be distributed in the Conclusion, which was not distributed in the Premises.*

478. By the First of these Rules the sixteen Moods with negative Premises are excluded from being valid in any Figure. By the Second, the sixteen with one negative Premise and affirmative Conclusions; and by the Third, the eight with affirmative Premises and a negative Conclusion. The First excludes sixteen Moods. Second, sixteen more. Third, eight more.

479. By the Fourth and Fifth combined, all those Moods in which both Premises are particular, are excluded; since if both are particular (and one must be affirmative), there can be but one term distributed in the Premises—and if both Premises are affirmative, there will be none. In this case there will be undistributed Middle. But if one Premise is negative the Conclusion must be so too, Fourth & Fifth, Six.

* The following hexameters have been found to assist the memory in retaining these fundamental requirements of simple Categorical Syllogisms:

Distribuas Medium: nec quartus terminus adsit
Utraque nec praemissa negans, nec particularis:
Sectetur partem Conclusio deteriorem:
Et non distribuat, nisi cum Praemissa, negetve.

and then we shall have either Illicit Process of the Major or Undistributed Middle.

Six more.

480. By the operation of the same rules, Fourth and Fifth, it will be found that if one Premise be particular there can be no universal Conclusion. (1st) Suppose the conclusion to be A; in order to that, the Premises must be both affirmative—and with one of them, Particular Affirmative—there will be but one term distributed in the Premises, if that be the Minor, we shall have undistributed Middle, and if the Middle we shall have illicit of the Minor. (3d) Suppose the conclusion to be E, one Premise must be negative, and all three terms distributed in the Premises. But there are no Premises that fulfil this condition, except A and E, and O and E. But O and E are both negative, and can have no conclusion; A and E are universal, and therefore do not come under this rule.

IEO.

481. By the same reasoning it will be found that IEO will involve an Illicit Process of the Major in all the Figures.*

Eleven valid.

482. The eleven valid Moods are—AAA, AAI, AEE, AEO, AII, AOO, EAE, EAO, EIO, IAI and OAO.

483. Not all of these, however, are valid in each of the Four Figures which we have just described.

III. The Application of Moods to the Figures.

Application of Figure. First Figure.

484. In the First Figures (1) if the Major Premise be particular we can have no Conclusion—for (*a*) if the Minor be Affirmative we should

* The Moods excluded by these Rules are:

By the First—EEA, EEE, EEI, EEO, EOA, EOE, EOI, EOO, OEA, OEE, OEI, OEO, OOA, OOE, OOI, and OOO—(16).

By the Second—EAA, EAI, AEA, AEI, EIA, EII, IEA, IEI, OAA, OAI, AOA, AOI, OIA, OII, IOA, IOI—(16).

By the Third—AAE, AAO, AIE, AIO, IAE, IAO, IIE, IOO—(8).

By the Fourth and Fifth—(1) OIE, OIO, IOE, IIA, III, IIO—(6).

" " (2) AOE, OAE, IAA, IEE, AIA, EIE—(6).

" " (3) IEO—(1).

In all 16 + 16 + 8 + 6 + 6 + 1 = 53.

have an undistributed Middle; and (*b*) if Negative, the Conclusion must be Negative also, and that would involve an Illicit Process of the Major.

(2.) If the Minor be Negative there can be no Conclusion; for the Major Premise would have to be Affirmative, and that would involve an Illicit Process of the Major.

Six valid—four useful.

Hence in the First Figure the Major Premise must be A or E, and the Minor A or I, and we may have AAA, AAI, EAE, EAO, AII, EIO.

But as AAI and EAO have particular conclusions, when we might have from the same Premises an universal one, they are useless and so dismissed from further consideration.

Names.

485. These Four Syllogisms are called *Barbara*, *Celarent*, *Darii*, and *Ferio*.*

Second Figure.

486. In the Second Figure. If both Premises are Affirmative we can have no Conclusion; since the Middle term, being Predicate in both, would be undistributed.

* As examples we may have the following:

Barbara. "Those who derive benefit from every exertion of their industry, are more likely to be industrious than laborers employed by the day. Journeymen who work by the piece derive benefit from every exertion of their industry; therefore journeymen who work by the piece are more likely to be industrious than laborers employed by the day."

Celarent. "No real hardship upon individuals should be authorized by legislative enactment. The impress of sailors is a real hardship upon individuals, therefore the impress of sailors should not be authorized by legislative enactment."

Darii. "Every thing which obstructs the free course of justice deserves the reprobation of the virtuous. There are modes of enforcing the strict letter of the law which obstruct the free course of justice; therefore there are some modes of enforcing the strict letter of the law which deserve the reprobation of the virtuous."

Ferio. "Those who endure dangers and face death merely for the sake of acquiring glory to themselves, without being influenced by any desire to benefit their country, are not possessed of true fortitude. But it cannot be denied that some of the heroes of antiquity endured dangers and faced death, merely for the sake of acquiring glory to themselves, without being influenced by any desire to benefit their country. Consequently several of the heroes of antiquity were not possessed of true fortitude."

And if the Major Premise be Particular there can be no Conclusion, since that would involve an Illicit Process of the Major.

Hence we have in the Second Figure—AEE, AEO, EAE, EAO, EIO, and AOO. But AEO and EAO have particular Conclusions when we might have universal, and hence they are dismissed as useless.

Six valid—four useful.

487. It will be observed, that all the Conclusions in this Figure are Negative.

No Affirmative Conclusions.

488. The four valid and useful Syllogisms in the Figure are called *Cesare*, *Camestres*, *Festino*, and *Baroko*.*

Examples.

489. In the Third Figure there can be no Universal Conclusion—for in order to such a Conclusion both Premises must be Universal; but if both are Affirmative, the Minor term will be undistributed, and hence a Universal Affirmative would be Illicit of the Minor; and if the Minor be Negative the Major Premise must be Affirmative, and that would give an Illicit Process of the Major in a Negative Conclusion. And for the same reason there can be no conclusion if the Minor Premise be a Negative.

Third Figure.

No Universal Conclusions.

490. Hence in the Third Figure we can have only AAI, AII, EAO, EIO, IAI and OAO.

Six valid names.

* For examples take the following:

Cesare. "No conscientious person wilfully violates a solemn engagement. Every careless clergyman wilfully violates a solemn engagement; therefore no careless clergyman is a conscientious person."

Camestres. "All those who are qualified for sea-service must possess some knowledge of the arts of navigation. Mere inland watermen do not possess any knowledge of the arts of navigation; therefore mere inland watermen are not qualified for sea-service."

Festino. "No man of sound sense can despise the study of the classics. Some modern pretenders to literature do, however, despise the study of the classics; therefore some of the modern pretenders to literature are not men of sound sense."

Baroko. "All the fixed stars emit light from themselves. Yet there are some of the heavenly bodies which do not emit light from themselves; therefore some of the heavenly bodies are not fixed stars."

The six Syllogisms of the Third Figure are *Darapti*, *Disamis*, *Datisi*, *Felapton*, *Bokardo*, and *Feriso*.*

491. In the Fourth Figure, with A for Major, we must provide for the distribution of the Middle term in the Minor Premise by making that Premise Universal. If then the Minor Premise be A, we may have I for Conclusion (A would be illicit of the Major). If the Minor Premise be E, we may have E and O for Conclusions. But O is useless. Hence AAI and AEE.

Fourth Figure.

With E for Major Premise the Minor must be affirmative. If A, we have O for Conclusion (E would be illicit of the Minor). If it be I, we have O also for Conclusion. Hence EAO and EIO.

With I for Major we must have A for Minor to distribute the Middle, and hence I is the only Conclusion. Hence IAI.

With O for Major we must have a negative Con-

* Examples:

Darapti. "To be ashamed of one's birth, profession, or rank in life, has been represented as the fault of modesty—whereas in reality it is a symptom of pride; so that even that which is a symptom of pride has been represented as the result of modesty."

Disamis. "Some practices which the divine law allows are under particular circumstances inexpedient. All practices which the divine law allows however are in themselves consistent with holiness; therefore some things which are in themselves consistent with holiness are under particular circumstances inexpedient."

Datisi. "Every kind of pride is wholly inconsistent with the spirit of religion. Yet there are several kinds of pride which are highly commended by the world, therefore there are feelings highly commended by the world which are wholly inconsistent with the spirit of true religion."

Felapton. "No conspiracies against the liberty of the country lay any just obligation on the conscience. All such conspiracies, however, have the nature of contracts; hence some contracts do not lay any just obligation upon the conscience."

Bokardo. "Some compositions of an imitative nature, calculated by sublimity of idea and beauty of diction to expand and delight the mind and to excite every noble passion, are not written in verse. All such compositions, however, are called poems; therefore some works justly called poems, are not written in verse."

Feriso. "No prejudices are compatible with a state of perfection—but some prejudices are innocent; therefore some innocent things are not compatible with a state of perfection."

clusion, which would involve an Illicit Process of the Major.

Hence in the Fourth Figure we have AAI, AEE, EAO, EIO, and IAI.

Five valid Forms.

492. The five valid and useful Syllogisms in the Fourth Figure are, *Bramantip*, *Camenes*, *Dimaris*, *Fesapo*, and *Fresison*.*

Recapitulation.

493. Of the Eleven valid Moods, we have AAA valid only in the First Figure; AAI in the First, Third, and Fourth, but useless in the First; AEE valid in the Second and Fourth; AEO in the Second and Fourth, but useless in both; AII valid in the First and Third; AOO in the Second; EAE in the First and Second; EAO in all, but useless in the First and Second; EIO valid in all Figures; IAI in the Third and Fourth; OAO in the Third.

Nineteen valid Syllogisms.

494. In the whole, then, we have Nineteen valid and useful elementary Forms in Pure Categorical Syllogisms;—their names have already been given. But for the convenience of remembering, especially for those who understand Latin Prosody, they have been arranged into the following lines:

BArbArA, CElArEnt, DArII, FErIOque, *prioris;*
CEsArE, CAmEstrEs, FEstInO, BArOkO, *secundae;*
Tertia, DArAptI, DIsAmIs, DAtIsI, FElAptON;
BOkArdO, FErIsOn *habet: Quarta insuper addit*
BrAmAntIp, CAmEnEs, DImArIs, FEsApO, FrEsIsOn.

* Examples:

Bramantip. "All diamonds consist of carbon—but all carbon is combustible; therefore some combustible substances are diamonds."

Camenes. "All the planets are opaque bodies. No opaque bodies are capable of transmitting light in any other way than by reflection; therefore bodies capable of transmitting light in other ways than by reflection are not planets."

Dimaris. "Some of the inhabitants of the sea have antennae and horny jointed legs—but all animals of this description are insects; therefore some insects are inhabitants of the sea."

The vowels printed in capitals will be recognized as indicating the Mood of the Syllogism, and the consonants besides making out the words serve another purpose, to be explained by and by.

SECTION III.

Of Indirect Conclusions.

495. There has sometimes been reckoned a class of *Indirect* Moods, but this is unnecessary; since all that are reckoned as Indirect Moods are merely some one of the Direct Moods with the Premises transposed. Indirect Moods.

Thus for example, All B is A,
No C is B,
∴ Some A is not C.

This is simply Fesapo with the Premises transposed, and the Indirect Conclusion.

496. An Indirect Conclusion is one in which the order of the terms of the Direct Conclusion is inverted, so as that the Subject becomes Predicate, and *vice versa*; and an Indirect Conclusion is valid when (1) it does not change the quality of the Direct Conclusion; nor (2) distribute any term in the Indirect Conclusion which was not distributed in the Premises. Indirect Conclusion the converse of the Direct.

497. It is worth while to notice, however, that in most cases we may have an Indirect Conclusion as well as the Direct.* Thus—Barbara:

Fesapo. "No vice is to be admitted as a species of relaxation suited to a Christian. Every species of relaxation suited to a Christian consists of a cessation from ordinary occupations. Wherefore there are cessations from ordinary occupations which are not vice."

Fresison. "No fallacious argument is a legitimate mode of persuasion. And some legitimate modes of persuasion fail of securing acquiescence; therefore some arguments which fail of securing acquiescence are not fallacious."

* In fact it will be seen that all the Conclusions in the Fourth Figure are but the Indirect Conclusion from the same Premises, regarded (by considering the Major term as Minor, and *vice versa*) as in the First Figure."

Indirect Conclusions in all Syllogisms.

All Y is X,
All Z is Y,
∴ All Z is X—or indirectly, Some X is Z.

Bramantip gives a more important Indirect Conclusion still:

All X is Y,
All Y is Z,
∴ Some Z is X—or indirectly, *All* X is Z.

In the Direct Conclusion the Major term appears as undistributed in the Conclusion, whereas it was distributed in the Major Premise.

Incidental validity.

498. Besides the above-named nineteen Syllogisms, any other of the valid Moods may have an *incidental* validity, if its terms are so distributed either by signs or the nature of the terms, or of the matter of the judgment as to secure us against Undistributed Middle and Illicit Process.

Analogy proved in Second Figure.

499. Again, if we have two affirmative Premises in the Second Figure, both extremes are in the same category—the Middle term; and then they must each of them have the Essentia of the conception which the term denotes. They have therefore so much matter in common—that is, so many points of identity, and consequently there is an analogy between the Extremes.

SECTION IV.

Of the Conversion of Syllogisms.

Aristotle's Dictum.

500. It has been thought that all Mediate Inference could be reduced to the celebrated Dictum of Aristotle, called the *Dictum* de Omni et Nullo*; that is, "Whatever may be predicated of a

* Aristotle appears to have thought that all Mediate Inference could be reduced to this one Canon. And so by Conversion it can. But later writers have given us *dicta* for each of the other Figures (Lambert, Neues Organon, Part I. ch. 4, § 232).

That for the Second Figure is called the *Dictum de Diverso:* "If a certain attribute can be predicated (affirmatively or negatively) of every class [the Middle term], may be predicated as Major term of whatever is comprehended in that class, as a Minor term; and conversely whatever may be denied of that class may be denied of whatever is comprehended under it."

501. This is substantially the same as the first Axiom of Mediate Inference which we have given (464); and to prove that all cases of Mediate Inference can be reduced to it, various expedients have been devised for reducing the Syllogisms of the Second, Third, and Fourth Figures to Syllogisms in the same matter in the First Figure.

502. If this were the only object to be gained in the Reduction of Syllogisms, as it is called, it would hardly be worth the time and pains which it costs, since the other axioms given above are as primary and as satisfactory as the Dictum of Aristotle itself. But there is a further practical importance in the Reduction of Syllogisms which makes it worth our while to examine the laws and processes by which it can be done. Such is the nature and imperfections of language that we cannot always express our judgments exactly as we would, and many an expression which suits all the requirements of Logic, fail to meet the demands of Rhetoric.

Objects of Reduction.

503. In order to effect this Reduction or Conversion, we need to resort to Conversion, Permutation, and Transposition of Premises, one or the other of them, and sometimes more.

Means of Conversion.

member of a class—any subject of which it cannot be so predicated does not belong to that class."

The Third Figure (1) *Dictum de Exemplo:* "If a certain attribute can be affirmed of any portion of the members of a class, it is not incompatible with the distinctive attributes of that class;"—and (2) the *Dictum de Excepto:* "If a certain attribute can be denied of any portion of the members of a class, it is not inseparable from the distinctive attributes of that class." He also gives what he calls a Dictum for the Fourth Figure, which he calls the *Dictum de Reciproco.* But it is hardly worth quoting. The Fourth Figure is at best but an inverse of the First, and depends upon the same Principle inverted. For the above quotations I am indebted to the Oxford edition of Aldrich, 1849, pp. 72 and 80.

Conversion and Permutation of Propositions have already been sufficiently explained.

Transposition of Premises.

504. Transposition consists merely in changing the relative position of the Premises; thus, for

M is P, S is M, ∴ S is P,	we shall have	S is M, M is S, ∴ S is P.

This it will be observed is not changing the Syllogism from one Figure into another. It is merely writing the Minor Premise first instead of the Major. Sir William Hamilton says that this was generally done for several centuries after Aristotle. And we shall see by and by that in practice, where we are guided by instinct and common sense, with no regard to Logical Formulæ, we usually state the Major Premise first in the Deductive Methods, and the Minor first in the Inductive Methods.

505. But as the transposition changes neither the quantity nor the quality of the Premises, nor yet the relative position of any of the terms in regard to the laws of the distribution of terms by Position, it can have no effect upon the concluding force of the Premises.

Different forms of the Conclusion.

506. In these cases we obtain the result in three different forms—we may get (1) the same Conclusion in the Converse as in the Exposita; or we may get (2) one from which that is derived as an Immediate Inference; and we may get (3) a Conclusion contradictory to that of the Exposita, but false; from which of course the truth of that in the Exposita is inferred immediately.

Signification of Consonants in the Names of Syllogisms.

507. It is with reference to this process of Conversion of Syllogisms, that the Consonants used in the names that have been given to them are selected; the Vowels are used to indicate the Mood. But the Consonants indicate the processes and means of converting them into Syllogisms in the First Figure.

All beginning with B, can be proved in Barbara.
" " " C, " " " " Celarent.
" " " D, " " " " Darii.
" " " F, " " " " Ferio.

The steps to be taken are indicated as follows:

"*m*" transposes Premises.

"*m*" denotes that the Premises are to be transposed.

"*s*" converts simply.

"*s*" denotes that in order to reduce a Syllogism to the First Figure, the Proposition signified by the vowel before the *s* is to be converted simply.

Thus the Minor Premise in Camestres—No Y is Z, is to be converted into No Z is Y.

"*p*" converts *per accidens.*

"*p*" denotes that the Proposition indicated by the vowel before it, is to be converted by limitation, or *per accidens.*

"*k*" gives a contradictory Conclusion.

"*k*" occurs in Baroko and Bokardo only. These are reduced to Barbara by what is called *reductio ad impossibile.* The reduction is effected by substituting the contradictory of the Conclusion for the Premise, indicated by the vowel immediately before the "*k*," and proceeding as before.* In this way we get a Conclusion contradictory to the Premise for which we have substituted the contradictory of the old Conclusion. If now the new Conclusion is false, or absurd, or impossible, the old one must have been true. We are in fact proving that the Conclusion is O, by the indirect method of proving that it cannot be A.

Change of Terms.

508. In the course of these reductions, it will be observed that the terms undergo several relative changes, so that Major becomes Minor, &c., and *vice versa.* In that case the name of the Syllogism ends in "*s*" or "*p*,"—as "Camenes," "Bramantip." The Middle term also in Baroko and Bokardo becomes one of the Extremes.

* These rules have been expressed in the following lines:
S vult simpliciter verti; *P* vero per acci-
M vult transponi; *K* per impossibile duci.

509. When in the course of the Conversion or Reduction of Syllogisms we get a Conclusion in the same quality as that in the Exposita Syllogism, the process has been called *Ostensive Reduction.* But if the Conclusion be in the opposite quality, the Reduction is called *Reductio ad Impossibile*, or *Reductio ad Absurdum.*

Ostensive Reduction.

Reductio ad Absurdum.

510. As examples in Ostensive Reduction, I will give only a few, as follows:

Examples.

	Cesare	to	*Celarent.*
	No X is Y,	*s.*	No Y is X,
Cesare.	All Z is Y,	the Minor stands,	All Z is Y,
	∴ No Z is X,		∴ No Z is X.

	Darapti	to	*Darii.*
	All Y is X,	the Major stands,	All Y is X,
Darapti.	All Y is Z,	*p.*	Some Z is Y,
	∴ Some Z is X,		∴ Some Z is X.

	Bramantip	to	*Barbara.*
	All X is Y, }		{ All Y is Z,
Bramantip.	All Y is Z, }	*m.*	{ All X is Y,
	∴ Some Z is X,	∴ Some X is Z, *p*	Some Z is X.

	Felapton	to	*Ferio.*
	No Y is X,		No Y is X,
Felapton.	All Y is Z,	*p.*	Some Z is Y,
	∴ Some Z is not X,		∴ Some Z is not X.

	Fresison	to	*Ferio.*
	No X is Y,	*s.*	No Y is X,
Fusison.	Some Y is Z,	*s.*	Some Z is Y,
	∴ Some Z is not X,		∴ Some Z is not X.

511. *Reductio ad Impossibile* is effected by means of *Contra-position* and *Excluded Middle.*

Baroko. Thus if we have in Baroko:

Every star is fixed.
Some luminous bodies are not fixed.
∴ Some luminous bodies are not stars (such for instance as planets, meteors, &c.)

Let us substitute for this Minor Premise the contradictory of the Conclusion and we shall have:

Every star is fixed.
All luminous bodies are stars.
∴ All luminous bodies are fixed.

But this Conclusion is false, consequently the Minor Premise of the first Syllogism, Baroko, its contradictory, is true. And if that Premise is true (the Major Premise also), the Conclusion is irrefragable.

In the same way we may test Bokardo.

512. Or again, we may reduce Bokardo by contraposition of the Major to Ferio; thus, Baroko to Ferio.

All X is Y,
Some Z is not Y,
∴ Some Z is not X.

All X is Y, we may state by contra-position and conversion in E.—No non-Y is X, then we have as before,

Some Z is not Y or non-Y,
∴ Some Z is not X,

which gives us the same conclusion in Ferio as we had in Baroko.

513. Again, we may reduce Bokardo to Darii, by permuting, and converting, and transposition, as follows: Bokardo to Darii.

Some slaves are not discontented. But
All slaves are wronged.
∴ Some who are wronged are not discontented.

We may have:

All slaves are wronged.
Some not-discontented persons are slaves.
∴ Some not-discontented are wronged.

514. This process of Reductio ad Impossibile may be applied to all Syllogisms, as well as to Baroko and Bokardo, on the ground that if we substitute for any given Premise the contradictory of the Conclusion, we shall obtain for a new Conclusion the contradictory of the Premise; or its contrary, in which, of course, the contradictory is included. Process applicable to all.

Barbara to Bokardo.

Thus *Barbara*	to	*Bokardo.*
All Y is X,	by contra-posi-	Some Z is not X,
All Z is Y,	tion of the Con-	All Z is Y,
∴ All Z is X,	clusion becomes	∴ Some Y is not X.

Thus from Celarent we may have Disamis in the Third Figure, and Festino of the Second.

Celarent to Disamis and Festino.

No Y is X,	Some Z is X, or,	No Y is X,
All Z is Y,	All Z is Y,	Some Z is X,
∴ No Z is X,	∴ Some Y is X,	∴ Some Z is not Y.

515. It is often very important in general discussions to disembarrass ourselves of the details of Mood and Figure, and speak of Terms and Premises in the most general way; even where the Differentia of the Figures would require, if they were recognized at all, a very important modification of our statement.

Omission of peculiarities of Figure.

516. For this purpose we always consider an argument, unless otherwise expressly stated, as made in the First Figure, and when we speak of the Major Premise we mean that which either is the Major in the First Figure, or that which would become the Major if the Syllogism were converted into that Figure. And for the same purpose we consider all Negative Propositions as Affirmative with Negative Predicates, as we have a right to do. And hence we may always speak of that term which either is or would become on conversion of the Syllogism into the First Figure the Predicate of the Conclusion, as the Major term. If the Conclusion be affirmative that is the Major term, and if not we substitute for the Predicate of the Negative Conclusion its connoted negative or privative, which of course becomes a Major to the others.

Indicates no uncertainty about Terms.

517. This may, perhaps, be thought to indicate a looseness and uncertainty with regard to the whole nomenclature of Mood and Figure, which does not exist. But we have to take an argument for the most part as we find it. And as it thus stands, it is no matter of choice or uncertainty which

are the Major and Minor terms by *position*. But to avoid the perplexity and the prolixity of continued repetition or detail, we may avail ourselves of the fact that all the Syllogisms may be reduced to the First Figure; that is, the fact that with the same matter as that given in the Premises, we may prove the same Conclusion in the First Figure, and thus adopt the simplicity and brevity of discussion which there would be if there were only the one Figure.

SECTION V.

Of Complex Syllogisms.

518. We have thus far in the investigation of the laws and formula of Syllogisms spoken only of the Simple Categoric Syllogisms. Although this is the simplest and primary formula, we but seldom meet with them in practice. In nearly every case one or more of the terms is complex. Hence a Syllogism in which one or more terms has a modal, is called a Complex Syllogism.

Seldom meet Pure and Simple Formulas.

519. Strictly speaking the simple term can be nothing more than a single word;* which is either a noun, an adjective, or a verb in the Infinitive Mood. In adjectives I include participles used adjectively.

Simple Terms.

520. But it often happens that several words are used as the definition of a term instead of the term itself. Thus we have the term Negro—but instead of it we may use its definition in any case—as "*men with dark skins and woolly hair*," &c. Now suppose that we had not the word "*Negro*" at all. In that case we should be obliged to use its

Definition for a Term.

* This must depend, however, somewhat upon the genius of a language. Perhaps the only exception, the only one that I have noticed in the English, is in those words which answer to the Aristotelian category "*where*." We say a man is "in the house,"—"on the ground," &c., &c. We have not in this respect any thing corresponding to the Greek termination θῖ as in ἀγρόθι, ὄικοθι, &c.

definition whenever we wish to use the conception as a term at all.

521. This is precisely the case with regard to a large part, by far the largest part of the conceptions which enter into our reasonings. There is no precise term for them; and therefore we are obliged to use, instead of the term, what is really its definition. The Definition gives first the Genus and then the Differentia one after another. Thus for "*Negro*" we have [genus] men,—[1st differentia] with dark skins,—and [2d differentia] woolly hair. Suppose we wish to speak of those Christians who adhere strictly to their faith and live pious and devoted lives, as a class distinguished from the rest, we have no one word by which to denote the class. Consequently when we want to express the conception, we are obliged to use the definition for want of a word to denote it.

Necessity for it.

522. In all such cases we may, if we please, regard the Definition as the Term and its Logical Modals, or as a simple term for all the ordinary purposes of deduction.

Definition a Term and its Modals.

523. All Modals which have any logical force at all, as has been shown, either limit the comprehensiveness of the subject in reference to quantity, or point out some condition, or time necessary to limit the scope of the judgment in order that it may be true. Hence the Modal will often make the whole of the difference between a Proposition that is true and one that is false.

Modals limit the comprehensiveness of the Term.

But as Rhetoric often requires some variety in expression, the phraseology of Modals must often be changed, and in these changes Fallacies often occur.

524. The Modal of a subject limits the scope of the judgment, by limiting the sphere of the subject itself. Now from the fundamental axiom, that the narrower the sphere the greater the amount of the matter of any conception, it follows that more may be predicated of a subject which is limited by a modal than can be predicated of the

Modals of the Subject limit the scope of the Judgment.

same term without the Modal. Hence the dropping of the Modal would in some cases render the Proposition untrue.

525. Suppose now that the Middle term is first used with a Modal, and is used in the next Premise without one, we have in fact a different term; and it will affect the formula differently according to its position. Middle Term with a Modal.

Let us then refer to the First Figure in which the Middle term is Subject of the Major Premise and Predicate of the Minor. If we drop the Modal in the Minor term we enlarge the sphere denoted by it, and by consequence it may become so large that the Major term could not be predicated of it. Thus, In the First Figure.

All *true* Christians enjoy the favor of God.
Hypocrites are Christians.
∴ Hypocrites—

But here it becomes obvious that the matter of the Predicate in the Major Premise could not be predicated of so comprehensive a sphere as "Christians;" that is, "*all* Christians,"—nor the Differentia of *true* Christians of the subject of the Minor Premise.

526. Now let us take an example of the opposite course:

All Christians believe in Christ.
The Waldenses were *true* Christians.
∴ The Waldenses, &c.

Here the conclusion is good. We include the Minor term by means of the Modal in a narrower and comprehended sphere than that which, as Middle term, we had included in the Major term in the Major Premise.

527. We have already seen that the Middle term must be once distributed in the Premises of a Syllogism, and in fact it is distributed in both Premises in two of them, Darapti and Felapton. But wherever it occurs as an undistributed term, it stands of course for a narrower though an undetermined sphere than if it

were distributed. We have the following Rules for the dropping or assumption of Modals in the same Syllogism.

Three Rules.

(1.) In all cases where the Middle term is undistributed, as always in the Minor Premise in the First Figure for instance, we may always make the indeterminate undistributed term a determinate distributed term, with a narrower sphere than the absolute or simple term, by joining to it its appropriate Modal. And when the Middle is twice distributed as in Darapti, and Felapton, and Fesapo, we may limit it in either Premise at discretion, but not in both unless it be with the same Modal.

First Rule.

(2.) And conversely a Modal that was introduced and used with the Middle term when used distributively, may not be omitted where it occurs in the other Premises as an undistributed term. This remark, for a reason similar to the one given in case of the last rule, does not apply to Darapti, Felapton, and Fesapo, in which the Middle term is distributed in both Premises.

Second Rule.

(3.) And finally, if the undistributed Middle occurs in the Major Premise, as in the Fourth Figure with a Modal, that Modal may be dropped when the Middle term comes to be used as a distributed term in the Minor Premise.

Third Rule.

(4.) If in the Major Premise a Modal is used, extending the comprehensiveness of the judgment to all possible cases, then either in the Minor Premise or in the Conclusion we may have one pointing to any special case or class of cases, included within the comprehensiveness to which the Modal of the Major Premise extended it. Thus:

Expansive Modals.

"No man is justified on any pretence in taking the life of one with whom he is living on terms of confidence."

"But Brutus was living on terms of confidence with Cæsar."

"*Therefore* Brutus was not justifiable in taking

Cæsar's life on *the pretence which he pleaded—of a higher obligation to his country.*"

(5.) In regard to the Minor term, if it was used without a Modal in the Minor Premise it was used in its most comprehensive sense; hence if we annex a Modal in the Conclusion we simply narrow the sphere of the subject, which as we have before seen does not render the Proposition untrue. But if the Minor term had a Modal in the Minor Premise, it may not be omitted in the Conclusion, since that would enlarge its sphere and possibly include thereby individuals of whom the predicate may not be affirmed.

Modals of the Minor Terms.

(6.) And in regard to the Major term the converse holds. If there was a Modal in the Major Premise it may be omitted in the Conclusion, as by so doing we enlarge its sphere and consequently include less matter. If therefore it was predicable of the subject before the enlargement of its sphere, then *a fortiori* it is afterwards. But if the Major term was in the Premise without the Middle, no Modal can be introduced into the Conclusion, except that which was spoken of above as changing the indeterminate undistributed into a determined distributed, denoting the individuals included in the scope of the subject as a species.

Modals of the Major Term.

Generel Rule for taking or assuming a Modal.

528. We may then lay down the general proposition that a Modal may at any time, and in any position be attached to an undistributed term, provided the Modal expresses the differentia or peculiar property of that part of the sphere of the term which is taken into the scope of the judgment by its undistributed use. We thus convert the indeterminate undistributed term into a determinate distributed one with a narrower and comprehended sphere.

General Proposition of the assumption of a Modal.

529. It is sometimes a matter of doubt whether a Modal shall be considered as belonging to the Subject or the Predicate of a Proposition.

It is not of so much importance to which it is considered as belonging as might at first sight appear, as the Modal can easily be transferred from one term to the other. Thus, "Drowning men catch at straws;"—"*Drowning*" is here a Modal of the Subject. But if we say, "Men catch at straws *when they are drowning*," the Modal is transferred to the Predicate, and the Proposition remains the same for all Logical purposes; although that which was the differentia of a species in the subject becomes the conditional of the genus in the Predicate, and *vice versa.*

Change of the Modal from Subject to Predicate, and *vice versa.*

530. We have yet another important class of Modals whose influence upon the deductive force of the Formulae we must consider. I mean those which indicate *Protensive* comprehension.

Protensive Modals.

531. Such Modals seem rather to limit the Copula than the terms of a judgment.

532. It is obvious that when the Copulas in both the Premises are taken with unlimited Protension—that is, with the adverb "always" or "universally" expressed or implied, we may have a Copula in the Conclusion with the same protension.

Absolute Protension.

Let us then consider those adverbial Modals which limit the Protension without giving a definite limit to it, such as "sometimes," "generally," "rarely," &c.

533. It is manifest that such Modals always limit the Subject, so that a Proposition in which one of them occurs cannot be regarded as universal. Nor is this all—they indicate that there is no one part of the Subject of which as a species the Predicate may be affirmed with unlimited Protension. It may be affirmed of any or all the individuals included in the Subject at some time, and at others perhaps it can be affirmed of none of them.

Limited Protension.

534. Now if there is such a Modal in both Premises, it is manifest that we can have no Conclusion. For example:

In both Premises.

M is sometimes P.
S is sometimes M.
∴ ————————

For it does not appear but that M may be included in P precisely then when S is not included in M, and *vicè versa*. The Minor term may be included in the Middle when, and only when the Middle is not included in the Major term.

535. But if the Modal is in either Premise alone it must be in the Conclusion also. For if either Subject is in its Predicate only sometimes, then the Conclusion can affirm the Minor term to be in the Major only "*sometimes*." And at any particular time it can predicate the Major of the Minor only in a Problematic or Probable Judgment. The Conclusion with such a Modal in either Premise, therefore, may assume either of the two following forms: In one Premise.

S is sometimes P; or
S may be P;

that is, it may be so without contradiction or logical absurdity.

536. We sometimes have a Protensive Modal, however, when we ought to have a differential or conditional. Thus: Protensive for Differential Modal.

"Testimony sometimes leads us into error.
The belief in miracles rests upon testimony.
Hence the belief in miracles may be only an error."

Here for "testimony sometimes" we manifestly ought to have "some testimony;" that is, "some kinds of testimony misleads us."

But when we substitute "some kinds of testimony," for "testimony sometimes," we have not got the full force of the Modal or the exact meaning of the Proposition. It does not mean to affirm that there are any kinds of testimony that *always* mislead. The Modal of the Copula must therefore be still retained in some other form. We may say, "some kinds of testimony *occasionally* mislead."

SECTION VI.

Of Compound Syllogisms or Sorites.

537. The Syllogism gives us a Conclusion but one step further removed from the intuitive judgments than the Premises themselves, having but one Middle term.

538. We may however have in the same Formula any number of Middle terms with a deduction for a conclusion, of a corresponding degree of remoteness from the Premises. Thus,

Sorites.

A is B,
B is C,
C is D,
∴ A is D.

This is called a SORITES or *Chain Syllogism.*

539. In the usual form the Predicate of each Premise becomes the subject of the next in a Universal Affirmative Proposition, until in the Conclusion we have the subject of the first Premise for subject as Minor term, and the Predicate of the last for Predicate as Major term.*

Order of Terms in the Usual Form.

540. In this Formula each successive term beginning with the Minor, has a wider and comprehending sphere until we come to the last. Consequently whatever may be predicated of the last or Major term, may be predicated of the first or Minor term just the same as if there had been but one Middle term.

541. It is manifest that as there can be but one Conclusion, so there can be but one Major and but one Minor Premise. But there may

One Minor and one Major Term.

* A Sorites, called the *Goclenian*, has been noticed also—consisting of Propositions in which the terms are arranged in the inverse order;

Thus B is A,
C is B,
D is C,
E is D,
∴ A is E.

And this form with the usual form given above, are all that have hitherto been recognized so far as I know.

be any number of Intermediate Premises introduced between the Minor and the Major instead of one—each Premise introducing a new Middle term, until the last becomes with the Major term either the Subject or Predicate in the same Proposition. Thus: Intermediate Premises.

All Z is A,
All A is B,
All B is C,
All C is "
All " is N,
All N is X,
∴ All Z is X.

542. But there is no necessity for confining the Sorites within such narrow limits as have usually been assigned to it. In fact we cannot keep it within these limits. Other forms and varieties are constantly occurring, and the business of Logic is rather to account for what is, than to determine what ought to be. More than one form of Sorites.

543. It is obvious, that if we can introduce one Universal Affirmative between the Minor and Major Premise of any Syllogism, we can introduce any number so long as the Subject of the one becomes the Predicate of the next, or *vice versa;* in which case each new Middle term will be once distributed.

544. Hence in any Syllogism, if after transposing the Premises, we can pass from the Minor Premise to an Universal Affirmative and from that again to the Major Premise, we may continue on with any number of Universal Affirmative Intermediate Premises, without changing the essential character of the Sorites. Any Syllogism may be expanded.

545. In this way we find that each of the nineteen Syllogisms may be expanded into Sorites.

546. In the expansion of the Syllogisms by this means we are to regard only the two Fallacies of Figure—Undistributed Middle and Illicit Process. Each Middle term must be distributed Cautions to be regarded.

once, and no term distributed in the Conclusion which was not distributed in the Major or Minor Premise.

547. It is sometimes the case that in the expansion of the Syllogism, we are obliged to resort to the inverse of the usual method, or to what is called the *Goclenian* method. Thus in the expansion of Camestres:

The Goclenian method of expansion.

No Z is A,
All B is A,
All C is B,
All X is C,
∴ No Z is X;

in which case the Subject of each Intermediate Premise becomes the Predicate of the next, and the inverse method would give an illicit of the Major.

548. The introduction of a Negative Intermediate Premise between two Affirmatives, or of a Particular between two Universals, will have its usual effects upon the quantity and quality of the Conclusion. Thus Darapti expanded by a Negative Intermediate Premise becomes:

A Negative Intermediate.

All Y is Z,
No Y is B,
All B is X,
∴ Some Z is not X.

549. The Sorites may be resolved into as many Syllogisms as it has Premises less one.

Sorites resolved into Syllogisms.

550. The first Premise containing the Minor term of the Sorites is the Minor Premise of the first Syllogism, and the second Premise is the Major. The Conclusion of the first Syllogism becomes the Minor Premise, and the third Premise of the Sorites becomes the Major Premise of the second Syllogism, and so on, each Conclusion becoming Minor Premise for the next Syllogism.

551. In this way each Middle term after the first serves as a Major term to establish the Minor Premise of the Syllogism in which it is to serve as a Middle.

Thus the most ordinary form of the Sorites is:

First Example.

All A is B,
All B is C,
All C is D,
All D is E,
∴ All A is E;

which is resolved into Syllogisms as follows:

1st.	2d.	3d.
All B is C,	All C is D,	All D is E,
All A is B,	All A is C,	All A is D,
∴ All A is C,	∴ All A is D,	∴ All A is E.

In this case each of the Syllogisms is in Barbara.

552. For another example take the following:

Second Example.

All C is A,
C is not D,
All B is D,
∴ Some A is not B; which is resolved as follows:

1st.	2d.
C is not D,	All B is D,
All C is A,	Some A is not D,
∴ Some A is not D.	∴ Some A is not B.

The first of these Syllogisms will at once be seen to be Felapton (3d Fig.), and the second is Baroko of the 2d Fig.

553. In most cases where Bramantip occurs in the course of resolving the Sorites into Syllogisms, it is necessary to use the indirect Conclusion for the Minor Premise to the next Syllogism. Thus:

The peculiarity of Bramantip.

All A is Z,
All B is A,
All N is B,
All N is X,
∴ Some Z is X.

(1)	(2)	(3)
All B is A,	All N is B,	All N is X,
All A is Z (ind. Con.)	All B is Z,	Some Z is N,
∴ Some Z is B,	∴ Some Z is N,	∴ Some Z is X.

The same thing occurs in Disamis, Bokardo, Bramantip, Dimaris, &c. &c.

554. In the statement of the Sorites, as in fact in the statement of the Syllogism, there is sometimes a rhetorical complication of terms, by means of which the Subject is kept more constantly before the mind than it could otherwise be. This is effected by converting each Proposition into a single cognition as we pass along according to the principle laid down [187]. Thus,

Combination of Terms in the statement of Sorites.

"All men are mortal.
All mortal men are sinners.
Christ died for all sinful men.

But the sinners for whom Christ died must exercise faith and repentance towards God in order to obtain the benefits of His death; *therefore* those who do not believe in Him and live a life of faith and repentance, will be left to the full consequences of their sins."

555. The only additional point to be secured in analyzing such arguments, is that no new term be surreptitiously introduced by this process of accumulation.

Caution against surreptitious matter.

SECTION VII.

Of the Incomplete Formula.

556. For the most part in ordinary reasoning one Premise and sometimes two are suppressed; that is, they are not stated in the course of the argument. The reason is often a rhetorical one. It would be tedious to be constantly repeating what is so obvious as to be known and admitted by all. Logic however never supposes any thing; it requires all the Premises to be stated, and hence we must examine these abridged forms of argument.

Premises often suppressed.

557. They are called *Enthymemes*, and may be of four kinds:

Four kinds.

(1.) When one Premise of a Syllogism is omitted. In this case we have the Conclusion and one Premise, but the Conclusion and the Premise contain

First.

only *three* distinct terms; as, All Y is X, therefore All Z is X.

Second. (2.) We may have the Conclusion and one Premise with *four* distinct terms; as, All A is B, therefore All Z is X. In this case the Enthymeme is an abridgment of the Sorites, and the given Premise is the Middle Premise.

Third. (3.) Or there may be a Conclusion given with more than one Premise, and yet not a complete Sorites.

Fourth. (4.) In the fourth case we may have several Premises in which there is one term common to them all.

Completion of Enthymemes of the first kind.

558. Enthymemes with three terms are easily completed into Syllogisms. The Conclusion necessarily contains the Major and the Minor terms. The given Premise contains the Middle term and either the Minor or the Major term, and determines the position of the Middle term as Subject or Predicate of the given Premise. From this we learn the Figure, the quality and quantity of the Premise to be supplied.

Thus, if the Conclusion be A, the Premises must be AA.

If the Conclusion be E, the Premises must be either EA or AE.

If the Conclusion be I, the Premises must be either AI or IA.—(AA of course would be valid but not necessary.)

If the Conclusion be O, the Premises must be either EI, OA or AO.

No Universal Premise introduced unless it is necessary.

559. We must always remember that we have no right to supply a Universal Premise in the completion of an Enthymeme when a Particular one would answer. This would be attributing to him who made the Enthymeme what he never said and what his argument does not necessarily imply. For this reason no Enthymeme can require to be completed in Darapti, as Disamis and Datisi are in

the same Figure, in one or the other of which any Enthymeme with a Conclusion in I in the 3d Figure can be completed.

560. If it is found impossible to complete the Syllogism—that is, to find a Premise that will connect the given Premise legitimately with the Conclusion, the Enthymeme includes or implies a fallacy which renders its conclusion worthless or worse.

561. Of Enthymemes with four terms there can be only the one variety given, except as the difference in quantity and quality may vary it:

Enthymemes with Four Terms.

All A is B,
∴ C is D.

Any variation of the relative position of these terms would produce no variety in the Formulæ. It could only change the term which a given letter represents.

562. If an Enthymeme has four distinct terms, two of them must of course be Middle terms, and it can be completed into a Sorites with three Premises; thus, A is B, therefore C is D.—"The state punishes no man for his religious opinions, therefore heresy is no crime."

Completed into a Sorites.

563. Here we have four distinct terms—"state," "religious opinions," "heresy," and "crime;" and the latter of the two Propositions is given as a Conclusion from the former. Let us then put A for state, B for religious opinions, C for heresy, and D for crime, and we shall have:

All C is B,
No A is B,
All D is A,
No C is D, or C is not D.

564. From which it appears that the Enthymeme implied the two following Propositions: 1st, the Minor Premise that all "*heresy*" is "*religious opinion*" of some kind or another.—2d, for the Major Premise whatever is a "*crime*" is "*punished by the state.*" Or as for rhetorical purposes one would be most likely to

express the same thing by contra-position—"whatever is not punished by the state is no crime."

565. But in the third case we may have the Conclusion of a Sorites with two or more of the Premises given and others suppressed. Enthymemes with more than four terms.

566. A fundamental maxim in the completion of these Enthymematic Formulæ, is that in completing them no term may be used that was not contained in the Elements of the Formulæ that were actually given. No new terms introduced.

If now we have—A is B,
B is C,
C is D,
D is E,
E is F,
∴ A is F;

it is obvious that if the 1st, 3d, and 5th Premises were omitted, we should have all the terms given, A, B, C, D, E and F. Thus, B is C,
D is E,
∴ A is F,

and we could easily restore the wanting Premises by principles with which we are already familiar.

567. But if one Premise were stricken out or omitted, the full form could not be completed. We should have:— All B is C, ∴ A is F. } or { All D is E, ∴ All A is F;

which would be completed thus:

All A is B,	or,	All A is D,
All B is C,		All D is E,
All C is F,		All E is F,
∴ All A is F,		∴ All A is F.

568. As the Middle term is usually a general term, that is a term denoting a class, it is obvious that the result will be the same if in a succession of Propositions we compare either of the Extremes with the individuals of which the Middle term is composed, as if we should compare that Ex- Enthymemes with Middle Term stated Individually.

treme with the Middle term as a Whole in a single Proposition, this gives a *Classificatory Formula.*

Classificatory Formula.

569. Thus let M be a genus consisting of the individuals *a*, *b*, *c*, *d* and *e*, we may thus predicate P of each of these; as,

a is P,
b is P,
c is P,
d is P,
e is P;

and then as whatever may be predicated of all the individuals of a class, whether genus or species, may be predicated of the class, we may have for these several Propositions, M is P; since by the supposition M is the general term whose comprehended individuals are *a*, *b*, *c*, *d* and *e*. With "M is P" we may have the Conclusion S is P—the two constituting an Enthymeme.

570. This it will be seen by and by is the Form in which Induction is usually stated; thus, the wolf, the fox, the cat are individuals which make up, or at least represent the class of animals called *Canidæ*, or animals with canine teeth. Now we may say:

The Formulas of Induction.

The wolf is carniverous,
The fox is carniverous,
The cat is carniverous,
∴ the Canidæ, or animals with canine teeth, are carniverous.

571. It will follow of course on the same principle, that if we predicate the several individuals of which the Middle is composed of the Minor term individually, we may predicate the Middle itself of that Minor, thus:

Cumulative Formula.

S is *a*,
S is *b*,
S is *c*,
S is *d*,
Therefore S is M.

572. This is the Formula of what is called the *Cumulative Argument.*

573. The Cumulative Formula differs from the Inductive in that the Cumulative Formula is an Enthymeme with the Major Premise suppressed.

Thus in Mr. Webster's argument in the case of the White murderers, we have:

"The prisoner was at the place at the time of the murder.

"He participated in the motives which led to the commission of the murder.

"He owned and usually carried with him the weapon with which the murder was committed.

"He shared in the means which were afterwards taken to divert attention from those who were actually engaged in committing the murder.

∴ the prisoner is guilty."

574. It will often happen, as in this case, that there is no one term in the language that will denote the genus, which these several terms predicated of the Subject taken as a Logical Whole, would constitute. But whether there is such a term or not they must be considered as making such a Whole, and one too which may be predicated of the Minor in the Inductive Formula, and of which the Major term may be predicated in the Cumulative Formula. In the case alluded to, Mr. Webster argued his Major Premise at some length; thus, "Whoever was present when the murder was committed had a motive and the means for committing it, and subsequent to its commission, endeavored to foil all attempts at discovering the murderer, must be held guilty." Here plainly for want of a single term of which to predicate "guilty," he enumerates the individuals of which it is composed—in short describes its sphere.

Sometimes there is no single term for the Middle.

575. In both of the above-named Formulæ it is necessary that the Premise which is thus individually stated, should enumerate all the coördinate parts of the Middle term as a Logical

Must enumerate all the coördinate parts.

Whole, otherwise it is manifest that we may have an *Undistributed Middle.*

SECTION VIII.

Of Epichirema.

576. Besides the Sorites we have sometimes Formulæ in which there is a Proposition, which is redundant so far as the purposes of that Formula are concerned. These Formulæ have been called *Epichirema.* The Propositions serve an important purpose, and are called either *Pro-Syllogisms* or *Epi-Syllogisms.*

577. The *Pro-Syllogism* is a Proposition thrown in either before or after one of the Premises as a Premise to that Premise; and of course, therefore, is a Premise which with the given Premise for a Conclusion constitutes an Enthymeme. For example: "Confidence in promises is essential to the intercourse of human life (because without it the greatest part of our conduct would proceed upon chance). But there could be no confidence in promises if men were not obliged to perform them; therefore the obligation to perform promises is as essential as the intercourse of human life."—(*Paley.*)

Pro-Syllogism.

578. Here the Pro-Syllogism, which is thrown in to confirm the Major Proposition, is enclosed in the parenthesis.

Again, we sometimes have a Conclusion stated immediately after the Conclusion of a Formula, and to which the Conclusion of the Formula is designed to serve as a Premise. This is called an *Epi-Syllogism.*

Epi-Syllogism.

As, Y is X,
Z is Y,
∴ Z is X,
∴ Z is W,
or ∴ M is X.

579. Here the Conclusion serves as a Premise to the Epi-Syllogism, and the two together are an Enthymeme.

SECTION IX.

Of Compound Judgments in Syllogisms.

580. We have seen in a previous Section how any compound Proposition may, for all the purposes of the Syllogistic Conclusion, be regarded as a simple Proposition with a Modal.

581. Such a process of course implies that the Judgments into which the Compound Proposition may be resolved, are either all false or all true together. When they are thus regarded however as simple Propositions with Modals, we proceed with them as though they neither contained or implied more than the one Judgment, and the law concerning Modals already stated must be observed.

All the Simple Judgments must be true or false together.

582. When either of the Premises is a Compound Proposition thus regarded as a simple one, the Conclusion may of course be a Compound of the same kind; only that it will appear as a Modal Proposition containing one modified judgment. This Proposition may be again resolved back into its component simple judgments by the same process, though in the inverse order—as it has been resolved from a Compound into a simple Modal Proposition. Thus,

May have a Compound Conclusion.

M is (X and P),
S is M,
∴ S is (X and P).

But the Major Premises may be resolved into "M is X," and "M is P." So also the Conclusion into "S is X," and "S is P."

583. But it is sometimes the case that the Conclusion depends upon only one of the simple judgments contained or implied in the Compound Proposition. In that case whether the Compound be either copulative or discretive, we must treat the judgment which is not taken into the scope of the Syllogism in the Premises, as in no other way belonging to it or affecting it. It is a mere rhetorical surplusage.

Only one of the judgments used in some cases.

584. *Causal* Propositions are properly Enthymemes, containing a Conclusion and one Premise. The Causal Judgment may be regarded as merely a *Pro-Syllogism.* We may also regard it as a mere Modal; thus,

Causal Propositions.

"Christians are happy *because they have faith;*
The early martyrs were Christians:
∴ the early martyrs were happy *because they had faith.*"

585. When the Major Premise is a Causal, if the Minor affirms the cause of any new Minor term, the Conclusion may affirm the Predicate of the Major Premise of the new Minor term. Thus we may say:

"Christians are content with their lot, *because they have faith;*
The Early Martyrs had faith:
∴ the Early Martyrs were content with their lot."

586. Now if this Conclusion be not true, it must be either because the Minor Premise is a *non vera* (untrue), or because the main Proposition in the Major Premise, "*Christians are content with their* lot," is untrue; or finally, because the cause assigned—"because they have faith," is not the cause, is a *non causa* PRO CAUSA.

587. The *Discretive*, *Exceptional*, and the *Exclusive* Propositions, as has been seen, agree in containing or implying judgment of one quality while they express a judgment of another. These judgments have one term common to them both. The Exceptionals affirm the Predicate of the subject and deny it of all other subjects. The Exclusives include the subject in the Predicate and exclude all other subjects from it. The Discretives affirm one Predicate and deny another of the same subject.

Discretives, Exceptionals, and Exclusives.

588. Hence these classes of Propositions may be regarded as negatives or affirmatives, according as we involve in our Syllogism the one or the other of the judgments contained in them. Thus for a Discretive:

A is B, but A is not C,
S is A, S is A,
∴ S is B, ∴ S is not C.

For an Exceptive take the following:

"All races of men except the Anglo-Saxons have failed to sustain free Institutions; Examples.
The Canadians are Anglo-Saxons:
∴ the Canadians have not failed, &c."—

or with a Negative Minor Premise:

"The Mexicans are not Anglo-Saxons;
∴ the Mexicans have failed, &c."

In the first case the Affirmative Judgment is used as Major Premise, and in the second the Negative.

589. Again, in the case of an Exclusive, we have the same phenomenon:

"Water is the only thing in the sea;
Fish live in the sea:
∴ Fish live in the water."

"Water is the only thing in the sea;
Hot-blooded animals do not live in water:
∴ Hot-blooded animals do not live in the sea."

In the above examples we have an Affirmative Conclusion in the 2d Figure, and a Negative Conclusion with an Affirmative Major Premise in the 1st Figure.

SECTION X.

Of Comparative Syllogisms.

590. It has been usual to regard Comparative Judgments as but Pure Categoricals with Modals. But the Modals of Comparative Judgments exert an influence upon the Formulæ essentially different from that of any class of Modals yet considered. Comparative Judgments, as already shown, are Formally different from any other; and constitute a class by themselves with differentia peculiarly their own.

Force of Modals in Comparative Syllogisms.

Thus we may have—M is P,
S is greater than M,
∴ S is greater than P.

Here we have a Modal to the Middle term in the Minor Premise, and none to it in the Major. We have also a Modal to the Major term in the Conclusion and none in the Major Premise; and yet we see at once that the Formula is valid.

Again we may have different Modals in each Premise, as:
Y is *greater than* X,
Z is *equal to* Y,
∴ Z is greater than X.

591. Comparative Syllogisms are of three kinds:—

Three kinds. (1) Simple Comparatives in Continuous Quantity; (2) Comparatives in which the difference of intensity is regarded as cause; (3) Comparatives of time, place, manner, &c.

I. *Simple Comparatives.*

592. In Continuous Quantity the reasoning depends upon the following Axioms:

(1.) Axiom of Equality. If any two things are

First Axiom. each equal to one and the same third thing, they are equal to each other. Thus, If A and B are each equal to C, A and B are equal to each other.

(2.) Axiom of Difference. If of any two things one

Second Axiom. is greater and the other less than or equal to a common third, then the one is greater than the other. Thus, If A is greater than C, and B is equal with C, A is greater than B; or if A is less than C, and B is equal with it, A is less than B.

(3d.) If two terms are both either greater or less

Third Axiom. than a common third term, no conclusion can be drawn concerning them by means of a comparison with that third term.

593. If, however, in cases coming under the last

Application of Discrete Quantity. Axiom we introduce Discrete Quantity also, so as to express *how much* greater or less each of the terms compared are, than that with which they are compared, a conclusion can be drawn—thus, three is two less than five, and six is one more. Hence six is three more than three.

The *two terms* of which we speak in these Axioms are the Extremes, Minor and Major, and the common third term is the Middle term.

Explanation of Signs.

594. We shall greatly facilitate our examination of the Formulæ of Continuous Quantity by introducing a method of notation somewhat similar to Sir William Hamilton's,—in which we will denote comparisons which imply the equality of the two Extremes of a Comparative Judgment, by parallel lines drawn between the Subject and the Predicate, as $S = P$, "S is equal to P." Comparisons of Inequality will be denoted by the *Convergent* when the Subject is larger than the Predicate, and by the *Divergent* when it is the reverse. Thus, $S > P$, "S is larger than P;" and $S < P$, "S is smaller than P."

Convergent & Divergent the Converse of each other.

595. The fact that Comparatives of Inequality are converted by transposition of terms and changing of the Comparative Modal for that which is in the same degree of comparison as the other side of the Positive, is indicated by the fact that the Convergent and the Divergent are but the converse the one of the other.

Notation of the Indefinite.

596. But the Indefinite Comparisons, as we have seen, affirm only that the Subject is as great as the Predicate. We might therefore always represent these Comparisons by the sign of equality—only remembering, however, that such Propositions cannot be converted.

597. But as such a mode of notation may lead to confusion in some cases, it will be well to denote the Indefinite Comparisons by two straight lines crossing each other, thus +.

Comparisons of Equality.

598. Now since in Comparisons of Equality the compared and the standard of the comparison are equal to each other, it will follow

that if both, or all the Premises are Comparisons of this kind, all Moods and all Figures must be valid.

1st, $A = B$, 2d, $A = B$, 3d, $B = A$, 4th, $B = A$,
$B = C$, $C = B$, $B = C$, $C = B$,
$\therefore A = C$, $\therefore A = C$, $\therefore A = C$, $\therefore A = C$.

Of Inequality in both Premises of the same intensity.

599. But if both are Comparisons of Inequality, unless they can be so converted or read as to come into the 1st or 4th Figure, and of the same intensity, there can be no Conclusion except by means of Discrete Quantity. Thus:

2d, $A > B$, 3d, $B < A$,
$C > B$, $B < C$.

In both these cases the Premises offend against the Third Axiom.

Of opposite Intensity.

600. But if the intensity be unlike in the 2d or 3d Figures we may have a Conclusion. In that case the Premise may be read either in 1st or 4th Figures, and so brought under the 2d Axiom—the Axiom of Inequality; thus,

$A > B$,
$C < B$,

becomes "A is greater than B," and "B is greater than C." Hence we may have the Conclusion "A is greater than C," or $A > C$.

Premises read in the Fourth Figure.

601. If the Premises are read in the 4th Figure, the Conclusion will be of the opposite intensity from that in the Premises, or, which is the same thing, the Conclusion here, as in Logical Quantity, will be the converse of that in the 1st Figure; thus,—1st, $M > P$, 4th, $P < M$,
$S > M$, $M < S$,
$\therefore S > P$, $\therefore S > P$.

Comparisons of Inequality.

602. If the Premises are Comparisons of Inequality, and of opposite intensity, they must be read in the 2d or 3d Figure; thus,

1st, $M > P$, and 4th, $P > M$,
$S < M$, $M < S$,

offend alike against the Third Axiom.

But 2d, $M > P$, and 3d, $P > M$,
$M < S$, $S < M$,
$\therefore S > P$, $\therefore S < P$.

603. We have seen that the Indefinite Comparisons cannot be converted, and must always be regarded as Comparisons of greater intensity, though it is very possible in any case that they are not so. Hence when such a Comparison occurs in such a place as not to fulfil the conditions of Figures just stated, we are obliged to regard the Conclusion as invalid; thus,

Indefinite Premises.

$$M > P,$$
$$S +- M,$$
$$\therefore S > P \text{ is valid.}$$

But $M < P$,
$S +- M$ gives no Conclusion, as the comparisons cannot be read so as to bring them under the Axiom of Inequality. We might indeed read thus:

$$\left.\begin{array}{l} P > M, \\ S +- M, \end{array}\right\} \text{ or } \left\{\begin{array}{l} P > M, \\ S = M; \end{array}\right.$$

but that would not improve the matter at all so far as their conclusive force is concerned, for we could not determine the comparison between S and P.

604. When but one Premise is a Comparative Judgment the Comparative may be regarded as a Modal, and we may proceed as in pure categoricals; thus,

One Premise only Comparative.

A is greater than B,
C is A,
∴ C is greater than B.

II. *Comparative Syllogisms in which the difference of intensity is regarded as a cause.*

Intensity as a Cause.

605. As an instance take the following from Kossuth's late speech in England on the War in the East:
"Napoleon failed to conquer Russia;
But Napoleon was superior to the Allied Powers:
Therefore the Allied Powers will fail to conquer Russia" (that is, if they pursue their present policy).

In this case we have a Comparative Judgment for

the Minor Premise, in which the Minor and the Middle terms are compared with reference to the intensity of some property which they have in common. In this case it is "*military force.*" But the Major term here is predicated of the Minor in the Conclusion, not on the ground of any of the Dicta of the Figures, but because the property common to both of the terms of the Comparative Judgment is conceived to be the cause or reason why the Major term is predicated of the Middle in the Major Premise, and therefore the reason why it may be predicated of the Minor in the Conclusion. But this implies the existence of that which is the cause of the Major term in the Minor also, and moreover that it exists in as great intensity at the least in the Minor term as in the Middle. And this is affirmed by the Comparative Judgment which is the Minor Premise.

Conclusion affirmed on the ground of sufficient cause.

606. In Syllogisms of this class the difference in intensity must be a real Cause, and one which necessarily implies the reality of the effect.

Comparisons of manner, time, place, &c.

III. *The Comparatives of manner, time, place, ratio, &c.*

607. These are all very simple, and are completed by expanding or explaining the Comparative Modal for the Minor Premise; thus,

The Boys are with their Father;
Their Father is in the city:
∴ The Boys are in the city.

A is to B as C is to D,
But A is one half of B,
∴ C is one half of D;

or, A is to B as C is to D,
But A is the Father of B,
∴ C is the Father of D.

The Comparative is the Major Premise.

608. It will be observed, that in all these cases the Comparative is the Major Premise.

609. We may also have an Indirect Conclusion; thus,

Indirect Conclusions in Comparative Syllogisms.

The Boys are with their Father;
The Boys are in the city:
∴ The Father is in the city.

SECTION XI.

Of Probable Syllogisms.

610. By the application of Discrete Quantity to the measure of Wholes in Continuous and Logical Quantity, we have a further modification of Formulæ and some new principles and rules to consider.

611. Arithmetic, Algebra, and the Calculus are but methods of calculation in Discrete Quantity. It will not of course be expected that we shall go into a discussion of the Rules and Formulæ belonging to these Methods in this place.

Calculations in Discrete Quantity.

612. There are but two fundamental Axioms in Discrete Quantity.

(1.) The sum of the parts of any whole is that whole itself.*

First Axiom.

The usual statement that the sum of the "parts is equal to the whole," though true, belongs to Continuous rather than to Discrete Quantity.

(2.) If from any whole a part be taken, the remainder is such a part as that together with that which was taken from the whole, it will make the whole itself.

Second Axiom.

* We do not say, "*equal to* that whole," for that would imply a want of identity in the terms or objects of the conceptions. We say that "a whole is equal to the sum of its parts" in Continuous Quantity, Geometry, &c. But in Arithmetic we say, "3 times 4 *is* twelve," not "is equal to twelve." Units, as such, have no differentia—and sums or wholes differ only in the number of units which they contain.

When, however, in Algebra and the Calculus, we use the sign of equality, and read our statements or Logical Propositions, "X is equal to A," it is because "X" and "A" stand for quantities which while they are equal to each other as quantities have other relations, which must be kept distinctly before the mind.

The first is the Axiom of *Addition*, and the last that of *Subtraction*.

613. Where several *equal* parts are to be added together to make one whole, the shorter method of *Multiplication* is adopted, and when several equal parts are to be taken from any whole the method used is called *Division*.

Methods in Calculation.

614. The Involution and Evolution of Roots, the Binomial Theorem, Fractions, Indeterminate Quantities, Logarithms, are all but short and convenient ways of finding values.

But it is important for us to investigate in this place the effect of the application of Discrete Quantity to Logical and Continuous Quantity.

Discrete Quantity applied to Continuous.

615. By introducing Discrete Quantity a Comparative Syllogism which offends against the Third Axiom, by having the two extremes either both greater or both less than the Middle term, and which consequently can have no conclusion by a comparison of Continuous Quantity alone, comes to have a valid conclusion; thus,

Three is two less than five,
Two is three less than five,
∴ Two is one less than three.

To Protensive Quantity.

616. Again, we may have an application of Discrete Quantity to Propositions which are protensively quantified, so as to give a valid conclusion to one that can have none without it; thus,

The cars stop at Waterloo *one half* of the time;
The cars carry the mail *three fourths* of the time:
∴ *Some* mail trains stop at Waterloo.

To Logical Quantity in general.

617. The principle involved here is the same as that which controls the influence of Discrete Quantity when applied to Logical Quantity in general. For example take the following:—At a certain extensive conflagration it is ascertained that,

Three fourths of the buildings in a city were of brick;
One half of the buildings were destroyed:
∴ Some brick buildings were destroyed.

618. When one of the Extremes is expressed in integral Discrete Quantity, it does not at all modify the Formula, as in the following examples:

Extremes in Discrete Quantity.

All that were in the Ark with Noah were saved;
Eight human beings were in the Ark with Noah:
∴ Eight human beings were saved.

All terms in which Discrete Quantity is expressed by the numerals, indicating simply how many are included in the terms are undistributed. Absolute Whole belongs to Logical Quantity, and it is a Whole which is not included as an alternate genus in any more comprehensive Whole or Sphere. Infinite belongs to Continuous Quantity, such as GOD, Space, Eternity, &c. But in Discrete Quantity we know of no number so large that it may not be a part of a larger and more comprehensive Whole, therefore none which is absolute; and of none so large that it may not be made larger by addition, and therefore none which is infinite. The Units have no properties by which they are distinguished as Individuals, or divided into Genera and Species. It is true that "one man" has such properties, but not as "*one*." It is only as "man" that he has differentia and peculiarities. Hence in Discrete Quantity there are no Logical Wholes.

Numerals not distributed Terms.

619. Since a term expressive of Discrete Quantity alone, as "six," "ten," "fifteen," &c., can never be a distributed term, such a Middle term can never help us to any conclusion. Nor yet can any term measured by Discrete Quantity serve as a Middle term, unless it expresses the ratio of the number expressed to the Discrete Quantity of the Logical Whole denoted by the term. For example:

If the Middle be merely Discrete Quantity there can be no Conclusion.

Three men got on the cars at the station;
Three men were killed in the cars:
∴ The men killed in the cars were the men who got on at the station.

620. The fallacy is obvious.—Nor from this statement can we infer any thing of the amount of the probability that any one of those who thus got on were among the killed. Nor should we gain any thing by using a much larger number for the Middle term.

The Middle Term must be either a Ratio or a Fraction.

621. It is only, therefore, when the Discrete Quantity expresses the ratio of those included within the scope of the judgment to the number of individuals included in the Logical Whole denoted by the term which this Discrete Quantity qualifies, that it can be available for the purposes of deduction.

Method of Notation.

622. We shall greatly facilitate our understanding of the principles upon which the conclusiveness of these Syllogisms depends, by resorting to Plouc-quet's Method of Notation, or at least a modification of it. Let a line be drawn, which by its length will indicate the unit of which the Middle term is a fraction, and another directly under it, in each case denoting the amount of the fraction.

How many at least.

623. Thus to take the example just given, let us denote the whole number of houses by a line, and then directly under it two lines more—the one one half and the other three fourths as long. And since we wish to know whether any, and if so, the least part of the Minor term that is necessarily contained in the Major, we will place one of the fractional lines even with the unit line at one end, and the other at the other; thus,

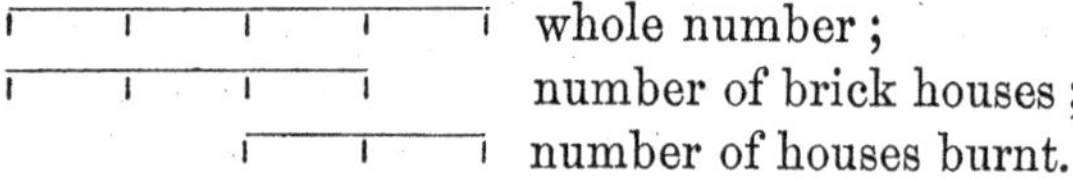

624. The reason for placing the lines as above, will be obvious from the fact that for aught that appears to the contrary in our statement, all of the not-brick houses were burnt, and only so many of the brick houses burnt as are necessary to make up the one half; that is, that the two spheres "*burnt*" and "*brick*,"

are as far as possible opposite. Hence the distance by which the lower line overlaps the one above it, will be the least part of the Minor term "*burnt*," which can possibly be included in the Major term "*brick*."

But the overlapping portion of the two lines is one third of the one and one half of the other.

625. Assuming then the term "brick houses" for the Minor term, we have for conclusion:

"*One third*, at least, of the brick houses were burnt."

Or taking "burnt" for the Minor term, we have:

"One half, at least, of the burnt houses were brick."

626. But if the two lines when thus placed did not overlap each other at all, there would be no assertive conclusion; that is, we could not say positively that any of the burnt houses were brick, or that any of the brick houses were burnt.

627. From the foregoing it is certain that unless the sum of the two fractional values used as Middle term is more than a unit, we have no conclusion.

Sum of the Fractions must be more than a Unit.

628. The Conclusion in these cases may be measured in Discrete Quantity, giving the precise number, which is the least that can have been included in the Predicate of the Conclusion as above, or we may have the undistributed Subject in Logical Quantity, "Some brick houses were burnt."

Conclusion Discretely quantified.

629. Or if we place the lines differently, we shall see how many *at most* could have been burnt.

How many at most.

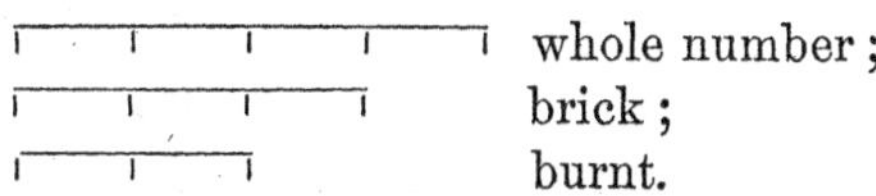

630. We place the lines thus because it is possible that the two spheres, "burnt" and "brick," are coincident to the extent of the comprehensiveness of the narrowest.

631. From this it appears that if the Minor term

has a sphere less comprehensive than the Major it may be wholly included in it.

632. Let us now pass on to consider the application of Discrete Quantity to the calculation of probabilities in Syllogisms.

633. There are three distinct classes of cases in the Calculation of Probabilities, which we will consider as involving all the Logical Principles which belong to that interesting but intricate and complicated subject.

634. (1.) We will first consider the effect of Discrete Quantification, expressed in a ratio or a fraction of the units of the Middle term, when one Premise only is a fraction and the other is unity; thus,

One Probable Premise.

All the houses in the city were brick;
One half the houses were burnt:
∴ All the burnt houses were brick;—or conversely, One half the brick houses were burnt.

And the quantity of the Conclusion will be the same as that of the *Major* Premise, as in the above examples. The two Conclusions from the first of these, as will be seen, results from our regarding the one Premise as Major in the one case, and the other in the other.

Quantification of the Conclusion.

635. (2.) The next class of cases are those in which the Premises are all probable, and several probabilities are dependent upon each other.

Dependent Probabilities.

636. Of these we have two kinds—(*a*) that in which we have several Premises, and the value of each is expressed in fractions of the common Middle term, as in the case just given:

Three fourths of the houses were brick,
One half of the houses were burnt;

and (*b*) that kind in which the value of each Premise (after the first) is expressed in fractions of the value of the preceding Premise.

637. (*a*) The probability that any particular house is brick, when three fourths of the whole are brick, is of

course three fourths. And the probability that any particular house is burnt, when one half of the whole are burnt, is of course one half of the whole. As the number of houses that are of brick, and the number that are burnt are each of them separately less than the whole, the probability that a brick house is burnt, or that a burnt house is brick, is of course less than the probability that any particular house is either brick—or burnt; that is, the probability that any particular house is *both* brick *and* burnt, is less than that it is either separately.

Ratio of Calculation in Fractions of a common Middle Teim.

638. We have seen that the probability that any particular house was burnt, when one half were burnt, is one half of the whole. Now of course the probability that any burnt house was brick, is one half of the whole number of the brick houses. But the whole number of brick houses is three fourths of the whole, the probability therefore that a brick house was burnt is one half of three fourths, which is three eighths of the whole number of houses.

639. The probability that any particular brick house was burnt, is of course the same as the number of brick houses that were probably burnt.

The probability of any one chance the same as the probable number of favorable chances.

This results from the principles laid down concerning the effect of classification upon predication; for each brick house is an individual, of which the brick houses burnt is the species. Hence whatever we may predicate of the individuals distributively, we may predicate of the species generally, and *vice versa* whatever we may predicate of the species we may predicate of each individual.

Or the point may be proved in another way, as follows:

640. The probability that any one house was burnt, is the same as the probability that any other house was burnt; so likewise the improbability. The probability that any house was brick, is as we have seen 3:1, three to one: again the pro-

Proved mathematically.

bability that any one house was burnt is 1 : 1, one to one against it—that is, one half. Now that fraction which sustains the same ratio to the number of brick buildings in the city that the number of the burnt does to the whole is $\frac{3}{8}$; thus $\frac{1}{2} : 1 :: \frac{3}{8} : \frac{3}{4}$—three eighths of the whole therefore must be the number of brick buildings that were probably burnt. And if more than three eighths of the whole number were burnt from among the brick buildings, then it would follow that since a larger proportion of brick than of the non-brick were burnt, the probability of any particular brick houses having been burnt is greater than the probability that a non-brick house was burnt.

641. (*b*) In the second class of cases we have successive Premises, in which the value of each is expressed in fractional values of the preceding Premise, as a whole or unity.

This Process implies the form of the Sorites already explained (554), in which each successive judgment expressed as a single cognition, becomes the subject to the one which follows.

642. Thus, suppose that a battle has been fought, concerning which we have the following particulars:

Ratio of Calculation when the ratio is in the units of the preceding Premise.

"*Three fourths* of the men in the army were in the engagement. *One tenth* of the men that were engaged in the battle were missing the next morning, and *one third* of the missing were killed." What is the probability that any particular man was killed?

643. It is obvious that $\frac{1}{3}$ of $\frac{1}{10}$ of those engaged were slain. But "those engaged" were only three fourths of the whole. Hence $\frac{3}{4}$ of $\frac{1}{3}$ of $\frac{1}{10}$ that $\frac{3}{120} = \frac{1}{40}$ were slain.

644. And from the reasoning already given, the probability that any particular man was slain on the *mere general ground* of probability, is $\frac{1}{40}$ or 1 : 39.

645. If, however, we have any particular class of

Special grounds of Probability.

men among whom the individual concerning whom we are making our calculation is included, and they are known to have been especially exposed, the probability of his being among the killed is rendered greater by the consideration of that particular ground affecting the amount of the probability.

646. (3.) We will next consider the several cases of independent probabilities:

(*a*) We have a class of cases in which we have a probability in one Premise, and an improbability in another. In that case we have only to subtract the one from the other, and the remainder will be of the same kind as the largest Premise.

Probability and Improbability combined.

647. But when we have a special improbability against an event to be combined with several probabilities in its favor, this special improbability must be computed by using its complement as a new probability, to be multiplied in according to the principle in the last named class of cases.

648. Suppose an individual to have belonged to a department of the army which is but slightly exposed, call this an improbability of $\frac{3}{4}$, then the probability that one in that department will be among the killed, will be of course but just $\frac{1}{4}$ of the probability resulting from the other probabilities $\frac{1}{40} \times \frac{1}{4} = \frac{1}{160}$.

General Probability and special Improbability.

(*b*) We will next consider the class of cases in which the question is of *one of several chances in the same event.*

One of several chances in the same event.

649. Thus, the die has six sides, and therefore six chances for each throw, and each throw is an event in which there are chances.

650. Now what is the probability that either of two, say the *ace* and the *deuce*, will turn up in any single throw or event? It is of course double the probability of any one side or chance $\frac{1}{6} + \frac{1}{6} = \frac{1}{3}$.

Ratio of the Calculation.

651. This is easily proved by supposing the question to be, what is the probability that some one of the six sides will fall up. By the rule $\frac{1}{6}+\frac{1}{6}+\frac{1}{6}+\frac{1}{6}+\frac{1}{6}+\frac{1}{6} = \frac{6}{6} = 1$ or certainty.

Proved

652. But we know previous to any computation, that one of the six sides will fall uppermost at each throw.

653. Hence in all cases where we have to inquire what is the probability of some one of several chances in the same event, we may add the sum of probabilities of the several chances.

654. These "several" must, however, be a part of some one whole, or totality of chances, as occurring in one event, otherwise their sum may amount to more than unity; which is impossible. Thus, suppose we have three probabilities, not included in any such unity, they may be $\frac{1}{2}$, $\frac{1}{3}$, $\frac{1}{4}$, then $\frac{1}{2}+\frac{1}{4}+\frac{1}{3}=\frac{13}{12}$ which is absurd.

Several must be parts of the same whole.

655. (*d*) This brings us to the last class of cases which we will consider—namely, that in which the question is concerning one chance in several events.

One chance in several events.

656. Of these there are two kinds—(*d* 1st) where the events are in the same totality of chances; and (*d* 2d) where they are in different totalities.

Two kinds.

657. (*d* 1st) For the simplest case in this kind, suppose we have the question, "What is the probability of throwing any particular number on a die in two different throws?"

Differentia of the first.

658. The probability of its being up in the first throw or event is $\frac{1}{6}$, and the independent probability of its being up in the second throw or event is also $\frac{1}{6}$.

659. Here the totality—the six sides of the die—is the same in both cases, the two throws are different events.

660. (*d* 2d) But for a case of the second kind take the following:

Two thirds of the pious are grave persons.

Three fourths of the studious are grave persons.

Here the different totalities are "the pious" and "the studious," and the question is what is the probability that one who is both "pious" and "studious" will be "grave."

Differentia of the second.

661. The principle or rule of calculation is the same in both of these varieties of this class of cases.

662. And we have two distinct questions to con-

sider—(1) What will be the average of the probability of one chance in any given number of events? and (2) What is that probability in any particular case?

The two Questions.

663. These questions are by no means the same. In any indefinitely large number of events, it is evident that each side would be uppermost—that is, each chance would happen just as often as any other one chance. Each side of the die therefore would come up just one sixth of the whole number of events. If now we divide this totality of events into pairs, then of course a given side would come uppermost just as often as before; that is, 1 : 5 in the whole. But the probability of any given side coming up once in every pair of events, on an average is one third as great as the probability of its coming up once in three times as many chances, or twice as great as that of its coming up in each chance; that is, $\frac{1}{6}+\frac{1}{6}=\frac{1}{3}$. So if we divide the events into triplets, the probability of any given side on the average of an immense number of events is three times as great as in the single event, that is, $\frac{1}{6}+\frac{1}{6}+\frac{1}{6}=\frac{1}{2}$.

By no means the same.

Ratio of calculating the average probability.

664. Now in this way the fraction can amount to more than unity, for as there are but six sides or chances, so if we ask what is the probability of ace, for instance, in sets of ten events, we have $\frac{1}{6}$ taken ten times or $1\frac{4}{6}$; that is, ace will come up on an average more than once in every ten throws. Otherwise ace will not come up so often as some of the other sides. But if it does not then there is some special reason or ground of probability, which is contrary to the supposition on which we started.

The result may be more than units.

Let us now consider the other question—what is the probability of any particular chance in a definite number of events.

665. It certainly can make no difference whether the events are in the same totality of chances or not,

since in the throw of the die, for instance, the probability of any particular side in each throw is certainly just as independent of each and every other throw, as it is of the probability of the head side of a cent's coming up in any throw of the cent.

Immaterial whether the events be in the same totality or not.

666. We may therefore consider the two kinds of cases in the class which we have named above (*d*), as depending upon the same principle and requiring to be calculated by the same rule.

Now we have two conditions to fulfil:

Two conditions to be fulfilled. 1st condition.

667. (1.) The probability of any chance in two events must be greater than it is in either one of them alone; thus the probability of the ace in two throws is greater than it is in one.

668. And not only so, but the probability in any number of combined throws must be greater than that of the sum of all the throws excepting any one of them; that is, two must be greater than any one in the two, three than any two in the three, four must be greater than any three in the four, and so on.

2d condition.

669. (2.) The sum of the combined probability can never amount to any more than unity—for by the very mode of reckoning probabilities they are but the fractions of unity. When therefore they amount to unity, they are no longer probabilities but a certainty, and there can be nothing beyond.

We cannot add the fractions.

670. Now in the case of the die, for instance, as there are six sides the probability of throwing any particular side, say the *ace*, at the first throw would be 1:5. or $\frac{1}{6}$. And in six throws it would be $\frac{1}{6}+\frac{1}{6}+\frac{1}{6}+\frac{1}{6}+\frac{1}{6}+\frac{1}{6}$ or $\frac{1}{6}\times6=1$ unity. And yet it is possible that the given side might not be thrown once in six times, or even in any greater number. There is a bare possibility that that side might not fall uppermost in a thousand times. Still, however, when the event is far from the sum of the probabilities (provided they keep within unity) in either direction—that is, greater or less; it creates

And yet cannot vary much from the sum of the probabilities.

a presumption and finally the unhesitating belief that there is some *special* cause influencing the chances, as that a die is loaded.

671. It appears therefore that we cannot calculate the probability by adding the value of each fraction, since that method would soon produce unity, and exceed it even.

We cannot multiply the Fractions.

672. Nor can we calculate it by *multiplying* the fractions. The value in each successive Premise is not a fraction of that of the preceding or of any other fraction. Each one is the fraction of a unity, and of a different unity, as the 1st and 2d throws in the first example, and "the pious," and "the studious" in the second. And besides the multiplication of the fractions would give us a constantly decreasing probability, when obviously we ought to have an increasing one.

By means of the Improbability.

673. If now instead of the probability in each Premise we take its complement improbability, and multiply them together as fractions, and then take the complement of that product for the probability of the conclusion, we shall have a method answering exactly the demands of the case.

674. Thus in the first case the probability of an *ace* in two throws is $\frac{1}{6}$ and $\frac{1}{6}$, the complement is $\frac{5}{6}$ and $\frac{5}{6}$, multiplying we have $\frac{25}{36}$, and taking the complement we have $\frac{11}{36}$. In five throws it becomes $\frac{4651}{7776}$, in six $\frac{31031}{46656}$, thus approaching but never reaching unity or absolute certainty.*

* For the gratification of those who would like to see this in a more purely mathematical form I give the following demonstration.

Let the probability of a particular chance in one event be $\frac{a}{b}$, and that of the same chance in another event $\frac{c}{d}$, certainty being unity. The combined probabilities can never be greater than unity, nor less than the sum of all minus any one of them.

Now multiply the complement of $\frac{a}{b}$ which is $(1-\frac{a}{b})$ by the complement

675. In the second case we have $\frac{2}{3}$, or $\frac{1}{3}$ complement in unity, and $\frac{3}{4}$, or $\frac{1}{4}$ complement. Multiplying, we have $\frac{1}{3} \times \frac{1}{4} = \frac{1}{12}$ or $\frac{11}{12}$ probability that the man who is both "studious" and "pious" is "grave." *

SECTION XII.

Of Conditional Syllogisms.

676. We are not to consider all sentences stated in the conditional form as expressing a conditional judg-

of $\frac{c}{d}$ which is $(1 - \frac{c}{d})$ and we have $\frac{(bd - (b-a)(d-c)}{bd}$ as the complement of the product, which is the combined probability. For as the numerator cannot be greater than bd, the fraction itself can never exceed unity.

Again this fraction may be put under the form $\frac{a}{b} + (1 - \frac{a}{b}) \frac{c}{d}$, a quantity which can never be less than $\frac{a}{b}$.

Now suppose that both independent probabilities are unity, then they are not probabilities; they have no complements and so of course they cannot be multiplied.

Again, suppose them to be indefinitely near to unity, then applying the doctrine of limits, they may be assumed as unity, and so will have no complements to be multiplied.

In either case the fraction becomes $\frac{bd}{bd}$ or unity, that is $1 \times 1 = 1$.

But suppose the probability in each case to be as near to unity as the nearest assignable quantity, then by this rule the product of two such probabilities would be nearer than any assignable quantity or indefinitely near. We may pursue the demonstration in this way for every assignable value to the fraction. If therefore there is any other rule that will give the same result, it is not another but the same. But if it gives a different result it cannot be true.

* I have taken no notice of the effect of *concurrence* upon the probabilities; this will be considered in the Chapter on Methods of Proof. But it will often happen that the concurrence of two very small probabilities will produce an amount of conviction but very little if any short of certainty. Thus, suppose two men whose veracity was nothing should come in and report to me a certain occurrence, the one after the other, and under such circumstances that I could know that there had been no collusion between them—the strength of the *combined* testimony might be but very slight—but the fact of their *concurring without collusion* would be very convincing, and all the more so, the more strange and unexpected the event which they narrate.

ment. It is often the case that statements are made in the hypothetical form where no *logical* dependence of one member upon the other is intended. Thus, "If on the one hand Greece failed by an excess of the popular element in its constitution, Rome on the other became purely a military despotism, the least favorable of all forms of government to popular liberty." Here manifestly the judgment concerning Rome is not intended to be made dependent upon the truth of that concerning Greece. We must regard the judgments therefore as being logically two entirely distinct categorical affirmations.

Not all Conditional Sentences Conditional Judgments.

677. Nor is it always the case where a Proposition is a Conditional Judgment that the deductive force depends upon the peculiarities of the Conditional Judgment.

The Conditional sometimes a mere Modal of a Categoric Premise.

As examples take the following:

Whatever comes from God is entitled to faith and obedience.

If the Scriptures are not an imposture they came from God.

∴ *If they are not an imposture* they are entitled to faith and obedience.

Or thus: All Y is X,

(If M is Z, A) is Y,

∴ (If M is Z, A) is X.

678. In this case the Conditional is merely the Modal of the Minor Term, and is treated accordingly. The Premise is used as a Complex Categorical rather than as a Conditional.

679. But when the Conditional Judgment is used as such, it is the Major Premise, and there are two ways of completing the Formula.

Conditional Judgment Major Premise in Conditional Syllogisms.

From the nature of Conditional Judgments it follows that:

(1.) If we affirm the Antecedent the Consequent cannot be denied.

Canons for Minor Premise.

(2.) If we deny the Consequent the Antecedent must be false; that is, the contradictory of the Antecedent must be true.

680. Hence we may complete in what is called the *Constructive Method*, or *modus ponens*, by affirming the Antecedent for a Minor Premise, and have the Consequent for a Conclusion; thus,

Constructive Minor Premises.

If A is B, A is C,
But A is B,
∴ A is C.

681. Or secondly, we may complete the Formula in the *Destructive Method*, or *modus tollens*,* by using the contradictory of the Consequent for Minor Premise, and then we shall have the contradictory of the Antecedent for Conclusion; thus,

Destructive Minor Premise.

If A is B, C is D,
But some C is not D,
∴ Some A is not B.

682. But by denying the Antecedent in simple conditionals we do not disprove the Consequent, nor by proving the Consequent do we prove the Antecedent.

683. But the Conditional Proposition is sometimes made an Exclusive Conditional by the insertion of "only," "alone," &c.

Exclusive Conditionals.

684. The effect of this exclusive is to show that the Consequent can have no other Antecedent, and could not exist without the one given in the Conditional. Thus, "If the Trojans came into Italy contrary to the will of the gods, they would then *alone* have deserved punishment.

But they did not come contrary to the will of the gods.

∴ They do not deserve punishment."—*Virg. Æn.* X. 31.

* The words "*posit*" and "*amote*" have sometimes been used to express these processes. Thus if we *posit* the Antecedent the Consequent must follow, and if we *amote* the Consequent the Antecedent must be false.

685. In this case by denying the Antecedent we disprove the Consequent.

And if we affirm the Consequent we establish the Antecedent.

They deserved punishment;

∴ They came into Italy contrary to the will of the gods.

686. But without the Exclusive Modal we prove nothing concerning the Consequent by disproving the Antecedent.

No Conclusion from the opposite Methods.

687. This will be obvious by the following illustration:—"If John has a fever he is sick." Hence if we prove the Antecedent, viz., that "John has a fever," the Consequent that "he is sick" will not be denied. But if we disprove the Antecedent and show that "he has not a fever," we have not proved that "he is not sick." He may be sick from some other disease.

688. For the same reason, though operating in the inverse order, if we prove the Consequent we do not thereby prove the Antecedent; that is, if we prove that "John is sick," we have not proved that "he has a fever;" his ailment may be something else for aught that would need to appear in our argument.

689. The whole force of Hypothetical reasoning in either method must depend upon the Sequence. There must be some such connection between the Consequent and the Antecedent in the nature of things and independent of our volition, that the truth of the one follows from that of the other.

The validity of the Conclusion depends upon the Sequence.

690. But as we have already considered the Sequence or ground of affirmation in Conditionals, we need not add any thing more concerning it here except to make the remark that the Premise of any Enthymeme may be made an Antecedent, and the Conclusion a Consequent in a Conditional Judgment, and then the other Premise will be the sequence; thus, If M is P, S is P.

Any Enthymeme may be expressed conditionally.

Completing as before we have:

If M is P, S is P,
But M is P,
∴ S is P.

691. But regarding it as an Enthymeme, we have:

M is P,
S is M,
∴ S is P.

Conditionals will through sequence become Categoricals.

692. In the same way, any Conditional by means of its Sequence is converted into a Categorical Syllogism.

Modified sequence.

693. It is sometimes the case that the Conclusion depends rather upon some modal of the general Sequence than upon the general sequence itself. Thus if I say, "If John has a fever he will die," the general sequence is "all that have fevers die," which is *non vera pro vera;* the Sequence, therefore, if there be one, must be found in some peculiarity of "John," to be expressed by a modal. The Sequence then would be, "All (*sub modo*) who have fevers die;" the *sub modo* denoting the differentia of the class to which the subject of the Antecedent belongs. This modal, however, should always be stated either in the Antecedent, or by giving the Sequence stated in such a form as to clearly point it out.

Conditionals with four terms.

694. If the Conditional has four distinct terms, of course the Sequence becomes double, and the Conditional as an Enthymeme is completed into a Sorites. Thus, If A is B, C is D.

And we complete thus, C is A,
A is B,
B is D,
∴ C is D.

Compound Conditionals.

695. In what is called the *Compound* Conditional, it is necessary to prove all the Antecedents in order to establish the Consequent. If, however, we disprove the Consequent, we show that some one or more of the Antecedents is untrue, without determining by the Formula which it is.

696. This makes the Minor Premise a compound compulative categoric Proposition. Thus,

If A is B, } E is F.
and If C is D, }
But A is B, and C is D,
∴ E is F.

697. In continuous Conditionals if we prove the first Antecedent all the rest will follow. Thus, If A is B, C is D;—If C is D, E is F;— If E is F, F is H, and so on; since each Antecedent after the first is the Consequent of the preceding Conditional, it is established by that first Antecedent. Continuous Conditionals.

And conversely, if we disprove the last Consequent we have disproved all the Antecedents.

698. We may also have Conditionals with Disjunctive Consequents. Thus, "If grain is cheap it must be either because the crops are large, the consumers are comparatively few, or the importations are extensive." Conditionals with Disjunctive Consequents.

699. Completing this Formula and we have a Disjunctive Conclusion. Thus,

If A is B, either C is D, or E is F,
But A is B,
∴ Either C is D, or E is F.

700. But if we complete in the Destructive Method, we must deny all the members of the Disjunctive Consequent. Thus,

If A is B, either C is D, or E is F,
But neither is C, D, nor E, F,
∴ Some A is not B.

SECTION XIII.

Of Disjunctive Syllogisms.

701. It has sometimes been held that there are two classes of Disjunctive Judgments—the Divisive and Comprehensive. Those which we have already considered are the Comprehensive Disjunctive Judgments. Comprehensive and Divisive Disjunctives.

702. The Divisives are rather categorical judgments, in which the divided whole is one term and the coördinate terms are the other. Thus, "All food is either vegetable or animal."

The Divisives are rather Compound Categorical.

But we will postpone the consideration of the completion of the Formula of this class until we have attended to the other, or the Comprehensive Disjunctives.

703. We have already examined the Disjunctive Judgments. They affirm that one of two or more judgments contained in the Disjunctive Proposition must be true without at all indicating which that one is.

704. But it is not always the case that the deduction depends upon this opposition of the parts, when a Disjunctive Proposition occurs as one of the Premises. Thus,

Deduction does not always depend upon the Excluded Middle.

Every conqueror is (either a hero or a villain);
Cæsar was a conqueror:
∴ Cæsar was (either a hero or a villain).

All Y is (either X or W),
All Z is Y,
∴ All Z is (either X or W).

Or the Disjunctive may be the Minor:

All Y is X,
Either (Z or W) is Y,
∴ Either (Z or W) is X.

Or finally, the Middle Term may be Disjunctive in one of the Premises. Thus,

Gold, silver, and platina are malleable;
All precious metals, are either gold, silver, or platina:
∴ All precious metals are malleable.

705. But in this case the Disjunctive Middle must enumerate all the coördinate parts, and in one Premise at least, as above, it must not appear as a Disjunctive.

For if we say—Either gold, or silver, or platina *is* malleable—as Major, and then write the Minor as above, we should manifestly

Not Disjunctive in both Premises.

have an undistributed Middle; and we might have the following as all the truth there would be necessary in the Formula:

Either gold, or silver, or platina is malleable; (suppose it to be gold only that is malleable):

All precious metals are either gold, silver, or platina; (suppose it to be silver and platina only that are precious metals), and then manifestly we should have no Conclusion, for the Major term was compared with gold and the Minor with silver and platina. This is in fact what is always done in the fallacy of undistributed Middle.

706. In all the above examples the judgment is not Disjunctive. It is merely a compound categorical judgment with a Disjunctive for either subject or predicate as the case may be.

707. We have seen that the ground of a Disjunctive Judgment properly so called, that is, a Comprehensive Disjunctive, is the Excluded Middle. It will follow, therefore, that if we deny one of the members the other must be true.

708. Hence in all Disjunctive Syllogisms the Disjunctive Judgment is the Major Premise. For the Minor we have the Contradictory of one of the Members, and for the Conclusion the other Member. Thus,

Disjunctive Judgment the Major Premise in Disjunctive Syllogisms.

Either A is B, or A is C,
But A is not B,
∴ A is C.

Or, Either A is B, or A is C,
But A is not C,
∴ A is B.

709. This is called by the Scholastic writers the *modus tollente ponens*.

Modus tollente ponens.

710. But if the coördinate terms are also coördinate parts of the divided whole, and not merely Alternate Species, we may also complete in the *modus ponente tollens*.

Modus ponente tollens.

Thus Either A is B, or A is C,
But A is B,
∴ A is not C.

This is either gold or platinum;
It is platinum:
∴ It is not gold.

The validity of this Conclusion depends not upon the simple Excluded Middle but upon the law of Division, that no individual can be in more than one of the coördinate parts of any divided whole at the same time and in the same respect.

The mode depends upon Division.

711. When there are more than two members we obtain only a compound categorical Proposition for the first answer. Thus,

More than two members.

Either A is C, or A is B, or A is D,
But A is not C,
∴ Either A is B, or A is D.

We may thus proceed with this as before, and then we shall get a simple categorical Conclusion. Thus,

Either A is B, or C is D,
But A is not B,
∴ C is D.

712. From the foregoing it will be seen that what are called the Divisive Disjunctives, can be completed by a Discretive Categorical alone. Thus,

Divisive Disjunctives completed only by Discretives.

All A is either B or C,
S is A but it is not B,
∴ S is C;

that is, we must include the Subject of the Conclusion in the Subject of the Major Premise, which is the divided whole, and at the same time exclude it from all the parts except one, which one is predicated of the Subject of the Conclusion.

713. Nor is the Method materially different when the divided whole is the Predicate instead of the Subject in the Disjunctive. As,

a b and c constitute M,
S is M but not a,
∴ S is either b or c.

SECTION XIV.

Of the Dilemma.

714. The Dilemma seldom needs or requires any completion. It differs from the Compound Conditional in that its Antecedents bear such a relation to each other as to constitute an Excluded Middle, and therefore some one of them must be true. And as the Consequent may be predicated on either one of them alone, it is immaterial which of the Antecedents is denied, as its denial affirms the other. **Dilemma.**

715. These Antecedents are sometimes called the horns of the Dilemma. **Horns of the Dilemma.**

716. The Dilemma is often Complex by having several Antecedents one after another.

Thus Demosthenes says:

"If Æschines partook in the public rejoicing he is inconsistent.

If he did not he is unpatriotic."

717. But in all such cases there is a real Consequent in which all the Antecedents or series of Antecedents unite. The obvious Consequent in the above case is that therefore "Æschines is unworthy of public favor and confidence." **A Consequent to the Complex Dilemma.**

The Formula may be thus expressed:

If A is B, A is C,	But If A is C,	A is E.
Or, If A is B, A is D,	And If A is D,	

718. Hence we may say, "Whoever committed this fault is either too ignorant to be our guide or too dishonest to be trusted—in either case he is unworthy of our confidence."

Which we may represent thus:

If A is B, A is not C,	And If A is not C,	A is not F.
Or, If A is D, A is not E,	And If A is not E,	

719. The Dilemma is not unfrequently stated in an inverted form. Thus, If A is B, either A is D, or A is F. "If he fails, it is because he is ignorant of his profession or inattentive to his duties."

Dilemma stated in an inverted form.

720. This may be regarded as an Enthymeme stated conditionally with a Disjunctive Conclusion, or a Major Term with a Disjunctive Modal similar to the instance already given, &c. Thus,

All B is either D or F,
A is B,
∴ A is either D or F;

or in the other form, Either A is D, or A is F.

721. It is not unfrequently the case that in stating the Dilemma, the Antecedents are alone stated in disjunctive opposition to each other, and the Formula is of course nothing more than a Disjunctive Judgment. But as the Consequent of the truth of either member is so obvious, and is in fact suggested by the circumstances and the occasion, the statement is considered a Dilemma nevertheless. Thus, "The Dilemma then presents itself to us anew: Either we must accept the doctrine of the *transmutation of species* and suppose that the organized species of one geological epoch were transmuted into those of another by some long-continued agency of natural causes; or else we must believe in many successive *acts of creation* and extinction of species out of the common course of nature; acts which therefore we may properly call marvellous."—(*Whewell's Indications of the Creator*, p. 39.)

The Consequent sometimes omitted.

Here we have the two members of a Disjunctive stated as a Dilemma, and so called; the first member is considered absurd and the second therefore as true.

722. Another form of the Dilemma is sometimes used; namely, one in which two Antecedents are affirmed with contradictory Consequents, from which it follows of course that

Antecedents with Contradictory Consequents.

one of the Antecedents must be false. Thus, "Lord Bacon opposed the English system of colonization;" therefore, "If Lord Bacon was right, the English system of colonization is wrong."

But if the English are right, their system of colonization is not wrong; therefore, If the English are right, Lord Bacon was not right. Or if Lord Bacon was right, the English are wrong.

CHAPTER IV.

OF FALLACIES.

Errors besides those in the Formula.

723. We have already noticed the difference between the Form and the Matter* of an Argument, and although the Analysis of Formula takes no account of the Matter, and supposes that the Formulæ are valid whatever may be the Matter, there are certain sources of error which a mere inspection of the Formulæ will never reveal to us. These have been called *Fallacies*. It is not easy to collect and classify them all, and yet something of the kind is indispensable.

Fallacies defined.

724. A *Fallacy* may be defined in its broadest and general sense to be any fault or error in an argument, by means of which it (1) fails to prove any thing; or (2) the Conclusion which has been assigned to it; or (3) the Conclusion which was demanded by the occasion or end in view.

Divided into four classes.

725. It has been customary to divide Fallacies into four classes.—(1) Fallacies in Form; (2) Fallacies in Diction; (3) Fallacies in Matter; and (4) Extra-Logical Fallacies. The differentia of these classes is not very distinctly given anywhere, nor are the specific names used with any great uniformity or clearness. We may perhaps define each species as follows:

* See Introduction, 14.

726. Fallacies are *in Form* when the Formula offends against any of the rules of the mere Form, and is perceptible without any consideration of the Matter of the Argument. Hence Fallacies in Form should rather be called *Faults* than Fallacies, and we shall so designate them hereafter; and then a Fallacy will be that which has the appearance of a valid Form, and deceives by its appearance of being Fault*less*. It does not *fail* to fulfil the formal conditions of a proof, but fails in the *essential* conditions which lie beneath the Form.

Fallacies in Form.

Called *Faults*.

727. The fallacy may be said to be *in Diction*, when the words in which it is stated are so used as to leave us in doubt as to the meaning, and in fact so as to have several meanings in the same Formula.

Fallacies in Diction.

728. The Fallacy may be considered as *in the Matter*, when one Premise or both of them are taken in a sense not intended, or when they fail to express the judgment adequately.

Fallacies in Matter.

729. And the Fallacy is *extra Logical* when it lies beyond the Province of Logic;* as when it states as a Premise a Proposition which is not true; or proves a Conclusion, which though true enough, is not to the purpose.

Extra Logical Fallacies.

730. It is quite possible that an Argument should offend in more than one of these points at the same time. We must however remember that a Fallacy is simply *a failure to prove*. It does not necessarily follow that because the Formula contains a Fallacy therefore the Conclusion is false; the Conclusion may be true after all, and all that can be inferred or predicated on the ground of the Fallacy is simply that the Conclusion is not proved. But it is not *dis*proved; for disproof implies a concluding force in the Formula of which the Fallacy has deprived it.

More than one Fallacy in the same Argument.

The effect of a Fallacy.

* See Introduction, 17.

Enumeration of Fallacies.

Including the *Extra Logical* we have seven distinct Fallacies, excluding Faults in Form from our number; *Ignoratio Elenchi*, *Petitio Principii*, and the five in the use of the Middle Term.*

* Aristotle [Soph. Elench.], and after him most other writers, reckons six Fallacies *in Dictione*, and seven *extra Dictionem*.

The six in Diction are: (1) *Equivocation*, as "the dog is an animal, Sirius [the star] is a dog, *therefore* Sirius is an animal;" (2) *Amphiboliæ*, as ἆρ' ὃ ὁρᾷ τις, τοῦτο ὁρᾷ, or as Aldrich gives it, *Quod tangitur a Socrate illud sentit; Columna tangitur a Socrate: Ergo Columna sentit*,—the amphibology is in τοῦτο, as being either accusative or nominative, and in the Latin example it is in the uncertainty as to the subject of *sentit*; (3) *Composition*; and (4) *Division*, as explained below; (5) *Accent*, as when putting the accent on the wrong word, or the wrong syllable in a word, we give it a meaning different from that which was intended; and (6) *Figure of Speech*, where on account of similarity of words one draws a false inference from one to the other, as because *Musa* is of the feminine gender therefore so is *Poeta*.

The seven Fallacies *extra Dictionem* are: (1) *Fallacy of Accidents*; and (2) *a Dicto secundum quid ad dictum simpliciter*, as explained below; (3) *Ignoratio Elenchi*; (4) *A non causa pro causa*, whether it be *a non vera pro vera*, or *a non tali pro tali*. As an example of the first, Aldrich gives, "A comet shines—therefore there will be war." This is a *non causa*, the comet being entirely innocent of causing wars. Of the second he gives, "Whatever will intoxicate is forbidden; wine intoxicates, therefore wine is forbidden." "Not at all," he adds, "but only the abuse of wine." Here wine is admitted to be a cause of intoxication, but it is prohibited only when it *is such*, that is, in sufficient quantity as to cause intoxication; (5) *Fallacy of Consequences*, as when a Conclusion is given which does not follow from the Premises—this in fact includes all Fallacies in Form; (6) *Petitio Principii*, when that is assumed as given which ought to have been proved; and (7) the Fallacy of *Plurium Interrogationum*, when several questions are proposed as if they were one, which are yet so related to each other as to require different answers. As, "Are honey and poison sweet? Have you left off your bad habits?"

These thirteen Fallacies have been arranged into mnemonic lines; thus,

ÆQUIVOCAT. AMPHI. COMPONIT, DIVIDIT, ACC. FI.
ACCI. QUID. IGNORANS, NON CAUSA, CON. PETIT. INTERR.

But I have preferred the classification given above in the text, for reasons I will not enumerate here; the 1st, 2d, and 6th are included under Ambiguous Middle; the 5th, *Accent*, does not belong to Logic at all—at least it is a mere trick; the same may be said of the 13th, *Plurium Interrogationum*; the 11th I have reckoned under the head of Faults in Form; the 3d and 4th I have recognized by name, as also the 7th, 8th, and 9th; the 10th, *Non Causa*, I have included under the more general head of the *Petitio Principii*.

SECTION I.

Of the Ignoratio Elenchi, or Mistaking the Issue.

Ignoratio Elenchi a Fault in Aim rather than a Fallacy.

The words *Ignoratio Elenchi* mean "Ignorance of the Proof" which ought to be given, and are applied equally to cases in which one is really and innocently ignorant, and to those in which one chooses to ignore the real issue to be met and the Proof necessary to meet it. In this view of it, therefore, it is not a Fallacy in Logic at all, but simply a fault in sagacity or honesty, or both. It is no fault in Form nor a fallacy in the use of Forms. It is no fault in Method, for the Formula and Method may both be faultless. It is therefore merely a failure to pursue the right End—a failure in Aim or End; as disastrous of course to the success of an Argument as any fallacy can be, but differing in kind both from Fallacies in the uses of Formula and Faults in Method.

Importance of the right End.

731. Nothing can be more important in the construction of an argument than a clear and adequate conception of the precise point to be proved. Without this we may deceive ourselves or be imposed upon by others.

Where *Ignoratio* is likely to occur.

732. The *Ignoratio Elenchi*, or mistake of the Question, is more pernicious when it occurs in a course of reasoning where an argument is introduced merely as subservient to some more general purpose or conclusion than elsewhere. In this case the deception is less likely to be detected, and the temptation to it is much stronger than any where else.

Illustration from Thucydides.

733. We have an illustration of this fallacy pointed out in the speech of Diodatus, given in Thucydides, in answer to Cleon, who had argued that it would be *just* to put the Mitylenians to death. Diodatus reminds him that that was not the question; the question really before them was whe-

ther it would be *expedient* for the Athenians in their present circumstances to undertake it.*

734. Mistakes of this kind will be found on a careful scrutiny of far more frequent occurrence than one would at first expect; and nothing but the most careful scrutiny and the most sagacious discrimination of things similar in appearance, but different in reality, can secure immunity from this kind of imposture.

Fallacies of this kind frequent.

SECTION II.

Of the Petitio Principii.

Under this head I shall include all forms of assuming for Premises what ought not to be assumed, or used as such without being first proved to be true in the sense and to the extent used.

735. Strictly speaking, the *Petitio Principii* is the fault in Method which consists in stating as a Premise a Proposition which contains the Conclusion, in such a way as that it can be evolved from the Premise by some of the processes of Immediate Inference.

Petitio Principii strictly a fault in Method.

736. In the popular sense it means simply the assuming as true that which we are expecting or wishing to have proved. It is seldom the case that both Premises of an Argument are disputed or questioned,† and when the one that is thus

The popular sense of the word.

* Thucydides, Book III, Year 5.

† For this reason some writers, and writers on "Logic," even, have maintained that every Syllogism is a *Petitio Principii*. They cite such examples as the following:

All men are mortal;
John Smith is a man:
∴ John Smith is mortal.

But, say they, the Major cannot be affirmed as true unless John Smith be mortal. They forget that they beg the question themselves—the question, to wit, whether John Smith is *a man* or not.

Let us take a case in which both Premises admit of doubt, or are at least denied:

questioned is assumed, the assumption is regarded as a begging of the principle or main Premise on which the Conclusion depends.

737. We have several forms of Premises unduly assumed, or untrue. We must, however, distinguish between a fallacy and a falsehood, or mere false statement. It is no part of Logic to ascertain whether Propositions introduced as Premises are true or false; thus, If a man affirms that A is B, when it is not so, the false statement is not a Fallacy for Logic to correct; but it is a misstatement to be corrected by investigation into the subject matter of the Proposition.* The truth is to be sought in

Falsity of Premises not a Fallacy.

No murderer hath eternal life;
All warriors are murderers:
Therefore No warrior hath eternal life.

Here we have a Major Premise which some professing Christians deny, and others would of course deny the Minor. Hence in the estimation of some persons one Premise might be affirmed without involving the truth of the Conclusion, and in the estimation of another class the other Premise might be affirmed without involving its truth. In this case, therefore, neither Premise can be regarded as a Petitio Principii. But this differs from others so far as this point is concerned, only in the purely accidental fact, that either one of its Premises are such as to be denied or doubted by any body.

* It certainly diminishes our reverence for ARISTOTLE immensely, to find that in his *Prior Analytics*, Book II, he has devoted three chapters, II, III, and IV, to the consideration of the cases and conditions in which we may have a *true* Conclusion from *False* Premises! If one could, he would disbelieve that these chapters ever came from the Stagyrite. But there is no help for it that I can see; I find no intimation of their spuriousness.

That there may be no mistake about the matter, and that the reader may see what cases the Father of Logic is discussing, I will give an example: "As animal is with no stone, nor stone present with any man, yet if animal is predicated of stone, and stone of man, we shall yet have the Conclusion, man is an animal." Thus,

"Every stone is an animal;
Every man is a stone:
∴ Every man is an animal."

The Conclusion is undoubtedly true; and it is *from*, and a good ways *from*, the Premises too. We might just all well substitute "*jack-knife*" for Minor term, and prove by the same formula that a "jack-knife" is a man.

It is no wonder that Logic has fallen into disrepute when we find the Father of the Science indulging in such ridiculous nonsense. Had this acutest of men got bewildered with the intricacy of his own system, aban-

History, in Science, in Observation, &c. &c. The whole realm of knowledge is to be put in requisition to determine the truth or falsehood of Propositions when used as Premises. Logic is responsible only for the truth of the Conclusion on condition that the Premises are true.

Classes of Assumptions.

The assumptions under this head are reckoned by the old writers as two:

Non vera pro vera.

738. (1.) A *non verâ causâ pro verâ causâ.* As when we say, "There is a comet, therefore there will be a pestilence." The completion of this Enthymeme would imply the assertion, that "comets *cause* pestilence," or "whenever there is a comet there is a pestilence;" the latter of which statements is simply untrue, the former assigning for a cause that which is not a cause of the effect. Hence a *non vera pro vera*, as it is usually written (omitting the word *causa*), is stating as a Premise that which is untrue.

Non tali pro tali.

739. (2.) A *non tali* [*causâ*] *pro tali* [*causâ.*] As, "Whatever is poisonous should never be taken. But opium is poisonous." In this case it is admitted that opium is poisonous—that it is a cause of death, *but* a cause of death only when taken in certain quantities or in certain ways.

To these we may add one or two others:

Other Forms of False Assumptions.

740. (1) When in categorical Premises the two relate to different points of time, as, "He who is most hungry eats most. But he that eats most is least hungry, *therefore* he that is most hungry is least hungry." These Premises refer to different points of time in relation to the act of eating; (2) then we may have want of sequence in Conditionals; (3) non-exclusion of Middle in Disjunctives; (4) want of sameness in kind in things compared in Comparatives.

doned his *a priori* light, and set himself to justify by hook or by crook, as best he could, every possible Formula to which a Conclusion which is true as an independent Proposition, though not as a Conclusion, might be attached? It would seem so.

SECTION III.

Of Ambiguous Middle.

741. Not only must the Middle Term be once taken as a Whole, but it must be used in both Premises *in the same sense;* otherwise we have the Fallacy in Diction of *Ambiguous Middle.*

Ambiguous Middle.

742. A word may be equivocal in itself, or intrinsically, as in fact many words are, so that we really do not know precisely what one intends by his Proposition, until we have heard him discourse long enough to render his terms perspicuous. Thus if one were speaking of "heat" in a scientific treatise, we should be in doubt whether by the word he meant that specific heat which is perceptible to the senses, or that latent heat which exists in all bodies to a greater or less extent and yet produces no effects upon the thermometer. And yet a Proposition might be true or false as the term was used in one or another of these senses.

Words intrinsically ambiguous.

743. But if the Middle Term is taken in a different sense in each Premise, it is the same so far as all purposes of deduction are concerned, as if these were two entirely unlike and different terms.

The Middle Term used ambiguously is the same as two Middle Terms.

744. "It is worth observing," says Whately,* "that the words whose ambiguity is the most frequently overlooked, and is productive of the greatest amount of confusion of thought and fallacy are among the *commonest*, and are those of whose meaning the generality consider there is the least room to doubt. It is indeed from these very circumstances that the danger arises; words in very common use are both the most liable from the looseness of ordinary discourse, to slide from one sense into

Words whose ambiguity is most frequently overlooked.

* Appendix, No. I.

another, and also the least likely to have that ambiguity suspected."

745. The Archbishop has collected some forty or fifty words illustrative of the foregoing remark. But its truth and force can be appreciated only after a long-continued habit of carefully noticing the meaning of words as they are used in ordinary conversation and in the printed works, especially those of a controversial character. A large part of all the controversy that has ever existed in the world has risen from persons calling the same thing by different names, or by their meaning very different things when they use the same name or term.

Habitual caution our only safeguard.

746. The Fallacy of Ambiguous Middle is spoken of in several different ways, but it is in all these classes (if we are to regard these different names as indicating different classes) essentially the same. Thus we have the Fallacy of *Equivocation* when the same word is used in different senses. The Fallacy of *Amphibology* when the word is used so as to admit of different senses in each Premise. The Fallacy of *Figure of Speech* when the Middle Term is used metaphorically in one Premise; and the Fallacy of *Paronomasia* &c.

Several varieties of ambiguity.

SECTION IV.

Of the Fallacy of Division and Composition.

747. This Fallacy consists in using the Middle Term in one Premise as a General Term, and in the other as a Collective Term.

If now we use the Middle Term as a Collective Term in the Major, and as a General Term in the Minor Premise, we have the Fallacy of *Division*; thus,

Fallacy of Division.

The Romans [collectively] destroyed Carthage;

Brutus was a Roman [that is, belonged to the Genus Roman]:

∴Brutus destroyed Carthage.

748. But if the Middle Term is used generally, or as a General Term in the Major Premise, and collectively, or as a Collective Term in the Minor, we have what is called the Fallacy of *Composition;* thus,

Fallacy of Composition.

Three and two are two numbers;
Five is two and three [collectively]:
∴ Five is two numbers.

749. "This is a Fallacy with which men are exceedingly apt to deceive themselves," says Whately; "for when a multitude of particulars are presented to the mind, many are too weak or too indolent to take a comprehensive view, but confine their attention to each single point by turns and thus decide, infer, and act accordingly. For example, the imprudent spendthrift finding that he cannot afford a certain great expenditure as a whole, resolves upon each of its parts separately, forgetting that *all of them together* will ruin him."

The spendthrift's Fallacy.

SECTION V.

Fallacy of Accidents and of Quid.

750. The first, *Fallacia Accidentis*, occurs whenever in the course of the syllogism a term has been predicated of another, in reference to its essential and inseparable properties, and taken as predicated of its *separable accidents*.*

Fallacy of Accidents.

What we buy in the market we eat;
We buy raw meat in the market:
∴ Raw meat is what we eat; or, "we eat raw meat."

Here the Middle Term is predicated of the Minor essentially, and thus by means of the Middle Term the Major is predicated of the Minor, as if the Middle had been predicated of the Accidents rather than the Essentia of the Minor.

* See Chap. II., 220.

751. The Fallacy, *a dicto secundum quid ad dictum simpliciter*, called for the sake of brevity the Fallacy of *Quid*, is that in which the Middle Term is taken in one Premise as used in its broadest signification, and in the other as used only with reference to some special subject or application.

Fallacy of *Quid.*

As for example, when it is inferred from the declarations concerning the Virgin Mary, that she was pure and immaculate [as a virgin], that therefore she was sinless [as an accountable being], and so must have been born without any taint of human depravity.

But the pureness and immaculateness *as to virginity* is one thing and absolute purity is quite another, and cannot be inferred from it. The fallacy is precisely the same as that made by the passenger in a railroad car when on seeing the notice, "No smoking allowed here," he inferred that the stove would not smoke.

As another illustration take the following:

Nebuchadnezzar ate grass like the oxen;
But the oxen eat grass standing on hoofs and chewing the cud:
∴ Nebuchadnezzar had hoofs and chewed the cud.

752. This Fallacy it will be seen arises from a disregard of the scope and design of a writer. In fact it is but seldom that any proposition is affirmed except when there is some special end in view, or some special object before the mind in reference to which it is true; while in an application to objects of another class it might be entirely false.

Most assertions limited in their scope.

753. Besides the foregoing Fallacies, Whately has enumerated several others which are merely Tricks of the Rhetorician's Art, and the consideration of which does not belong to a Treatise on Logic.

We have defined Faults as failures to fulfil the Formal conditions of an Argument, and Fallacies as failures to fulfil the Essential conditions lying beneath the mere form. But a Trick is something which fails to be a Fault even.

Tricks as different from Faults or mere Fallacies.

A Fault can always be reduced to some Formula, one of the sixty-four Moods, though an invalid one. But a mere Trick has not the elements to complete any Formula. It cannot be put into the form or shape of an Argument, however successful it may sometimes prove in carrying a point and producing the legitimate results of sound reasoning.

PART II.

OF LOGICAL METHODS.

CHAPTER I.

OF THE ELEMENTS OF METHOD.

SECTION I.

Of Method in General.

754. METHOD is the way in which the means to any end are used for its accomplishment. Consequently Method always supposes an End or object in view, Matter in which it is to be accomplished, Means to be used in its accomplishment, and an Agent to use them;—the word is from the Greek μεθ' ὅδου. Thus if I wish to be in a neighboring village, the road by which I go thither is my Method, while the carriage in which I ride, or my feet if I walk, are the Means which I use by the way.

Method defined.

Supposes an End, Matter, and Means.

755. Method itself, however, may be resolved into several elements; as, (1) Method, properly so called, that is, the way by which one shall go, as in going from one place to another; (2) the Order in which the several steps shall be taken, as which first, and which next, and so on; and (3) the Manner in which each step shall be taken. In going

Elements of Method.

to a neighboring village there is no room for choice, as to which step shall be taken first in order, but one might take it into his head to walk sideways or backwards. In this case his Method and Order might be perfectly good, but his Manner would be very awkward. In a general sense, however, all three of these elements are included in Method; and Order and Manner themselves become but the Method of the subordinate parts of any whole with reference to which the word Method is used.

756. Method gives unity of plan and efficiency in the use of means towards the attainment of any end. It is not always the strongest man that can accomplish the most work in a given time, nor the fleetest of foot that can make the quickest race. Inferior force is often rendered the most efficient by the superiority of Method. Method has to do with every thing. Method is the result of mental power and application. It indicates capacity and attention, as its absence indicates the want of them.

Method gives unity and efficiency.

757. Hence Method must form an essential part of any trade or art that is to be learned. It is in fact the conversion of Science into Art, the passing from knowledge to practice.

Method is the reduction of Knowledge to Practice.

758. The beauty of any operation depends upon the Order and Method pursued in it, and the pleasure or the pain with which any accomplished performer in any department of human activity watches the acts of another depends upon the presence or absence of Method in the operator. And a quick insight into the Method of any act or series of actions is called genius for that kind of actions.

Beauty of operation depends upon Method.

759. In writing or speaking, not only the order in which the sentences follow one another, but also that in which the words are placed relatively to each other in each sentence, depends upon Method; and upon this arrangement depends the beauty and force of what is said or written. In a mathematical demonstration there is a cer-

Force of writing and arguments depend upon their Method.

tain method or order in which the steps should be taken—and we should hardly call that a demonstration, which although it had included all that was necessary, had thrown the parts together in entire disregard of the order in which they ought to follow each other. Such a demonstration, if demonstration it could be called, would demonstrate the want of capacity in the demonstrator rather than the truth of the Proposition to be proved.

SECTION II.

Of Order as an Element of Method.

760. Method always implies an End, and yet it is not concerned in the selection of that End. It is concerned merely with its attainment. The End may be determined for us, or we may be left to choose it for ourselves. Ethics determine Ends for us when it specifies certain acts as being of moral obligation, and which therefore we are not at liberty to do otherwise than pursue. Theology determines Ends for us by showing acts which by the Will and Command of God are obligatory upon us. Polity determines Ends for us, as when the State commands certain acts by its positive enactments. Necessity determines Ends for us when by a fixed law of our nature it is ordained that we must eat to live, and must work in order to have something to eat. But in regard to many of our acts we are left to select our Ends for ourselves, as Pleasure, or Interest, or Benevolence may incline us.

Ends determined by Necessity and by Choice.

761. Order, however, is an important element in Method, and there can be no Method without Order. The Principles of Order however are very few and simple, and the same in all departments of human activity. Always there is a place to begin, a place to end, and intermediate steps to be arranged. That step or act which presupposes

Order necessary to Method.

others cannot well be taken first, and that which is necessary to the succeeding cannot well be postponed to the last. The mason cannot lay the wall until the stone, and lime, and sand have been drawn and the mortar made. The carpenter cannot dress the timber and fit each piece to its place, until the trees have been felled and the boards hauled to the place where they are to be used. So in studies—the alphabet must be learned first, geometry must be learned before trigonometry, and grammar before rhetoric; and he that should undertake the calculus before algebra, or history before he knew any thing of geography, would find that he had made a mistake in Method, which would render all his studies and his efforts unavailing.

Order to some extent determined by necessity.

762. That fault in Method which consists in inverting the true order of the steps, or successive acts in any series of actions, has been called by the Greek writers a ὕστερον πρῶτον, that is, a *later-first*.

The Fault of *later-first.*

763. In every process there are some of the steps or elements whose position is fixed by the very nature and necessities of the case. Thus in the erection of a house the materials must be hauled to the spot before the walls can be put up. But in every process also there is a large number of elements or steps, the position of which is not so determined by the nature and necessities of the case as that there may not be varieties in the order; and their disposal furnishes a sphere for the exercise of tact and genius.

The Order of many steps left to choice.

764. The five great Canons of Order are:

Five Canons of Order.

(1.) Place that first which presupposes nothing as having preceded it.

(2.) Put that last which presupposes all the rest, and neither conduces to nor implies any thing to follow it.

(3.) Put each intermediate step after that which it presupposes, and before all those which depend upon it.

(4.) Omit as extraneous matter whatever is not conducive to the End in view.

(5.) If there are intermediate steps requiring to occupy the same place, they may be arranged with regard to convenience or taste merely.

765. Method can never be discussed and treated in any full and satisfactory way, except in connection with a discussion of the Means and the Matter, or at least by presuming that they are already known. To teach the Method of any trade or art would be to teach the trade or art itself. We could not teach the Method of ship-building, for instance, without teaching the whole trade of building ships. For the order in which each act should come, each material be used, and the way in which these details should be disposed of, must depend upon the character of the details themselves to such an extent as to involve Method and Means most inextricably in the same discussion.

The discussion of Method implies a knowledge of the Matter and the Means.

766. For this reason it will be necessary to limit ourselves in the discussion to some special and definite sphere. This we shall best accomplish by considering those influences which are external to Method itself properly considered, but which do nevertheless determine it, and constitute species and varieties in Method.

Means of limiting the Subject.

SECTION III.

Of the Ideas which determine Method.

767. I have said that Method is the result of mind in its application to the attainment of any End.

768. But there may be several Ways or Methods to the same End. If I wish to go to the neighboring village, for instance, I may wish to go as quickly as possible; in that case I should select my means and my method or way with reference to quickness of time. If the time is no object, the ease

Several Methods to the same End.

with which the journey may be accomplished may determine me to select other means and another route. Or again, if pleasure be the leading object, I may select still different means and still a different route from what I should if speed or ease alone were to be consulted.

769. There are FIVE Ideas which determine the mind in its choice of a Method—two of them are relative—Ideas of the Understanding, as the Germans would call them; and three are absolute—Ideas of the Reason. The two former are PLEASURE and UTILITY; the three latter are the GOOD, the BEAUTIFUL, and the TRUE.*

Five Ideas that determine Methods.

770. The two former, Pleasure and Utility, I have called relative Ideas, because they always relate to the person by whom the Method is determined. What is *pleasant* is pleasant not absolutely and in itself, but only because it is found to afford pleasure to him who experiences it; the same thing, as we often see, may be pleasant to one and unpleasant to another.

Pleasure, why relative.

771. So of Utility. Nothing is useful in itself or absolutely. It is useful only to some end; and the end by comparison with which we judge a thing to be useful is also personal and of time. If we ask why a thing is useful, we always come round at last as the final answer to the fact, that it conduces to some worldly object which we wish to have accomplished.

Utility also relative.

772. But the Good, the Beautiful, and the True are absolute. To say that a thing is Beautiful because it pleases, is merely to give our means of knowing a thing for the reality of

The Good, the Beautiful, and the True, absolute.

* There may be good reasons for reckoning the *Plausible* as sustaining the same relation to the True that the Pleasant does to the Beautiful, and the Useful to the Good. But I have chosen not to do so; but rather to look upon the Plausible as merely one subordinate species of the Useful; namely, that which is useful for conviction and persuasion, irrespective of the truth of that which those whom we address are to be persuaded or convinced to do.

the thing itself. To say that an act is good because it is useful is to change the standard altogether. The absurdity of the change is seen, when instead of speaking of moral excellence or the character of God, we say that it is Useful instead of it is Good.

773. The life of man is for the most part controlled and directed by the relative Ideas of Utility and Pleasure. Devotion to the absolute Ideas implies something of self-forgetfulness and self-immolation that rises into heroism and religion. It implies an elevation and dignity of character which is by no means every where to be met with.

The Relative Ideas most prominent in the ordinary life of man.

774. These several Ideas when developed into practical precepts, give rise to systems or codes of action. Thus the Idea of Pleasure becomes the Epicurean theory of Ethics. Pleasure is the Highest Good, and Virtue is only the wise and prudent pursuit of Pleasure. The Idea of Utility gives rise to the system of expediency, the Happiness of Man; and each one's happiness is for himself the Highest Good which he can propose to himself to accomplish. Hence whatever is useful towards the accomplishment of this end is right, and the pursuit of it is virtue.

These Ideas developed into rules of action.

775. The Idea of the Beautiful is developed into what has come to be called ÆSTHETICS; and the Idea of the Good determines ETHICS, or the law of right action. And LOGIC in its comprehensive sense is determined by the Idea of Truth. Æsthetics says this must be so because it is *beautiful*. Ethics says this must be so because it is *right*, and Logic says this must be so because so it is *conformed to Truth*.

Development of the Absolute Ideas.

776. These Ideas sustain towards each other a sort of *sub-contrary* opposition, in consequence of which one may prevail and control the Method without influence from the others, and yet no Method can be formed in which all of the Ideas can

Relation of these Ideas to each other.

be combined, each in its perfection. At least, man in his present state has never been able thus to combine these ideas, and we are satisfied with any object when in determining its method that idea has had the ascendency which in the common estimation ought to have the controlling influence in such cases. Thus in an act, the moral character of which is strongly marked and of an unalterable character, as parental affection, filial duty, gratitude to benefactors, fidelity to an engagement, &c., we are shocked and indignant if considerations of Æsthetics, or of expediency, are allowed to take precedence of that controlling influence which Right and Good ought to have in such cases. In the fine arts, on the other hand, the artist entirely fails of his object unless he subordinates all other considerations to that of the Beautiful. The same holds true in regard to objects whose final cause is Utility. Any attempt or pretence of motives of conscience in matters which are indifferent in themselves, as in the cut of a coat, the color of a hat, the shape of a house, &c., &c., is but ridiculous fanaticism; just as any attempt at the display of ornament in cases where utility alone is sought for is an offence against good taste, which implies either a want of culture or a want of sensibility. The man who should attempt the ornaments and pleasantries of poetry in a mathematical demonstration, would be considered hopelessly bad in respect both to taste and good sense.

The Beautiful and the Useful how combined.

777. Still however the Ideas of the Beautiful and the Useful are so related, that we seldom pursue the one without some regard to the other. Seldom do we so far abandon ourselves to the luxurious emotions of delight, awakened by the Beautiful either in nature or in art, but that considerations of economy and utility come in for some share in the control of our actions. Nor is it often that the iron rule of necessity so far breaks down the spirit or paralyzes the wings of the fancy, that we are content with fulfilling the conditions and requirements

of utility alone. The commonest tool of the mechanic, the utensils of the housekeeper, and even the implements of the boy who cleans the stables, are all fashioned and finished with some regard to beauty of shape—some regard to good looks—some considerations of taste.

The desire of the maximum of Beauty and Utility combined.

778. In most of the transactions of life the desire to combine as much of usefulness and of beauty as practicable, is a leading and controlling motive. In building a dwelling-house, or a church, for instance, utility is the first object. But we often sacrifice something, and sometimes much of utility, for the sake of realizing some conception of beauty which has entered into our plans. And always do we superadd much to what utility alone would require, for the sake of making our structure pleasing to the taste. The same remark holds equally true in regard to articles of dress, of furniture, equipage, and whatever circumstances we may choose to surround ourselves with. And rarely do we become so hurried with business, so engrossed with care, so jaded with over exertion, or broken with affliction and disappointment, that we become entirely indifferent to the appearance of things about us.

SECTION IV.

Of the Matter of Logical Methods.

Matter as determining Method.

779. The second element to be considered as that which determines Method, is the Matter on which effort or labor is to be bestowed. This must precede a consideration of the Means, because different matter will require different means. The "tools" (which are but the Means of the artisan) of a shoemaker, a hatter, and a stonemason, for instance, are as unlike as the material upon which they are to work, and the Means themselves must be determined by the Matter.

780. For this reason we will hereafter confine ourselves to the consideration of those Methods which concern the discovery, proof, and communication of knowledge.

Limitation of the Subject.

781. We have already reviewed the Matter of Logic so far as the investigation of the Formulæ can command.* But its relation to Method requires a reconsideration of it from another point of view, and with reference to another end to be accomplished.

Analytic and Synthetic Judgments.

782. When a Judgment affirms of its Subject only a property which was necessarily implied in the conception of the Subject itself, the Judgment is called an *Analytical* Judgment. But if it adds to or affirms of the Subject a property which was not necessarily implied in the conception of the Subject, the Judgment is called *Synthetical*. Thus, "Every triangle has three sides," is an Analytic Judgment, we cannot conceive of a triangle without three sides. Nor can we form a conception of a triangle at all without thinking of its *three-sidedness*. Hence Analytical Judgments, while they serve to amplify our knowledge and put our conceptions into Judgments for deductive purposes, do not increase our knowledge at all. But the Proposition, "The angles of a triangle are equal to two right angles," is a Synthetic Judgment. For although this is a necessary truth, yet the property affirmed in the Predicate is not a part of the matter of the conception of a triangle, as is obvious from the fact that we may know what a triangle is without knowing this property of triangles. Hence a Synthetic Judgment always adds to the stock of our knowledge.

Analytical Judgments do not increase Knowledge.

783. An Analytic Judgment affirms of a Subject only what was necessarily implied in the conception of the Subject. But it is one thing to be implied in the conception of a Subject, and another to be implied in the existence or

Matter of the Conception and Matter of the Reality of Objects.

* Chap. I. of Part. I.

reality of the Subject; thus, to take the example just given, "*three-sidedness*," is necessarily implied in the conception of a triangle. But "*the equality of its angles to two right angles*," though necessarily implied in the nature and reality of the triangle, is not, as we have seen, necessarily implied in the conception of it. A triangle however could no more be a reality, that is a triangle, without the equality of its angles to two right angles, than without its three-sidedness.

Necessary Matter.

784. Now the Matter of all Judgments, whether Synthetic or Analytic, which affirm of any Subject only what is necessary to its reality as an individual in any particular genus, is called *Necessary Matter*. Or in other words, all Judgments based upon the principle of contradiction are in *Necessary Matter*. Hence, if we deny the Predicate we necessarily exclude the Subject, not from reality, but from the genus which the Subject denotes. Thus if I predicate of a circle that its radii are not all equal to each other, it may be a figure and a curve, but it is not a circle.*

Effect of contradiction.

* There is no simple term that may not be affirmed as a Predicate of something either real, possible, or impossible in the abstract; though not always in the concrete (Part. I. 279, 280). Thus we may not always be able to predicate "*walking*" in the concrete of any individual, but in the abstract we may always predicate it not only of man but also of other beings, as a property which we conceive as belonging to them *in posse* if not *in esse*—ἐν ἐντελέχεια if not ἐν ἐνέργεια. Hence when the Predicate is a simple term, the Principle of contradiction can only exclude the subject spoken of from the genus denoted by the name given to it, and used as a subject in the Proposition. As when we say, "this circle has unequal radii," the Principle of contradiction, if applied, would exclude the figure spoken of from the genus "circle," though it might leave it in some other genus of realities—as the ellipse for instance.

But we sometimes have a complex Predicate, which, by the Principle of contradiction, would exclude the Subject not only from reality but from possibility also. Thus if one should say, "this figure is a two-sided triangle,"—"two-sidedness" and "triangularity" cannot be combined as predicates of the same subject. Hence their combination produces a complex term, which can be affirmed of nothing, whether real or possible, and the Proposition affirms no judgment. It is mere non-sense. It will be found that the number of such that one meets with in his intercourse with human minds, whether orally or in books, is vastly greater than he would at first expect.

785. It is manifest, however, that Judgments in Necessary Matter may affirm of a Subject something more than the Essentia of its conception. Most of the properties of the figures with which Geometry is concerned, are properties conjoined in some such way with the Essentia of their several genera, and yet they are not Essentia, for they are not known as soon as the conception of the class is formed. One knows what a circle or an ellipse is, for instance (so that he could never be mistaken in deciding with regard to any figure, whether it is a circle, or an ellipse, or not), long before he knows all the properties which are implied in the very nature of those curves.

Judgments in Necessary Matter may affirm something more than the Essentia.

786. But if we pass from the consideration of such matter to the consideration of the realities of being, we find there that any object of thought has properties which not only are not contained in its class-conception (as the Essentia of the proximate genus has with propriety been called), but which do not appear to us to be in any way necessarily connected with the matter of that conception. Such in fact are most of the properties of the objects of the natural world; they constitute what is called *Contingent Matter*—for it seems to be contingent or dependent upon the will of the Creator, whether they should have such properties or not.*

All objects have properties not contained in this class-conception.

Contingent Matter.

* Necessary Matter is that which is affirmed or denied on the Principle of Identity or Contradiction.

But there is a class of philosophers who either ignore or deny the difference between Necessary and Contingent Matter. Among those is MILL in his *Logic*. Prof. WHEWELL has affirmed the distinction on two grounds:

(1.) That Necessary Judgments affirm what has never been a matter of experience, as when we say, "Two straight lines can never inclose a space."

To this Mr. Mill replies, that what we can construct *in the imagination* is as much a matter of experience as that which we may have seen in the reality of being. We can imagine two straight lines infinitely extended, and yet not inclosing a space.

(2.) Prof. Whewell said also that the Judgments which we call Neces-

787. Now all Judgments, whether analytical or synthetic, in Necessary Matter are called Judgments *a priori*; that is, Judgments which are affirmed from a consideration of what was contained or necessarily implied in the very conception of the object. But all Judgments in Contingent Matter are called Judgments *a posteriori*; that is, Judgments which are and can be known to be true only *posterior* to and after an acquaintance with the Subject as existing among the realities of being.

Judgments in Necessary Matter *a priori*.

Judgments in Contingent Matter *a posteriori*.

788. Necessary Matter, therefore, consists of the conceptions of realities of truth; and Contingent Matter, in what is added thereto to constitute them realities of being. Thus, suppose I form a conception of a point in space—as a point it has no extension. It is a reality of truth but not of being. I conceive that point to move directly towards another point in space—the path which the point is thus conceived to describe, I call a *straight*

Necessary and Contingent Matter in the same conception.

sary, differ from the Contingent in that we cannot even imagine or conceive of an exception to the Necessary, whereas all Contingent Propositions actually have exceptions.

But Mr. Mill replies, that this rather proves the limited capacity of our powers than any thing else. Many things have now become true which not long ago were not and could not have been conceived as true or possible.

Without deciding upon the merits of this controversy thus waged, I will add for the consideration of those who think with Mr. Mill, that all men perceive a difference in the kind of certainty which they feel in the truth, that "every triangle has three sides;" and those Contingent Propositions which we are continually offering. Thus I say, "The rose is red—the apple is unripe—the horse is gray—that man has ten fingers,"—every body sees that the one may have ten fingers and yet be a man, that a horse may cease to be gray without ceasing to be a horse, that an apple may be unripe, or a rose yellow. But if the (so called) triangle has not three sides, it is *mis*called, it is no triangle, and the Proposition cannot be true. Change the quality of the Copula and you destroy the Logical Essentia of the Subject. But in the other examples given, this change in the quality of the Copula may be made without changing the Essentia of the Subject at all, and thus causing it to cease to be of the species to which by its name we had referred it. No one, I suppose, will deny the difference thus pointed out between those two classes of Judgments—we make it a Differentia of the Species, the one Necessary and the other Contingent Judgments.

line—the line also is only a reality of truth. I suppose the point to move again towards another point not in that straight line. It generates another straight line. I conceive it to move again directly to the point from which it started. It has now generated a third line in such a relation to the other two as that it joins them, and they then make a *triangle*. The triangle is a reality of truth; and I conceive of it, that is, have a conception of it, as a figure with three straight sides, including three angles. These two properties are the matter of my class-conception. From this I deduce *a priori* the further property, that the sum of its angles are just half as much as the sum of all the angles that can be formed around any one point in space; and that if I know the size of any one of its angles and the two adjacent sides, or if I know the length of one side and the size of the two adjacent angles, I can determine the size of the other angles and the length of the other sides. In the same way, I may construct in my mind a rectangle, a circle, an ellipse, &c., and of each I can ascertain *a priori*, many properties which did not enter into the class-conception of those figures.

A priori deductions from the class-conception.

789. But if I take up my crayon, before a blackboard, and make a dot, calling that a point, and make a mark as straight as I can, calling that a line, &c., these figures on the board are not the realities of being of which I had formed the conception, and of which I had demonstrated, or of which I could demonstrate those propositions. These marks may *represent*, but they *are* not the point, the line, the triangle, &c. I can predicate much of those marks that could not be predicated of the realities of being which they represent. Thus the mark has breadth, the line none—the mark has color, and is upon a ground of a different color—a white mark on a blackboard, for instance; the line has no such properties. These realities of truth, the point, the line, &c.,

The Conception drawn in a Diagram.

More can be predicated of the Diagram than of the Conception.

The difference in Contingent Matter.

have been *done* or *made* into facts—realities of being in the outer world. They have been clothed upon with visible forms, having properties of their own in addition to those contained in their class-conception. Now all these properties are Contingent Matter. It depends upon my will whether I will give to my conception of a triangle an outward expression on the blackboard or not; and whether that expression shall be with a white mark or a mark of another color; whether the mark shall be small and smooth, or broad, rough, and irregular, &c.

Creation.

790. Let us pass to another class of objects. Suppose the Divine Mind to have constructed a conception or an idea of the various classes of beings included in the Creation. As existent substantial reali ties each individual must consist of Matter, extended so as to fill limits in space and to be impenetrable; be composed of particles, every one of which should have an attraction for every other particle, and this substantial matter must be without life or capacity of originating motion or of acting, except as it was acted upon by a spirit either within or from without each individual object.

A priori inferences from the conception of Matter.

791. Now, here we have the class-conception of the objects which have a material existence. From this we can deduce *a priori* many of the fundamental principles of the Natural Sciences. From extension must follow the divisibility of all material objects; from attraction must follow density and the phenomena of gravitation; from inertia the three laws of motion may be deduced, and so on. We should, however, know nothing of the phenomena of light, of color, of electricity, of sound, of chemical combination, &c., from these mere class-conceptions.

Contingent Matter necessarily implied in the reality of being.

792. But let this Divine Conception pass into reality of existence—be done into a fact, and each piece of matter necessarily takes upon itself, or rather its Creator puts upon

it properties and relations not implied in the class-conception or resulting therefrom; but which are, however, necessary to the reality of each individual object among the facts of existence. The specific color and shape of each piece of matter, for instance, though it must have some color and shape, were to be determined by the will of the Creator, and not necessarily implied in the conception or the resolution to give it reality of being. Those properties of the outward form of the conception—its material body—are like the diagrams by which we represent our conceptions of a triangle, a pyramid, &c., matters of choice and chosen by ourselves, and can never be known by any other mind until he has learned them either by revelation—that is, verbal communication from ourselves, or by an inspection and study of the diagram which we have drawn.

Contingent Matter how known.

793. From the foregoing considerations of the Matter of Judgments, we may divide the Properties of Objects again with reference to Method on another principle and into other classes.

A new classification of Properties.

794. Thus all of those Properties which are included in the class-conception may be called *Material Properties;* as *three-angledness* and *three-sidedness* of a triangle, *extension* and *inertia* in matter, &c. Then all of those Properties which are necessarily implied in, and deducible *a priori* from these Material Properties may be called the *Implied* Properties, as the equality of the angles of a triangle to two right angles, divisibility from the extension of matter, and the laws of motion from its inertia.

Material Properties.

Implied Properties.

795. Those properties of bodies which serve to make the species of objects in the reality of being, such as *two-footedness* of man, *canine teeth* or the carnivora, *web-footedness* of aquatic birds, *unsupportedness* of falling bodies, &c., may indeed be assumed as Material Properties in our conception of the class, and as such we may reason

Properties of the reality of being may be material.

from them *a priori* to other implied properties, just as from the *three-angledness* of a triangle in Mathematics.

796. But for the most part, and always for all the purposes of science, these properties are learned *a posteriori*, from actual observation of the individuals existing in the reality of being. Each of these properties, however, is connected with and is suggestive of a Final Cause, for which it was bestowed upon individuals of that class; the two-footedness of man was designed as a means to the upright position in which he walks; and so throughout the material world we connect those properties which are differentia of species with something in the habits or modes of the individuals of the species, as *two-footedness* with erectness of stature—*canine teeth* with carnivorousness, &c.

Properties indicative of a Final Cause.

797. Now in reference to this fact we may call the former Properties which are indicative of the Final Cause the *Formal* Properties; and those which are thus connected with them and implied in their reality, we may call the *Modal* Properties. And all those Properties which are susceptible of more and less, as *size*, *temperature*, *density*, *might*, &c., we may call *variable* Properties.

Call Formal Properties.

Modal Properties.

Variable Properties.

798. It will be observed that Material and Formal are not coördinate terms, but only terms denoting alternate conceptions. Material and Implied are the coördinates in *a priori* Matter. Formal and Modal are the coördinates in *a posteriori* Matter. Then besides these we have the Accidental and Variable Properties. These, however, may become either Material or Formal. But when they do become so they cease so far forth as they are Material or Formal to be accidental to the individuals into whose class-conception they have thus entered. Thus, the "unsupportedness" of bodies which fall is but an accidental

Material and Formal not coördinate terms.

Accidental and Variable Properties may become either Material or Formal.

property of those bodies as masses of matter. But we assume it as a Formal Property with reference to the Modal Property denoted by the word "*falling;*" when we say that "all bodies which are unsupported, fall to the ground." So too "right-angledness" is but accidental to "triangle;" but when we take it into our class-conception we have "right-angled triangles," and then it becomes Material.

The Contradictory of Judgments in Necessary Matter absurd.

799. Now as the Matter of all *a priori* Judgments is *necessary* Matter, if the Judgment be affirmative, its contrary or contradictory is called an *absurdity*. It is not merely an error. Of this kind are all mathematical and all analytic Judgments. If the Judgments be negative, the affirmative would give a *nihil purum*—that is, an impossibility; as that two and two make five, two straight lines may inclose a space, an effect without a cause.

Immediate Inferences from Judgments in Necessary Matter.

800. In Necessary Matter if the subaltern is true, its universal must be true also. That is,

If I is true A must be true also.

If O is true E must be true also.

And all contraries are virtually contradictories, and only one of the sub-contraries I and O can be true.

801. Contingent Matter is also divided into Natural and Moral.

Knowledge of Contingent Matter *a posteriori.*

Although the order of Nature seems to be perfectly stable and uniform, we conceive this order as having been established by an Intelligent Author as the choice of His will. In many respects we can conceive of it being different from what it is, and for the most part we know nothing of its facts, principles, or laws until we have observed and studied them from actual facts and occurrences. Hence clearly the knowledge of Nature is *a posteriori*, and the Matter itself is contingent.

802. But so great is the uniformity and constancy of its operations and processes, that we consider its

laws as almost as certain as the deductions of mathematics themselves. But the certainty is not quite so great (since there always may be exceptions), and it is different in kind. Hence we call it a *physical* certainty. And the contradictory of any proposition enunciating a physical truth or certainty would not be an absurdity, but simply a falsehood or error.

Physical Certainty.

803. But in the actions of man there is no such uniformity as we find in Nature. His moral freedom places his acts at the disposal of his will, rather than of any law which operates uniformly in all similar cases.

Moral Matter.

804. Hence in the actions of man there is not a necessity of any kind, in the proper sense of the word. Since, however, the will of man is influenced in some measure by motives external to itself, any strong combination of motives will usually induce a particular kind of action; and hence this class of actions are said to constitute a sort of *moral necessity*. The objects in Nature are not conceived as having any liberty to choose what they will do, or any power to act except as they are acted upon.—Hence the physical necessity. On the other hand, man is conceived as having the power to choose what he will do, to act in accordance with external forces or against them; and hence his acts are not under the same law as that which determines the motions, the facts, and events in Nature.

Moral and Physical Necessity.

805. Still, however, there is some uniformity in the acts of men under similar circumstances; and hence a knowledge of the circumstances always gives a strong *probability* as to the course one will pursue. This, when it exists in but a low degree, is called merely probability. But when the probability becomes very great, it is called a *moral certainty*.

Moral Certainty.

806. The same principles are also extended to the events of Providence; that is, future events which are

not, so far as we know, under the control of any physical laws and causes, but which are supposed to depend upon the overruling Providence of God. What the probability lacks of certainty in the two cases, however, depends upon two entirely different grounds. In the case of man it depends upon the fact that he does not always act consistently with himself, or as he ought. But in the case of the acts which are conceived as depending upon the will of God, the uncertainty in our minds arises solely from our not understanding His ways, and the laws and principles upon which He acts in His government of the world.

Moral Certainty only in the acts of Providence.

807. There are some cases, however, in which even man may acquire such a character, as that we feel a certainty as great, though different in kind, as though it were absolute with regard to the course he will pursue. We know that Washington will be patriotic, Ney will be brave, Howard benevolent, and that St. Paul will hesitate in view of no peril to himself in doing what he regards as the will of God.

Circumstances increasing the force of Moral Certainty.

808. So too in forecasting the conduct of masses of men, we can calculate with almost a physical certainty—almost as surely as the motions of the heavenly bodies. Masses can never differ from one another so much as one individual may differ from another. Nay, when masses become quite large, the Political Economist and the Statesman can, from knowledge of the circumstances, determine beforehand in general terms what course men will pursue, and what result they will arrive at, almost as certainly as the astronomer can determine the return of a comet.

Certainty in regard to the conduct of masses of men.

809. The Matter which thus determines Logical Methods admits of being resolved into several elements, to which we will refer for a moment, in order to get a little more distinct conception of them.

810. Every object of thought, regarded merely as

an object about which our thoughts are occupied, and over the existence of which in the past and in the present we have no control, may be regarded as a FACT. Thus, what one has been, said, or done, and even the intention of that which was intended but left undone; whatever exists or has existed, whether in the mind alone or embodied in some external form, is a *fact*.

Facts.

811. The word "*fact*" is from *facio*, to do, and is used with reference to something *done*, or something which has been brought into the reality of existence.

812. We distinguish a fact from an *event* by applying the word "*fact*" to that which remains as the result of the making. But by an "*event*," on the other hand, we mean the happening or occurring itself, even if it leaves no fact, or *factum*, thing done, behind. But an "event" is the mere happening, it is a mere phenomenon; it appears in time, is instantaneous, and then ceases. Hence the same thing may be regarded as both a fact and an event; the birth of Napoleon, for instance, was both an event and a fact. As an event, it happened or occurred on a certain day, at a certain hour and moment—was real as an event then and then only. But as a fact, a thing done—a thing that is remembered, enters into and forms a part of history, it is as real now as it ever was, and must remain so forever.

Event.

Events pass into Facts.

813. Again, we distinguish "facts" from mere realities of truth. A point, a line, a triangle, would hardly be called facts; they are rather realities of truth than of being, of which the mind forms conceptions by means of its own activity. The dot, the mark, &c., are not points and lines, they only represent them.

Facts distinguished from Conceptions.

814. We also distinguish "*facts*" from Ideas. We could hardly speak of time, of space, of cause, of substance, of truth, as facts. We do not conceive of them as made, but rather as neces-

Facts distinguished from Ideas.

sary and eternal realities anterior to any act of creation, any act of making or conceiving them.

815. We distinguish "facts" from "fancies" or "phantasms" also. The facts are supposed to have an objective reality of being. The phantasm or fancy has none. It is a mere combination of properties in the mind, to form that which is the representation of nothing that exists or is supposed to exist.

Facts distinguished from Fancies.

816. Any facts which attend upon or surround another fact as their principal are called *circumstances*.

Circumstances.

817. Facts, as they first become objects of thought, are complex wholes. We do not perceive color, size, shape, density, &c., each separately and one after the other; and then combine them by any conscious or voluntary operation into the perception of an object. But we perceive the object as a whole, and then by an act of reflection we consider these properties separately.

Facts at first complex.

818. The process by which we resolve the perceived whole into its parts is called ANALYSIS; and the act of considering one of the parts alone, and by itself is called *Abstraction;* and the name by which the part is thus designated is called an *abstract* term.

Analysis.

Abstraction.

819. Analysis has different methods in different kinds of matter; thus the chemist has one kind of Analysis, the mathematician another, and the metaphysician another.*

Different kinds of Analysis.

* "ST. JOHN DAMASCENE says there are three kinds of Analysis; the *first* resolves compounds into their simple elements; the *second* resolves the syllogism into its several parts; and the *third* or mathematical, consists in admitting the correctness of a certain principle in order to arrive at the knowledge of an important truth."—BLAKEY'S *Hist. of Int. Philosophy*, vol. I. p. 274.

PAPPUS, a mathematician of Alexandria, A. D. 400, and author of "Mathematical Collections," says in the preface to his seventh book:— "*Analysis* is the course which setting out from the thing sought, and which for the moment is taken for granted, conducts by a series of consequences

820. Logical Analysis, of which alone we are now speaking, consists in resolving the conception of any object of thought into those elementary parts which go to make up the adequate conception of that object. The Analysis is called *proximate* when the parts, any or all of them, admit of further analysis. Thus the Analysis of the conception of any object into substance, attributes, and modes is proximate. For the attributes and modes admit of further analysis. But when the Analysis can go no further, because there is no part that admits of further analysis, it is called the last analysis, and the parts given out by it are called ultimate parts. Thus, I analyze my conception of a piece of gold before me into the *substance*, which I will call gold; the *properties*, which I will call extension, yellow, ductile, &c.; and into the *modes*, as *polished*, *coin*, *ornament*, *utensil*, &c., &c.

Logical Analysis.

Proximate Analysis & Parts.

Last or Ultimate Analysis.

821. By a process which is the reverse of Analysis, called SYNTHESIS, we put together these ultimate elements to construct the complex whole. Thus, as by analysis the chemist reduces water to oxygen and hydrogen, so by synthesis he puts these elements together and combines them into water again.

Synthesis.

822. So also in Logical Synthesis we put together in the unity of consciousness the elements of which a conception is composed, and form the conception. It is by this process of analysis and synthesis that a conception passes from one mind to another. Again, with the substance for subject and any one of the properties or modes for a predicate, we

Synthesis of Conceptions.

to something already known, or placed among the number of principles admitted to be true. By this method, therefore, we ascend from a truth or a proposition to its antecedents; and we call it Analysis or resolution, as if indicating an inverted solution. In *Synthesis*, on the contrary, we set out from the proposition, which is the last in the Analysis." In the method of Analysis, "If the result is true the proposition which we assumed at the outset is true also, and the direct demonstration is obtained [synthetically] by stating in an inverse order the different parts of the Analysis. If the ultimate consequence is false the proposition was false also."

unite them into a judgment; these judgments we combine into a syllogism, &c. And a set of judgments combined into a whole by means of the unity of their several subjects is called a "*System.*" The word is from a root of similar import as "*synthesis.*" System.

823. Now when the evidence or grounds upon which any system is based is such as to leave no doubt of its truth, as in mathematics, we call it a *truth* or *the* truth. But if its truth be still doubtful, and received by those who accept it, on grounds which are not satisfactory, or not generally acknowledged as such, we call it an *Opinion.* Truth is supposed to rest upon grounds which are entirely independent of choice, passion, prejudice, or any wishes or feelings of a personal character. Opinion, on the other hand, is always supposed to be indebted for its reception in some measure to the good will or wishes of those who hold it; that is, they hold it from choice in part at least, and not altogether from the unbiassed convictions of their own judgments, or the necessary laws of belief. Truth. Opinion.

824. When any system of judgments, or a judgment singly is regarded as explaining a fact or a series of them, it is called a *Theory.* Thus we have the facts of bodies falling to the earth; and we have the *theory* of gravity—namely, that the Earth *attracts* them. But the agency or efficacy here attributed to the Earth is a mere theory. It may be consistent with the facts. But it is after all a theory, and a theory only. We have theories of light, theories of electricity, &c.; that is, some explanation of the facts, which goes beyond the facts themselves, and serves to give them a scientific unity and completeness; and it is sometimes the case that the facts remaining precisely the same, two or more theories will each of them explain the facts so far as they are at present known as well as the other. This I believe to be the case with regard to the two theories of light—the emanation and the undulation theories; Theory. Several Theories for the same facts.

and the two theories of electricity—the theory of a single fluid and the theory of two fluids.

825. When before we have facts enough to form a theory, we guess at what the true theory or explanation of the facts will be—this guess is called a *Conjecture*.

Conjecture.

826. From the foregoing definition it is evident that the collection and analysis of the facts must always precede in the order of a correct method, the synthesis or putting them together into a system, or combining them for the construction of a theory or an argument.

Analysis precedes Synthesis.

827. But as the accumulation and careful analysis of facts is slow, men often desire to construct a theory or system before this preparatory work has been done. In this case they are often compelled to guess at what the fact would be if it were known. Such a guess is called a *Hypothesis*, or something placed under to support our theory or system.

Hypothesis.

Our subject will henceforth divide itself into the four chief parts—(1) Methods of Investigation; (2) Methods of Proof; (3) Methods of Disproof or Refutation; and (4) Methods of Instruction.

Division of the Subject.

828. These subdivisions of the present part of our Treatise are rather alternate than coördinate parts. There is no investigation that does not carry with it some conviction of the certainty of its result; that is, some kind and amount of proof. So, too, there is no method of proof that is not in some measure an investigation into the truth of what it undertakes to prove. Disproof is of course a method of proof. And Instruction, or the construction of the things known into systems and sciences, implies something of investigation and proof.

These Parts rather Alternate than Coördinate.

Still, however, a division seems to be desirable; and I shall refer the various methods and topics to one or another of the four class terms, according as that which I have announced as the leading subject in each, is or is not the prominent trait in the Method to be discussed.

Principle of Classification.

CHAPTER II.

METHODS OF INVESTIGATION.

SECTION I.

Of Investigation.

829. I remarked in Part I. [451], that where the Question is concerning the Copula, it is to be answered by some one of the Formulæ. The Formula, however, presupposes all the Terms as given. In the case of Immediate Inference, as well as in all Intuitive Judgments, there is no Term needed except those which appear in the Judgment or Conclusion itself. But we may often have a Judgment to be proved, with no Exposita from which it can be deduced by Immediate Inference, and no Middle Term given by means of which it can be proved as a Deductive Judgment. Hence we may have occasion to find a Middle Term. And in all cases where the Question is concerning the Major Term that Term is still to be found.

Necessity for finding Terms.

830. The finding of these Terms is what we call *Investigation.** Whether the Term to be sought be to

* The subject which we treat in this Chapter is to a considerable extent the same as that which Aristotle and the ancients generally treated under the head of "*Topics*" or "*Loci;*" for the reason, as Mansel observes, that "it is the *place* in which we look for Middle Terms." Instead of *the place where we may* find them, I have made it a Treatise on *the Methods of finding* them.

Of these *loci* the Schoolmen made two classes: "*Maximæ*"—that is,

be used as Middle Term or not, it must be found as a Predicate to the subject of our inquiry. In the Methods of Investigation, therefore, we are seeking some term which we may predicate of a given subject; and if we wish to use it as a Middle Term to establish a Copula, it must be such an one as can be used as subject to that Term which we wish to affirm as Predicate of it as Major Term. Thus, if we wish to prove that S is P, we must find a Term as M, which we can predicate of S (S is M), and of which we can predicate P, as M is P, and we then can affirm our conclusion S is P in the First Figure.

Investigation is the finding of Predicates.

831. The point then in which all the Methods of Investigation unite is this: that they are Methods of finding what may be predicated of any given subject.

Point common to all Methods of Investigation.

832. Methods of Investigation, therefore, always presuppose the subject to be given; that is, we must have something to investigate; and we may have it given by its sphere only, or by the matter of its class-conception determining its sphere. Thus I may remember that something occurred without remembering what it was [52, 53]. I may know that there is something in a given room or place without knowing what it is; that is, I have the sphere of the conception only.

Subjects given by the sphere only.

833. In this case the first thing is to learn *what* the subject is. This we do by acquiring the matter of its class-conception. I may test it by my own senses—see it, touch it, taste it, smell it, handle it, &c., in which case I form the conception directly from the object itself. This Method is called *Observation*. Or I may ask some one

The first thing is to acquire the class-conception.

By Observation.

Maxims; *Differentiæ Maximarum*." The former, as the word denotes, were Maxims; that is, the highest generalization of truth (Maxima Genera)—to be used as Major Premises in Processes of Deductions. As such, they of course contained the Middle Term, and furnished thus the means of proving the Copula of the desired Conclusion. The *Differentiæ Maximarum* consisted of one or more words expressive of the point in which one Maxim differed from another.

else *what* the subject is, and receive from him either its name or a description of it. In either case I form the conception from the observation of others—that is, from their *Testimony;* in which they communicate to me what they have observed. This is the Method of *Testimony;* and the only difference between an answer giving a name to the subject and a description is, that the former implies what is expressly stated in the latter.

By Testimony.

834. At the first observation we cannot determine whether the observed property be any thing more than a separable accident or not. On a second observation of the same individual, we decide at once that all of the properties that were different in the two observations were but separable accidents of that individual. And a third and fourth, as well as each successive observation may, and most likely will add to this list of separable accidents some properties that had not been so regarded before.

Distinction of Properties made at the second observation.

835. But as soon as our observation has extended to two objects, these objects are referred to a class. The properties which they have in common are for the present assumed as Formal, constitutive of the class; and those in which they are unlike, after deducting what we have seen to be separable accidents in each, are regarded as peculiarities or individual properties of each.

And a Classification also.

836. A wider observation embracing more individuals always brings a new classification. Perhaps the bringing in of a third object may give us two classes—one including two of the three objects, while the other will be so unlike them as to be regarded as not of the same class with the other two. And any change in our classification changes our view of the properties; that which we considered an individual peculiarity in one classification, becomes a Formal property in another and Material in still another.

A wider observation makes a new classification.

837. In the process of classification we soon come

to find that one property which we had made Formal of one class, is always connected with another, which of course therefore may be predicated of all the individuals in that class as a mode of their existence. We see, for instance, that all animals that have sharp claws are predacious. "Sharp claws" is a Formal property, and "predacious" is a Modal, indicating their mode or manner of life. "Unsupported bodies fall to the ground;"—"unsupportedness" is the Formal property—"falling to the ground" is the Modal property, indicating something concerning their mode or condition of being, while objects belonging to the class of "unsupported bodies."

Recognition of some properties as Formal.

838. But "unsupportedness" itself may be and in fact is only an accidental property. The same object may be "supported" at one time and "unsupported" at another, and *vice versa*. Hence the Modal property "falling," will be accidental also.

Accidental properties may be Formal.

839. But we soon find that some of the properties which are not in the class-conception, and of course therefore were not known to us at our first acquaintance with the object, are not only inseparable from the object so far as we have seen or known, but that they are inseparable from it absolutely. They are *Implied* properties necessarily resulting from the combination of the properties which are included in the class-conception, as the laws of motion, for instance, in the conception of Matter *as inert* [791].

Recognition of properties as implied.

840. This distinction, however, between the Modal and the Implied properties cannot be shown *a posteriori*, or by any of the Methods of Investigation.

Distinction between Implied & Formal properties not shown *a posteriori*.

841. Methods of Observation are therefore, and of necessity *a posteriori*, with regard to all the Accidental and Modal properties of objects.

Investigation of Accidental and Implied properties *a posteriori*.

842. But in the case of the Implied properties, it is for the most part in actual experience no less so.

These properties are not included obviously in the first perception of an individual object. But we first observe the property, or something which suggests it, and then we prove its reality *a priori*. Thus, suppose I have a circle before me, I observe its radii; I see that they are equal to each other, or at least more nearly so than any difference that I can measure by my eye. I start with the hypothesis that they are equal, and measure them; this is *a posteriori* method of proof. It can, however, never approach to any thing more than something less than any *measurable* difference between the radii. But by *a priori* demonstration we can prove that they are equal as a fact, because of necessity they must be so.

Implied properties also investigated *a posteriori*.

And proved *a priori*.

843. So too with the Formal property of any species. The web-feet of aquatic birds, for instance. We may conjecture from the examination of such feet that they are designed for *swimming;* and hence indicative of the Modal property "aquatic," as applied to birds. We form the hypothesis [*fingo hypothesin*], "that web-footed birds are aquatic." We appeal to observation—that is, we investigate the hypothesized predicate *a posteriori*, and find it true.

Modal properties may be conjectured *a priori*.

844. Then Analysis of the class-conception, further Inquiry and Observation, Measurement, Calculation and the various other Methods of Investigation, will give us further predicates to the subject. We will therefore proceed to treat these Methods separately.

SECTION II.

Of Observation and Testimony.

845. Observation is the first and most primary of all the Methods of Investigation. From the moment that we open our eyes upon the objects of this world, we begin to be observers of what is taking place in it.

Each of our Senses is an avenue through which information is constantly coming in.

846. But of the psychological powers and of the grounds of belief in what we thus observe, it is not my design to speak here. We all *perceive* external objects, we form conceptions of them immediately, we classify them, we believe in their reality, and never do or can seriously distrust the testimony of our senses.

847. Our primary Method of obtaining a knowledge of the facts and events of the external world, and of the properties and relations of the objects existing there, is *Observation.* When by our own agency the facts which we wish to observe are either brought into existence or under our observation, the Method is called an *Experiment.* Experiment, therefore, is a Method of Investigation differing from Observation only, in the purely accidental circumstances of the observed fact having been voluntarily produced by ourselves for the purpose of the Observation.

Observation the primary Method.

Experiment.

848. For the observation of the facts of the external or material world we have the five senses: *Sight, Touch, Hearing, Smell,* and *Taste.* For the facts of the interior world, those which pass within the Soul, we have the single faculty or interior sense called *Consciousness.*

Means of Observation.

849. In both these cases the same faculty gives us both the Subject and the Predicate included in the one perception, and with the *intuitive* judgment affirming the one of the other as property of a Subject. Thus, I *see* a rose and that it is red, I smell that it is fragrant, I touch that it is soft and velvety. I am conscious of thinking, and that my thought is dull or active; I am conscious of admiring, and that my admiration is profound; I am conscious of envy, and that envy makes me unhappy.

Subject and Predicate seen as one.

850. From these intuitive perceptions of the senses there is no appeal, or if there is there is no means of

settling that appeal. One sense may indeed sometimes correct a judgment based upon another. Thus, by a touch I may find that what I had supposed from sight alone to be a peach, is but a piece of stone so carved and colored as to look precisely like a peach. But in this case it is only one sense acting in its appropriate sphere, furnishing means to correct the too hasty judgment based upon the data furnished by another. Nor is there any reason to trust one sense any more than another, when each are exercised within their appropriate spheres.

No appeal from the intuitive sense perceptions.

851. So with consciousness. If I am conscious of believing, or doubting, or remembering, there can be no appeal from my consciousness. The fact may be miscalled. Thus, I may call the feeling of which I am conscious humility, when all others will see that it is but spiritual pride. The mistake, however, is in the name and not in the fact that I have *some* feeling.

No appeal from consciousness.

852. The Predicates of any Subject may express either (1) the Implied Properties affirmed in Synthetic Judgments *a priori*. (2) Modal Properties expressing the Final cause of any Property included in a class-conception considered as a Formal Property; and (3) Accidental Properties denoting (*a*) that which distinguishes one individual from another, or (*b*) that which distinguishes an individual from itself in another condition or at another time; (4) (*a*) the Cause, or (*b*) Effect, and (5) the Quantity.

Matter expressed in the Predicates.

853. Now as all investigation begins with individual objects, a property when first brought to our minds cannot be referred to any of these classes; for at first we do not know that it is any thing more than a separable accident, nor in fact do we know that it is not.

854. In the course of our investigations we may occupy either of two different positions in relation to the Subject. We may be investigating it *de novo*, or we may be merely following an inves-

Investigation of Subjects and of Authorities.

tigation made by some one else before us. In this latter case we are learning from Testimony or Authority, from the Force of Terms or from the Common Sentiment of mankind. In all these cases we are not investigating the subject, but we are looking for the result of an investigation made by some one else.

Use of Hypotheses in Investigation.

855. But if we are investigating the subject itself, and looking for properties and relations which are not obvious on the first sight, it will be found necessary in almost all cases to form some hypothesis or conjecture of what this property is to be. This hypothesis serves something the same purpose as the x, which is the representative of the unknown quantity in Algebraic Equations. Thus, suppose one is trying to discover the Cause of any phenomenon; he would need to make a supposition beforehand, and proceed to test its correctness by facts and observations. Few discoveries have in fact ever been made except under the guidance of a shrewd guess, conjecture, or hypothesis of what the truth or fact is to be when it is found.

Having noticed the principal Methods by which we can investigate subjects by the direct application of our faculties to the subjects themselves, let us consider Testimony, or the Means by which we avail ourselves of the exercise of the faculties of others upon the subject of our inquiries.

Kinds of Testimony.

856. Of these we have two distinct classes: (1) Subjects which we might investigate directly ourselves if we had the opportunity and means; and (2) the Predicates which depend upon Authority, or the expressed Will of another.

Testimony as a means of using the Observations of others.

857. For by far the largest part of what we know, or at least by far the largest part of the facts upon which we have to depend in forming our opinions, constructing our systems, as well as for the practical purposes of life, we are obliged to depend upon the observations of others;

their statements of what has come within their experience and observation is called *Testimony*.

858. The use of Testimony supposes that others have the same faculties and means of knowing as ourselves, and opportunities which we have not had. This fact, however, leads us to investigate the nature and value of Testimony. And I shall at present speak of Testimony only by itself, referring to a subsequent Chapter in which I shall speak of the *Concurrence* of Testimony, as giving demonstrative force to simple Testimony.

The use of Testimony supposes opportunities which we have not had ourselves.

The value of Testimony is to be estimated by the following tests:

Tests of the value of Testimony.

859. (1) The nature of that concerning which the testimony is given.

Some facts are obvious in themselves, easily seen, and not easily misunderstood—snow on the face of the earth, a mountain, a desert, a loud noise, and such like facts, are too obvious to diminish aught on that ground from the value of testimony to their reality.

Nature of the subject matter.

860. But in a large variety of cases, the *fact* is beyond the reach of human faculties, and that which is reported as the fact is merely the inference from the fact. Thus, take all the reported cases of demoniacal possession, witchcraft, second-sight, &c. The fact really testified to is beyond the reach of the senses—a mere inference from what was seen. One might see that another was acting strangely and report those acts, but to see that there was demoniacal possession, the presence of the spirit of one departed, or any of that kind, is of course quite impossible.*

Reporting theories for facts.

861. So too in reporting the acts of another. A

* Of course I am not questioning the reality of such facts, and especially demoniacal possessions *when properly vouched for*. The testimony of our Lord in the New Testament is of course that of a competent witness. But for all persons who have nothing beyond the ordinary *insight* of mortals, the demoniacal possession, witchcraft, &c., must be only a theory to explain the observed facts.

witness might speak of his motives as facts that he had observed, and testify that such a person was angry, or jealous, or benevolent, &c., when the moral states could be nothing more than inferences from what was seen. The facts which could be seen and testified to, and the inferences from those facts, must be carefully distinguished.

Motives for the acts.

862. (2) The intelligence of the witnesses. In many cases this is of slight importance, since the fact may be so obvious as that no one could mistake. But in others it is far otherwise. The testimony of a physician, for instance, to a disease with which an invalid is suffering, would be of vastly greater value than that of one who knew nothing of medicine, and had scarcely ever seen a sick person in his life.

Intelligence of the witness.

863. (3) Opportunity to know is reckoned as one of the fundamental points in the value of testimony. One should speak of what he has heard and seen. If he only reports what he has heard others say of what they have heard or seen, the testimony becomes of constantly less value at each remove from the original witness.

Opportunity to know.

864. (4) Integrity or moral honesty in the witness is of course an important element in the value of testimony. Without it the witness may be only imposing upon us the fictions of his own imagination instead of any outward realities.

Moral character of the witness.

865. (5) And finally, since there are but few if any persons without some prejudices, feelings of personal interest or passion, or attachments to theory, which will very much influence the value of testimony, it is seldom if ever safe to take the testimony of any one without knowing something of his *animus* in regard to the subject-matter, and guarding against its influence upon the testimony itself. There is scarcely any event or fact that has not two sides to it, and its appearance will depend very much upon the side which is presented to us, or from which we choose to view it. A traveller with aristocratic notions,

Freedom from prejudice.

travelling in Europe, and constantly received into aristocratic circles, and receiving the kindest civilities from that class of the population, seeing every thing from their position and with their eyes, would report a very different class of facts from one who should walk on foot, associate with "the toiling millions," and see life as it passes with them.

866. We must also remember that testimony to be of any value must be positive. More mischief has been done by the neglect of this fact, obvious as its importance is, than one would at first believe.

Testimony must be positive.

A good illustration of this mistake is seen in the case of the Irishman, who is said to have complained, because he was convicted on the testimony of *one witness, who saw him commit the offence*, when there were hundreds that did not see him commit it.

867. Omissions of this kind are most likely to occur in the midst of statements, where other circumstances or occurrences are mentioned. Thus a very common case, in theological controversy, is in the testimony of an ancient Father, that "in Alexandria, from the days of St. Mark, the Presbyters were accustomed to select one of their number, place him on the throne, and call him their Bishop." No mention is here made of his having been ordained, as a part of the process by which he was placed in the office of Bishop, and hence it has been argued that there was no ordination.

Omissions when most likely to occur.

868. The mere omission to mention the occurrence of what was customary, is no proof that it did not occur. History, from the necessities of the case, is full of such omissions. It is impossible to state all that occurred, and if it were stated no one could read the books that would be written, nor could the world contain them. Hence writers do not usually mention that which is so common as that it is never omitted, and is perfectly well understood by those to whom the writings are addressed.

Omission no testimony or proof.

What facts most likely to be omitted.

869. But even positive testimony to a negative proposition can never be equal to positive testimony to an affirmative one. Positive testimony to a negative proposition, like negative testimony, is for the most part only the absence of testimony.

Positive Testimony to a Negative Proposition.

870. Positive testimony, supposing there is no fraud or mental hallucination, can be accounted for only on the ground of the reality of that which was seen, heard, &c. Testimony to a negative, however, may always be accounted for on the ground of inability or inattention on the part of the witness, as well as by the absence of that which he did not perceive. If, however, one man should testify that he had seen an extraordinary phenomenon, and a large number of others—even two or three other persons, having their attention directed to the same object or place, and occupying a position equally favorable as that of the man who pretended to see it—did not see it, this conflict of testimony would always raise the question of the sanity of the mind and faculties of the affirming witness, over and above the question of his veracity. In all such cases the contradiction in the testimony must be in some way accounted for before either can be received, unless it be in cases where one side is vastly preponderant against the other. Such a disparity may in itself, unless it can be accounted for otherwise, be taken as a sufficient guarantee of the accuracy of the testimony on that side. But in all these estimations, *ceteris paribus*, the preponderance is always on the side of the affirmative testimony.

Negative Testimony, how accounted for.

871. Again, we must always distinguish very carefully between what is seen and the inference from it. Perhaps there is no case that illustrates this so well as the common belief and testimony to the fact that the sun rises and sets. The fact is a relative change in position—the motion of the sun is but an inference or a theory to account for that fact.

Fact and inference from the Fact.

The fact we take as indisputable, the theory we reject whenever we can show that there is a better one or that it is unnecessary.

872. The truth of *a priori* propositions we conceive to be independent of any Will or of any Mind even. They are *necessary* truth, and therefore absolutely true. Their truth depends upon no condition whatever. Hence, in Necessary Matter we seldom make use of Testimony, or the authority of others.

Testimony not used in Necessary Matter.

873. But with regard to physical truths, although their being true depends upon the Will of the Creator or First Cause of them, yet we know the Predicate from an observation of the Subject itself. We have but to look at a rose to see that it is red, to taste an orange to see that it is sweet, &c. From this observation of the properties in the effect, we infer the intention or will of the Intelligent Cause, which is the Creator. In Physical Matter, therefore, Testimony can be properly used only to *facts*. It can never establish theories or opinions, but only facts; the fact that this, that, and the other man held the theory, and upon what grounds he held it.

In Physical Matter Testimony to Facts only.

874. But in Moral Matter we can never learn the properties of subjects by any mere investigation of the subject itself. They depend upon the will of him from whom they proceeded. Of these things, therefore, our only means of knowledge is the Testimony of some one who knew the will and intention of the Authority from which they emanated. Thus, in Revelation we have Sacrifice, Baptism, the Holy Eucharist, the Lord's Day, &c. Of these no one knows or can know what is to be predicated of them in certain respects except from Revelation itself. And Revelation is a Testimony to the Will of God concerning those elements of Religion. Of Baptism, for instance, we can know what it is; how, by whom, and to whom, it is to be administered, and

Testimony in Matter resting upon Authority.

what is its efficacy upon the worthy recipient, only from the Scriptures. All of these are questions that never can be answered by any study of the subject, Baptism, itself; but only by a study of the Revelation, which is Testimony to the Will of God concerning it.

875. So it is in every society and organization of men. There are, and of necessity must be, some positive rules and institutions not dependent upon any one's sense of propriety, but ordained by the consent of the collective whole; or at least by the authority that acts for that whole. And these statutes, constitutions, canons, by-laws, &c., by whatever name they are called, become the Testimony by which we investigate the properties which may be predicated of the subjects treated of in those documents.

Positive institutions in all societies.

876. Again, Lexicons, Dictionaries, and such like compilations, are Testimonies which we use as a means of investigating the meanings and definitions of words. Analysis is often of great service. When a word is compounded of two or more, or is used in a derivative form, we can often get an important suggestion towards its meaning from an analysis of the word into its parts—or as grammarians say, from its *Etymology*. But the real force and meaning of a word after all will depend upon the *usus loquendi;* and a Dictionary or Vocabulary is but a Testimony to that usage of a language which determines the meaning of words.

Dictionaries Testimony to the meaning of words.

SECTION III.

Of Measurement and Calculation.

877. Measurement as a Method of Investigation requires a mention, although there is but little to be said of it. It is the Method by which we find the Predicates that answer the questions "how many?" "how much?" "the time when?" &c.

878. We may have a definite answer, or only an indefinite, or comparative one. Thus, if one ask how high Mont Blanc is, he may obtain the indefinite comparative answer, "It is the highest of the Alps." Such answers give of course but indefinite answers, by comparing the thing which is unknown to the inquirer with something which is or is supposed to be known to him.

Definite and Comparative answers.

879. But for a definite answer in Quantity, it is always necessary to assume some unity or standard, and to give the answer in the number of the units of the assumed standard, comprehended in the object to be measured. Hence we have our tables of unities in long measure, as "inches," "feet," "furlongs," "miles," "leagues." We have also unities of measure in time, in weight, in solid quantity, &c.

Assumed Unit.

880. Some such Method is, I apprehend, that which in fact gives us the first hypothesis, or hypothetical knowledge of the implied properties of the subjects treated of in the sciences of Continuous Quantity, Geometry, Trigonometry, &c. Such implied properties there are in every class-conception. They are likely to be brought to our knowledge first by some one of the Methods of Investigation (and may be brought to our mind by any of them). But when they are so brought to our minds, they must be proved by Demonstration, which we have treated as one of the Methods of Proof. Thus, I may learn at first *from actual measurement*, that the square of the hypothenuse of a right-angled triangle is equal to the sum of the squares of the two other sides, and then prove it as a necessary and invariable property of all right-angled triangles *a priori*. Such, I suppose, has been the method in which most of the Predicates that are now affirmed *a priori* were first discovered; they were first learned *a posteriori* by observation or measurement, and then affirmed on *a priori* grounds.

Measurement as a means of learning the Implied Properties of Geometrical Figures.

881. It is not, however, the Method of their Discovery but their Proof which determines between the

Synthetic Judgments *a posteriori* and those which are *a priori.*

Counting a Method of Investigation in Discrete Quantity.

882. When the question relative to quantity is, "how many?" we have as preparatory to calculation "*counting*," as a means of enumerating the number of individuals in any Logical Whole. In this case the unity is not *assumed* but is given. It is the logical individual.

Methods of Calculation.

883. Arithmetic, Algebra, and the Calculus are but Methods of Investigation in Discrete Quantity. They presuppose counting or enumeration by individuals as units of number.

884. Of course we cannot go into a consideration of these Methods in detail here. To do so would require a Treatise on Arithmetic, Algebra, and the Calculus. I will in this place therefore specify only what is essential to all of them.

Methods in Mathematics determined by the Idea of the Useful.

885. The Methods described in the works on these subjects, are determined rather by the Idea of the Useful than by the Idea of the True. They all come to the same result, and the superiority of the one over the other consists in its superior usefulness; that is, it is a shorter and more useful way of doing what may be done in some other way.

Logically but two Methods.

886. So far as the Idea of the True determines them, there are but two radically distinct Methods of Calculation: (1) when the parts are given to find the whole; and (2) when the whole with some of the parts are given to find the other, or others if there be more than one.

Conditions of the first Method.

887. For the first Method or Addition it is necessary that all the parts be given: one of them at least a Discrete Quantity; and the others so as to be ascertainable by means of the one thus given; thus, $\frac{x}{2}+\frac{x}{3}+4=x$.

In this case the three terms $\frac{x}{2}+\frac{x}{3}+4$ are the parts, and x represents the whole, which is still an unknown quantity. By the Method of Addition we find that quantity and substitute it for x, and say $x=24$, or twenty-four is the whole.*

* As illustrating this point we may refer to the old Sophism of Achilles and the Tortoise.—"They start at the same time from points one mile apart, the Tortoise being ahead. While Achilles is running that mile the Tortoise will have run one-tenth of a mile. But while Achilles is running that one-tenth of a mile the Tortoise will have run one-tenth of one-tenth, that is, one-hundredth of a mile, and so on; therefore Achilles will never overtake the Tortoise."

Leibnitz first proposed as a solution of this sophism, and it has been repeated by Coleridge and De Quincey, that it implies the infinite divisibility of space, without taking into account the equally infinite divisibility of time also. I am not authorized to say that this solution is not satisfactory, I suppose, but I really cannot see that it has any meaning that is to the purpose. Whately says that Aldrich and the old Logicians answered by proving that the Conclusion is false. But as he justly remarks that is no answer, if the Premises are admitted and the Formula is unquestionable. Whately answers by saying that the Argument cannot be stated Logically at all; that is, in any Logical Formula. But to this we reply, so much the worse for the Formulæ. If there is, as he admits, "a seeming demonstration," there must be a Formula to which it can be reduced, though it may be of course an invalid Formula. Otherwise it must be reducible to a Formula valid in itself, without fulfilling the conditions of that Formula.

The Sophism can be reduced to a Categorical Formula as well as any other Algebraic Equation. The expression in these Formula is awkward and unnecessary. Mathematics is the Logic of Continuous and Discrete Quantity. Nor is there the slightest necessity of bringing their arguments within the Formula of Logical Quantity. But if one will insist upon such a statement of the Sophism before us, it will then be found that the word "while" is used in each successive Premise in different senses. Hence the Fallacy of Ambiguous Middle.

Thus,—The first period is "while;"
"While" is the second period:
∴ The first period is [equal to] the second.

That is, it takes as long to run the mile and the tenth, as it does the tenth and the hundredth—and if so Achilles will never overtake the Tortoise.

But in the Methods of Discrete Quantity the fallacy is in requiring a Whole without giving any measure of the parts. The Whole is "the quantity of time from the moment of their starting until that of their overtaking." Now undoubtedly the time of Achilles running the mile is one part of that Whole. But its value is not given either relatively to the Whole nor in Simple Quantity. So, too, the time of running the tenth and the one-hundredth is a part of the Whole; but we are not told what part, nor how long it is in Simple Quantity.

880. If there are two unknown quantities, the Method of Adding is different; but the Method of Investigating the Discrete Quantity of the Whole, or finding the Predicate is the same, namely, it is Addition of the Parts.

889. Or again, if we have a Whole and some of its Parts given, to find the other part, we have the Method of Subtraction. Thus,

Second Method.

$$6 - 3 - 2 = x.$$

Here 6 is a Whole, and 3 and 2 are parts of the Whole, and x represents the other unknown part which is to be found. By Subtraction we find it and say,

$$x = 1.$$

890. But Multiplication, Division, Involution, Evolution, &c., &c., are only more *useful* because shorter Methods to the same results; that is, to find a whole from the given parts, or a part from a whole—the rest of the parts also being given in Discrete Quantity.

Multiplication, Division, &c.

891. When I speak of the parts and the whole, &c., being given, I mean that they are virtually given. As in the first example above one part alone was given in pure quantity, 4; but it was given in such a way that the value of the others could be obtained from it. It was given, and its fractional value in relation to the whole was also given. And this will always be found to be necessary. If the parts are not given in simple quantity they must be in or reducible to some fraction or multiple of the whole.

The Parts how given.

892. The whole must of course also be homogeneous. Thus, if we add 6 and 8, the whole, as all wholes in pure quantity are, is homogeneous.

Parts must be homogeneous.

Now from such a statement we can simply have no answer, because the Premises are inadequate. But the Sophism instead of saying as it should, that there is no answer, gives a negative answer, which is of course a very different thing.

But let us give a value to either of these parts and the answer is easily obtained. Suppose that Achilles runs at the rate of twelve miles an hour, and an acquaintance with the first principles of Algebra is all that is required to find the answer.

It is merely 14—not fourteen *men* or fourteen *dollars*, or any thing of the kind, but fourteen simply.

893. But if we have six *men* and eight *dollars*, we cannot add them into a whole, which will be expressed by any name in the English language. Suppose, however, we have six horses, eight cows, twelve sheep, we may add them, and then the homogeneous whole is not horses, cows, or sheep, but it may be denoted by a generic term including these parts as species. Such a term is the English word, "cattle" or "stock."

Sometimes produce a higher Whole.

894. And for the same reason in Division the divisor, and in Multiplication the multiplier, must be pure number; while the dividend and the multiplicand may denote any objects in Logical Quantity.*

Divisor and Multiplier must be pure number.

SECTION IV.

Of Average and Exclusion.

895. It is sometimes the case that we cannot obtain an exact observation of a fact which we wish to use in our calculations. And again, there are many facts differing from each other in many points, that are either based upon and indicative of a law, or at least afford results of great importance, which, however, none of our inductive processes can reach. Such facts and results are obtained by what is called the Process of Average.

The use of Average.

896. Average is obtained by adding together several results, and dividing the amount by the number of results—these results must of course, therefore, be stated in Discrete Quantity.

How obtained.

* The Method of investigating or calculating Probabilities has necessarily been anticipated in the preceding Part, p. 87 *et seq.*, 157 *et seq.* The justification for such an anticipation is in the fact that the amount of probability is in these cases an essential part of the Copula, and therefore implied in the formation of the Judgment, as much so as the inclusion of the Subject in the sphere of the Predicate in Pure Categoricals, the Sequence in Conditionals, or the Excluded Middle in Disjunctives.

Observations at sea.

897. For example, the mariner at sea is desirous of getting the precise position of a heavenly body. But from the rocking of his vessel it is impossible to get two observations precisely alike. Let him take several and take the average.

In the use of the Barometer.

898. Again, suppose we wish to ascertain the pressure or weight of the atmosphere. We find that the Barometer does not indicate exactly the same pressure twice perhaps in a whole month. Heat, the time of the day, the currents of the atmosphere, all affect it. But let there be made observations several times a day for a year, for instance, add them all together, and divide by the whole number, and we have an average approaching the truth, just in proportion to the extent of the observations.

In collecting Statistics.

899. This Method is of vast importance in the collection of Statistics, and has given us some of our most useful facts and estimates in Political Economy, in the doctrines of Insurance, and in fact in every department of business and of legislation.

Statistics of Deaths.

900. Thus it is found by Statistics that out of every one hundred thousand infants born in England and Wales, fifteen thousand die the first year, five thousand more in the second, about one in four of the whole number before they would have reached their sixth year, and scarcely one-half reach the age of forty years. Now suppose results similarly obtained from other places, other races of people, other modes of treating their infants, to differ in the proportion of deaths from those in England and Wales, we should have this difference as a fact to be accounted for, and its investigation could scarcely fail to lead to knowledge of the greatest importance.

Vitability.

901. In the same way Physiologists, by dividing the whole number of population between certain periods, of five years say, as from twenty to twenty-five, from twenty-five to thirty, and so on by the number of deaths of persons of that age, obtain a

number which will of course vary with the proportion of deaths to the whole population. This is assumed to represent what is called the *vitability** of men and women, during these different periods of their life. In some of these periods the vitability of the males is greater than that of the females, as from fifteen to twenty, and from forty to forty-five. In others that of the males is greater than the females. In this way definite results are obtained, which are of the greatest value in the investigations of many of our most useful as well as interesting sciences.

902. Even those matters which are supposed to depend chiefly upon the will, such as marriage, and suicide, are found to yield results astonishing from their uniformity. Quetelet,† the Belgian statistician, affirms that the Belgian people pays its annual tribute of marriage with more regularity than that of death. Not only does the total number of marriages, as well in towns as in the country, follow a constant mathematical law, but the same regularity is observed in the numbers which indicate the marriages between bachelors and maids, bachelors and widows, widowers and maids, and widowers and widows. So in respect to the ages at which marriage is contracted, there is an astonishing uniformity in the annual returns. In regard to suicides the statistics of France‡ for a period of twelve years exhibit a similar uniformity. Their number varies but little from year to year. It is less in December than in any other month. From December it increases to June, when it attains its maximum and then diminishes regularly until December again.

In moral matters.

Marriages.

Suicides.

903. These facts, which can be obtained in a form to be of use by the Method of Average only, doubtless imply some causes extrinsic to the will of man, and which therefore are

Imply causes extrinsic to the Will.

* Carpenter's Human Physiology. † Du Systeme Social, p. 67.
‡ Annuaire de l'Economié Politique, 1851, p. 200.

within the legitimate sphere of scientific investigation. They furnish a case for the Methods of Elimination (Section VII. below).

904. Now where there is uniformity in results, there must be of course a cause acting under a law or from some settled design. And in the case of intelligent causes, the design itself gives the law to its activity and determines it. But in Nature, where the Causes are considered as mere Forces, acting without intelligence of their end or of their law, uniformity is always considered primarily and especially as implying law—an unchanging rule guiding the activity of the Force.

Uniformity in this law.

905. In this view, the Average of a single series of figures might indeed be valuable in many cases, as those for instance specified in 889 and 890. But still its great value as a Method can be seen only in its application for the purpose of comparing the average results of different series of figures relating to the same matter, at different times or under different circumstances, as in the cases specified above (894).

Comparison of Averages.

906. The Method of Exclusion is used for abridging processes of investigation by the exclusion of whole classes of objects as individuals from the necessity of examining each one separately. The exclusion is effected by means of properties assumed as differentia of species, and may be of two kinds.

Method of Exclusion.

(1.) The exclusion of one fact or species of facts after another from any given Predicate assumed as the Differentia of a species, in order to include a remaining fact or class of facts in the sphere of that Predicate.

First variety.

(2.) The exclusion of one fact or subspecies of facts belonging to any Proximate Genus from one after another of the coördinate species in that genus, in order to include it by this means in some one remaining species.

Second variety.

907. The first makes or implies a statement in the

form of a Disjunctive Judgment with the Predicate common and the Subjects coördinate, as either A or some non-A is B [410].

Based upon a Disjunctive Judgment with coördinate Subjects.

908. The second of these varieties makes or implies a statement in the form of a Disjunctive Judgment with the Subject common and the Predicates coördinate, as A is either B or C, or D, &c. [408].

Disjunctive Judgment with Coördinate Predicates.

909. This Method has been called the *Abscissio Infiniti*, and is of great use both in investigation and in proof. It partakes in fact so fully of the Differentia of both classes of Methods that we are in doubt with which of them to place it in our present Treatise. We put it here, however, because we are treating of Methods of Investigation before Methods of Proof.

Called *Abscissio Infiniti*, its use.

910. Perhaps the best illustration of the first form of Abscissio for our present purpose, is the one which we have already made use of in examining the validity of Moods and Figures of Syllogisms [478 *et seq.*]. Thus we said (or rather used the implied Disjunctive), "Either those with negative Premises, or some of those that have not both Premises negative, are valid," we completed by the *modus tollente ponens;* proving that those with negative Premise could not be valid. We then divided the remaining coördinate, "those which have at least one Premise affirmative," into two coördinate parts, and said or implied again, "Either those with Particular Premises," or "some of those whose Premises are not both Particular are valid;" and proceeded as before until we come to the species of which alone "validity" could be predicated.

Illustration of the first variety.

911. In this case we knew at the outset that some of the individuals included in the divided whole—that is, some syllogisms, were valid. But if we had not known this we could even then have proceeded in the same method until we had found that there was no individual in the

This Method may be used even where the Disjunctive is not valid.

divided whole of which "*valid*" could be predicated. In that case we should have ascertained that "*valid*" is a Differentia incompatible with the Essentia, which is constitutive of the Logical Whole as a genus; that is, with the Material Properties of the Logical Moods.

912. But in this case there would have been only the form without the reality of a Disjunctive Judgment. The Disjunctive would have been merely suppposititious, designed or supposed for the sake of the Method, since a true and valid Disjunctive always implies that one member at least shall be true.

913. This Method is often of great use as a Method of Proof in Geometry. Thus in the Theorem, "A line let fall from any point perpendicular to a straight line, is the shortest distance between the point and the line. For either the perpendicular is the shortest line or some *not perpendicular* is the shortest." But as the perpendicular makes a right angle with the line, any other line would be the hypothenuse of a right-angled triangle, of which the perpendicular is one of the legs. Hence no non-perpendicular line is the shortest. Consequently the perpendicular is the shortest. This Method is of course vastly shorter than that by which we prove of each possible line, not a perpendicular, separately—that it is not the shortest.

Used in Geometry.

914. But let us now take a case of the other kind, in which we have an individual or several forming a sub-species, and are desirous of finding to which of the species it belongs—in short to find *what* it is.

Illustration of the second variety.

915. Let us take for an illustration a case of chemical analysis. We there say this is *either an acid or an alkali.* We test it and find, let us suppose, that it is not an acid. It is therefore an alkali. We must say this is either potassa, or soda, or ammonia, &c., enumerating all of the alkalis. We proceed as before and test it for potassa, for soda, &c., until by proving that it is not one or the other in turn,

we come to the last. But of course it is quite possible that we shall find which species of alkali it belongs to, that is, what kind of an alkali it is, before we have tested it for all. Or again, as in the former case, we may test a metal, for instance, for each of the alkalis in turn, and disprove each member of the supposed disjunctive in turn, and thus find that it is not an alkali at all. Here, as before, the Disjunctive form was merely suppositious—made for the occasion, without knowing before-hand that the individual was included in the Logical Whole at all.

SECTION V.

Of Analysis.

916. We may have two kinds of Analysis: (1) Analysis of the Conception, and (2) Analysis of the Object of that Conception. The former is *Logical* Analysis and the latter is *Physical* Analysis.

Analysis of Conceptions & of Subjects.

917. We have seen that every conception of a reality contains as its matter certain properties of that reality. These properties make up its Essentia and Differentia; its Essentia as including it in the next superior Natural Genus (thus showing what it is); and its Differentia limiting or determining its reality by showing what it is not;—thus giving the boundaries that separate it from other objects.

The Matter of Conceptions.

918. The Analysis of this Conception therefore gives us each of these properties as separate predicates, which may be affirmed of the conception of the object as a Logical Subject, and consequently of the object itself, if the conception justly and properly represents it. Thus we may say of a triangle, "it has three sides;" since three-sidedness is necessarily included in the conception of a triangle.

The Analysis of Conceptions gives us Predicates of the Object of the Conception.

919. So too in Contingent Matter. The Matter of any superior and comprehending genus is always contained in the conception of a lower and comprehended species, and it may therefore be evolved as a predicate to that conception by Analysis. Thus I may say of a tree, "it is a vegetable;" of an ox, "it is an animal," &c., since "tree" and "ox" are but species of the proximate genera "vegetable" and "animal." Or we may predicate any one of the essential properties of the higher genus, as of animal, the circulation of the blood—of the tree, its growth from a seed, &c.

Analysis of Conceptions of Conting'nt Matter.

920. So far as Predication on the ground of Analysis is concerned, it is of but little if any consequence how the conception which we analyze was formed. It may have been that which we formed instinctively on our first comparison of one object with another, or it may have been that more elaborate and scientific class-conception formed by scientific investigation. In either case we may analyze the conception, consider the elements of which it is constituted separately, and separately they are Predicates which we may affirm of either the class-conception or of any individual comprehended under it.

Elements of a Concepti'n may be Predicated of the Conception itself.

921. The only possibility of mistake is in the formation of the conception itself. If the judgment is untrue the conception was ill-formed. Thus, if I should say that "horses have wings," the judgment would show that my conception of "horse" was inadequate or erroneous. Or in popular language, one would say that I did not know what I was talking about.

And of the Object of the Conception *if* the Conception be adequate.

922. But in Geometry, the Mathematics of Continuous Quantity,* we speak only of the conception;

* In Mathematics we deal with the conception exclusively. The very names which we use denote the conceptions and not the diagrams. But in what is called contingent matter it is not so. The names denote the individuals as they are in the reality of being or existence. With these the

and that conception is one which we have formed in our own minds *a priori*, and by a conscious process of construction. Hence in our analysis of such conceptions we merely evolve what we had consciously and designedly put into it, and there is no liability to error. Conceptions cannot be communicated from one mind to another. Each mind must form them for itself,* and as the process of forming the conception of a triangle, for instance, is the same in all minds, the conception itself of all geometrical figures must be the same in all minds.

In Mathematics no inadequate or erroneous Conceptions.

923. But in forming class-conceptions of the objects in the external world, different properties of the objects themselves will seem most conspicuous and characteristic to different minds. Hence the matters of those class-conceptions will be different to some extent, and may be different for each mind. Or if we undertake to reconstruct in our own minds the conceptions which others have formed from their description of the objects comprehended under that conception, the description never is and never can be quite adequate. Nor will it be understood by all minds alike. Every one has a conception of "apple," for instance, and yet who has analyzed that conception so that he can enumerate and describe precisely every element of its matter? We can all tell an apple from a pear, but who can describe precisely and exactly all the points of difference between them? Some of the most striking points all persons can give; but no one, I apprehend, can give them all.

Source of the error in Contingent Matter.

924. The question will always arise, therefore, whether the elements of our analysis be predicable of the individuals comprehended under our class-conception;

thoughts are occupied, and while in the former case we ignore the differentia between the diagram and the conception—in the latter the mind is chiefly occupied at first with those Formal Properties, and it is only by a slow process, and one that is at best liable to error and mistake, that we arrive at the class-conception as it actually existed in the Divine Mind.

* See Part II. Chap. IV. Sec. I.

not, however, in consequence of any fault or fallacy in the analysis, but on account of the doubt or uncertainty about the formation of the conception itself. And many persons are charged with intentional falsehood when the fault is not the moral one of uttering what they know to be false. It is merely the misfortune of having so conceived the subject as that predicates which do not belong to it are included in their conception of it.

False Conceptions source of unintentional false statements.

925. This analysis of our conceptions is carried on by the Reason itself; and the Reason possesses a faculty of insight or immediate intuition for the facts of consciousness, precisely as the external senses do for the facts of the external world. Thus, if I see that my class-conception of horse includes the property of *solid-ungularity* [having but one hoof for each foot], I can no more doubt that *my conception* of horse includes that property, than I can that the horse before me has but one hoof for each foot when my eye is distinctly fixed upon the object itself.

Reason the Agent of Analysis.

And the ultimate judge of its correctness.

926. But let us pass to the consideration of the analysis of the object itself. We cannot here give any precepts or rules for accomplishing such analysis. Those rules are not and cannot be reduced to any simple system. Success depends to a great extent upon original gift. It is a matter of quickness of insight in the Reason, just as the perception of colors and of sounds is matter of difference in the constitutional peculiarities of the eye and the ear. No rules can be given which will enable one to distinguish between the different shades of color, or the different tones of the diatonic scale in music. If one cannot make the discrimination without rules, no rules will enable him to make it.

Analysis of the object itself.

927. In chemistry, however, analysis forms so large and so indispensable a part of its Methods, that the rules and tests for analysis have been extensively systematized and recorded.

Rules and Methods in the Natural Sciences.

Nearly every science has done something of the kind. But the most that can be reduced to rule and formula, will in all cases be but a comparatively small part of what is to be done.

928. An analysis of this kind is always an experiment, and the elements evolved are objects of observation; and we can of course predicate them of the object analyzed as having been contained in it. Thus common salt is analyzed into chlorine and sodium. Hence we may say, "common salt contains chlorine,"—"common salt contains sodium."

Analysis an experiment.

929. There is no appeal from the result of an analysis. We may mistake the *name* of the subject analyzed, and also that of the element given out. But the things themselves cannot be mistaken. The greatest danger is in the too hasty inference from the analysis. We may suppose the example which we analyzed was a fair specimen of all the individuals of its class, and contained nothing which was not in them all and an essential constituent, when in fact it was not so. Hence we may predicate of a class as one of its constituent elements that which was only a foreign substance, accidentally in the specimen which we had subjected to our analysis.

The certainty of Analysis.

Liability to mistakes.

930. It is evident from these considerations that the analysis of any object may give us elements of its constitution of which we were ignorant before the analysis. Thus the analysis of water gives us hydrogen and oxygen. And it is especially characteristic of chemical analysis, that the elements evolved are totally unlike the compound that was subjected to the analysis.

Analysis gives us elements not before known.

931. It will be observed that analysis can give as results nothing except that which was in the analyzed compound. Thus if we analyze water we get oxygen and hydrogen, and whatever else there may be in the water—but nothing more. Otherwise we have no certainty in our results.

Analysis can give only material properties.

932. But we often find *on* analysis what we do not and cannot find *in* analysis. This is especially true of the analysis of our conceptions. By the analysis we get primarily merely what was contained in our conception as the material properties. But after the analysis has been completed, we are able to contemplate each element by itself, and also their relations to each other; and thus we gain an insight of many implied properties, which of course were not contained in the conception.

It enables us to see the implied properties.

933. This distinction between what we get *in* an analysis and what we get *on* analysis, is very generally overlooked or omitted in speaking of the results. This, for instance, is very constantly done by Cousin, who is certainly one of the most skilful and lucid in his analysis of all the metaphysicians that the world has ever seen.

The distinction often overlooked.

934. But as the conceptions which we form of objects in the reality of being are liable to differ somewhat from those which existed in the Divine Mind before their creation; and as the conceptions which one mind forms of objects in the reality of being will differ somewhat from those formed by other minds of the same objects, and as analysis of the conception can give only what is contained in the conception, the results of these analyses by different persons will be as various as their conceptions; agreeing necessarily in some of their elements while they differ in others.

The results of the Analysis of Conceptions may be different for different minds.

935. So, too, that which may be expressly contained in one man's conception as a material property in contingent Matter—that is, material to his conception, may be only implied in another and *vice versa.*

Material and Implied Properties may be different for different minds.

936. This results from the fact that our minds are imperfect and limited, "*Variasse est erroris.*" And there is probably no intellectual endowment in respect to which men differ more than in their powers of analysis. A Newton or a Pascal could see

Difference in the powers of Analysis.

at a glance into the relations and properties of geometrical figures, what men of ordinary powers can *see*—for to understand is to see—only after hours of study and a long process of demonstration. And to an infinite mind the result of the longest and most complicated calculation must be as evident at the first glance, as the first axioms of Geometry are to us.

SECTION VI.

Of Induction and Analogy.

937. The words Induction, and Analogy, are each of them used to denote Methods of Investigation, and Methods of Proof also. In one sense of the word they are regarded as furnishing Predicates, in the other as proving them to be true. In this latter sense I shall consider them in the next Chapter.* Induction and Analogy Methods of Investigation & Proof.

938. Induction† is the Method by which we colligate several facts, having identity of Formal Properties as a species, and in consequence of these facts agreeing in some other property not at first conceived as Formal, we predicate that fact of all individuals in that species, or of the species as a whole. Induction.

939. But when the facts of any two opposite species agree in any of their Formal properties (123), and we affirm a predicate of the second, on the ground that we had found it true of the first, we call this the Method of Analogy.‡ And the Method is said to be Analogy.

* Part II. Chap. III. Sect. V.

† ARISTOTLE Top. Book I. Cap. XII. defines Induction to be ἡ ἀπὸ τῶν καθ' ἕκαστον ἐπὶ τὰ καθόλου ἔφοδος, "the way of passing from particulars to universals."

‡ WHATELY has defined Analogy as being a "resemblance of ratios;" and quoted Aristotle for it [λόγων ὁμοιότης]. But this definition does not seem to me either correct or sufficiently definite to answer any good purpose. We certainly speak of "facts" as analogous, as well as "ratios" or "relations."

But is the analogy in the relations at all? Is it not in all cases and necessarily in the facts? Thus suppose A and B each entertain a similar that of Contraries when we affirm unlike or contrary predicates on the ground of contrariety of Formal properties.

Contraries.

940. Not only do many of the facts or objects in Nature have such properties in common, but these properties are taken as Formal at pleasure, and thus become matter determining a sphere, and the facts are *subsumed* under that conception. The word "subsumed" which I have just introduced, has been pretty extensively used to denote the inclusion of individuals within the sphere of a conception.

Objects in Nature classed by Formal Properties.

941. But no sooner do we find that we have thus constituted a class of individuals, by their subsumption under any one of their properties, than we find that there are other properties also which are common to all the individuals of this class.

Other Properties common to the class besides the Formal.

942. By this fact both science and memory are greatly assisted. One can learn as quick, remember as easily and as long a general statement like this: "All resinous bodies produce negative electricity," as he could the specific statements predicating the same thing of each kind of resin separately; or even the individual statements predicating it of each particular piece of resin—the specific statements would be quite numerous, the individuals innumerable. But the general statement occupies no more space on the written page, and requires no more time in enunciation and committing to memory, and no more effort to retain it, than each of the individual statements taken separately.

Classification saves time and labor.

relation to C, is not the analogy between A and B? If not, Analogy can answer only for illustration, and never for investigation and proof. We infer the relation of B to C, for instance, from (1) the known relation of A to C, and (2) the known analogy of B to A in that particular point which thus connects A to C. But if the Analogy be in the relations and not in the facts, the relation must be known before the Analogy; and hence Analogy as a means of investigation or proof is a ὑστέρον πρῶτον, a "later-first," or as some might prefer to call it, a *Petitio Principii.*

943. Hence it is of the utmost importance to science that such classifications should be made, and that in each case the generalization should be as high—that is, the sphere of the subject as comprehensive as the matter of the predicate will allow.

Should be carried as high as possible.

944. But we see objects one by one and individually. Nowhere are species and genera objects of direct observation and intuition. We can never therefore find any one of the contingent predicates of a class by direct intuition of the class-conception. We must have some other Method of investigating their properties.

No direct perception of the properties of classes as such.

945. We have three classes of cases coming under what is commonly called Induction. The first is that in which we have the Formal Properties of some class given to find the Modal Properties common to the individuals in that class. Or secondly, we may have the Modal property as our starting-point, and reason from it back to the Formal; and thirdly, we may have some event or phenomenon regarded as an effect to find the class of objects that will produce that effect.

Three cases.

946. (1) In the first place we fix upon the prominent and striking features which certain facts have in common. We give them a general name, and have made the Properties the Essentia of a Genus. Then we group together other facts in the same way into another Genus, based upon plain and obvious properties as Essentia.

Giving a class name.

947. But suppose we have a Whole to be embraced in our classification. Take for example the domestic animals of a farm. We then complete the classification already begun by division. We refer all having the properties which we had assumed as the Essentia of horses, for instance, to the class "horses;" all having the Essentia of cows to the class "cows;" and so on with all the classes which we had formed. But starting from the idea of a

We complete the classification by division.

Whole, all the individuals in that Whole must be included in some one of the classes which were in the other process regarded as so many genera, but which are now in this process regarded as coördinate species. And if in our process of division we find any individuals not included in any class which we had previously constituted, we either constitute that at once into a new coördinate species or change our principle of division, and classify on other differentia than those with which we had commenced.

Change of Principle of Classification.

948. Thus in all the Natural Sciences different principles of classification have succeeded each other with every important step in advance which the science has taken. New discoveries or a more careful analysis has brought to light new facts and new relations of fact to fact, and suggested a better principle of classification and nomenclature than was possessed before. In Botany, in Zoology, in Crystalography such changes have frequently occurred.

Often done in the Natural Sciences.

949. Now in this process of classification the Formula used is that described above (569), in which a common predicate denoting the Essentia of the Genus is affirmed of the individuals comprehended under it individually. When this has been done we give to the individuals a class-name, and then the matter of this class-conception gives the limits to its sphere, by including in it not only the colligated individuals which had been named in the process of the classification, but also all others which have the Essentia of the colligated individuals, and which constitutes the matter of the class-conception.

Formula of Classification.

950. We now come to the next step in the Induction. We find that several individuals in the genus thus formed have a Modal property common to them all, which however was not so obvious as the property upon which our classification was based, or which at all events was not included in our class-conception. We then predicate this property

Common Modal Properties predicated.

of the individuals in the class, one after another as above (571), and then predicate this property of the class as a whole. And this deductive judgment affirms the Modal property of the species as in the example given (570).

The wolf is carnivorous;
The fox is carnivorous;
The cat is carnivorous, &c.:
∴ The *Canidæ* are carnivorous.

951. And when we have thus affirmed a property of a whole class we speak of it as a law of Nature. It is in truth, however, but a general fact, and wants much yet of being what can properly be called a law.* General Facts.

952. There are three steps in Inductions of this class which it will be well to notice separately; not indeed as involving or depending upon different principles, but as being different and wider applications of the same principle. Three Steps of Induction.

953. (*a*) For the first let us take the following:

We learn of an individual animal a property which was not included in its class-conception, as of the horse, the fact that he sheds his hair every spring. We soon learn of the next horse that we become acquainted with, that he also sheds his hair in the same way. After learning this fact of a number of individuals in the species horse, we predicate the fact as a general fact or law with regard to the species, that "horses shed their hair every spring." First Step.

954. This may be regarded as illustrating the first and primary step in Induction. It is a process which we all go through with in reference to many of the most common species of facts, long before we reflect upon the process at all, or study its laws. This process universal in the acquisition of knowledge.

955. (*b*) Then for the second step take the case in which we extend or widen our induction by including several species. Thus, The Second Step.

* See Part II. Chap. III. Sec. V.

The cat has canine teeth;
The dog has canine teeth;
The wolf has canine teeth;

therefore the dog, and the wolf, the cat and *all animals* which have canine teeth constitute a natural genus, which we will call the *Canidæ*.

But the dog is carnivorous;
The cat is carnivorous;
The wolf is carnivorous;

therefore the Canidæ, or all animals with canine teeth, are carnivorous.

Third Step.

956. (*c*) For the third step we take the fact or law thus developed as a Formal property, and constitute upon it a species of "Carnivorous Animals;" and in the course of our investigation we find that their habit of life is always accompanied by a peculiarity of the digestive organs and alimentary canal, the stomach being smaller and the canal much shorter than in herbivorous animals. We have now established another fact. We may make this fact a Formal property and proceed with our investigation as before, showing that all animals with this kind of digestive apparatus possess more energy and activity, and stand higher in the scale of being, if we will measure their rank by the power of control. Thus the lion and the tiger, though much smaller, control the elephant, camel, &c.

The second class: cases in which we begin with the Modal Properties.

957. (2) If now our investigations had began at the other end, if we had seen the animal eating flesh, and so known that he was carnivorous before we had discovered the peculiarity of his teeth, we should have regarded this Mode as some indication of what could be found in the constitution—that is, among the Formal properties of the animal. It would then become a case for the investigation of a Formal property indicative of this Mode of life; the Method then becomes the same as that for finding the Cause when we have an effect given.* Canine teeth,

* See the next Section.

however, cannot be regarded as a Cause, notwithstanding they may be the Sign, of that mode of life.

958. Having by this Method ascended from the Modal to the Formal property, we reverse the order and predicate the Mode of the species upon the ground of the Formal property which is its sign, just as when the Formal property had been our starting-point in the order of time.

Having found the Formal Property we reverse the order.

959. (3) There are cases in which we have a phenomenon occurring, which we regard not as a Modal property, but merely as an occasional effect. For an example take the case of electricity excited by resinous bodies. The appearance of the electricity is not a mode of the resinous bodies, it is merely an effect of their excitement by silken or woollen surfaces.

Third class: Induction upon occasional effects.

960. In this class of cases the Induction is scarcely any thing more than a classification with a view to the general fact. We find one kind of resins, shellac for example, susceptible of negative electricity. But we cannot find in our analysis of shellac any thing which seems to us likely to cause electricity, any thing by which we can predict *a priori* on finding the same property in substances of another kind that they will excite the same kind of electricity. We soon find, however, that other resins do excite negative electricity, and thus far in our experience all known resins agree in this peculiarity. But why, or what is the property in them by which they produce an effect so unlike other substances under the same circumstances we cannot tell. Chemistry reveals to us many such cases, and it is quite possible that they point to something yet to be discovered, but which is at present beyond even the forerunning conjectures and hypotheses of science.

Induction in these cases scarcely any thing more than a classification.

961. And yet when the nature of electricity is better understood we may be able to see something in resins—some element common to them all as a constitutive or Formal principle

Further knowledge may convert them into complete Inductions.

of the class, which we shall then understand to be as naturally adapted to the production of that particular state of electric excitement which we call Negative Electricity, as the canine teeth of the Canidæ are to the carnivorous habit of life. The Analogies of Nature and the developments and progress in the history of Science lead us to expect such a result.

962. But as it is, we place much less dependence upon the inductions of this class than upon those of either of the others. We regard them in fact as but mere classifications of particular facts into a General fact, preparatory to an induction and prophetic of it, which, however, we are not fully prepared to make.

These Classifications suggestive of Inductions.

963. In the course of our induction we for the most part find some exceptions to the general fact which we first deduce in this way. And so strongly are we attached to the fundamental ideas under which we pursue any science, that when the exceptions become very numerous we abandon the classification upon which the induction was based, and classify anew and on another principle. Thus the old philosophers predicated the property of "*falling*" of *heavy* bodies only, such as earth, stones, metals; and they supposed that light bodies, as air, vapor, and smoke belonged to an opposite class, of which "ascending" could be predicated by the Method of Contraries. But it has been found that light bodies also tend to the earth, and now a new classification has been made, and "falling" is a property predicated of all bodies having the common Essentia of being "unsupported." And we state it as a general fact, that "all bodies left unsupported fall to the earth."

Exceptions becoming numerous lead to new Classifications.

964. We have already remarked that those properties upon which the classification of natural generas are based, are not generally those which are subject to comparisons of intensity, as *color*, *size*, *density*, &c., among material properties; virtue, wisdom, courage, &c., among spiritual

Natural Classifications not often based upon variable properties.

properties, but rather those which do not admit of any such comparison. In the case just given, bodies either are or are not supported. If one is supported, it remains where it is, if not, it falls. We take no notice of the fact of the support being adequate to sustain a body many times as large; that fact has no bearing upon the classification or the deduction based upon it. Nor if there be something under it which is not sufficient to support it, do we take notice of that fact—the body is simply "unsupported."

965. But in the previous classification in which it was affirmed, that "all heavy bodies fall," the classification was based upon a property which admits of comparisons of intensity. Bodies are more or less heavy. "*Heavy*" and "*light*" are not, like "*supported*". and "*unsupported*," contraries, but they are simply *sub-contraries;* and the Induction based upon *that* classification was fallacious. It stated the truth, indeed, but not the whole truth; and the *suppressio veri* was for all purposes of science just as bad as a false statement.

Analogy but an incomplete Induction.

966. Analogy stops short of an Induction of the second degree (955), because for the most part the objects of the class to which the inference is drawn—that is, the subject of the Conclusion is beyond the reach of actual Observation and Experiment. But if we could investigate the individual to which we reason by analogy, we should convert such Analogy into an Induction of *observed facts* in the same species.

Analogy may extend to fields of inquiry where Induction is impracticable.

967. In all the Inductive Sciences there are many of the fields of inquiry from which by the nature of the case we are excluded, and there are others which neither our telescopes nor our microscopes can reach. In such cases Analogy is our only guide and furnishes our only light—a light indeed of inestimable value, but still a light which needs to be most cautiously followed. In the anatomy of the human frame, for instance, we have

the facts for an induction before us. But in physiology and biology many of the facts are such that they never can be brought under inspection and observation. Comparative Anatomy, however, has shown an analogy between man and animals; and we may often subject them to an examination into the functions of reproduction, life and death, which we can never make in the case of man.

968. All substances are brought by their Formal properties into relation to the laws and sequences of nature. Thus bodies that are transparent, are by this property connected with an important class of phenomena and laws in optics. Resinous bodies, by a property common to them all, but which has no distinctive name, are connected with the science of electricity in one way; and vitreous bodies, by a property common to them, are connected with the other kind of electricity. Iron by a peculiar property is capable of important magnetic phenomena, and the laws of terrestrial polarity. Dense bodies, by their density, are connected with the laws of gravitation. Opaque bodies, by their opacity, with reflection of light and the phenomena of color. Thus every Formal property of a body connects it with some general law or fact—some class of phenomena more or less comprehensive; and those relations are the basis of the natural genera and species upon which all science and all knowledge depends.

The Formal Properties of all Species bring them within the field of Analogy.

969. Each property of a body is thus connected in the concatenation of nature's laws and sequences, with some law and with some phenomenon, which as a consequent is regarded as an effect or a mode.

970. Now when in such a natural species we find one property which is regarded as Formal, connected with a certain law and producing certain effects, we infer by analogy that any individual in another species, having the same Formal property, must sustain a like relation to that law, and have the same modal property or effect.

Application of Analogy.

971. Thus the physician knows that a certain drug is a deadly poison to some of the animal tribes. He infers from analogy between the animal and man that it will prove so to man. He knows that there are many points of identity between man and the animals—they have an Essentia in common; he knows that *most* drugs produce the same effects upon men as upon animals. But with regard to this particular drug's influence upon man, or whether man and beast are identical in that particular property, in consequence of which that drug is a deadly poison for the beast—he knows nothing anterior to experience of its effect upon man except what he can infer from the analogy between the man and the beast.

By the Medical Practitioner.

SECTION VII.

Of Elimination.

972. The facts of Nature have not only a lateral connection, so to speak, by which they admit of classification into Genera and Species, with a view to general facts and laws, but each one had something before it which is regarded as its Cause, and will be followed by something which will be regarded as its Effect.

The facts in Nature have relation of antecedent and consequent.

973. Causality is not a property inhering in any substance that can be cognized by any of the senses. We can see antecedence in time, but the causality is a matter of inference.

Causality not a property perceptible in itself.

974. *Causality*, however, is something more than mere antecedence and necessary connection.* Day and night follow each other, the successive steps of the pedestrian, the

Causality something more than mere antecedence.

* The Fallacy which we sometimes hear spoken of as the Fallacy of *post hoc ergo propter hoc*, consists in inferring that because one event is after another, therefore it was caused by that other. Bishop Latimer exposes this fallacy in some who attributed the laxity of morals in his time to the Reformation, by narrating the anecdote of a countryman who accounted

days of the week, the months of the year, all succeed each other, and yet no one supposes that each is the *Effect* of that which preceded or the *Cause* of that which follows. So the antecedence is a fact in the reality of being; the causality, where there is any, belongs to the reality of truth alone. It seems to direct the thought into the unseen realities of truth; and the Reason, by an intuition peculiar to itself, sees there what is not expressed in the sensible properties of external objects.

975. By means of Induction we may always find the Invariable Antecedent in the phenomena of Nature. But the distinction between a mere Antecedent and a Cause, is what no processes of *a posteriori* investigation can give. It is something which the Reason superadds to the results of our investigation in certain cases, just as in Induction the Reason superadds that which distinguishes a General Law from a mere General Fact. By the insight which Induction enables us to get into the Class-conceptions and Final Causes of the Creator, we are enabled to affirm the concomitance of certain properties of objects as Laws arising from that physical necessity which is based upon the volitions of the Divine Will. So, too, by Induction we establish certain antecedences and consequences in Nature as general facts, upon which the Reason infers or rather superadds the relation of Cause and Effect.

Invariable Antecedence established by Induction.

976. All investigation of Causes must of course end at last in the Absolute or First Cause (108). But the Method which we are now describing must proceed step by step, and from any one fact or event it can give us only that which next preceded it in the order of time and of causality. This becomes

The Causes in Nature only secondary.

for the sands that obstructed the Goodwin Harbor—by the building of Tenterden Steeple—"There were no sands," said he, "in the harbor; that is, none that gave trouble, until just after the steeple was built on Tenterden Church." Hence the good people of Tenterden supposed that the steeple had caused the sands in their harbor.

in its turn an Effect to be investigated in like manner, until in like manner "*omnia exeunt in Deum*" (all things lead to God). Then and then only do we find an Efficient Cause for the facts and phenomena of Nature.

977. This results from the fact that Matter is always regarded as inert, and incapable of acting except as it is acted upon. Even the imponderable agents, heat, light, electricity, &c., can hardly be regarded as exceptions to this rule. As yet we know not what they are. But the Reason refuses to regard them as any thing more than means, Instrumental or Second Causes in the hands of an Intelligent or First Cause.

And Instrumental.

978. Our inquiry into Causes therefore can be only an investigation into the antecedents of any event, along which the mind conceives that the efficiency which brought that event into the reality of being may have passed. And the only conditions which the Reason imposes are, (1) that that which is to be regarded as a cause be an invariable antecedent; (2) that it be a true cause; and (3) that it be a sufficient cause [*causa vera* and *causa sufficiens*].

The three Conditions required by the Reason.

979. Of the first we need say no more than the self-evident proposition, that a cause must precede its effect in point of chronology.

First: Antecedence in Time.

980. Of the second, we can only say that a true cause must be a substance acting through some of its properties. A mere state or mode of a substance is no cause, although of course it will often be an antecedent. Thus "day" is a mere mode of light, and is no cause of the succeeding mode which we call "night." One of the steps of a pedestrian is merely one condition or stage in his progress, and no cause of the succeeding one. "*Day*" and "*step*" are not substances in the metaphysical sense of the words at all (Part I. 55 and note), but merely modes or stages of certain substances. Thus

Second: a Substance.

A Mode no proper Cause.

the step that crushes the worm cannot be regarded as the cause of the crushing. Not the step but the man who steps is the cause; and the word "step" denotes merely the accidental condition or mode in which the cause happened to be when it exerted its efficiency. It may be well, therefore, for the sake of having a name, to call the former the *Substantial* or *Substantive* Causes, and the latter the *Modal* Causes.

Substantive & Modal Causes.

981. But not only must the antecedent which we are to regard as a cause be a substance, in order to be a *vera causa*, it must also bear some proportion or relation to the effect in order to be a sufficient cause, or *causa sufficiens*. Thus, a boil on one's hand may be a *vera causa* of a good deal of pain and annoyance, but it would not be regarded as a sufficient cause of the death of an individual, if one having such a sore should be found dead.

Cause must bear some proportion to its Effect.

982. The *substantiality** (38) of causes must be affirmed by an ultimate intuition of the Mind itself. One can no more *prove* that a "*day*" is no substantial cause than that the sun is round, or a rose is red. If our faculties do not so see these objects, there is no help for us in one case any more than in the other. The fault is an individual infirmity, and can be regarded as requiring no diminution of the confidence which all persons whose faculties are in their normal condition are entitled to place in the exercise of those faculties.

The substantiality rests on ultimate intuition.

983. But the *sufficiency* of causes in Nature is what we can learn only from observation. Of Primary Causes, as of the Infinite Mind, and of the human mind, from the very conception of them we can predicate certain events or phenomena as effects. We know that Infinite Wisdom

The sufficiency of Causes in Nature learned from Observation and Induction.

* When we speak of a cause as being necessarily a substance, we must be understood as speaking not of mere antecedence, but of causality. An antecedent need not be a substance, but a cause must.

will know all things—Infinite Power can do all things, that Mind or Reason can understand, that Will can choose, and determine the formal character of actions. And so in Nature we may predicate *a priori*, on the class-conception of certain objects something of their concatenation in the antecedents and consequences of Nature. But this class-conception is itself obtained *a posteriori*, and the nature and efficiency of their causality is a part of that which we learn by observation, and through which we are enabled to arrive at this class-conception. It is certainly very possible, and perhaps we had better say that it is probable, that the causality of all objects was an element in the class-conception which preceded in the Divine Mind the act of their creation.

Sufficiency of Cause includes two Elements.

984. In the *sufficiency* of causes we have two distinct elements to take note of—the *adequacy* in amount and *homogeneity* in kind. Thus wine is the sufficient cause of intoxication. But a single wine-glassful would be inadequate in quantity. But if one should attribute a scarlet fever or the small-pox to the use of wine, he would mistake the homogeneity of the cause to the effect which he ascribes to it. Wine is a cause, a *vera causa*, and a *causa sufficiens* of a variety of phenomena, but not of the diseases just named.

Causality often depends upon the mode of the Substance.

985. As every cause must be a substance, and every substance is known only by its properties, so also it is known only as existing in some certain condition or mode; and this condition or mode is often inseparable from that antecedence to the effect which renders the substance a cause of it. Thus wine is a cause of intoxication only when taken into the stomach and in a certain quantity. The Air is a cause, but it causes the uprooting of trees, and the other effects of tornadoes only when it exists in the mode of violent motion.

Four classes of words used to denote Causes.

986. Hence we have four classes of words or terms which are used to denote causes:—(1) Simple words denoting substances, as

"heat," "electricity," "light," &c., substances whose efficiency as causes is always active wherever the substances themselves are found; then (2) we have such words as denote merely the condition or mode in which the cause exerts its influence, as when we say that "walking fatigues one,"—"the succession of day and night causes great changes in the temperature," &c. Then we have (3) those complex terms which express both the cause and the mode or condition upon which the production of the effect depends, as "*the* SPARK *falling upon gunpowder* caused the explosion." Or sometimes (4) we have single words which in themselves express the substance and its modes, as "earthquake," "hurricane," "lightning," &c.

987. Words or terms in order to express a cause adequately should always be of this last-named kind. They should express not only the substance which is the cause, but also the mode or condition on which the efficiency as cause is exerted.

The last kind only express the cause adequately.

988. The immediate Antecedent of any phenomena will sometimes be complex, consisting of several elements, and at others simple. Thus Heat is a simple antecedent. It admits of no physical analysis. But the sun—a burning lamp—acidifying vegetable matter—the mixing of sulphuric and nitric acids—are all complex antecedents, compounded of the simple antecedent or cause, heat, among others.

Simple and Complex Antecedents.

989. We must remember also that in regard to many of the compound facts in Nature, as elsewhere, the causality is not to be found in any one of the ingredients or elements alone and by itself. Thus, it is not the charcoal, nor the nitre, nor the sulphur which causes the explosion when a spark falls upon that combination of these three elements which constitute what is called gunpowder. Neither of those elements are explosive alone and by

The Causality often depends upon the complexity.

itself.* Not any property of either of the substances, therefore, is the cause of the explosion—the combination itself is the cause.

990. When therefore the combination is the cause, and not any one of the simple elements in that combination, the complex antecedent is to be regarded as the cause. But it is often the case that some one element in the complex antecedent may be the cause, and it will in many cases be found of the greatest importance to ascertain which of the simple elements in any complex antecedent is the real cause of the phenomena which we are investigating.

No Elimination to be made when the Causality depends upon the complexity.

991. For this purpose several Methods have been resorted to, which have been called Methods of *Elimination*. They consist in removing entirely or varying in quantity certain of the elements in any complex antecedent or consequent for the purpose of ascertaining its relation to the supposed Consequent or Antecedent.

Elimination.

992. Elimination depends upon the four following axioms:

(1.) No two simple causes will produce the same effect and the converse. Hence identity of effect implies identity of cause, and diversity of effect implies diversity of cause.

First Axiom.

993. Several complex antecedents may be followed by the same effect. Thus a wax-taper, an oil-lamp, a coal-fire, the concentrated rays of the sun, may each be the cause of the melting of sealing-wax. But in these complex antecedents, there is identity in one simple element "heat," by which the effect is produced.

994. And so strong is the belief in this axiom of identity of cause, where there is identity of effect,

* This has recently been disputed in regard to Nitre. But I believe that its explosiveness has not been proved. But even if it has it will not affect the propriety of the illustration; since if it is explosive at all, it is not explosive under any such circumstances as those contemplated in the text.

that scientific men cling to it even when facts seem to be against them, and the belief in its infallibility has often led by means of an analysis of the complex antecedent to the discovery of what would otherwise, perhaps, never have been suspected to exist. And in investigations of the phenomena of Electricity, Galvanism, and Magnetism, the identity of effects produced in many cases have led very generally to the belief that these forces are but one and the same thing, acting in different ways and under different circumstances. Nay, so far has this matter gone, that it has been suggested that this one cause "Electricity," if that be the name of it, is the cause of heat and light, and the medium through which the mind exerts its control over the body.

Influence of this belief upon the minds of men.

995. As we know nothing *a posteriori* of substances except through their properties, so we know nothing of causes *as causes*—that is, nothing of the causality of objects in Nature, except by inference from their effects. As we have already said, a cause must be a substance, it must be adequate and homogeneous to its effect. And as the identity of objects in Nature depends upon the identity of their inseparable properties, so the identity of causes as such must depend upon that which constitutes their adequacy and homogeneity to the effect produced. Hence the proposition already laid down, "the identity of effect implies identity of simple cause."

Axiom proved *a priori.*

996. (2.) The second axiom is, that if the cause is removed the effect will disappear. Otherwise we should have an effect without a cause, which is absurd.

Second Axiom.

997. (3.) The magnitude of the effect varies with and is determined by the magnitude or intensity of the cause. Otherwise we should have some portion of causation without any effect, or some portion of effect without a cause.

Third Axiom.

998. (4.) And fourthly, that *cæteris paribus* the same cause will always produce the same effect.

Fourth Axiom.

999. The effect always depends very much upon the substance or matter upon which the cause exerts its force. Thus heat expands iron, and contracts clay; and as has been said, "what is one man's meat is another's poison."

Efficiency depends upon the subject matter.

1000. This leads us to mention the fact that Consequents as well as Antecedents are complex also, and as such the result of more than one simple cause. Thus, for example, an eclipse of the Moon, considered in its essence as an eclipse, and in its modes as occurring on such a moment and visible only at such a place on the Earth's surface, is a complex result, caused by the various forces of the diverse attractions of the different heavenly bodies. In this case the cause of the eclipse was one thing, the cause of its occurring at precisely that moment rather than another, or so as to be visible on one part of the Earth's surface rather than another, are each of them different causes, and may be called Formal Causes. In this case, however, we use the name Formal Cause in a sense somewhat different from what we have given to it in reference to logical classifications, and yet not so different as to occasion any confusion or error.

Consequents also complex or simple.

1001. Let us now proceed to consider the several Methods of Elimination. Of these we may have five that are specially useful, arising out of the axioms already mentioned as applied to the different cases which may arise for investigation.

Five Methods of Elimination.

1002. The first law of Elimination in the order in which I shall name them is the following:

(1.) *By the Elimination of any one element in the complex antecedent, its appropriate consequent or effect will disappear also.*

First Method.

1003. Thus suppose a physician administers a prescription consisting of three ingredients, camphor, and morphine, and ipecac—and finds unpleasant symptoms ensue that can be ascribed to nothing but the dose which he had prescribed. Suppose now that he administers two of the ingredients without the third,

Illustration.

or the two combined with some others, and the unfavorable symptoms do not ensue, he would doubtless ascribe those symptoms as an effect to that ingredient in the dose which in the second administration he had omitted.

1004. (2.) *When there is a uniform disagreement in several Antecedents in all the elements except one, that one must be regarded as the cause of any unvarying element in the Consequents of those diverse Antecedents.*

Second Method.

1005. Thus suppose we have an Antecedent A, consisting of elements *x*, *y*, and *z*, and a Consequent C. If now we can form or avail ourselves of new combinations as *w x* and *v*, or *s x* and *t*, having *x* alone common to them all, and the Consequent C following in each case, we should have no doubt that A is the cause of C, by reason of its element *x*.

Illustration.

1006. Such cases occur not unfrequently in Chemistry, when we have to deal with agents which we either cannot get in a separate and pure state, or if we could their use would be inconvenient or unsafe. The same thing holds true also in Medical practice. Some of the most indispensable of the medical agents, in fact nearly all of those that are the most efficient can never be used except in combination with others. Hence their effect can be ascertained only by forming them into different combinations, varying in each experiment every other ingredient.

Of use in Chemistry and Pharmacy.

1007. (3.) *By diminishing or increasing the cause, a corresponding increase or diminution of the effect will ensue.*

Third Method.

1008. This law of Elimination supposes a case in which the element in the compound Antecedent cannot be wholly eliminated.

1009. Thus "*heat*" is an agent of this kind. There is no absolute of cold or total absence of heat. But we can increase or diminish the intensity of heat to a very great extent. Thus we find that

Illustration.

nearly all bodies expand—become liquid, and finally vapor, and even gas, under intense heat; and in the absence of heat all bodies contract, condense, and become solid. Hence heat is assumed to be the cause of fluidity. The same may be said of density. There is no body without some density; and as the gravitation of bodies, so far as we can ascertain, varies with their density—we assume that density is the cause of the gravitation of bodies, or that all bodies gravitate in proportion to the quantity of matter.

Fourth Method.

1010. (4.) *If, from any pair, consisting of a complex Antecedent and a complex Consequent, we separate the elements in the Antecedent, whose effects in the complex Consequent are known, and find an element in the Consequent whose cause is not contained in the Antecedent, it is called a* Residual Phenomenon, *for which a cause must be sought.*

Residual Phenomena.

In the return Comets.

1011. We have many cases in which the several elements of a complex Antecedent have been so far examined, as that their effects both in quality and quantity in the Consequent are known, and yet something remains to be accounted for. The return of a Comet may be regarded as such an effect. Now among the causes which determine its return we know many—the attraction of the Earth, the attraction of the Sun, and of each of the other heavenly bodies to which it approaches in its path near enough to be influenced by them. These different attractions are the elements in the cause of its return, considered as a complex Consequent, including its return at a precise day and hour, &c. If now we begin and abstract from the Cause each element, deducting from the Consequent also its appropriate effect—appropriate both in character and in amount, in quality and quantity, and after thus abstracting each element in the Cause with its element in the effect, we find something remaining in the effect still unaccounted for—we have what Sir John F. W. Herschel called a *Residual Phenomenon*. Thus if we have Antecedent compound of *a*, *b*, *c*, and *d*; and Consequent consisting of *w*, *x*, *y*, *z*, and *s*; and abstracting *a* from the Antecedent removes *w*, *b* removes *x*; *c*, *y*; and *d*, *z*. We have *s* remaining as a Residual Phenomenon, for which a cause is yet to be sought, and to be added to our enumeration of the elements *a*, *b*, *c*, and *d* in the Antecedent. For the elements in any Cause must be adequate to the Effect, and the whole of it both in Substance and in Form.

The existence of a resisting Medium proved as a Residual Phenomenon.

1012. The existence of a resisting medium filling all space, and yet so rare as not to exert any perceptible influence upon the motions of the planets and satellites of our system, has been supposed to have been discovered as a Residual Phenomenon, effected by means of this Method in accounting for the return of comets at a period somewhat less than that assigned them by the calculations of astronomers. But whether there be such a medium or not, the Residual Phenomenon shows that there is some agency at work of which as yet we possess no satisfactory knowledge, and which will need to be investigated before the science of Astronomy will be complete.

Necessity for a Fifth Method.

1013. (5.) Again and finally, there may sometimes a doubt arise as to which of the two phenomena are to be regarded as cause and which as effect. Thus, it is always observed in cases of snow-storms, that just as the snow begins to fall the mercury in the thermometer rises a little. Now, is the change in the temperature the cause or the effect of its beginning to snow? In thunder-storms, a flash of lightning is sometimes attended by an increase in the quantity of rain that is falling; which is cause and which is effect?

The doubt settled in some cases by *a priori* knowledge of Causes.

1014. In many of these cases we can answer from our knowledge of the nature of the phenomena themselves. And there are many cases in which we can make no experiments of Elimination. But when elimination can be made, the case comes under the second axiom. Hence we have as the fifth rule of Elimination,

1015. (5.) *Remove one of the phenomena, and if the other disappears also, that which was removed is the cause and the other is the effect. But if the other does not disappear, that which was removed was the effect and not the cause.*

Fifth Method.

1016. For an illustration of this law it is very common to refer to the case of Dr. Wells' researches into the phenomena of dew. It was found in the course of his experiments that those surfaces on which dew collected, were colder than those upon which there was none. But which was the cause and which the effect, the cold or the dew? By substituting metal surfaces, which do not easily become cold in the position in which he placed them, for glass, which being a bad conductor does easily become cold, he found that the glass surfaces and not the metal were covered with dew, whence he inferred that the cooling of the surface was the cause of the dew, and not the dew the cause of the cooling of the bedewed surface.

Illustration.

1017. Having in these ways learned the nature of objects considered as causes, we can often reason or investigate into the future from causes to their yet undeveloped effects.* Reasoning in this Method, however, is always attended with something of danger. We seldom thoroughly comprehend all the properties of a Cause, or the influences which may be exerted upon its efficiency by its combination with other causes. Nor can we ever see far enough into the future to enable us to take into our account all of the contingencies that may arise to modify the course of events. Thus we can predict the fall of an unsupported body from our knowledge of the law of gravitation. But another law, as magnetism or electricity, &c.,

Reasoning from known causes into the future.

* This has also been called "*reasoning a priori*."—WHATELY'S *Rhetoric*, Part I. c. II. 32. It is not, however, *a priori* in the sense in which we have thus far used these words.

may interpose between the cause and the effect and break the connection.

1018. But yet there are many cases in which this is the only Method by which we can penetrate the future. The astronomer reasons upon it in predicting the rise and set of the sun, the changes of the moon, the recurrence of eclipses, comets, conjunction of the stars, &c., &c. And he feels perfect confidence in his conclusions.

Sometimes our only means of forecasting the future.

In Astronomy.

1019. The chemist reasons in this Method when he designs an experiment. He knows the effects which certain agents as causes generally produce. He reasons from this knowledge to the effect which those agents will produce in the new case, and trusts to this calculation to produce the test or crisis which he wishes to determine by his experiment.

In Chemistry.

1020. The physician reasons on this principle when he prescribes his remedies, and looks for the desired change in the condition of the patients as the effect of what he had prescribed.

In Medicine.

1021. The legislator has to rely on this Method in the discharge of his duties, as legislator, to a very great extent. It is often his only guide in devising laws and institutions for the welfare of those for whom he is called upon to legislate. And the causes whose influence he has to calculate, are moreover often of the subtlest and most evanescent or incomprehensible character.

In Legislation.

1022. It will have been observed from the foregoing remarks—that in speaking of the cause of any fact or event, we refer to a compound object within which one element alone was *causal* of the effect. Hence reasoning from effect to cause, we can reason only to that element, and not to any one of the combinations into which it may enter. Thus heat is the cause of fluidity. If now we start from fluidity, as an effect, we can argue to the existence of heat as a cause. But as this heat may have been produced by the sun, by a spirit-lamp, by a chemical

Reasoning from Effect to Cause limited.

decomposition, by friction, &c., &c., we cannot argue to the reality of any one of those combinations of heat from the mere fact of fluidity. Hence we can investigate and argue much more specifically from cause to effect than from effect to cause.

1023. In some of the most important inquiries which we can have to make, however, we have no other Method that we can pursue, but that from effect to cause. In Medical diagnosis, for instance, this is for the most part the only means of ascertaining the nature of the disease to be cured.

Limited in many cases to reasoning from Effect to Cause.

1024. The physician is called to see a patient—the prominent symptom is we will suppose a headache—this is an effect which may proceed from a variety of causes. If it were the first case of headache, and had never been investigated, there would be no other Method that could be pursued with success than those we have already described. But in the present state of the science almost all causes, and varieties of causes, have been investigated. The causes which may produce such results are pretty well known and recorded.

Illustration.

1025. Each cause also, for the most part, produces some other effects also besides the one that is chiefly conspicuous; and no two causes ever produce effects which are all of them precisely alike in all respects. Hence the physician is to look for the other effects, or "symptoms," as he will call them, until he finds one or more that is peculiar to one of the causes of headache. This one becomes, what Bacon proposed to call an *experimentum crucis*, or a test fact. And in the pursuit of such a test, he will often find it necessary to experiment with tests voluntarily applied, as well as to observe the facts that already exist without his procurement.

Each complex Antecedent has several Effects.

Experimentum crucis.

1026. In our attempt, to reason into the future of

human conduct, however, the moral freedom of man and the uncertainty as to the determinations of his will, render our conclusions peculiarly liable to error. Investigation or reasoning in this way, however, is much more reliable when applied to masses than when applied to a single individual (800, 801).

Reasoning from Cause to Effect in Moral Matter.

CHAPTER III.

OF METHODS OF PROOF AND REFUTATION.

SECTION I.

Of Proof.

1027. Methods of Proof presuppose both terms of the Proposition, whereas, as we have seen, Methods of Investigation presuppose merely the Subject. By Proof, then, we mean the establishment of the Copula, affirming or denying the relation between the given Subject and Predicate. From what has been said (431), it is evident that no proof is required of Intuitive Judgments. Hence in all our inquiries into Methods of Proof, we are understood to have reference to the Proof of Deductive Judgments only.

Proof.

1028. In the preceding Part of this Treatise, we have examined the ways in which Cognitions and Judgments can be so combined as to serve as Means of Proof. We have here now to consider the ways *in* which these Means or Formula may be used, with an especial reference to the Matter *on* which they are to be used.

Methods of using the Formula.

1029. I have already remarked that Methods of Investigation are, to some extent, Methods of Proof also. In Investigation we expect to find as the result, that with which we start as a Proposition in Methods of Proof. But besides being thus in respect to Methods the converse

Methods of Investigation to some extent Methods of Proof also.

of each other, their Differentia as Alternate Species of Methods is as stated above; the one *gives* (Whately would say proves)* the Major Terms, and the other *proves* the Copula.†

Direct and Indirect Methods of Proof.

1030. Methods of Proof may be either *direct* or *indirect.* Direct Methods prove the Proposition to be established; the Indirect prove its contradictory to be untrue, from which we have the desired Proposition by Immediate Inference.

Direct Proof.

1031. Direct Proof is effected by whatever Means or in whatever Method, wherever we show that the Subject of the Proposition has or has not the essential matter of the Predicate. Since whatever has

* Rhetoric, Part. I. Chap. I. § 1.

† We have in popular use the words Induction and Deduction, which are understood to denote Methods of Proof the reverse of each other. Both, however, may be regarded as Methods of either Investigation or of Proof, since even Deduction may give a new Major Term for a subject (see Part II. Chap. III. Sec. III.); and the word Induction is also used to denote a Method of proving the truth of the generalization which it effects. But the contrast between the two Methods in the common estimation just referred to, is between Induction and Deduction as *Methods of Investigation.* No contrast or comparison between the former as a Method of Investigation, and the latter as a Method of Proof, would ever be made with any view to a disparagement of either Method. The contrast for the disparagement of "the Deductive Method," as it is called, was undoubtedly occasioned by the misuse of it as a Method of Investigation, which seems to have had its origin to some extent at least in the "*Organon*" of Aristotle; and was encouraged by the schoolmen and philosophers generally until the time of Bacon, the famous author of the "*Novum Organon.*"

But there is no occasion for such a contrast. Induction as a Method of Proof is itself deduction from the very necessities of the case, as we shall see in our inquiry into the grounds of its validity as a Method of Proof. But regarded as Methods of Proof, Induction and Deduction differ in one of their more obvious properties which has not yet been mentioned.

In Deduction the General Principle or Major Premise is most conspicuous and will be made most prominent. In Induction the particular facts or cases—that is, the Minor Premise is made the most conspicuous. So that Deduction and Induction are both of them for the most part made by means of Enthymemes; the former suppressing the Minor and the latter the Major Premise. In Deduction the inclusion of the Minor Term or Subject of the Syllogism in the Subject of the Major is considered too obvious to need express statement. In Induction the general principle of all Induction—the uniformity of Nature is assumed as too obvious and undisputed to require explicit recognition.

the Essentia of any class, is of necessity included in that class, and *vice versa.* To render Direct Proof possible, therefore, two conditions are necessary:—(1) that the Proposition to be proved must have a Positive Term for its Predicate; and (2) that there may be a conception occupying a middle position in Logical Quantity between its Subject and its Predicate.

Its two requisites.

1032. Without this last condition the Proposition must be either intuitive (431), or incapable of proof.

1033. Thus for the first case—Every Effect has a Cause. This is something more than a simple Proposition in A, as stated; for it results from the nature of the Matter, that whatever has a cause is an effect. Hence the Subject "every Effect," and the Predicate "has a Cause," are coextensive spheres, and both distributed. Hence there can be no Middle Term in Logical Quantity between them. The one is not included in any species which is comprehended by the other.*

Judgments with no Middle Term.

1034. For the second case, take any Proposition which affirms what is not true, as "apples are gingerbread." It is seen at once that although these articles may be made coördinate species in a comprehending genus, as "*food,*" for instance, yet in no way can one of them be made to be a comprehending sphere to the other, and conse-

Judgments incapable of Proof.

* We may, however, need to have the terms of an Intuitive Judgment defined or explained before the mind can assent to them. This processs, however, is not to be mistaken for, or confounded with, *proof* of the *Proposition* expressing the judgment. Thus in the case above given, one would hesitate at the judgment until he might obtain an adequate conception of what we mean by "cause," and what by "effect." In that case he would be in want rather of *instruction* than of *proof.*

And such in fact will be the case universally when one of the terms is but a synonyme of the other, or both are but alternate conceptions of the same subject (460). In this case the Syllogism which we may construct is rather for instruction than proof, designed to explain our terms rather than to prove that the Predicate may be affirmed of the Subject of the Conclusion.

quently there can be no conception coming between them in Logical Quantity.

1035. Without the first condition, namely, that the Proposition to be proved must have a Positive Term for its Predicate, there can be no direct proof, since Positive Terms only denote their spheres by their matter (134). Hence if the Predicate be not Positive it has no matter, or rather it gives none, by which we can determine whether the given Subject be included in it or not.

Propositions with Negative Predicates.

1036. The Indirect Proof depends upon the Principle of Excluded Middle (400), and is accomplished by proving the falsity of the contradictory of that which we wish to prove. But as the contradictory of an Affirmative is always Negative, the Indirect Method is seldom used to prove Affirmatives, except in three classes of Propositions, which do not admit of the direct Method; namely, (1) Intuitive Judgments; and (2) those in which the words "infinite" and "eternal," &c., are used as Predicates; or (3) Affirmative Propositions with Negative Predicates.

Indirect Proof.

1037. It has commonly been held, that Axioms expressive of Intuitive Judgments *a priori*, are incapable of proof. This must be understood of Direct Proof only—for of Indirect Proof they all admit. It consists in this case in showing that the contradictory violates either the Principle of Identity (422), and Contradiction (423), or of Sufficient Cause (425). If it violates the first it destroys the Subject (784 and *note*); if the second, it involves an absolute scepticism or unbelief, by impeaching the veracity of our means of knowledge. It thus removes the very foundation upon which we can pretend to know any thing; and so the very ground upon which we would base the assertion by which we seek or expect to accomplish our object. Thus if one denies the proposition, "the foliage is green," he asserts a proposition contradictory to the sense of sight, concerning matter in regard to which we have

Axioms incapable of Direct Proof.

May be proved indirectly.

absolutely no means of knowledge but the sense of sight. Hence if that sense cannot be relied upon, his assertion cannot be relied upon, and we know nothing of colors. And so of all other propositions asserting the primary sense-perceptions.

Eternal and Infinite used as Predicates.

1038. The words "*eternal*" and "*infinite*," have been sometimes regarded as Negatives. At others they are claimed as Positive. But for all the purposes of deduction, they can be used only as though they were negatives. They predicate of the Subject no essentia, except the *absence of* bounds or limits in Continuous Quantity.—Hence "eternal," "infinite," Negative and Privative Terms generally, are all in the same category. Denoting no sphere by means of its essence, they can be proved of a Subject only by the Principle of the Excluded Middle. We predicate of the Subject the Positive Term, which is coördinate to the Privative or Negative, and thus show that it has not the Essentia of that Positive.

Illustrated in reference to the word "*Space*."

Thus if we say, "Space is infinite," we suppose that space is "finite," or "has a limit;" that is, a limit in Continuous Quantity. If so, beyond or outside of this limit space is not or it is not space. But even if it is occupied by material substance, it is still space; and we have space occupied and space unoccupied. Hence the judgment that that which is outside of any limit is not space, is a contradiction in terms. If it be not space, there is no such 'outside of the limits." Hence as the Proposition, "space is finite," is absurd, a contradiction in terms—its contradictory, "space is infinite," must be true. In the same way all Affirmative Propositions with Negative or Privative Predicates must be proved (429).

Positive Predicates in Negative Judgments.

1039. If, however, the Predicate be a Positive Term, and the Copula Negative, we still have the Essentia of the Predicate given, and must prove that the Subject has not that Essentia, if so be it has not, by either Observation, Testimony, Analysis, or the *Abscissio infiniti;* since none of the other Methods of Investigation give negative results directly, or in any other way than by Immediate Inference on the ground of the Excluded Middle. We can neither count, nor measure, nor average what is not. Induction, Analogy, Example, and Elimination are all based upon the properties which the objects of inquiry do possess, and not upon those which they do not.

1040. But Testimony comes at last to Observation and Authority. The Abscissio is based upon Observation and Analysis. And Analysis of Objects is based upon Observation; and Analysis of Conceptions upon the Intuitions of the Reason. Hence in the last analysis of our means of proving Negative Propositions with Positive Terms for Predicates, we have Observation, Authority, and Analysis—Methods which give both the Predicate and the Copula in the one act and at the same time.

Proved only by Observation, Authority, or Analysis.

It is a question which it will often be important to have answered, when are we to regard any Proposition as proved?

1041. Most Premises will be Conclusions of previous Syllogisms; that is, they will be themselves but Deductive Judgments—and so lead us to consider the Premises from which they are deduced.

Premises for the most part Deductive Judgments.

1042. But there can be no infinite retrogression. We must come at last to something that cannot be proved (directly), simply because there is no Middle Term that can come between its Subject and Predicate by which it can be proved. Such are Axioms or Intuitive Judgments. When we have got back to these the mind is satisfied. The question, Why? which always implies a belief in an anterior judgment, will and can be no longer asked. The judgment is intuitive, and affirmed by all minds as soon as the cognitions of which it is composed are apprehended by the mind.

There must be first Principles.

The mind is satisfied with them.

1043. Yet in practice we seldom need to go through

this whole process. We may always assume something as known and admitted—something as having been already proved to the satisfaction of those whom we address; and which, consequently, like the succeeding theorems in Mathematics, are as certain to those who have been over them thoroughly, as the ultimate axioms and facts themselves.

In practice we may start from Deductive Judgments.

1044. But as we have seen already (186), it is unimportant whether we come to an ultimate fact, or to an Intuitive Judgment or Axiom; for the fact can always be transferred into a judgment by predicating of its sphere, any one of its properties which we wish to make the Major Term to a Syllogism.

Facts and Axioms resolvable into each other.

SECTION II.

Of Demonstration.

1045. The words "*Demonstration*" and "*demonstrate*," are often used in popular language, with reference to the absolute certainty of the conclusion, rather than to denote the method of argument by which it has been attained.

Popular sense of Demonstration.

1046. Demonstration, however, in the proper sense of the word, is that Method of Proof in which we establish the truth of a Proposition by means of the matter necessarily contained in the conception of its subject. Hence the Predicate must always be either (1) a Material Property, in which case the Proposition expresses an Intuitive Judgment which is analytic *a priori;* or (2) an Implied Property—and in that case the Proposition represents a Deductive Judgment which is synthetic *a priori.*

Strict sense of the word.

1047. In each case the judgment is *a priori*, and implies an analysis of the conception. In the first case it affirms what is given *in* the analysis; and in the second it affirms what is seen, *on* analysis, to be implied in the matter of the conception. And the judgments at each

Based upon Analysis, and constructed of Intuitive Judgments.

step, from the analysis to the conclusion must be intuitive; and of course capable of proof, on the Principle of Identity and Contradiction.

1048. In practice, however, we for the most part adopt a previously made analysis of the conception; and instead of taking each of the steps, one by one, we adopt the results of previous demonstrations. Thus in the successive Theorems in Geometry, we adopt the results of the analysis—that is, the Definition—given in the first two or three pages; and in each successive theorem, we adopt as our starting-point some proposition proved in a preceding theorem.

Use of preceding Propositions.

But beside the Analysis of Conceptions we have also the meaning of words, or *force of terms*, as it is sometimes called, furnishing us the matter for demonstrations.

1049. The force of terms or names is often very great in determining our conceptions of things, and in contributing to our stock of knowledge. Most names instead of being an arbitrary sign for the representation of things, have an etymological force or meaning from which we can draw some inference as to the idea which they are designed to convey—the conception of the thing itself, which was in the mind of the persons who first gave the name to the thing. This is sometimes called the Argument or Inference, *ex vi termini*. It is however strictly demonstrative.

Arguments from the force of Terms.

1050. Demonstrations, *ex vi termini*, may be based either (1) upon the necessary matter of the term, or (2) upon its etymology, or (3) the common acceptation of its meaning.

Based upon the etymology of a word.

1051. We have already seen (212), that whatever is contained necessarily in a term may be predicated of that term. Thus it is *ex vi termini* that a triangle has three angles—that a quadruped has four feet, &c.

On the necessary matter of the term.

1052. And universally the Essentia of any class,

considered as a genus, may be predicated of any individual of that genus. In necessary matter this ground of predication, moreover, extends to all the properties which are common to the class; as from the nature of the matter there can here be no exceptions to a general rule—all triangles must have three angles and three sides—and the sum of their angles must be equal to two right angles, &c.

Difference between necessary and contingent matter in this respect.

1053. But in Contingent Matter this ground of Demonstration must be regarded as most strictly limited to the Essentia of the class. Otherwise it might be applied to an exception from the general rule and result in error.

1054. When this argument is based upon the etymology of the word, we must take heed to the changes which words undergo in their signification, by lapse of time or the peculiar circumstances of their use. Thus *allegiance* is *ad legem, to the law.* But if one should argue, *ex vi termini,* that therefore it does not bind him to his king or chief magistrate, he would err about as widely as if he should argue that because Mr. Mason is Speaker of the House of Representatives, he is the man who does all the speaking in the House.

Arguments based on Etymology unsafe.

1055. The conclusive force of this argument is of course still less, where it is based upon the mere common acceptation of the meaning of terms. Such meanings are often given or taken very much at hap-hazard, or varied when they have once been given by very insignificant and accidental circumstances.

Those based on the common meaning of words still more so.

1056. In order to the absolute certainty which the Demonstration is capable of producing, it is necessary that there be no mistake in regard to the Material or Essential Properties of the Conception from which we demonstrate. And in Mathematics there is for the most part no difference of opinion in regard to them, and of course no possibility

Requisites for an absolute certainty.

of mistake; the essential properties of a triangle, or a circle are the same in the estimation of all men. Every class-conception of necessity has such properties. But in the class-conceptions which we form of objects in the reality of being, there is always also some contingent matter included; and hence there will be diversity in the estimates which men will form of the properties included in the conception—some regarding those as essential, which others will regard as merely accidental and contingent. In this fact is great liability to error, and the great source in fact from which errors in Demonstration proceed.

Reason why it cannot be had in Contingent Matter.

1057. We must also remember that a property which is only accidental to the conception of an object for one purpose, may become essential to its conception for another. *Right-angledness*, for example, is accidental to the conception of triangle, but essential to the conception of the class or species which we call "*right-angled triangles.*" So "unsupportedness" is purely accidental to the conception of ponderable bodies. But it is an essential property of the class-conception, formed for the purpose of investigating and proving the fact, and the law of gravitation.

Accidental Properties become necessary.

1058. And as a general rule, we may say that any property by means or on account of which we may include its substance in any predicate, is an essential property in the conception which we form of that subject with reference to the use of that predicate.

General Rule.

1059. When we enlarge the matter of any class-conception, and thereby narrow its sphere by taking into our class-conception another as a Material property, we are enabled to proceed still farther and demonstrate still other implied properties, which have been brought in by means of the newly admitted Material property. Thus, suppose to the Material properties of triangle, which are two,

Increasing the Necessary Matter, enlarges the sphere of Demonstration.

three-sidedness and *three-angledness*, we add the one more, *right-angledness*. We now have a narrower sphere, but we are able to demonstrate many properties of right-angled triangles—the species—which we could not demonstrate, and which were not true of triangles—the genus merely.

1060. But besides Mathematics, a large part of Astronomy, Mechanics, and what are called the *Mixed Sciences* generally, are largely indebted to Demonstration. The same is true in Logic, in Ethics. These are, and of necessity must be to a very great extent, if not wholly *a priori* and demonstrative sciences.

Demonstration in all Sciences.

1061. Logic has especially been called "the Mathematics of Thought." And in Logic, as in Mathematics, we must prove the legitimacy and force of both our Formulæ and our Methods *a priori*, before we are entitled to place any confidence in the Conclusions or results to which they may lead us.

In Logic.

1062. We have already remarked that Arithmetic, Algebra, and the Calculus, are but Methods of Investigation in Discrete Quantity (883). But we are obliged to justify the Methods by Demonstrations. Take the Rule of Addition, of Subtraction, of Multiplication, of Division, of Involution or Evolution, or the Binomial Theorem, or any other, and we see at once that they are but Methods of finding results. But the Methods are all justified *a priori*, by inferences from the Necessary Matter of the Conception; that is, from the Material Properties of the Methods themselves. We say, for example, that the square of any Binomial, as $a + b$, is the square of the first term plus twice the product of the two, plus the square of the second, or $a^2 + 2ab + b^2$. And this is shown to be true from the nature of the Process or Method itself, as will be seen by a reference to any treatise on Algebra, where the Binomial Theorem is discussed.

Methods must be justified by Demonstration.

1063. So in Ethics. We lay it down as a rule that

the communications between man and man should be based upon veracity and benevolence. We prove it from the class-conception of society, having proved or assumed that man, as a species, can live only in society. Thus, suppose the contrary, that deception and hate were the conditions or laws of human association. Deception and hate would destroy society, not only by rendering association among men impossible—but hate would take the life of man, beginning with the weakest and most defenceless, until only one, and he the strongest, were left alive. But one does not make "*society*." Hence, on the principle of contradiction (422), we affirm veracity and benevolence to be necessary rules of morality.

Demonstration in Ethics.

1064. The same holds true of all class-conceptions in every department of knowledge. There are certain properties not contained but implied in the class-conception, which may be predicated of every individual comprehended under that conception. I have instanced the laws of Motion as predicable on the class-conception of Matter (791).

Demonstration in all departments of knowledge.

1065. In Theology, also, we may predicate "*sin*" of the class-conception, man, as a being having the power of choice, finite in capacity, surrounded by objects of desire, some of which are prohibited.

Illustration from Theology.

1066. Now in every department of knowledge, just in proportion as our class-conceptions become distinct, definite, and adequate, including all that belongs to the class-conception and nothing that does not, does our knowledge of the objects in that department become a matter of insight, or of *a priori* intuition and affirmation. And upon this part of what we know of the objects in any science, does the science itself depend for its existence as a science.

Sciences become a matter of insight as they become more perfect.

1067. It is worthy of note that Demonstration being occupied with necessary matter exclusively, we may have a universal conclusion when,

A Universal Conclusion from Particular Premises.

as is usually the case, the Minor Premise is Particular, or rather Individual, including in fact only one instance. Thus in regard to the side of the triangle,* and the position of a straight line,† we have no hesitation in including in our conclusion all sides of all possible triangles and all possible straight lines, although in our demonstration our attention may have been confined to a single case alone. This results from the nature of the matter, and is more obvious in general practice than in the statement just made, for then a diagram is usually drawn, and the line, &c., is designated as line AB, or by some other such sign.

1068. It is obvious from this slight examination that Demonstration is not a Formula, but a Method in which any Formula may be used as bests suits the taste or the matter at our disposal.

Demonstration a Method in which any Formula may be used.

1069. It should be distinctly observed, however, that nothing accidental enters into the Demonstration—that is, nothing except what was either contained or necessarily implied in the class-conception of the subjects of the several propositions. Thus when we speak of a triangle, all the matter that is contained in the conception is "a figure made by three straight lines so meeting as to make three angles." The Differentia right-angled, isosceles, equilateral, scalene, &c., does not enter into the Demonstration, concerning triangles merely. But as triangle is the genus which includes all of these species, when we have proved the proposition of the genus, it must hold true of every included species.

No Contingent Matter enters into the scope of Judgments in the Process of Demonstration.

1070. The Demonstration, moreover, holds true only of the reality of truth, represented by the Conception, and not by any means or necessarily of any diagram

* "Any one side of a triangle is less than the sum of the two other sides."

† "A straight line let fall from any point without a straight line perpendicular to that line is the shortest line that can be let fall from the point to the straight line."

which we may draw, or of any piece of matter which may be brought into the form of a triangle. For not the diagram nor the piece of matter was the subject of our Demonstration; they serve only to illustrate and represent it at most, and the conclusion holds good of them only in proportion as they conform to the conception.

1071. An Hypothesis, as we have seen (827), is a supposition or guess put into the place of a fact or a judgment, in the structure of an argument or system of any kind.

Hypotheses fraudulently used.

Of the case in which hypotheses are unintentionally mistaken for facts or ascertained truths, or of those cases in which they are intentionally but fraudulently and surreptitiously introduced instead of fact and truth we have nothing here to say: the first constitutes a fallacy in matter, and the latter is a mere trick of sophistry.

1072. But there is a legitimate use of hypotheses in Demonstrations. Thus in Mathematics we have a theorem enunciated—we suppose cases, for the sake of testing it. We may suppose the contradictory of the theorem and disprove it, thus proving the theorem. Or we may suppose various cases to test the comprehensiveness and adaptability of the principle enunciated. In the first-named case either the hypothesis or the theorem is impossible and absurd, and the method adopted enables us to determine what is absurd and by consequence which is true. In the last case the only limit to the right to make suppositions is that they be possible. For as in necessary matter there can be no exceptions, so any rule or principle must meet all conceivable cases coming under that rule or principle. If, therefore, we can suppose one that is possible, it is just as good for the sake of any argument claiming to be based on *a priori* grounds, as if instead of being merely supposed, it were actually real. For in necessary matter all conceivable things are possible, and so must be included

All possibilities real in Necessary Matter.

within the comprehensiveness of the class-conception.*

1073. But in contingent matter it is far otherwise. Here we are hardly competent to judge of the possibility of what may become or may have become real. And in moral matter the danger of resorting to hypotheses is still greater.

Not so in Contingent Matter.

1074. In contingent matter we may use hypotheses or supposed cases for the sake of illustration. But even then we must be careful that they are not only supposable but also possible. We never do and never can understand sufficiently the designs of the Creator and the limits to the possibility of the realities of being, to be very confident in our opinions as to the possible and the impossible in contingent matter. There are always influences and principles at work of which we know but very little, and others of whose very existence we know nothing, except the constant appearance of unaccountable events and facts—events and facts which in our ignorance of these principles we ascribe to chance—to render a resort to hypotheses as elements in the construction of arguments and systems in all cases of contingent matter unsafe.

Legitimate use of Hypotheses in Contingent Matter.

1075. From the account which we have now given of Demonstration, it will be seen that while in some cases, as in Mathematics, Logic, Ethics, &c., it will constitute the whole of the Proof, it will also enter more or less extensively into all the other Methods as subordinate parts. For in all there must be some reliance upon or reference to the force of the terms, some analysis and development of the matter necessarily contained or implied in the conception of the subject of the Argument. It is this part of an argument which gives it much of what it has of clearness and cogency. If it does not give the

Demonstration in all Methods of Proof.

* In fact it has been held by one class of philosophers that Mathematics is based wholly on hypotheses.

argument force, it makes the force which it has, felt, and often carries conviction where it would not otherwise be produced. I know of no illustration of this remark so good as is to be found every where in WEBSTER's Argumentative Speeches. And no mind, so far as I have known, has ever surpassed his in the capacity to see what was necessarily contained or implied in the conception of any subject, and to develope it with overwhelming force of conviction.

Necessary in all sciences as proof of its fundamental Principles.

1076. And in all sciences it will be found that before the facts can be constructed into a science at all, some fundamental Principles or Axioms* must be evolved by analysis of the conception of subject-matter, and proved by Demonstration. Methods of Investigation may be necessary to precede this step in order to give us adequate conceptions of the subject-matter from which to evolve and demonstrate the fundamental principles. But these principles themselves must be demonstrated *a priori* before the science can receive any permanent or satisfactory form.

SECTION III.

Of Deduction.

Deduction.

1077. By Deduction we mean the Method or Process of proving a Proposition with a less comprehensive subject, as a Conclusion from one with a more comprehensive subject, by the subsumption of the less under the more comprehensive—the Predicates of both being common. Thus in Barbara:

M is P,
S is M,
∴ S is P.

* The difference between an *Axiom* and a *Maxim* is, that the latter is a *general* truth obtained by classification and induction to a maximum genus; whereas an Axiom is a *necessary* truth, and may be either intuitive or obtained by demonstration from the necessary matter of the class-conception of the subject.

Here S is subsumed as a class under M in the Minor Premise, whence it follows that M is the more comprehensive Sphere of the two, and that P is predicable of S if it may be predicated of M.

1078. Deduction forms a large part in the development and completion of any science. A few leading principles are ascertained from observation and experience, and from them deduction is made to particular facts with much more ease and certainty even, in most cases than an observation of the fact itself could be made. And in many cases, as in Physiology, the fact is beyond the reach of any observation; or in others, as in Astronomy for instance, it will not come round in centuries perhaps. Thus the details of any science will be made out to a considerable extent by deduction from its general principles.

The Sphere of Deduction.

1079. In the practical application of sciences the Method is always deductive. Even those books which are written with the most especial reference to application to practice, never do and never can mention and enumerate all the *individual* cases. The most they can do is to specify classes of cases, and the more nearly in their enumeration of classes—that is, in their division and classification—they approach to the *Infima Species*, the more practical do they become in the ordinary sense of the word.

The Method is always deductive in the application of science.

1080. In that case the Infima Species is the Middle Term, the particular individual case to which the application is to be made is the Minor Term, and the other term, whether Subject or Predicate, which enters into the "Precept," as it is called, with the Infima Species as the Middle Term, is the Major Premise.

1081. Thus the physician examining a patient decides the case to be intermittent fever. His science has taught him that quinine is required in intermittent fevers. Accordingly he prescribes quinine. His reasoning, stated at length, is as follows:

Illustration in Pharmacy.

Intermittent fevers require quinine;
This case is an intermittent fever:
∴ This case requires quinine.

1082. It will be seen at once that this is precisely the form in which the principles of science are applied to useful purposes.

1083. In the same way established principles and laws are applied to new cases. For example, in Astronomy the laws of motion, the relation of distance to time in the periodic revolutions of planets, comets, &c., are so well known that the moment a new one is discerned, the astronomer proceeds by way of demonstration to determine from those elements of its sphere nearly all that can be known about it, without waiting for the much slower and more tedious process of observing these revolutions, as they occur in the course of centuries of our years.

In Astronomy.

1084. It will have been observed that one leading object in Methods of Investigation is to determine definitely and adequately the class-conceptions which are based upon the nature of things in the reality of being. It has been remarked* that just in proportion as any science progresses from its inception and the first rude accumulation of elementary facts, does it become more and more deductive and even demonstrative in its Methods. Our class-conceptions of its subject-matter by this means become more distinct, definite, and adequate—more conformed to the constitutive Idea of the classes, more comprehensive of individuals and of phenomena—and our confidence in the results and teachings of that science become proportionally great.

All Sciences become more deductive as they become more perfect.

* MILL'S *Logic*, Book II. Chap. IV. § 6.—See also DEVEY, Book V. Chap. I. §. 5.

SECTION IV.

Of the Argument from Authority.

1085. There are many Propositions, which from their relating to subjects above our comprehension, or from their being beyond the reach of our observation, and differing so far from what we can observe and know in this state of being that Analogy fails to be a safe guide, can be proved only by an appeal to the Authority of God in the Revelation which He has been pleased to make.

Authority of Revelation.

1086. Then we have also another class of Propositions in which *stat pro ratione voluntas*, where the will of some Authority so determining, is the ground and the only ground on which we are obliged to receive them as true, because they have been so declared by a competent authority.

Authority of Governance.

1087. Of this kind are the *laws* of a State, whether enactments of the legislature, or decisions of the courts, for all citizens; the laws, canons, rubrics, &c., of a Church for all its members; the constitutions, rules, and by-laws of any voluntary society or corporation for economical, social, moral, political, philanthropic or religious purposes, upon the members of those societies or corporations as members and during their membership.

Authority of only limited obligation.

1088. Propositions of the kind now under consideration are authority, and therefore to be received as true only in relation to the particular things which come under the jurisdiction of the authority, and for those persons over whom that authority justly extends. Thus Revelation is final to all the creatures of God to whom it is made; the authority of the state to all citizens and subjects; that of a voluntary society to those only who voluntarily belong to the society.

1089. There are some spheres in which by the very nature of the case this Means of Proof is made necessary, and is the only one that is proper. In Statute Law and Theology, for instance, the *dicta* of the proper Authority must be an end to controversy. Any arguments on general grounds, as to what *ought to be true*, can do nothing more at most than to create a presumption in favor of any doctrine.

Authority our only ground in some cases.

1090. Besides the foregoing, the common sense or consent of mankind, as well as the admissions of those against whom we are arguing, become first principles of the nature of authority within certain limits, and to certain persons the argument from the admissions of parties *ex concessis*, is scarcely any thing more than an *argumentum ad hominem*, and for that I will refer the reader to Sec. XI. of this Chapter below.

Concessions and common opinion.

1091. But the common opinion of men is an Authority or first principle, on which a large part of our most important deductions are based, especially in practical matters, and among those whose minds have never been trained to look into the *philosophical* grounds of their actions.

Extent of Common Opinion as a Principle.

These are commonly called Arguments from Common Sense, *sensus communis omnibus*, and their value has been very variously estimated.

Common Sense of various values in different Spheres.

1092. In matters of Religion, if man is to be regarded as a fallen and depraved being, it is to be distrusted and scanned very closely. In fact it can never be used except as confirmatory of the Argument from authority, or as serving the rhetorical purpose of removing a prejudice or supposed antecedent improbability. But if man is not fallen or depraved, his common sense must be as infallible an indication of the law and will of God (*vox populi vox Dei*), as the facts and changes of the physical world are of His laws and will in relation to matter.

Religion.

1093. In Polity and Ethics the common sense of man is of more value; for they relate to matters that are more comprehensible, and which have of necessity been not only subjects of reflection, but also and moreover they have been tested by the experience of all and in all ages. What has been thus found to be best and true, is most likely to stand the trial to which it can be brought. The latter schools of philosophy have professedly regarded this common sense as of great value as a standard of truth.

In Polity and Ethics.

1094. In the Natural Sciences it has been found to be an unsafe guide. It always depends upon the appearances of things, while in many cases the reality lies much deeper and is often very unlike the appearance. The contrast between the common belief in regard to the motion of the Sun and the Earth is familiar to all, and a case in point.

In the Natural Sciences.

1095. But in matters which depend upon *a priori* conceptions or upon facts, the appeal to common opinion is out of place. By authority, however, in this connection, I do not mean testimony to the reality of facts. Such testimony we must use and depend upon. But testimony to a fact is one thing, and opinion or inference from the fact is quite another. And the difference between them is one of the things which it is most important to notice. Testimony is the means by which we know what are the Principles which have been established by Authority. Thus in Religion, God himself is the Authority; and the Scriptures are the Testimony which make known to us what has emanated from that Authority. In Law, the State is the Authority; and the statute-books and the decisions of the Courts are the Testimony from which we learn what are the laws established by that Authority.

In the Pure Sciences.

Distinction between Authority and Testimony.

1096. Hence, although we may use testimony in the Natural Sciences, in History, &c., Authority, strictly speaking, we do not use. We use testimony as a means of ascertaining facts, whether they be the facts which any Authority has made such, as when a State enacts a law, that enact-

Legitimate use of Testimony.

ment is a fact; or whether they are the facts evolved in the history of man and the world, or finally the facts of Nature.

Testimony often called Authority. 1097. Yet even Testimony is often called Authority—an authority for believing the facts to which it bears witness only. We speak of believing a fact in Roman history on the authority of Livy or of Tacitus, when in strictness of language we mean the testimony of those writers. This distinction between Authority and Testimony is indispensable to a right apprehension of Methods of Investigation and Argument in which they are used. In what sense.

In what way Testimony can prove an opinion or law. 1098. Testimony can prove facts only, and a law or an opinion only as the facts themselves prove the opinion. Testimony may prove the acts and words of our Lord, as recorded in the Holy Scriptures. But these acts and words, *as facts*, must prove the Revelation, and that that which is given as a Revelation of the Will of God is really His will. Testimony can prove the enactment of a law, or the issuing a command—but the enactment itself, and the giving of the command, as facts must prove, if it is proved at all, that the law enacted and the command given are laws and commands of Authority.

Testimony when a ground of belief. 1099. Hence in Mathematics Testimony is never used as a means of Teaching or of Proof. All must rest on the personal intuition of the learner. In the Natural Sciences we have to depend upon Testimony for a large part of our facts. But the facts speak for themselves. Testimony cannot even prove an *opinion*, but only the fact that such and such an one held it as an opinion. It does not prove the opinion to be true; and all that can be gained by the opinion of others in the fields of scientific inquiry, is at most a *probable ground of action, when we must act and can have nothing better to act upon.*

And of Action. 1100. Thus a physician, in a critical case, may act upon a mere opinion of a distinguished *physician*, provided there is no prescription for it which experience has satisfactorily proved, and where, if he does not act at all, only the worst of consequences can ensue.

1101. In all appeals to Authority, and to Testimony also, howsoever and wheresoever expressed, the true meaning of the words in which it is expressed is of material importance, and of course one of the first things to be obtained. Language itself is but an imperfect instrument for the expression of thought, and often it is used without clearness in the mind of him who uses it, and without any successful effort to make it as adequate to the expression of the thought as its capabilities would allow.

Necessity for Interpretation in the use of Authority.

1102. The process by which we evolve a man's thoughts from his words, is called *Interpretation* or *Hermeneutics*. Something of interpretation is always necessary when we read. But when such words are used as we are familiar with, and the clear thought is clearly expressed in familiar phrase, the process of interpretation is performed so quickly and so easily, that we are wholly unconscious of it. It is only when it becomes difficult, and takes time, and causes delay and doubt, that we become conscious of the effort, and feel the need of rules and principles to guide us.

Interpretation or Hermeneutics.

A few of these leading and most important principles we will now briefly specify.

1103. (1) In the first place, wherever there is one plain and obvious meaning to a passage, that is to be adopted.

Words must be taken in their obvious meaning.

Seldom, indeed, will it be expedient or allowable to go behind the text itself to any evidence or indications of what the author may have *intended* to say, provided his language is clear and appears to have been used by one who knew how to express whatever thought he may have intended to communicate. The choice of words and expressions was with him, and he must be responsible for what he has clearly and plainly said.

1104. (2) But secondly, where language is ambiguous, or the meaning of a passage is doubtful, we are to interpret in accordance with truth and right sentiment if possible.

Ambiguous language, how interpreted.

This rule is charitable enough, and may sometimes give one more than his due. But it is better to do so than otherwise. Let the error, if there be one, be put down to the account of charity.

1105. (3) Thirdly, we must take heed to the *usus loquendi:*

The usus loquendi.

(*a*) Of the author himself.

(*b*) Of the sect or people to which he belongs.

There is scarcely a writer or speaker who has not some peculiarities in style, and in the use of some of the words which will occur in the course of his writings or speeches. The exact meaning of such words, as used by any man, is best obtained from a study of his own writings; or secondly, in case there are none, in those of the sect or school to which he belongs. Thus the word "Idea" means one thing, in Plato's use of it, another in Mr. Locke's, and still another in the writings of some modern philosophers, as Kant and Cousin. If, therefore, we should undertake to read the writings of any one of these authors, with the sense which the other attaches to the word whenever it occurs, we not only should fail to find our author very clear and intelligible, but we should deduce from his statements conclusions which his words, when understood *as he intended them*, would not justify. It would be easy to accumulate a long list of words, illustrating this point, but we have not room.

1106. (4) The fourth rule is, that technical terms must be explained by the science to which their use belongs.

Technical Terms.

Every science has, and of necessity must have some terms to which those who are proficient in that science will attach a meaning, somewhat different from that which it has among those who are unacquainted with its scientific use. The word "switch," as used by boys at their plays, and by a railroad manager, has two entirely distinct senses. In fact no one can read any treatise on a scientific subject with which he is unacquainted without finding new words, and old words used with new significations. Lexicographers, in preparing their Dictionaries, derive their definitions from the sources now indicated, or at least should do so. But in no case can a Dictionary give all the technical words with all their meanings. Let any one, for instance, attempt to find in any Dictionary a definition of the terms used by sailors at sea, by printers in the printing-office, to say nothing of the technicalities of Law, Medicine, and Theology, and he will see the necessity and reasonableness of the rule of interpretation now laid down.

1107. (5) All language used in deeds, wills, and other documents, conveying property from one to another, are to be interpreted in favor of the grantor, if there is any of ambiguity.

Language of giving and conveying.

The obvious reason for this, is that the right of property requires that no one should be presumed to have intended to give away any more than he expressed his intention to give.

1108. But to this there are several modifications; and the first is in conveying away any object, we convey with it whatever is inseparable from it, even though it be not mentioned; and secondly, as a grant is seldom if ever made except for a consideration of something in return, the amount of this consideration may sometimes be taken into account to determine the true sense of the grant.

Modifications to the rule.

1109. (6) Oaths are always to be understood (*in sensu imponentis*), in the sense of the authority which imposes the oath.

Oaths.

Oaths are given to secure the fidelity and truthfulness of those on whom they are imposed. But if those who receive the oaths may take advantage of any obscurity or ambiguity which may exist in the language of the oath itself, or which by ingenuity and prejudice persons interested can cause to exist, the obligations of an oath and the very purposes for which they are imposed will be at an end. One has a right to know, before taking an oath, what it means and what it is designed to impose upon him. And although he would be justified in some cases in refusing the oath and submitting to the consequences, yet in no case would one be justified in taking the oath and then perjuring himself, under the plea that the oath is susceptible of another construction, than that designed by the authority imposing it, or that he chose to put another construction upon it.

Laws, Edicts, restraining liberty.

1110. (7) All laws, edicts, &c., restraining personal liberty and the right of private judgment, are to be interpreted as favorably as possible to those who are thus restrained.

All law and authority is of necessity and essentially a restraint upon the personal liberty of those who are subject to the law or authority. We seldom speak of it in this light, however, except where the restraint becomes greater than there is any good reason for. But as such restraints should be as little as the cause of order and morality will allow, we are to interpret all laws which go beyond those requirements in favor of the subject, and give him the benefit of any ambiguity that there may be in the language in which the laws are expressed.

Commissions and patents of privilege.

1111. (8) Commissions and other documents conferring authority or privilege, are to be regarded as Exclusives (*expressio unius, exclusio alterius*). This is substantially the same as the fifth rule above, in a different application. No one is *presumed* to have any authority over another, or special privileges and exemptions. If he has them there must be proof of it, and the mention of one or more in the words that confer the authority or privilege, leaves the others in possession of no more than they would have had if no such document had been issued. The commission of one man in a company does not constitute all the privates captains. Nor does the appointment of one man to be a justice of the peace make the whole neighborhood to be esquires.

1112. (9) When the quantity of a proposition is doubtful we are to take it at its least value, unless the conclusions of the argument, or the truth of the statement require otherwise.

The Quantity of a Proposition.

Thus in Wayland's Political Economy occurs the remark, which is universal in its form, "*All men are not merchants.*" But truth requires that it be considered as particular negative—that is, "Some men are not merchants." And again; from the connection in which it occurs, it appears to have been designed as a contradictory of a supposed preceding universal affirmation, "All men are merchants." Again, the following occurs in a work before me, "Abstinence from eating flesh had reference to the divine institution of sacrifice;" the author's argument, as well as the ordinary principles of interpretation, require that the proposition should be regarded as universal. But the truth of the proposition would in that case be a matter of doubt at least, and most likely the proposition would be false if taken universally. But if the proposition had occurred where no use was made of it, requiring it to be regarded as a universal proposition, it would have passed without notice as a statement generally true, perhaps, but yet only the expression of a particular judgment, "Abstinence" being regarded as not a distributed term; the abstract term being used for the concrete plural.

1113. (10) Parables and metaphors are to be construed with special reference to the design for which they were used.

Parables and Metaphors.

Parables, metaphors, fables, and all of that kind of illustrations, are based upon analogy and not identity of cases. But in all analogies there are points of diversity, and the case upon which the parable is based is assumed to be identical only in the point to be illustrated by it. In that point there must be identity, else the illustration fails; beyond that point there must be some diversity. These points must not be brought into the illustration, nor may its force and appropriateness be objected to on their account.

1114. In the Parable of the Rich Man and Lazarus (Luke xvi.), for instance, the main design, undoubtedly, was to show the impossibility of changing one's doom by repentance after death. And it would be unsafe and unwise to attempt to infer any thing further from it concerning the condition of man in the future state. We can hardly go so far with safety, (I think,) as to infer from it that the two classes of persons represented by Lazarus and the Rich Man, are in a condition to hold conversation with each other, or with those of the other class at all.

Obiter dicta.

1115. (11) Mere *obiter dicta* are never to be regarded as of equal authority with the assertions made to the point directly before the mind.

In nearly all discourse and reasoning there is *a* leading object, to which the attention is especially directed. The assertions bearing directly on that point are always to be regarded as the most mature and carefully guarded opinions of the author. But there are almost always expressions dropped by the way, called *obiter dicta*, on incidental and collateral matters, to which the attention is not directed with so much energy as to the main point, and consequently these *obiter dicta* are less valuable as expressions of opinion or authority, than those to which the attention is mainly directed.

Special Rules in nearly every department.

1116. The science of Interpretation is a comprehensive one, and cannot be fully treated in this place. And as in each special department of inquiry, where we have to depend upon Testimony and Authority, some special rules and cautions are found necessary, I have aimed above to give only such general rules as seemed necessary to my present purpose, and of the most extensive application.

SECTION V.

Of the Appeal to Facts.

1117. The Appeal to Facts, as a Method of Argument, is in some respects the converse of the foregoing Methods. We reason from Facts to Principles rather than from Principles to Facts.

Appeal to Facts.

1118. These Facts may be introduced by way of Induction, Analogy, Example, or as Contraries, Exceptions,* Circumstances, Cause or Effect. But in all cases they require the force of Principles lying deeper than the facts themselves, in order to render their argumentative force of any value.

Facts how introduced.

1119. I have already in the last Chapter (Section VII.) said concerning reasoning from Cause to Effect—that is, concerning the appeal to Facts as Causes or Effects, all that I shall deem it advisable to say in the present Treatise. I will, therefore, proceed at once to consider the general Principles involved, and the Methods of proceeding in reasoning from Facts in the various other conceptions of them.

Cause and Effect.

1120. An important distinction is made between a law and a general fact. Thus it is a general fact, proved by Induction, that "all Canidæ are carnivorous;"—"all bodies gravitate towards the Earth." But that which lies under this general fact and determines the manner in which the Cause shall act, is called the law. Hence the law of gravitation is that which accounts for the general facts of gravity. It is the law which produces, or rather guides the cause in producing the general fact of a carnivorous habit of life in animals, constituted by their Creator

General Facts and Laws.

* For facts introduced by way of Exceptions, see Sec. IX. below. Since they always presuppose that to which they are exceptions, I have chosen to consider them as means of disproof; that is, disproving the universality of that rule in view of which alone they can be regarded as exceptions.

for that habit of life. Hence the law always implies the fact and the fact the law, and the two are often confounded.

Induction must go beyond a mere classification.

1121. We place but very little confidence, however, in any mere induction of facts, unless we can go a little farther. The Formula of Induction itself, as will be seen (569), is an undistributed Middle, and becomes valid at all only by a sort of transfer of the matter over into the domain of *necessary matter*.

How accomplished.

1122. This we accomplish by means of principles, logically antecedent to all induction, and lying deeper in the subject-matter than Induction itself can reach. By this means we can extend our predication from what is and has been to what will be. We pass from the general fact to the law.*

The first of these Principles which we shall consider is the UNIFORMITY OF NATURE—the second is that of FINAL CAUSES.

"Nature" in what sense used.

1123. We use the word "Nature" [*Natura*, from *nascor*], as a collective term, including all those realities of being in the external world, whose existence is contingent, and which are not the product of human agency as their Efficient Cause. Thus a blow with the hand would not be a fact in Nature, since it proceeds from the will of man as its

* We have given above, p. 249 *n.*, Aristotle's definition of Induction, TOP. B. I. Cap. XII. In the Prior Analytics, Book II. Cap. XXII. Aristotle speaks of Induction as a means of proving one extreme through the other, i. e. to prove the Major Term *of the Middle*, by means of the Minor. Thus he gives for example :

Men, horses, and mules are long lived ;
Men, horses, and mules are void of bile.

If then, says he, (men, horses, and mules) and (long-livers) may be converted "without excluding the Middle,"—that is, if (long-lived) is not a more comprehensive sphere than (men, horses, and mules), we may have the conclusion :

All animals void of bile are long-lived ;

But this is the very difficulty ; the Major Premise can never be converted in that way. The Predicate is always comprehensive of more than the inducted particulars, and it is precisely this peculiarity of induction that we wish to account for and justify.

Efficient Cause. But the growth of a blade of corn would be a fact in Nature, although the growth might depend upon the fact that man had planted it, or still keeps the soil in a condition to continue its growth towards maturity. In this case man is not the Efficient but only the Occasional Cause.

1124. By the *Uniformity* of Nature we mean what may be stated generally as the fact, that the same causes acting under the same laws, and *cæteris paribus*—(that is, all the modifying circumstances being the same,) will produce the same effects.*

What is meant by "*uniformity.*"

1125. But let us try to get a little more definite idea of this uniformity, and the grounds upon which it rests.

It is, doubtless, first suggested by the facts in the external world. Thus, for instance, a tree always produces leaves and fruit of the same kind. So, too, with the offspring of animals. Each new individual is not the germ of a new class or species. Nor does it even belong to a species different from that from which it derived its origin. In short the objects of nature at once suggest the classifications, by means of Essentia and Differentia, which have already been spoken of as so advantageous to science.

The idea of Uniformity how first obtained.

* Mr. Mill thinks (besides expressing some doubts about the Uniformity of Nature) that what we know or believe of it we have learned from experience. In a certain sense this is true. And using words still in the same sense all that we ever know is learned from experience. But then we may easily get to be wiser than our teacher. We learn *from* experience a great deal more than there is *in* experience. Experience is confined to the past, and generalizations upon its facts can give us only what has been. But by induction from the facts of experience we infer what is to be in the future, and every where in the reality of being constituted like that in which we are placed. From *mere* uniformity we do not expect its continuance, as Mr. Mill has indirectly shown. From the fact that the first five or six of the Presidents of the United States retired from office at the age of sixty-six, the people of the country formed no expectation whatever that such would continue for ever to be the uniform fact with regard to the age of the retiring Presidents. Hence it is something not given *in* experience which leads us to expect a continuance of this uniformity in some cases and not in others. This "something," call it what you will, is what we are now inquiring after, and it must be *a priori*.

1126. But if they suggest to our minds these classifications, it must be because they proceeded from a class-conception in a mind like our own, at least in respect to the faculty of constructing such conceptions. If the words I use suggest to the mind of the reader or hearer a thought, it must be because they proceeded from the same thought, and are used as a means of expressing it in my own mind.

Implies a creating mind *essentially* like ours.

1127. Let us then consider the operations of the human mind. Take the case of an artisan. He forms the plan of a piece of mechanism, a watch for instance—that plan is his class-conception, his object being not to produce one watch only but a number—a supply for the demand of his customers. Hence we have a species of watches agreeing exactly with each other, so far as the properties included in the class-conception are concerned, but differing in the accidents of having been finished at different times, by different hands perhaps—made in part of different materials, some having gold and others silver cases, &c.; and differing also in size and ornamental decorations. Now, suppose the same artisan to form a different plan or class-conception, one differing therefore in some of the essential parts of a watch, as in the form of the escapement, &c., and we shall have from that model another species of watch.

An analogy in the operations of man.

1128. Now before creation, the Creative Mind must have formed such class-conceptions for each species of created objects; and each individual in a species is like all the others in all the properties which were included in that class-conception; and differing from others only in those which, from their not being included in the original class-conception, are called accidental.*

The class-conceptions of the Creative Mind.

* This illustration of the operation of the Divine Mind might be carried much farther. One point more only, however, will I notice in passing.

It is not altogether voluntary with man what elements he will include

1129. We may then say that *the uniformity of Nature consists in the agreement of all objects within the same species in the matter of their class-conception.* And our Induction is but the process by which we make our conceptions of the material species adequate. We get one of its elements. We classify upon that; then find another property common to all the individuals in that species which have fallen under our observation—predicate this latter property of the species by means of the specific name which we have given it, and call the Proposition so made a statement of a law of Nature. It is an indication of the Divine will and conception; and therefore we expect all individuals in any class to conform to the essentials of that class—which essentials we are learning one after another by Induction. If there were no such class-conception, there could be no classification; no Uniformity of Nature; consequently no Induction.

The Uniformity of Nature stated.

in his class-conceptions. Having fixed upon some which are material to it, there are others that are necessarily implied, and others that are accidental—over which, however, he has no control, any further than his own hand may be employed in making the objects in the class. Thus in a watch, if he would have a lever escapement, he must have a hair-spring, whether he would or not, he must have wheels and pinions to graduate the motion; and he must have the liability to break, to wear, &c., as inseparable from all the materials that man has at his command to use. And as all the watches of that species are to be made by himself, or under his control, he can control the purely accidental properties of size, ornament, &c. But beyond that he has no control over what is accidental.

In Nature, however, there is but one Creator and Producer. All those properties of the objects of nature, therefore, which so far as we can see, are only accidental to the class-conception, are yet under the control of the Will of Him who designed and still produces them; and in all of them, therefore, He can secure a perfect uniformity, and make them to be for all practical purposes, not accidental but essential.

Hence individuals in the natural species, as apples, pears, peaches, dogs, horses, men, &c., &c., do not differ so much from each other, or from their idea or class-conception as the works of man, watches, hats, boots, coats, &c., &c., nor even so much as the diagrams which we draw to represent the mathematical figures, triangle, circle, ellipse, &c., differ from one another, even among those which are designed to represent precisely the same conception. Always do they come short of the conception to some extent, come short of realizing it as an idea; and go beyond it in presenting to the mind for its consideration, properties which were not contained in the conception.

1130. Now whatever is necessary to the proof of any Proposition is in some way a Premise to that Proposition. Hence the Uniformity of Nature being necessary to the belief in the result of any Induction, that uniformity must enter in some way as Premise to the Conclusion from the Induction, when announced as a Law of Nature.

Whatever is necessary to a Conclusion, is a Premise to that Conclusion.

1131. Using these principles as Premises, we are able to complete the Induction into a Syllogism as follows. For Major Premise we have, "All similar instances in Nature are governed by the same law."

Induction completed into a Syllogism.

For Minor Premise we may say, "The cat, the dog, the wolf are instances of carnivorous animals, similar in having canine teeth."

∴ All animals with canine teeth, will be instances of the same law, viz., carnivorous animals—that is, "All animals with canine teeth will be carnivorous." *

1132. But if the Major Premise were removed or

* It has been pretty extensively held that Induction is a Method of Argumentation totally unlike the Syllogistic, and one which can never be reduced to a Syllogism. Sir William Hamilton was of this opinion. Now there can be no doubt that Induction, *as a Method of Investigation*, is a Method radically different from *Deduction* or the Syllogism. But the Induction, as an investigation of the predicates of Natural Species, is a very different thing from the verification of that Method, or the use which we make of the Induction as a means of proof. The Binomial theorem is one thing, the use we make of it in practice quite another—and the reasoning and principles by which we verify the theorem is another still—and quite as distinct from the theorem itself.

Now Methods of Investigation cannot be reduced to the Logical Formula. The Formulæ are the Means to be used in the Methods of Proof, and whatever can be proved must be proved by some Formula—one that has been catalogued and examined, or one that yet remains to be entered upon our list. But Methods of Investigation *prove* nothing.

There can be no need of the accumulation of authorities or of argument to show, not that the Induction, but that our confidence in its results—and hence Induction, as a Method of Proof, depends upon the uniformity of Nature. This point is nowhere denied or doubted. If this be so, this Uniformity, stated as a Principle or Premise, must be the Major Premise in all Proof from Induction; and the basis of the verification of Induction itself as a Method of Investigation.

denied, no confidence whatever would be placed in the Conclusion. That is, take away the Uniformity of Nature, and we should place no confidence in Induction as a means of Proof, or as indicating a law upon which we could base any predictions or expectations for the future.

No Induction without the Major Premise.

1133. We have seen that Induction is the Method which most appropriately belongs to the facts in the reality of being, and within the range of what is called Nature—including as it does all facts which are not considered as depending *directly* upon the will and volitions of a moral agent. But inasmuch as the will of man is subject to no such law of necessity and uniformity, as the course of Nature, and inasmuch as the courses of events in God's providential government of the world are to such an extent above our knowledge and comprehension, the facts or events in each of these two Spheres are hardly to be considered as within the province of Induction. We can indeed in this way learn much of the nature of man, and of the plans and principles of God's moral government, but not enough to enable us to speak with the same confidence as we may use in regard to the facts of Nature. That God is just, we know indeed as well as we know any truth of Natural Science, and that He will punish any particular sin we may also know with the same certainty. But the particular time, way, and means we cannot infer from any induction of the past with any thing that approaches a physical certainty.

Induction belongs to Physical Matter.

But not to Moral Matter.

1134. So, too, from an observation of human nature, we see that men for the most part are governed in their actions by a regard to their own interests. But we cannot therefore say, in any particular case, with any thing like the certainty of an induction, that this man will be controlled by considerations of self-interest. There are not only too many exceptions to the rule to allow of such a certainty, but we recognize in all men a capacity to resist

Moral freedom destroys uniformity.

all such considerations whenever they choose to do so; not only for the purpose of following their passions, but also in many cases for the heroic purpose of sacrificing themselves and their own interests for the truth and the good of others.

Induction cannot prove accidental properties.

1135. The next condition, limiting the sphere of Induction, is that the Predicate be *not* an *Accidental* property, but such as are regarded as *inseparable* properties. Induction does not extend to separable accidents or properties. If they are inseparable it is because there is some law or necessity connecting and binding them to a concomitance with the more obvious properties which make up the Essentia of the class-conception. But if they are separable their connection with the individuals of the genus is regarded as merely accidental, implying neither necessity nor law; and the connection remains, for the present at least, an isolated fact. Further discoveries, however, may find relations which indicate law and design, and then a new genus will be formed to which this property will no longer be an accident but an inseparable property.

Properties now considered accidental may be found to be essential.

Cousin's illustration from history.

1136. But until that is done and we gain some insight into the will and designs of Providence, farther than the mere Induction of facts can give, we hardly call our investigation an Induction at all. Thus M. Cousin has observed that great events take place in the *middle* of centuries. He speaks of the Middle of the Fourteenth as remarkable for the discoveries and revival of learning; the Fifteenth as remarkable for the fall of Constantinople; the Sixteenth for the Reformation; the Seventeenth for the English Rebellion, &c.; and yet no one regards this as an induction establishing a law, that the middle of every century will be accompanied by some great event in history. Again, five of the Presidents of the United States—the first five, went out of office when they were sixty-six years old. No one regards this, however, as an induction that establishes a general fact or law, that all Presidents shall hold office until they are sixty-six years old.

1137. And yet there is undoubtedly an important sense in which the facts of History constitute a field for inductive investigations.

Facts of History, how constituting a field for Induction.

One of the most striking and extraordinary illustrations of this that I have ever seen, is Spelman's History and Fate of Sacrilege; in which, after deducing the law of God upon the subject from the Scriptures, he runs over the whole of History, and especially the History of England since the Reformation, to show how the facts of History indicates principles the same as those educed from the Scriptures.

1138. This use of History assumes that God has a plan and a purpose in History, and governs the moral world by laws as completely as He does the natural world; and that from the facts evolved, His will can be learned in the one case as certainly as in the other.

This use of History assumes a Moral Government of the world.

1139. Induction, therefore, becomes a ground of Proof, or belief in the result obtained by our classification, only as it approaches to the condition in which we could demonstrate the conclusion which we reach by our inductive investigation from the class-conception. In Mathematics we get the class-conception by constructing in our own mind the figures which are comprehended under it. But before the creation of the world, the Creator must have constructed the same class-conception of all objects to be comprehended under each species of being that He would create. These conceptions are what Plato called Ideas, and Aristotle called Notions (τὰ νοητὰ), or as we render the word, "conceptions."

Induction approaches to a Demonstration.

1139. Induction helps us to these Ideas or Conceptions, and puts us, so far as it is successful, into the position which the Creative Mind occupied with regard to them before creation. It puts us into the same relation in

Induction limited to properties implied or contained in the original class-conceptions.

regard to objects in the natural world as we sustain to the Figures of Geometry, which we have constructed in our own imagination, or those conceptions of the various machines and implements of human contrivance with which the abodes of civilized man every where abounds. And from the matter of the Ideas or class-conceptions, as Material Properties, we see that other properties are necessarily implied. And it is a matter of doubt if there is or can be any Induction which deserves to be so called—that undertakes to prove any property of a species in natural objects which is not implied in the Matter of its class-conception, as that conception existed in the Creative Mind.*

* Since these pages were put into the Printer's hand, I have met with a report of the doings of "*the American Association for the Advancement of Science*," held at Providence, R. I. In the report of the doings for August 16th [1855], there is an account of PROF. AGASSIZ' paper of "The System in Zoology," from which I make the extract below.

I have long regarded Prof. Agassiz as the most philosophical of all our naturalists; perhaps more so than any other scholar in that department now living. And it affords me great pleasure to find that after some twenty years study and effort at an attempt to classify, and so proceed with his Induction on some other principle than that to which I had arrived on philosophical grounds, he has at last found by his experience that it is impossible to do so. And, aside from the pleasure which it affords me as a confirmation of my view on the subject, I cannot but regard his announcement as not only a great triumph of philosophy in general, but also of Christian Faith in particular.

I give his words as I find them in the Report (N. Y. Daily Times, Aug. 18, 1855). Even the Italics are given as I copy them.

"Even as late as the last classification of the animal kingdom by CUVIER—a system which has made his name so famous—that distinguished naturalist depended more upon arbitrary groupings than upon critical observations of natural affinities. To be understood well, the true relations of the system of Nature ought to be considered *as an analysis of the thought expressed by the Creator*. Classification is in reality nothing but the expression of that thought. We may no longer speak of *our* system. We may only speak of our readings of that thought which constitutes the animal system; which has gone on developing through countless ages. No longer do naturalists consider the Animal Kingdom without reference to the cause of existence. They are all driven to one point. They are compelled to ascribe existence of animal forms, either to physical causes or to an intelligent Maker. Between these two there is no medium point, no other alternative. The classes of animals are either the result of the general forces which we observe in Nature, or they are the work of an intelligent Being. Do we see in these classes the evidences of physical force—or thought! And now,

Thus if carnivorousness was an element in the class-conception of the Canidæ, just as equality of radii is in that of the circle, then canine teeth were as necessarily implied as a property of the Canidæ, as the Formulæ and Propositions of Trigonometry are in the conception of the Triangle.

1140. We can also accomplish our object of passing from the facts of Nature to a law by means of the conception of Final Causes. A Final Cause, as has been defined, is that for which any thing is or is done.

We may also pass from fact to law by means of Final Causes.

1141. We are conscious of acting from purpose or design. Our actions are conformed to our designs and reveal them to others. We can also see in the motions, features, and acts of other persons indications of their designs. We can often see in the structure of a piece of machinery or an implement of any kind, the design which its framer intended and expected it should accomplish.

Origin of the Idea of Final Causes in Nature.

1142. Precisely so in Nature we see, and cannot help but see marks of design—proofs that the Creator had an end in view—that He created from regard to Final Causes. If now we find by our induction that animals with canine teeth are carnivorous, and can moreover see that that kind of teeth are especially adapted to that kind of food, we have scarcely less doubt that all animals with canine teeth are carnivorous, than if we had seen them all in the pursuit of that mode of life—or if the Omniscient Creator Himself had revealed to us the fact.

Nature indicates Design.

1143. When then our induction leads us to see any connection between the Essentia of the Genus and the Property predicated of it, as is implied in the doctrine of Final Causes, or as the necessary correlates of each other, we feel

Final Causes point to a law based upon the will of the Creator.

when we come to consider the Animal Kingdom practically, as a process of Zoological Investigation, it comes first in order to ascertain whether, in the combinations already ascertained, we can read that thought, or whether any other result can there be read."

confident that we have found a law, which if it be not based upon the necessary nature of the things, is at least based upon the will of the Creator, and will not therefore be changed while the present order of things remains.

1144. But so expressive are the works of Nature every where of purpose and design, that long before we come to conscious reflection upon the subject, we have come to believe that whatever exists as the work of the Creator, was made for some purpose, or "Nothing was made in vain." The Formal properties—that is, those properties in any object which are regarded as constituting it an individual in the species between itself and the next subaltern species or genus, which is in our minds at the time, put us on the inquiry to ascertain what are the implied properties which accompany these Differentia or Formal properties; and what are they for; what fact or law in regard to the individuals of their class do they indicate.

Nothing made in vain.

1145. Now this way of regarding the Formal properties of objects is not the result of any system of philosophy. It exists before philosophy. One of the first questions that the child learns to ask with regard to any thing new that atatracts its attention is, "What is it for?" Thus to take the case already spoken of—we see certain animals with teeth of a peculiar shape; we see one of them using these teeth to tear the flesh of some animal which it has just caught, and devouring that flesh as food. The adaptation of the teeth to the end for which we see them being used, is such that we have no doubt that such was their design or Final Cause.

The idea of Final Causes exists before Philosophy.

1146. One case is enough. It seems to let us into the secrets of Nature—the counsels of the Creator. We feel as though we knew why He had so made the animal; and we predicate that mode of life of all animals having the same Formal property, as a general fact. We hold it as a physical

One case sufficient to suggest the belief.

certainty—but not as an *absolute* certainty. For not only may the nature or formal properties change in some respects, but influences may exist in some cases which will turn individuals and even whole species from the course of nature.

1147. There are sometimes cases of individual deformity. Most of the species of domesticated animals have been changed by domestication; and some of them so much that it is now difficult to ascertain precisely what they were in their undomesticated state. Man, we see was made for veracity, benevolence, and virtue; but his history shows that there has been a very general departure from what his nature shows that he was intended for.

Cases of deformity.

1148. The Fundamental Principle of this doctrine of Final Causes is, that whatever exists in the domain of Nature exists for some end or purpose, and consequently where its constitution and use indicates a purpose, we infer that that was the purpose designed, and consequently the law of its being which was imposed upon it by its Creator.

Fundamental Principles in this doctrine.

1149. Now taking this Principle for our Major Premise and we have:

That for which any thing in Nature was evidently designed it will accomplish.

Canine teeth were evidently designed for a carnivorous habit of life.

Therefore, Animals with canine teeth will always be carnivorous.

1150. Hence as Induction always implies that whatever is or occurs, is or occurs for some purpose or design; so it implies also a Wisdom which comprehends all things and events, and never errs—and a Power which can accomplish all that that Wisdom can design.

Induction always implies an Intelligent Creator.

1151. In the domain of Nature it is immaterial, so far as the result is concerned, whether we begin with the constitution of the object as seen in its Formal Properties, or with the

In Physical Matter we may reason from Modal Properties to the Final Cause.

Final Cause as seen in its Modal—the result is in each case and alike the same. But with man it is not so. We see from his constitution that he was designed for virtue. But we see much in his Modal properties—that is, in his thoughts, feelings, and actions—that is not in accordance with the Final Cause of his being; much which therefore we pronounce to be wrong, or at least abnormal.

But not in Moral.

1152. So too in Nature, there are abnormal cases in which we cannot infer from the individual the design or law of the mode of life which his species was intended to pursue. If we should find a man, without legs from his birth, it would not answer to infer from him that all men were designed merely to sit or to crawl, and that walking is a violation of the law of man's being. Such anomalies occur in nearly all species of being. And HUGH MILLER* has suggested that there may be, and that in fact there are reasons for believing that there are, in Nature whole species which have been degraded from their idea or normal condition. Of such he thinks that serpents, venomous insects, and insects with stings, are examples. His remark would include all those which have means of injury to other beings not necessary as either means of defence or of taking their prey.

Abnormal cases in Nature.

1153. The Argument from Examples, or a Fact as an Example, is evidently but an induction from a single inducted fact; as when we argue from the fact that Astronomy was opposed by religious bigotry, when it first began to be cultivated by the Christian Philosophers in the Middle Ages, that Geology will be in like manner opposed as subversive of the Christian faith.

Facts as Examples.

1154. It is evident that the particulars denoted by the terms "*Astronomy*" and "*Geology*" in this case, must have a resemblance, consisting of identity in the properties on which the comparison or argument is based. And in estimat-

There must be Identity in the point of Comparison.

* Old Red Sandstone, final Chapter.

ing the force of an Argument of this kind, the first step in each case is to consider whether there really is that resemblance or identity or not.

1155. But we are at present concerned only with the Method and its proper force. The Argument stated in brief is this:

Astronomy when first introduced was opposed as adverse to religion.

∴ Geology when first introduced will be opposed as adverse to religion.

1156. This is manifestly an Enthymeme, in which the Minor Premise is suppressed.

A is P,
∴ G is P.

We may complete the Formula by affirming A of G. Thus,

A is P,
G is A,
∴ G is P;

that is, by saying that "Geology is Astronomy." But that is not true. Astronomy and Geology are not identical; nor is Astronomy a species within which Geology is included. All we can say, and all that the Argument from Example means to say, is that they are alike. But as this does not affirm either identity of spheres, or include the one in the other, no inference can be drawn by means of such a proposition in a categorical Syllogism.

1157. The Force of the Argument from Facts as Examples, therefore, must be sought in the point of resemblance, considered as the Formal Properties of a Species.

The Inference depends upon that identity.

Thus Astronomy, when first introduced, was a new science, contradicting some of the prevailing theological opinions.

But Astronomy was opposed by the religious when first introduced, *because* it contradicted, &c.

Therefore all sciences which contradict the prevalent theological notions, will be opposed when first introduced.

1158. With this Conclusion for a Major Premise, we introduce "Geology is a new science, contradicting the prevalent theological nôtions;" and we have the conclusion, *therefore* "Geology will be opposed," &c.

Example an Induction from a single Fact.

1159. It will be seen that in form this is but an Induction from a single Example as an inducted fact, and as such depends for whatever value it may have either as a Method of Investigation or of Proof, upon the principles and laws of Induction, and the extent to which it fulfils them.*

Seldom called Example except in Moral Matter.

1160. This Method is seldom, if ever, spoken of in common use of language as an Argument from Example, except when it is applied to Moral Matter. In that case the value of the Method is much less, since there is no such uniformity of Causes and Laws in Moral as in Physical Matter.

* WHATELY, in his Rhetoric, Part. I. Chap. II. § 6, has given the Argument from Example in a form which is, perhaps, more striking than that in the text, as follows:

Astronomy was decried at its first introduction as adverse to religion:	Geology is likely to be decried, &c.:

Every science is likely to be decried at its first introduction as adverse to religion.

But this Major Premise is untrue, and can be saved only by the Modal, inserted above: "Every science *which contradicts the prevalent religious opinions*—" In this case the Modal not only limits the subject to an included species, but is also in fact assigning the Cause, and we might therefore have the Causal Argument.

Astronomy was decried *because* it opposed the prevalent religious opinions.
Geology opposes the prevalent religious opinions.
∴ Geology will be decried.

And in fact the inference of a General Principle from a single fact as Example, or many, as inducted particulars, must always be limited in one of these two ways—namely, either to instances of the same kind only, or to instances in which the same cause is at work upon matter which is essentially the same.

1161. The Induction of Facts by way of Example, is but a loose and vague way of reasoning, and is seldom satisfactory. For in all contingent matter, that there are exceptions to all rules is proverbial; and the Argument from Example often has the appearance, and is in danger of the reality, of being based upon the exceptions rather than upon the individual facts coming under the Rule. Thus if one should attempt to prove from Examples of dreams coming to pass, that dreams are to be regarded as generally prophetic, or signs of what is to take place, he would most manifestly be arguing from the exception to the general rule. Yet Examples of what he is trying to prove can undoubtedly be produced. Nor in fact is there any proposition in Contingent Matter, however absurd, which may not find some Minor Premise, which by way of Example, will connect it in the fulfilment of Formula with some indisputable Major Premise, and thus prove it to be true with all the force of which the Argument from Example is capable.

Argument from Example seldom satisfactory.

1162. Two affirmative Premises in the 2d Figure constitute an Analogy between their subjects. As,

Analogy how constituted.

A is B,
C is B.

A and C must therefore be analogous, or identical in the Matter of the conception B.

1163. But if we take that Matter as a Formal Property, and then predicate of A or C some other Modal Property in a compound Causal, assigning B as its Cause, we may predicate that Property also in an Argument from Analogy of the other of those subjects. Thus,

Formal Property taken as Cause.

A is C,
B is C.
But A is X *because* it is C,
∴ B is X.

1164. Thus Bishop Butler argues from the analogy between the death of man and the chrysalis state of the worm, that the soul of man is immortal. The chrysalis and the man have but few points in common. Yet some such points or properties they have—and the analogy is in this case somewhat remote; and in consequence requires much greater scrutiny, and can never in fact produce the same degree of certainty as the closer analogies.

Bishop Butler's argument.

1165. This Argument put into Form would stand thus:

Man has a principle of life.

The worm has a principle of life.

The worm lives through an apparent death, *because* it has the principle of life.

The Argument completed.

Therefore man will live through the appearance of death at the dissolution of his body.

1166. Or without the Causal we may have the Problematic Conclusion, (which is in all cases valid of the Affirmative Premises in the 2d Figure,)

Problematic Conclusion.

Therefore man *may* live through the apparent extinction of his being at the death of his body.

1167. There is sometimes a presumption, but nothing more, arising from the fact that two individuals which are known to agree in many points as a common Essentia, will agree in a certain other point in regard to which it is not yet known whether they agree or not. But arguments based on such supposed analogies are of but little value. Thus a man and a horse agree in a vast number of points of the animal economy, but still they may disagree in regard to that property by which a certain plant is food for one and a poison for the other. The probability is against any such proposition on the ground of general analogy, but still it is only a probability; and the proposition may be true, as we know that it is true in a vast number of instances.

Analogy in some points not always a safe ground of inference to analogy in others.

1168. The reason for the inferiority of the Argument from Analogy to an Induction, results as will be seen from the inadequacy of the class-

Why Analogy is inferior to Induction.

conceptions which we have in our own minds—an inadequacy which Induction and Analysis properly used are all the while removing, and the removal of which converts the Induction into Demonstrative Sciences just as fast as it progresses.

1169. There is another use of Analogy which is of great value, and which we ought not to fail to notice in this place. It consists in removing antecedent objections and improbabilities, in interposing objections to too hasty inductions, or inferences from inductions too broad for the inducted facts.

Analogy as a means of removing antecedent objections.

1170. Any inference which is too broad for the facts—that is, an inference including a Genus comprehending several species from facts gathered from one species alone, must comprehend the facts of the other species also as being necessarily analogous to the extent of their common Essentia. If, therefore, such analogous facts can be adduced, which are not in accordance with the inference, they are an answer to it. This is the case with Butler's Analogy. It refutes the Major Premise of the sceptic, by substituting a new Minor Term, "the Chrysalis" for "Man;" and with the same Middle and Major Terms, the Bishop deduces a Conclusion which is contradictory to an indisputable fact.* But as the new Minor Premise cannot be disputed, the Major Premise is proved thereby to be untrue, and consequently the inference from it to the death of the soul of man, is invalid.

In what way.

* The Infidel had inferred from *the appearance*, that man's being terminated at the death of the body. His argument was that:

Man appears to end his being at death.
Therefore his being does end, and the immortality of the soul is but a dream.

But the Bishop says, Your principle, Major Premise, proves too much; for the worm when it goes into the chrysalis state, *appears* to die, as evidently as man, and yet the worm comes out a butterfly. Man *may*, therefore, notwithstanding the appearance, come out of the apparent death a purely spiritual being, with powers and faculties which he does not now possess.

1171. In the same way the antecedent objection to a miraculous revelation of the will of God in Christianity, is answered by the fact that there has been an interposition at the creation of man; and if there has been one such interposition, there can be no antecedent presumption against another's being made when there is sufficient occasion for it.

Removes also antecedent objection to Revelation.

1172. Both Testimony and Circumstances are to be regarded by Logic as Facts. The reality and value of which, individually and separately, are to be determined by principles which do not belong to the sphere of Logic. But the force of *concurrence* in testimony and in circumstances, is a fact which it becomes important to consider in this connection.

Testimony and Circumstances as Facts.

1173. By *Concurrence* we understand such a connection between two or more circumstances, or pieces of testimony, as that one did not cause the other; nor does the one serve to explain and account for the reality of the other, except through or by means of the principle which they are adduced to prove.

Concurrence.

1174. Thus two witnesses testifying in the presence of each other, or after an interview between them on the subject of their testimony, could hardly give what would be fairly considered *concurrent* testimony. It would be *accumulated* testimony, and worth just as much additional force as the moral character of the second witness, and his opportunity to know could give it. But the testimony of the second *might* be accounted for on the ground that he knew what was the testimony which the first had given or was about to give. It could be a case of concurrence, and have the force due to a concurrence only on condition, that the two witnesses had had no opportunity of knowing what each other had testified, or were about to testify to.

Of Testimony concurrent and accumulated.

1175. And so of circumstances; when one will account for the existence of others, there is no

Concurrence of Circumstances.

concurrence. It is merely an accumulation of circumstances, and in fact of but little value.

1176. This is the Method of Argument upon which, for the most part, the conclusions of the Historian—that is, the series of statements which make up what he calls his history, depend. Such is the infirmity of human testimony—man's liability to error in perceiving—his susceptibility to the unconscious influences of prejudice and passion, and worse than all his perverse inclination to mistake and misrepresent others, that the cautious student of history will seldom believe even the most explicit testimony of a single witness, unless there are other witnesses or material circumstances *concurring* with his statement. And if the influence of this concurrence be *against* any man's testimony clearly, and with any very great force, we set it aside with the charitable judgment that it was a mistake of his.

The sphere of its use.

In History.

1177. In the criminal jurisdiction of our Courts also, concurrence of testimony, or *Circumstantial* Evidence, as it is called, is for the most part all that can be had. The criminal never surrounds his acts with witnesses who can testify to his guilt. On the contrary he seeks to be as far removed as possible from such means of convicting him of the crime.

In Courts of Criminal Jurisdiction.

1178. Moreover, as showing the value of this kind of testimony, there are some crimes of which a man cannot be convicted on the testimony of a single witness, without a strong concurrence of circumstantial evidence, as perjury for instance; and in many cases concurrence of circumstances is sufficient to destroy entirely the direct testimony of an individual witness.

Concurrence superior to single direct testimony in some cases.

SECTION VI.

Of Progressive Approach.

1179. There are certain Methods of Argument which, while from their nature they are incapable of establishing an absolute certainty, do nevertheless answer a good practical purpose; and for certain extraneous reasons are preferred in some cases to Methods which could give a different kind or degree of certainty. There are other cases where absolute certainty is unattainable, though we may make some approach to it. All these Methods we call Methods of *Progressive Approach;* of which there are several kinds.

Occasion for the use of Progressive Approach.

1180. (1) *A posteriori* efforts to prove an *a priori* proposition.

1181. Suppose we take for illustration the first law of motion—"A body in motion will continue to move for ever unless it be stopped by some force external to itself."

First case. Illustration.

This proposition contains terms and elements which can never be justified by any *a posteriori* Method. In the first place we can never remove *all* the external forces that act upon any body, so as to see it in motion uninfluenced by any thing external to itself. Always there will be some friction, some resistance of the atmosphere, &c. But in the second place if we could fulfil this condition, an observation or experiment could never extend through the time implied in the Proposition to be proved, "*for ever.*" We might, if the first condition was fulfilled, see it move a long time—but "for ever" is not only somewhat longer than any individual observer will live to test the matter; but, even if that difficulty could be satisfactorily disposed of, the proof of the proposition by this method could not be completed until it would be too late to be of any practical utility.

A posteriori proof inadequate to the terms of the Proposition.

1182. Our only resource, therefore, is to approach the conditions as nearly as possible. We set a body in motion with a given amount of friction and retarding forces—it goes a certain length of time. We start the same body, or another precisely like it, with less of friction, and it keeps moving much longer; and the less there is to retard it, the longer it moves—and we *infer* that if it had nothing to retard it it would move for ever.

We can only approximate by *a posteriori* means.

1183. The Proposition can be proved *a priori* from the property of inertia, which is contained in the class-conception of Matter as a material property.

It may be Demonstrated.

1184. But *a posteriori* we can prove only general truths, with the possibility of exceptions to them, while the absolute certainty of universal truths, which admit no exceptions, can be proved only *a priori* by Demonstration.

Absolute truths proved only by Demonstration.

1185. (2) A second modification of this Method is afforded in the mathematical doctrine of limits. That is, "Whatever is true of any point indefinitely near to any limit, is true at that limit."

The Doctrine of Limits a Progressive Approach.

1186. Thus if we have the question of the quadrature of the circle, What is the ratio of the diameter to the circumference? We can answer only by Progressive Approach. We can construct a polygon within the circle, whose sides are near to the circumference of the circles, but not coincident with it. We may then bisect the sides of that polygon, and so on, but the polygon can never become a circle. It can only approach it indefinitely near. So, too, the number that expresses the ratio of the radius to the circumference becomes a decimal 3.141, and extending indefinitely, but it can never become complete.

The Quadrature of the Circle.

1187. Arguments from the force of Terms, from Testimony, from Concurrence, from Circumstances, in fact Cumulative Arguments, and Probable Arguments of all kinds, are but

Cumulative and Probable Arguments Progressive Approaches.

Progressive Approaches towards the absolute certainty of the truth of the Proposition which they aim to establish. A jury in criminal cases, for instance, is bound not to convict a criminal so long as there is a reasonable doubt left of his guilt. And yet the records of criminal jurisdiction furnish many instances in which persons have been convicted, who were afterwards found to have been entirely innocent.

Progressive Approach often more satisfactory than Demonstrative.

1188. In speaking of Arguments of this kind as but Progressive Approaches to certainty, we must be understood to refer to their Logical character rather than to their practical effect. In point of fact the mass of minds are sooner and easier persuaded by a Progressive Approach than by a Demonstration, even in those cases where a Demonstration is possible. It requires a peculiar mental constitution, or at least much practice, to be so familiar with the Method of Demonstration as to be fully under the influence of its power.

Danger of depreciating Progressive Approach.

1189. And on the other hand, minds which are particularly accustomed to the Methods of Demonstration, or which are constitutionally peculiarly susceptible to its force, not unfrequently acquire a contempt for what is called moral reasoning, and a distrust of its conclusive force, which is entirely unjustifiable. And it is, perhaps, one of the most difficult branches of practical Ethics, to determine where the force of a Progressive Approach becomes a sufficient ground for the responsibility of action.

SECTION VII.

Of the Argumentum ad Ignorantiam.

Argumentum ad Ignorantiam.

1190. This Argument consists in proving that a given Proposition is true, because we know of no reason why it should not be true, or why the truth should be otherwise.

1191. An instance of this occurs where we should least of all expect it, in Herschel's Discourse on the Study of Natural Philosophy. He says that on the old principle, "that Nature abhors a vacuum," as accounting for the rising of the mercury in a Barometer, and such like phenomena, "We know of no reason why Nature should not abhor the vacuum as much on a high mountain as in the plain below." Therefore the Barometer ought to stand as high on a mountain as in the plain below. This of course assumes that if there was any reason for its being otherwise, he or we should know it; or which is the same thing, that we know all the reasons for whatever phenomena may come before our minds.

Illustration.

1192. Now there are undoubtedly cases in which one's ignorance of any fact or phenomena, is a presumption at least of its non-existence. Thus an alleged fact in any science of which none of those most familiar with the science had any knowledge, would be looked upon with great suspicion. And so universally just in proportion to one's opportunity to know, is his ignorance a ground or principle of proof of the non-reality of the alleged fact.

Ignorance of a fact or principle sometimes a proof of its non-reality.

1193. The Ad Ignorantiam labors not only under the disadvantages of Negative Testimony, and of Positive Testimony to a Negative Proposition (858–863), but also under peculiar disadvantages of its own. For what man adequately conceives and knows, is an indefinitely small amount when compared to the infinitum of the knowable; and the value of the Argumentum ad Ignorantiam increases from nothing up towards certainty, only as our knowledge advances from total ignorance up towards omniscience.

Value increases with our knowledge.

1194. There are some cases, however, in which this element enters pretty largely into our Methods of Investigation and Argument. In investigating Causes, for instance, both Final and Efficient,

Use in investigating Causes.

so strong is the belief in their reality, that we often affirm the causality of a particular Antecedent or Mode, not because we can see any connection between the facts, but simply because we can see no other fact of which to affirm it. We can see no connection, for instance, between the resin and the kind of electricity that it excites. But Induction having established the invariable antecedence, we affirm a causality simply because we believe that there is a cause, and we do not know of any thing else that could have produced the observed phenomena, except the resinous substances.

1195. Such reasoning can hardly be said to be based upon any general principle which comprehends the facts of the case; or in more exact terms, any principle, the statement of which furnishes a Middle Term, as a means of proving the Predicate of the Subject in the Conclusion.

Want of Principle.

SECTION VIII.

Of Refutation.

1196. Refutation supposes a foregoing proposition already asserted or assented to, which it is desirable to disprove. As this foregoing proposition can hardly be an axiom or intuitive judgment, it must be regarded as a conclusion to a course of reasoning, or at least as resting on Premises or grounds, which must in some way be removed before we can expect those who have adopted the conclusion to give it up, or justify ourselves in dissenting from it.

Refutation supposes a Conclusion of a foregoing Argument.

1197. In cases where there has been an *Ignoratio Elenchi*, or the proof of a Proposition which is not to the purpose, we have no occasion to show that the conclusion is untrue, by any method. It is enough to show that it is not to the purpose. This is not in fact so much a refutation of the Argument or

Ignoratio a Refutation.

Conclusion, as the rescuing our cause from the effects of a false and improper attack.

1198. Setting this case aside, therefore, as not strictly belonging to Methods of Refutation, we may divide all our Methods into three classes:— (1) the Direct; (2) the Indirect; (3) Personal Refutations. Three Methods.

SECTION IX.

Of Direct Refutation.

1199. The first form of Direct Refutation to be considered, is that in which we prove the contradictory of the *Proposition*, which may have been affirmed without regard to any Premises or means of Proof which may have been given to prove its truth. First Method.

1200. No Proposition and its contradictory can be true at the same time. If now we have any Universal Proposition asserted, we can refute it directly if we can find what is called an *Exception*—that is, a fact included in the sphere of its Subject, with which the Predicate of the Proposition cannot be connected by a Copula in the same quality as in the original Proposition. If that Proposition was affirmative, its Predicate must be denied of the Exception; or if negative, it must be affirmed of it. Thus if I say that all the men in a given company are sitting down, the Proposition would be refuted if one could show that there was so much as one exception, one individual that was not sitting down. Universal Propositions refuted by Exceptions.

1201. The mere inability to affirm the Predicate could hardly be regarded as a refutation. It would be a piece of mere negative testimony (see 860). A caution.

1202. In all such cases the appeal is always to some of the primary means of investigation, which, because they are primary, are both investigation and proof (1040). Exceptions how proved.

1203. We must remember that Individual judgments always precede Universal or General judgments, and that general judgments are based upon the individual.*

Individual Judgments first and surest.

And by no principle can the general judgment be made more certain, than the least certain of the individual judgments comprehended in it; as the chain can never be any stronger than its weakest link. Hence the assertion of an exception to any Universal Proposition is but an appeal to the primary judgments; and of course, therefore, it must have a greater degree of certainty than the Universal Proposition itself.

Exceptions do not refute General Propositions but only Universal.

1204. An Exception, however, never refutes a mere *general* Proposition, since in all contingent matter it is a recognized principle that all such admit of exceptions. "*Exceptio probat regulam*," has come to be an axiom.† But an Exception is a refutation to a Universal Proposition. It destroys its Universality, and therefore its Formal character. Of course it is immaterial whether the Proposition was affirmative or negative, so far as the effect of the Exception is concerned.

Refutation of a Particular Proposition.

1205. But if the Proposition to be refuted be Particular rather than Universal, then of course it can be refuted only by the Proof of its contradictory Universal. And this can be proved in one of two ways only: (1) first by an *a priori* demonstration in necessary matter; or (2) by an actual inspection of all the individuals included in the sphere of the Logical Whole; a part of which constitutes the subject of the Particular judgment which we wish to refute.‡

* The Individual judgment is always first in point of time, and if we proceed from that by Induction we get a General judgment; but if we evolve the Predicate from the necessary matter of the conception of the subject, our judgment becomes a Necessary one.

† Of course it is not the Exception that proves the rule, strictly speaking: but the fact that it has been noticed *as an exception*, proves that the general Proposition, to which it is contradictory, has been recognized as a rule which is true in general.

‡ In the first case we obtain a judgment, which is Universal, *ex necessitate rei;* in the second it is only Universal, *de facto*—as in fact there is no necessity that it should be so or always remain so.

1206. But there may be many cases in which neither of these modes of direct refutation are practicable, where we can have no *a priori* demonstration—nor yet submit the individuals included within the sphere of the subject to the test of observation and experiment.

Refutation of the Proposition not always possible.

1207. In all such cases we may release ourselves from the obligation to assent to a Conclusion *by refuting the Reasoning*. This we accomplish not by disproving the Conclusion, but by showing that it is not proved by the Premises; we show in fact from the Premises themselves without referring to any matter not contained in them, that the Conclusion is invalid, and ought not to have been drawn from those Premises. It may be true as a Proposition, but is not proved as a Conclusion.

Second Method of Direct Refutation.

1208. This may be done in four ways: (1) in the first place we may have a simple *Non sequitur*, as in all cases of Fault or Fallacy in Form. In this case the Premise may be true and the Conclusion true, and yet no connection between them; or the Premise may be true and the Conclusion false. Thus if any of the five Canons (477) be violated, we have a simple *Non sequitur*.

Non sequitur.

1209. So, also, if in Conditionals we deny the Antecedent to destroy the Consequent (682), or from the denial of the Consequent infer the contrary and not the contradictory merely of the Antecedent. Or if in Disjunctives, we apply the *Modus ponente tollens* (710), where the excluded Middle is produced by the opposition of alternate rather than coördinate species or parts. In short any Fault or Fallacy in Form will give a *Non sequitur*. Hence it is always a sufficient refutation to point out such a fault.

Non sequitur in Conditionals and Disjunctives.

1210. (2) In the second place we may have a *Sequitur per Fallaciam*—using the word Fallacy in its strictest sense—as indicating some deceptive use of a Formula, where the Premises, each taken

Sequiter per Fallaciam.

by itself is true, and the conditions and requirements of the Formula are fulfilled. Of these it will be seen (Part I. Chap. IV. Sec. 3,) that there are five: (1) Ambiguous Middle; (2) Division; (3) Composition; (4) Accidents; (5) Quid.

1211. Any one of these Fallacies of course destroys the validity of an Argument; and although the Conclusion may still be true, we are no longer bound to receive it as a Conclusion after such a Fallacy has been pointed out in the process by which one has arrived at it.

The Conclusion may be true notwithstanding the Fallacy.

1212. (3) In the third case we may have a *Sequitur per non veram*, in which case there is neither fault in Form nor Fallacy in the use of matter, but simply the assumption of Premises, one or more of which are not true.

Sequitur per non veram.

1213. This will be seen occurs in the case of *Non causa pro causa*, as stated in Part I. (738), together with the assumption of Sequence where there is none, non-exclusion of Middle, &c., &c. In all these cases a Proposition is assumed as true, which is not so. And whether it be expressly stated or implied as the suppressed Premise of an Enthymeme, the Sequence of a Conditional, &c., it is equally mischievous; and needs to be distinctly evolved if it were not expressly stated.

Cases of *Petitio Principii.*

1214. It thus becomes a Proposition, which we shall need to disprove—unless its falsity be obvious without any proof. This can be done of course only by proving the contradictory of the False Premise.

The False Premise will need disproof.

1215. (4) But finally, we may have a Fault in Method, or a misapplication of Method to Matter; as if we should attempt to apply Demonstration to contingent matter, and determine realities in being from our conceptions, stated as definitions. This was the great fault that prevailed among the students of the Natural Sciences from Aristotle down to Bacon.

Fault in Method.

1216. But in modern times we have a tendency to the opposite error. One writer* has attempted to apply Induction to the religious history of the world, and to prove the falsity of Christianity from the fact, that all religions except that contained in the Scriptures have been delusions.

Volney's Fault.

SECTION X.

Of Indirect Refutation.

1217. This consists in proving a Proposition untrue, by showing that it contains or comprehends that which is false.

Indirect Refutation.

1218. In the first place we may show a Proposition to be false by evolving from it, *by Immediate Inference*, an untruth. Thus, one writer says that the human souls are propagated by "decision;" and the context shows that by "decision" he means the cutting off of a part. But "decision" or division implies extension, and extension is a property of matter and not of spirit.

By Immediate Inference.

1219. In the second place we may refute one's reasoning by what is called the *Reductio ad Absurdum*. In this process we introduce other matter, which is either admitted as true, or which admits of proof beyond further question, and combines this new matter with that part of which was given before, which we wish to show to be false.

Refutation by a *Reductio ad Absurdum.*

1220. This Method is often spoken of as the process of showing that one's "Principles" or "argument proves too much." Thus the infidel's argument, that the apparent death of the body implies the death of the soul and the cessation of existence, as Bishop Butler shows in his Analogy, "proves too much." It proves that the larvæ of the Metabolians die when they go into the chrysalis state; whereas

Popular names for the Method.

* See Volney's Ruins, or Meditations among the Ruins of Empires.

they do not die but only change their mode of existence.

1221. Now if any general Proposition, that is, a Proposition with a general term for a subject be true, its Predicate must be true of every species included in the genus denoted by the subject. If then we can discover a species, of which the subject of that general Proposition can be predicated, while its Predicate cannot, the general Proposition itself must be untrue.

Fundamental Principle of the Indirect Refutation.

1222. Thus to recur to Bishop Butler's argument again. The infidel had asserted that the soul dies with the body—the assertion was based on the appearance of death—and hence implied the Major Premise, that "in all cases of an apparent death of the body, there is a total cessation of the existence of the individual."—Using this Major Premise, we may complete the Formula thus:

Illustration.

Whenever the body dies there is a termination of the individual existence.

The body dies in what we call the death of man.

∴ In what we call the death of man there is a termination of the individual existence.

But says Bishop Butler there is a death of the body in the larvæ of Metabolian insects. Using this for a Minor Premise to the Major Premise just given, and we have for Conclusion:

∴ There is a termination of the individual existence of each Metabolian when it goes into the chrysalis state.

This Conclusion, however, is confessedly untrue, and yet the Major Premise is the same as the infidel had used; the Minor Premise is indeed different, but then it is a Proposition that no one can dispute. Hence the Major Premise, common to both Conclusions, must be untrue.

1223. By this we do not mean to say that the Proposition had no element of truth in it, or that this Reductio has shown that the Predi-

The disproved Premise may be partly true.

cate is not true of any individuals included in the subject; but only that inasmuch as the Proposition is not true of all, we cannot admit it to be true of any, until it is modified by some modal which shall give either the Differentia of an included species of which it may always be affirmed, or expressive of a term or a condition in which it may be affirmed of any one of them generally. And until this has been done by the infidel the refutation is complete.

Indirect Methods always imply a Direct Method to the same Conclusion.

1224. The Indirect Methods of Disproof as well as the Indirect Method of Proof imply that there is more than one way of knowing the truth of the Proposition which it is sought to disprove. Otherwise there would be no means of disproving. Thus, as we have seen, we may disprove a Proposition by proving directly its contradictory. This gives us two methods to the same Proposition, since from any Proposition to its contradictory is an immediate inference.

The same in the Reductio ad Absurdum.

1225. Or again, we may disprove a Proposition as a Premise by the *reductio ad absurdum.* But this implies that we have some other means or method of proving that Conclusion or its contradictory, as the case may be. Otherwise we should not know which of the two Conclusions was right. We cannot pronounce our Proposition to be absurd or false, until we have ascertained that it is contradictory to another which we know to be true. Affirmative judgments are antecedent in point of time to the Negative, and the test of a theory or Method is that it gives results in accordance with what we know to be true, independent of the Method or theory in all those cases of which we know any thing, except by means of the theory or Method itself.

The Refutation depends upon the certainty of the new Matter.

1226. The value of the Method will of course depend upon the certainty of the newly introduced Premise or Matter, and of course is worth nothing unless that Premise be more certain than the common Premise which it seeks to redargue.

1227. What is called the *Argumentum ab Absurdo* is merely the inference from the Absurdity of the Conclusion, that one or the other of the Premises, or both of them must be untrue. This can seldom be of any further use than a mere appeal to prejudice, since one is not likely to announce an absurd opinion without some force of Premises to support it which may need a Refutation.

The *Argumentum ab Absurdo.*

SECTION XI.

Of Personal Refutations.

1228. There are certain Methods of Refutation, which, while they have no conclusive force of a general character, are often of great rhetorical efficiency in putting a stop to further controversy. These I have called *Personal Arguments.*

Personal Refutations.

1229. (1) The *Argumentum ad Hominem* consists in appealing to a man's acts, or previous declarations, or avowed principles, as being inconsistent with the position he is at present maintaining.

Argumentum ad Hominem.

1230. The *ad hominem* proves nothing categorically. The opinion of the Respondent is used as a Premise against himself. It may effectually annoy or even answer him; but it can prove nothing more than that such and such is his opinion, or results from his opinion. The Conclusion can have no more truth than the subjective Premise or personal opinion of the person to whom the Argument is addressed.

What it proves.

1231. (2) The *Argumentum ad Verecundiam* is an appeal to the opinion of an authority which the person against whom the argument is used is bound to respect and follow, on the score of modesty.

Argumentum ad Verecundiam.

1232. This argument also can hardly be said to prove any thing categorically. It is used and very well serves to embarrass an antagonist.

Its force.

Beyond this it has but little force. It gives for a Premise the opinion of the individual or authority cited, and the Conclusion can have no force except what results from the respect due to that authority; a force which may have far greater *moral* than logical weight.

Argumentum ad Invidiam.

1233. The *Argumentum ad Invidiam* as it is sometimes called, is really no argument at all. It consists in appeals to the passions, prejudices, or feelings of people, for the purpose of exciting emotions unfavorable either to a cause or the person of him who advocates it. However effective this may be in a rhetorical point of view, it accomplishes nothing logically; and proves, if it proves any thing, only that those who resort to this mode of argument are better skilled in Rhetoric than in reasoning, and know more of the Formulæ of Billingsgate than of Logic.

CHAPTER IV.

METHODS OF INSTRUCTION AND CRITICISM.

SECTION I.

Classification of Sciences.

1234. It may not be inappropriate to give a Classification of the Branches of Human Knowledge before proceeding with the appropriate topics of this Chapter. Such a classification has been already anticipated in some measure, and seems very generally to have been considered as belonging to this part of Philosophy.

1235. We have already referred to the early division of human knowledge into three branches: Physics, Ethics, and Logic (5). But a slight advance in science, however, rendered this classification inadequate and unsatisfactory. It must however be, to some extent, the basis of all divisions. The first department, Physics, including all branches of knowledge that have for subject-matter material objects in the concrete; Logic, including all branches that treat of the intellect, and are based upon the elements furnished by it, the realities of truth, and the *a priori* conceptions; and Ethics, including all that relate to man as having a destiny to accomplish, implying society, religion, and the state with its institutions and vested rights, as of Property, &c., as a means of accomplishing that destiny.

Early classification soon becomes inadequate.

1236. It would not be worth the while to follow the history of these classifications minutely if we had time. One or two of the classifications, however, it may be well to notice. ARISTOTLE divided all knowledge in the first place into two coördinate parts, the *Immediate*, in which we learn every thing in particulars and each by itself (τὰ καθ' ἕκαστα), and the *Mediate*, in which we acquire a knowledge of universals (τὰ καθ' ὅλου). From the Immediate in his theory, we deduce by means of Logic the knowledge of the Mediate. Hence Logic is the instrument or organ of all science, so far as its form is concerned. With another view he divided all knowledge into Philosophy and History. Philosophy he divided into Speculative and Practical. The Speculative becomes *Physics* or *Mathematics*, or what is afterwards called *Metaphysics*, according as it advances in abstraction; and *relatively to its end*, it is divided into Physics, Cosmology, Psychology, and Theology. Practical Philosophy includes Ethics, Politics, and Economy.

Aristotle's classification.

1237. In the Scholastic Philosophy of the Middle Ages we have the division into the TRIVIUM and the QUADRIVIUM; the first including *Grammar*, *Rhetoric*, and *Logic*; and the latter including *Arithmetic*, *Music*, *Geometry*, and *Astronomy*. They were described in these mnemonic lines:

Scholastic classification.

> "GRAM. loquitur; DIA. verba docet; RHE. verba ministrat;
> MUS. canit; AR. numerat; GE. ponderat; AS. colit astra."

1238. These seven sciences constituted what in the University distribution was called the Faculty of *Arts*. And besides these were three others: *Divinity*, *Law*, and *Medicine*. The first is regarded as including whatever concerns Religion and its duties; the second whatever relates to the State and its administration of affairs; and the third was understood to include the Physical Sciences generally.

University distribution of the Faculties.

1239. BACON proposed a new classification, dividing

all Sciences into three classes, as they refer to either *Memory*, *Imagination*, or *Reason*. But this resulted in great confusion, as there is scarcely any branch of knowledge in which all these faculties are not called into use; and as has been remarked, "his classification would put Boswell's Life of Johnson in the same class with the labors of Cuvier, and the researches of Hunter." Botany and Zoology were classed with Metaphysics, and Painting and Music among the "*artes voluptuarias*," were ranked with Cookery and Cosmetics.

Bacon's classification.

1240. LOCKE gave a much more sensible classification, as follows:

Locke's classification.

1. PHYSICA	Experimental	Natural History, Physiology.
	Rational	Theology, Ontology.
2. PRACTICA		Economics, Politics, Ethics.
3. SEMEIOTICA		Logic, Rhetoric, Grammar.

1241. DUGALD STEWART believed a classification of the Sciences impossible, at least in his day. COLERIDGE attempted it as a basis for the *Encyclopedia Metropolitana*, which was constructed on his plan. But as a confession of failure, he was obliged to give an "*and so forth*" at the end; or rather a chapter of "*Miscellanies*," which could not be included in any part of his division. This reminds us of the Treatise of Smalgruenius, entitled "*De Omnibus Rebus*," with a supplement, "*De Quibusdam Aliis*."

Stewart and Coleridge.

1242. AMPÈRE, however, elaborated a classification which is perhaps complete enough. But it is too complicated. Coleridge had failed by so classifying, as to make his exceptions too numerous. Ampère made his parts too numerous, and had to create names and sciences which were never before heard of. His division does not recognize those names

Ampère's classification.

and divisions which are already in use. Nor is there the remotest probability that the progressive development of Science will take the form and divisions that he has pointed out. He makes *one hundred and twenty-eight* sciences in the last subdivision, or third order, as he calls it—and *thirty-two* of the first order. He first divides into two kingdoms:—COSMOLOGICAL, including (1) *Mathematics;* (2) *Physics;* (3) *Natural Sciences;* (4) *Medical Sciences;*—and NOOLOGICAL Sciences, including (1) *Philosophics;* (2) *Dialegmatics;* (3) *Ethnological Sciences;* (4) *Political Sciences.*

1243. COMPTE has given a classification also in his Positive Philosophy, as follows: Compte's classification.

I. INORGANIC	Astronomy, Physics, Chemistry,	II. ORGANIC	Physiology, Sociology;

and then, as preceding and implied in all, he gives MATHEMATICS or the Science of Numbers.

1244. This classification, as will be seen, does not include many of those which have thus far always been regarded as distinct sciences. Nor is the division sufficiently minute to be of much service. His Theory of Knowledge and his Philosophy are too hopelessly bad to allow of any useful classification being based upon it.

1245. In the following classification which I shall give, I divide first into three classes with reference to the end in view; and in the subdivisions I have followed the received divisions and names. Each class naturally divides itself into two departments, differing in the first class both in the starting-point and in the Method. In the second class they differ in the starting-point only; and in the third class the two departments differ chiefly in the object in view—the one producing objects of Beauty and the other objects of Utility. The Sciences in the departments in the first class are necessary to those in the second class, and those in the second are necessary to the third. A new one proposed.

CLASS I.—THEORETICAL,

including those Sciences the object of which is "*to know.*"

DEPARTMENT I.

*Exact Sciences** (purely physical), based upon

Primary Phenomena		in the Atmosphere	METEOROLOGY.
		above the Atmosphere . .	OURANOGRAPHY.
	of facts	in the structure and Nat. History of the Earth . .	GEOLOGY.
		on the surface of the Earth	GEOGRAPHY.
		in the analysis and combination of the simple Elements . . .	CHEMISTRY.
		in the form and Nat. History of Solids on the Earth's surface . .	MINERALOGY.
		in the structure of living bodies . .	ANATOMY.
		of the internal functions of Life .	PHYSIOLOGY.
		in the structure and varieties of Vegetable Life	BOTANY.
		in the varieties and habits of Animal Life	ZOOLOGY.
		in the varieties and migrations of Men	ETHNOLOGY.
	of mind	as exhibited in Consciousness . . .	PSYCHOLOGY.
		in the external acts of man	HISTORY.†

* Beginning first with the facts of Observation, we have what are the strictly Inductive Sciences. I have called them the *Exact Sciences*, in accordance with the popular usage; not because they are any more exact than others, but because (if any reason can be given) they depend upon and require the greatest exactness of Observation—they depend upon Observation and Testimony.

† History, properly understood, will of course include a knowledge of ancient Geography, the Languages of ancient as well as foreign nations of the present day. It will also imply a knowledge of the systems of religion and modes of worship that have prevailed, and the progress that man has made in the Arts and Sciences, in Philosophy and Literature.

DEPARTMENT II.

*Pure Sciences** (purely metaphysical), based upon

Primary Conceptions		
	of unity	ARITHMETIC.
	of forms in Space	GEOMETRY.
	of combination of Symbols representing Constant Quantities .	ALGEBRA.
	of combination of Symbols representing Fluxional Quantities .	CALCULUS.
	of the meeting of lines and planes in a point	TRIGONOMETRY.
	of visible representation of Equations	ANALYTIC GEOMETRY.
	of the combination of Conceptions in Syllogisms	ANALYTICS.
	of Matter as modifying processes of Thought	METHOD.
	of the conditions and forms of Knowledge †	ONTOLOGY.‡

* Then in the next place I start with that other great coördinate in all knowledge, the elements of thought which exist nowhere in the reality of being, but which the Reason itself furnishes; and where all possible things are assumed as real, or rather the distinction between the possible and the real entirely disappears. Even the varieties of Method are based rather upon the varieties of Matter conceived as possible, than upon the results of experience in matter, although as the two coincide there is no necessity of observing the distinction in discussing Methods.

† By Ontology we mean the science of being, and it should include the discussion of the necessary law or forms of thought under which we know and believe whatever is supposed to exist out of the individual mind of the thinker. It will thus be found to furnish the fundamental and axiomatic principles of all the Exact Sciences, and in fact give to them their form or their Formal Cause.

‡ The Sciences in this Department are purely instrumental and valuable as Means and Helps to the construction of the Materials given in the preceding Department into the Sciences in the next two Departments, and in applying them to use as in the Departments in the third Class.

The six first named, *Arithmetic*, *Geometry*, *Algebra*, *Calculus*, *Trigonometry*, and *Analytic Geometry*, constitute the Department of MATHEMATICS; while of the other three, two, *Analytics* and *Method*, constitute LOGIC; and the three together, with one from the first Department, *Psychology*, constitute what is ordinarily called METAPHYSICS.

CLASS II.—PRACTICAL,*

including Sciences the object of which is "*to do.*"

DEPARTMENT I.

Mixed Sciences † based upon the Conception of

Matter and Motion	in solid bodies	on the Earth	MECHANICS.
		in the Heavens	ASTRONOMY.
	in liquids	at rest	HYDROSTATICS.
		in motion	HYDRAULICS.
	in gaseous masses		PNEUMATICS.
	in bodies as affecting	the hearing	ACOUSTICS.
		the vision	OPTICS.

DEPARTMENT II.

Ethical Sciences ‡ based on the conception of

Man and Action	in relation to the Idea of the Good		ETHICS.
	as exercising authority in temporal affairs		POLITY.
	as under Divine Providence		NAT. RELIGION.
	as under Authority	the State	JURISPRUDENCE.
		the Church	ECCL. POLITY.
		a Revelation from God	REV. RELIGION.

* The sciences in the second class are those which develope and state the laws of motion and of action. I have called them Practical because their End is Action; they all assume more or less of the results of the Theoretical, or sciences included in the first class. They proceed from the results there obtained by demonstration to the evolution of rules or laws.

† These sciences I have called Mixed, since although the laws of Matter are determined from the conception of its nature and constitution alone, yet the law itself is in point of fact for the most part first ascertained by observation. But it is soon found to be implied in our conceptions, (1) of Matter (as opposed to Mind); (2) of Force (as opposed to Motive); and (3) of Motion (as opposed to Thought).

‡ In the second Department we consider the laws which man *ought to* obey. These are derived from a consideration of man as he is (Psychology and Physiology), and of the destiny, which, by his voluntary activity, he ought to attain. But as this destiny implies as a means of its accomplishment Society or the Family, and the State, that is, a society having sovereignty over individual men, and a Providence or Moral Governor of the

CLASS III.—PRODUCTIVE,*

including the Sciences the object of which is "*to create.*"

DEPARTMENT I.

The *Fine Arts* † or Sciences which guide the expenditure of labor, directed to the production of

The Beautiful	in the Soil	GARDENING.
	in the construction of Edifices .	ARCHITECTURE.
	in solid representations of Life .	SCULPTURE.
	in perspective representations by Color	PAINTING.
	in the combination of Sounds . . .	MUSIC.
	in the use of Language . . .	POETRY.

world, to whom man is accountable, and whose final approbation is an essential part of his destiny, we evolve by Analysis and Demonstration from these conceptions Society, State, and Providence—the rules which man ought to obey. Hence Ethics, Polity, and Natural Religion, are based upon Reason alone. And the realization of Religion implies a Church having authority in matters of faith. Hence we have, besides the authority of GOD over us, the two others, State and Church, which we find that He has recognized and sanctioned as guides and authority, each within its appropriate sphere, and we have both Jurisprudence and Ecclesiastical Polity as rules of action within certain limits.

* In the third class I have included all those sciences the end of which is to aid man in the accomplishment of results out of himself, and have divided them into two classes, the Beautiful and the Useful. The Subjects included in this Class are more commonly called *Arts* than *Sciences.* They are, however, *Sciences of the Arts;* that is, branches of knowledge which teach how to produce results, the production of which is called Art. Art is distinguished from mere Instinct by this fact—namely, that it is guided by a scientific comprehension of its principles and processes, whereas Instinct has no such comprehension.

† I have not regarded the Methods of Æsthetics as properly coming within the province of Logic. They are determined rather by the Susceptibility than the Reason. Their ultimate Facts are only experimental; we can only refer to the fact that a beautiful object *does* excite the Emotions, which we call the emotions of Beauty; and we judge an object to be beautiful because it does excite such emotions. We cannot prove that it ought to do so. We can discover no necessity in the nature of the case for its exciting such emotions. Its judgments in fact are all Relative, while Logic deals with the Absolute alone.

DEPARTMENT II.

*Useful Arts** or Sciences which guide the expenditure of labor, directed to the production of

The Useful	in the Soil			AGRICULTURE.
	in objects beneath the Soil			METALLURGY.
	in the manufacture of the raw material			TECHNOLOGY.
	in multiplying the products of mind	expressed in	written Language	TYPOGRAPHY.
			works of the Fine Arts	ENGRAVING.
	in the increase of value by Exchange			COMMERCE.
	in the promotion of Health			MEDICINE.
	in the expression of thought by Language			RHETORIC.
	in promoting pecuniary prosperity			POLIT. ECONOMY.
	in promoting the National Defence			WAR.

1246. Of course all the above-named or described Sciences admit of being greatly subdivided. In fact any author has the right to take any part of any one Science and treat it as a Science by itself, if he chooses to do so. This is, in fact, making a subdivision of some part of the division of Science as it previously existed. In this way the names on our Catalogue of Sciences become more numerous, and may in fact extend beyond any known or conceivable limit. I have not thought it worth while, however, to follow the subdivisions already made, any further than they are given in the preceding three Tables and the Notes accompanying them.

Each Science in the above Tables admits for subdivision.

* But in the second part of this Class we have the Useful Arts. They take the results of the General Facts obtained by the Sciences in the First Department of the first Class, and the Laws obtained in the corresponding Department of the second Class, and by Deduction apply them to the results which minister to man's physical and temporal wants, as being subservient to the purposes of life; which purpose again is the attainment of that End or Destiny for which his Creator placed him in this state of existence.

SECTION II.

Of the Conveyance of Ideas from one Mind to another.

1247. All Methods in so far as they belong to the Sphere of Logic, are determined by the Idea of the True. They aim merely to satisfy the demands of comprehension and conviction. But most, if not all, the Methods of Argument and Instruction come also within the Sphere of Rhetoric. They aim not only to convince, but also to please and to persuade; and in Instruction especially, to save time and labor, and to facilitate the ease with which we remember what we have once learned. But the Methods of Rhetoric are determined by the Idea of the Useful. Its precepts are valuable only because they are useful—useful for pleasing and persuading—useful for the perspicuity of statement—lucidness of illustration or impressing upon the mind a sense of the importance of what is communicated.

Methods of Logic and of Rhetoric.

1248. It is obvious, therefore, that by far the largest, though by no means the most important, part of what properly belongs to any adequate discussion of the Methods of Instruction, must come within the appropriate sphere of Rhetoric. I shall, therefore, make but a very short Chapter on the Method of Instruction in this place.

Methods of Rhetoric in instruction.

1249. By Instruction we mean not merely the communication of the knowledge which we have obtained. Our attention is much more completely fixed upon the means of *Construction*, or the putting it into a system, and so arranging the parts as that they may best fulfil the conditions of a thorough comprehension of the general subject by those who are unacquainted with it.

Instruction and Construction.

1250. I regard it as a controlling fact in regard to Methods of Instruction, that a conception cannot be conveyed or transferred, as a whole, from one mind to another. Each one

Conceptions cannot be communicated as Wholes.

must be formed *de novo* in each mind. No one can convey his sensation to another; we can describe them to those beings, and those only who have had sensations of the same species—the sensation of color, for instance, which I have when I look at the object before me, I cannot communicate to any other person. If he can see, I can describe it to him so that he can form a conception of it. But if he be blind, he cannot conceive of a sensation of color, nor can one be conveyed into his mind.

Judgments may.

1251. A judgment may be conveyed from one mind to another, provided both minds have the conceptions which constitute the matter of the judgment. Thus if I affirm that "gold is yellow," the person hearing me does not need to *judge* whether it is yellow or not, in order to understand my judgment, or the proposition affirming it—the proposition conveys the judgment to his mind, and he may then affirm or deny it as he pleases.

Conceptions may be recalled by using a known for an unknown word.

1252. But a conception cannot be conveyed in that way or in any way. It is necessarily constructed by and within every mind in which it can exist at all. Thus suppose I have a conception of an object, and use some word in an unknown tongue to express it, that word is just as good *in itself* as any other, and just as good *relatively* to all who understand the language to which it belongs. But it has no power of itself to convey or suggest the conception. If the conception is one which has been already formed, and is in the mind of the person to whom I am speaking, all that I need to do is to *define my word* by giving its synonyme in the language which he uses. If I had used the word "*caleb*," which is Hebrew, I have but to give the English word "*dog*," and I have defined the word and recalled to his attention the conception which the two words are used to represent in their respective vocabularies.

1253. But suppose the conception be entirely new

to the person addressed, no mere definition of the word by which I denote it will suffice. I must give him first the Essentia of the object by referring it to the Proximate Genus, and then the Differentia, which distinguishes it from the coördinate species in that Genus. And then further if it be an individual object, I must give some of the individual marks or inseparable accidents.

Verbal Definitions will not convey conceptions.

1254. The person addressed then *takes up together* (for that is the meaning of the word "*conceive*"), all the matter which I have given and puts it together in his own mind, as I gave it to him, and he has the conception which I had. But he has formed it anew in his own mind; I gave him the material only. I defined my conception by an analysis of its matter, and he constructed his by a synthesis of the same matter.

The person addressed reconstructs the conception.

1255. But each of these elements into which I resolved my conception by analysis, and out of which he constructed his by synthesis, are also conceptions; and if they are conceptions which he has not already formed, he is not prepared to synthesize out of the material which I have given him. My Definition has not been sufficiently elementary, I must go back one step further and define the elements of which he has not yet formed a conception.

Conceptions analyzed in Definition into more elementary conceptions.

SECTION III.

Of Definition and Description.

1256. The predicating of any subject its Essentia and Differentia is what is called Definition. Thus if I say, "Mahomet was THE MAN *who founded the religion called by his name*," I give first the Essentia—what he was—"a man;" and secondly, the Differentia, which distinguishes him from all other men "*who founded the religion*," &c. By these words I have given an adequate definition.

Definition.

Where *adequate.*

1257. But suppose I had omitted the Essentia, and said, "he was the founder of the religion," &c., this would be a specific definition; but the question might still recur as to his Essentia, whether he was "man," "angel," or "demon." In that case the definition would have been inadequate, inasmuch as "founder of the religion," &c., may be the Differentia of Species in several different Proximate Genera, as "man," "angel," &c.

Specific Definitions inadequate.

1258. Or again, suppose I had merely said, "Mahomet was a MAN *of Arabia*." Here the Essentia "man" would be satisfactory to give me a distinct conception, but the words "of Arabia," are no Differentia of an individual man, since there are many "men of Arabia." The Definition would be inadequate. It would not be definite. It would give the Essentia with the Differentia of the species, but no peculiar or distinguishing mark of the individual.

Definitions of Individuals must give the individual marks.

1259. A Definition is either of a name or of the conception which we have of a thing, or of the thing itself by means of its conception or name.

Definition of a name, of a conception, or of the thing.

1260. When we define a name or a word, we explain its meaning by other words having the same meaning. Thus we define φιλέω in Greek and *amo* in Latin, by the word "*love*" in English. We explain the name "sulphuric acid," by saying that it is the "oil of vitriol." This is called a *Verbal* Definition, as merely defining words.

Definition of a name.

Verbal Definitions.

1261. A *real* Definition is one that defines the thing itself of which the conception is formed. But as we know the thing or subject-matter only by the conception which we form of it, we can of course define it only by means of that conception. To define any thing, therefore, is to define or give by analysis the conception which we have of it. Our conception may be compared by this means with those

Real Definitions.

which other persons have of the same object, and corrected, if found to be erroneous or inadequate, by means of theirs. This correction, however, implies that their means and opportunities of investigation have been superior to ours.

1262. We may, however, sometimes enable another to form a conception of the thing itself, without the intervention of any conception which we may have formed of it ourselves. This we do by a *Description* pointing to the place in which it is situated, the time when it occurs, or the circumstances by which it is surrounded. In this case we simply refer to the sphere of its conception, and leave others to learn the matter for themselves by their own observations or investigation.

Descriptions as a means of conveying conceptions.

1263. It has been very generally held that there are certain simple Ideas and ultimate elements in all conceptions which cannot be defined. And the reason given for the opinion is, that being simple or ultimate elements they can be divided or analyzed no farther.

1264. But this is evidently a mistake. We do not analyze *the object* in our definition, but only our *conception of it.* Now a conception *ex vi termini* can never consist of a simple element. It is *the taking together* of several properties as Essentia and Differentia into a Logical Whole which to the mind represents the object denoted by the term which represents the conception. We get a conception of an object only by its Essentia and Differentia. And here the conception, including these elments, can be analyzed and so defined.*

No Conception that cannot be defined.

* We must remember that it will often happen that the Differentia of any object, or class of objects, as we form our conceptions of them, will not consist of properties which can be predicated of the objects considered solely and by themselves. They are rather *relative* properties. Thus we may predicate "hardness" of iron in and by itself; but "magnetism" is but a relative property, since we could never know its reality except by the relation which the magnetic body sustains to others which are attracted by it while in that condition. So with "causality," and many of the other elements which enter into our conceptions; they indicate rather the relations which the objects sustain to others, than any properties which are directly perceptible by themselves.

1265. The difficulty however is *in us*. It is often the case that we have a distinct conception without its being definite in our own minds. We never have analyzed it, and perhaps cannot analyze it so as to name each element of its matter, and say what precisely is its Essentia and what its Differentia. Thus I suppose all persons have a pretty distinct conception of an *apple*. But I doubt if any one can give the Differentia of it so as precisely to draw the line between it and the *pear* for instance.

Reasons why we are sometimes unable to define.

1266. Again there are objects the definition of which is made difficult, and practically impossible in some cases, by our having no well known Proximate Genus to which to refer them as expressive of their Essentia. Thus Prof. Loomis, in his Geometry, in attempting to define a "straight line," says, "It is the *shortest* PATH *between two points*." The Differentia, "shortest between two points," is faultless. But the Essentia, "path," sounds strangely. A line is not a "path" in any sense in which we are accustomed to that word; that is, a "geometrical line" does not belong to any genus which we are accustomed to denote by the word "path."

Want of general terms.

1267. This is in fact a difficulty often met with. We may have the Differentia of a conception at our command, but not its Essentia. In all attempts to define "*consciousness*," for example, the same difficulty is encountered. Shall we call it a "faculty," a "function," or simply a "state" of the mind?

A frequent difficulty.

1268. The usual resort in such cases of our inability to define that of which, however, we have a definite but no distinct* conception, is to describe the sphere by means of the Differentia, and leave the Genus or Essentia undetermined.

The usual resort.

1269. But *an adequate* Definition defines its object by referring it to its species and genus. Thus we say

* It may be well to remark that the Essentia makes a conception "*distinct*," the Differentia makes it "*definite*."

that "Iron is a METAL *of great malleability, density, and of a darkish gray color.*" When we say it is a "metal," we refer it to the genus "metals;" and of course we may thereafter predicate of it all the Essentia of metals. By saying "it is of great malleability, density, and of a darkish gray color," we refer it to each of the species whose Differentia are respectively "malleability," "density," and "gray color."

What constitutes an adequate Definition.

1270. We are said to define a conception *generally* or *generically*, when we refer it to its genus, as "man is an *animal;*" *specifically,* when we give the Differentia of the species without the genus, as "man is *rational,*" or "a being with reason;" *accidentally,* when we give merely some accidental property of the object; *physically,* when we enumerate the physical parts, as "man has two hands, two feet, erect form;" and *metaphysically,* when we refer to the invisible nature, as "man is a spiritual being, with reason, intellect, memory, conscience," &c.*

Generic Definitions specified.

Accidental.

Physical.

Metaphysical.

1271. In defining a Genus, as such, the Essentia only can be given.† But in defining a Species, both the Essentia and the Differentia must be given; and in defining an Individual there must be added to the Essentia and Differentia the peculiarities which distinguish the Individual defined from others of the same species.

What Definitions can be given.

1272. But when a Definition fails to fulfil these conditions, as if in defining a Species, there is an omission of the Differentia; or in defining an Individual an omission of the peculiarities, the definition is *inadequate.*

Inadequate Definitions.

* What is sometimes called a *Negative* Definition, or defining negatively, is no definition of the subject at all. It consists merely in naming the Differentia of the coördinate species, and saying that they are *not* properties of, and do not belong to the Species which we are defining.

† We may of course refer it to the next higher of the subaltern Genera, in which case it becomes a Species to be defined as such by the Essentia of its Proximate Genus and its own Differentia.

1273. Definition, therefore, always implies a classification of the thing defined, by referring it to its Genus and Species. Hence it appears that we can cognize the Individual only through the Species. Each property which we ascribe to it or see that it possesses refers it to a class, whose Differentia is the property thus ascribed to the individual object.

Definition implies Classification.

1274. One of the readiest and best illustrations of this principle is afforded in the conjugation of the verb. The verb itself is the Genus, and its Essentia the meaning of the word in its most general sense. The Species is the voice, as active, passive, &c., whose Differentia is the mode of the action of the verb in reference to the agent and the object. Mood is the first sub-species, the Differentia of which is the mode of affirmation as declaring (Indicative), representing it as possible, &c. The second sub-species is Tense, and its Differentia is the relation of the action to the time in which the word is used by the speaker. The next sub-species is "number," indicating as its Differentia whether the subject of the verb included one or more; and the infima species is the "person," limiting by its Differentia the subject still further, by showing whether the subject is the person speaking, the person spoken to, or some person spoken of. And the word itself, as it stands on the written page, or is heard in oral speech, is the individual.

The Conjugation and Declension of Verbs an illustration.

1275. It is very likely to happen that the terms used in any Definition will also need to be defined. In this case the laws of Definition are the same as before; we define by Essentia and Differentia still. Thus if I should define the palm as "an *endogenous* tree," &c., one might be wholly unable to construct the conception, because he had not previously the conception for which "*endogenous*" stands. I should then be obliged to define that conception by giving its conception, as applied to plants—GROWTH *by succesive additions to the inside.* But suppose my definition were not yet sufficiently elementary,

We may need to define a Definition.

and that he had no definite conception of "growth," I should be obliged to define it as a species of the genus "increase," giving the Differentia which distinguish it from the coördinate species—*accretion*, *agglomeration*, &c. Or suppose the words "by successive additions to the inside," represented a conception not previously formed in the mind of the person addressed, I should have to explain or define them in the same way, either showing what an "addition" is, or the difference between the kind that is "to the inside," and that which is "to the outside," its coördinate.

Ultimate Conceptions.

1276. Hence as each Definition may need a definition of its terms, there must be a constant retrogression until we come to some ultimate conception, which is formed at the first sight of the object; or to Description, pointing out the sphere of the object of which the conception is to be found.

A Description never furnishes the Matter for a Conception.

1277. A Description, therefore, does not furnish the material for the construction of a conception. It merely informs us when, or where, or how we may find it for ourselves. And the process of finding it is one of the original Methods of Investigation. It brings us back, therefore, to primary or elementary conceptions.

Primary Conceptions spontaneous and necessary.

1278. These primary or elemental conceptions of external objects are formed spontaneously, and of necessity are the perception of the external senses. And of invisible objects, such as geometrical figures, &c., they are formed by the Reason constructing them in the mind itself. Thus suppose I imagine a point moving from one position in space always at the same distance from another point, until it comes back to the place of its departure, I have formed the conception of a circle by constructing the circle itself. It is for Genus A FIGURE IN SPACE, and for Differentia it has *a circumference every point of which is equally distant from one and the same point within it.*

1279. But this Genus, "figures in space," cannot be a primary conception for us, since we never have the Differentia denoted by the words "*in space*," except as a counterpart to objects having shape and outline in the external world or *in place*. I do not deny that the conception would be possible without such observation. That is a question of metaphysics with which we have nothing to do in this place. But as a fact, *all* mortals here on Earth, do not form conceptions of the invisible realities of truth, until after experience of the visible realities of being in the material world.

Conceptions of the reality of truth imply a previous perception of realities of being.

SECTION IV.

Of Natural and Artificial Classifications.

1280. The conception of each individual object—for with the individual we always begin in actual experience—is formed by means of the Essentia and Differentia. I see an object before me which is yellow and round; if I call it an "orange," I refer it to a conception already formed, and consequently this is not a primary one. It is, however, the point at which each of us who live at the present day begin with the formation of our conceptions. We learn the names that have already been given to things, and base our classifications and conceptions upon those that have been made before us.

Conceptions first formed upon the basis of those made by others.

1281. The primary classifications are always of necessity very simple and unscientific. They are based on some property immediately obvious to the senses, as color, shape, odor, &c., for their Essentia. The next step is a division of the Genera, using different colors, odors, shapes, &c., as Differentia. This classification is almost instantaneous if not quite so, at the first instant when the mind is awakened to activity by the presence of material objects to our senses.

Primary classifications very simple.

1282. From these first and purely accidental principles of classification, we pass on in our progress of comprehension, at each step adopting as permanent and useful such as have been found so in times past, and because they have been so found have received those common names which constitute the basis of all languages, as "common names."

Some of them remain as the basis of language.

1283. But no sooner do we begin our scientific investigations than we find in most cases that a new classification becomes requisite, one requiring for its construction a new analysis of the objects to be included in the classes.

Necessity of new Classifications.

1284. Hence the distinction between natural and artificial, or scientific classifications. Natural classifications are such as are formed at once instinctively and of necessity by the mind. They are based upon the more obvious and conspicuous properties of the objects, and denoted by such words as the common names of all languages. The scientific classifications, on the other hand, are such as are based upon less obvious properties, and are devised for the purpose of expediting Science. They are, for the most part, denoted by what are called the technical terms of a language or science.

Distinction between Natural and Scientific Classifications.

1285. The problem in all scientific classifications is to group together in one species those facts which have the greatest number of properties in common, and to classify on those properties which are regarded as Formal with reference to those which are Modal. The fewer the classes therefore the better, provided that in reducing the number of classes we do not increase the exceptions to each, so as to make the aggregate of Species and Exceptions greater than in some other classifications.

The problem in Scientific Classifications.

1286. Thus to take an example from Ethnology. If we divide men into three coördinate classes, red, black, and white, not only are the Modal properties common to each species in classification few, but the exceptions to any statement that might be made concerning any one of the species are

An illustration from Ethnology.

very numerous. As the result of much investigation, it has been found that if we class them as woolly-headed, bearded, and beardless, the number of statements, including both the rules and the exceptions, requisite for a full treatise on the Natural History of Man, is greatly reduced. Of course, therefore, that natural history when thus presented, is much more easily and much more quickly learned, and longer remembered than when presented to the mind of the learner by means of any other classification.

Illustration from the history of Botany.

1287. To take another illustration. In Botany the primary classification of its objects was into Trees, Shrubs, and Plants. CÆSALPINUS proposed the first scientific classification based on "the number, position, and figure of organs," as "the flower, the seed receptacle, and the seeds;" for the purpose, as he said, of "ranging them into brigades, regiments, and companies, like a well-ordered army." Soon after BAUHIN undertook another and simpler classification. RAY proposed another; and in 1687 TOURNEFORT proposed to classify on "the regularity or irregularity of the flowers in form, and by the situation of the receptacle of the seeds below the calyx or within it." Then LINNAEUS appeared and classified by "the pistils and stamens of the flowers." And finally, we have the system of the JUSSIEUS, based on "the number of the cotyledons and the structure of the seeds, and subordinate to this the insertion of the stamina, as over, about, or under the germen."

The limit to the reduction of the number Species.

1288. A primary object is undoubtedly to make the number of the species as small as practicable. And the limit to this reduction, as has been said, is the number of exceptions and abnormal peculiarities which always increases with the reduction in the number of classes, so long as we adhere to the same principle of classification. And that principle which will give us the smallest aggregate of species and of exceptions, is said to be the simplest or to simplify the classification the most.

1289. Now wherever we begin in our instruction, whether with the most general subject, as in the Synthetic Method—or with the individual, as in the Analytic, we must define our subject, and each subject as we pass along, by referring it to the natural and well-known classifications. And if we have adopted a scientific classification, we need always to give the common one also, and explain ours by the difference between them. Thus a chemist would say, "chloride of sodium is the muriate of soda of the old classifications—the common salt of the common use. It consists of so many parts of sodium, so many of chlorine," &c., &c.

We must define by reference to both Natural and Scientific classifications.

1290. In the course of our classifications we shall sometimes encounter a phenomenon which we have not yet noticed—namely, the recurrence of the same Differentia of Species in different Proximate Genera—these we may call *Recurring Species*.

Similar Differentia in different Proximate Genera.

Recurring Species.

1291. Thus in Mathematics we have "*curved* lines" and "*curved* surfaces," in which the Genera "lines" and "surfaces" comprehend Species, whose Differentia is "*curved;*" as "*curved* lines," and "*curved* surfaces." Again in Grammar, in the conjugation and declension of the Verb, we have three voices, for instance, Active, Passive, and Middle. Now taking these as Proximate Genera, we have in each of them the same Differentia of Mood, Infinitive Mood, &c.; and the Differentia, that is, the signification and force of Mood is precisely the same in one voice as in the other, although modifying a different Essentia. So, also, each Mood has different Tenses, as a Present, and Past, and a Future. The force or Differentia of Tense is precisely the same in one Mood as in the other. It is defined as determining "the time at which the Verb represents the act as taking place;" the Present represents it as taking place at the time of speaking, whether in one Mood or mode of representing the action or another, and irrespective of the Differentia of voice.

Illustrated from Mathematics and from Grammar.

SECTION V.

Of the Division of the General Subject.

1292. The subjects of which we treat have extension in two different directions, Comprehension and Protension. If we are treating a general subject, as Chemistry, Mechanics, &c., it has Comprehensive Extension, and admits of course of division into subordinate parts. If we are treating of an individual subject, as the history of a nation, the biography of an individual, it has Protensive Extension only.

Two kinds of Comprehensions in a General Subject.

1293. In this latter case there is no logical necessity for a division at all. A division is only a convenience, and one that is often of very great importance both to the writer and the reader. And as it is one that is required and determined rather by the idea of Utility than the idea of Truth, we will leave its discussion to the Rhetoricians.

No logical necessity for a division of Protensive Extension.

1294. But in treating of a general subject a division becomes necessary, in consequence of the fact that much which it is necessary to say, may be predicated of a part of the included individual subjects which cannot be predicated of the whole; and much of some parts which cannot be predicated of others.

Division of a General Subject necessary.

1295. If the subject will admit of a division into coördinate parts, it is best to divide in that way. And then the division is to be determined by the law already laid down for scientific classifications; namely, so divide as that the aggregate of the number of the parts and of the exceptions to the predicates affirmed of the parts, will be the smallest that the nature of the matter will allow.

Coördinate part preferable.

1296. The reason for this rule is the same as that given above. The instruction can be given in fewer words, consequently in shorter time, is more easily and sooner understood and better remembered, than when the mind is encumbered by a multiplicity either of subdivisions or of exceptions to the statements made for general. Each coördinate and each subordinate part, as well as each exceptional case or individual, becomes a separate and distinct subject of predication, which it takes as long to teach and requires as much, and often more, effort to remember than the most comprehensive statement in the whole science.

Reason for the Rule.

1297. But there are cases in which no division into coördinate parts can be made unless it be a very clumsy one. Our present general subject (828), "Method," as has been already said is such an one. Again, if one were treating of the Literary Men of a nation, it would be impossible to make a coördinate division that would answer any good purpose.

In some cases division into coordinate parts impossible.

1298. In such cases we must divide into Alternate Species. As in the case just named, we might divide the Literary Men into Historians, Poets, Essayists, Philosophers, Naturalists, &c. This would be a useful division. But the same man might be distinguished in more than one of the classes named, as for instance, the English Southey as a poet and as a historian; Coleridge, a poet and a philosopher; Macaulay as a poet, historian, and essayist.

Division int Alternate Spe cies.

1299. And with regard to the number of Alternate Parts into which the General Subject should be divided, the same rule holds as above: it should be the minimum aggregate of parts and exceptions.

The same rule governs the number of Alternate as of Coördinate Species.

SECTION VI.

Of the Order in the treatment.

1300. In the first acquisition of knowledge we are obliged to begin with the individual and concrete, and, examining them one by one, we ascend to the general and the abstract. Thus the knowledge of human nature is acquired by an acquaintance with individual men one after another, analyzing, abstracting, and omitting what is peculiar to each, and retaining as the matter of the conception to be expressed by one general term "*man*," all that is common to all men.

We begin to know with the individual.

1301. So, too, in acquiring the knowledge of any particular or individual object, we may perceive its properties, many of them at a time. But we have to learn or study them, property after property, one at a time.

We also learn Properties one by one.

1302. Now in teaching others, which is instruction, we may pursue the same method; beginning with the individual and the concrete, and proceed to the general and abstract. This is called the Analytic Method of teaching. But it is generally found tedious, uninteresting, and unsatisfactory. And it moreover requires an examination of each of the individuals separately and in detail, which is in some cases impossible on account of the number, and in others they are inaccessible.

The Analytic Method in teaching.

1303. Still, however, in some branches of science this method is preferable, and perhaps even indispensable. In Botany, in Chemistry, in Anatomy, and such like sciences, which consist almost entirely of details, and in which there are comparatively but very few general principles as yet established, we must of course confine ourselves to teaching the facts as they are known, and as far as they are known. The Causes and Laws which determine those facts are as yet unknown to us, if not altogether beyond the reach of our faculties.

In some cases the only Method.

1304. In the Analytic Method of Teaching, the subject of which we speak is, of course, an individual, and we pass from one to another as fast as we have predicated of each what we know of it, or at least that portion of what we

Analytic Method speaks of the Individual Subject.

know of it which our purpose requires us to communicate.

1305. But in the Synthetic Method we begin with the general subject which comprehends the individuals. We predicate of it whatever belongs to it as a general subject, then divide it into its coördinate parts, and those parts again into their subordinates, and so on until we come to the individuals included in each part.

The Synthetic Method.

1306. As each part is less comprehensive than its whole, and so on until we come to the individual, each part will have something to be said of it which could not have been predicated of its superior and comprehending part in any previous sections, and which ought to be predicated before we proceed to its subordinates.

Each Part requires special predication.

1307. These two Methods differ much less in relation to the fulfilment of the Logical conditions of Method than would appear at first sight. There is but one way of forming a conception of a subject, whether that subject be the general subject of our treatise or the special subject of any subordinate chapter, section, or paragraph, even down to the individual. In all cases we form, and must form, our conceptions by means of classification. By classification also, and by that only, can we communicate our conceptions to others. In the Analytic Method we teach by means of the natural classifications which all make naturally and necessarily; while in the Synthetic we teach by means of those scientific classifications which are the results of reflection, and some degree at least of advance towards the maturity of Science.*

Difference in the Methods not great.

* For an illustration take the following. Suppose a writer treating of Zoölogy synthetically, he would begin by defining his general subject, "animals;" giving its Essentia as "living beings," its Differentia "with material organizations, and living only on organic matter, either vegetable or animal." The first clause limiting against spiritual beings, angels, &c., and the second against the vegetable kingdom. He would then divide into

1308. Our conception of an object may be analyzed into its Essentia, Differentia, Accidents, Quantity or Comparison, Cause and Effects. This order is not in all its successive steps *strictly necessary*. It is, however, the most convenient. The conception is completed by the two first, Essentia and Differentia, in all that is essential to its *completeness*. The others are necessary to its *adequacy*.

Matter of Conception divided with reference to the order of communication.

1309. The Essentia and Differentia give us all the matter which is necessary to enable us to form the conception of any object of thought. They are, therefore, all that is necessary to the adequacy of the conception for all the purposes of *a priori* Methods of Investigation or Proof, as in the Analysis of a Conception, giving us the Matter of Analytic Judgments and in the Demonstration of the reality of Implied Properties.

The Essentia and Differentia alone necessary for the *a priori* Methods.

1310. But our conception of an object is never adequate, nor can our Science be completed until we have ascertained by the Methods of Investigation the Accidents—including the separable and inseparable—and the Continuous or Discrete Quantity and its Protensive Relation to its antecedents and consequents.

The Accidents, Quantity, &c, necessary to the Conception for Science.

1311. *Comparison* is by no means a necessary element in the formation of our conception of an object. It may serve instead of Quantity. Thus if the question be asked, How large are the Hottentots? The answer may be definite

Comparison not always necessary.

four "Departments,"—Vertebrata, Articulata, Mollusca, and Radiata, each department into Classes, classes into Orders, orders into Genera, genera into Species, species into Varieties, and varieties (the infima species) into Individuals, describing each in its order; and in describing the individual he would refer it to the species, and thereby in effect predicate of it all that had been said of each subaltern species or genera up to the highest. Its specific name would at once classify and describe all that for the most part we care to know of it. But in the Analytic Method he would begin with the first animal he might meet. He would have to begin with saying, "this *dog*," "this *cat*," "this *worm*," &c., as the case might be, in all cases, however, referring to the common and well-known class-names of the individual he might be examining.

in Quantity—"*four feet and a half;*" (which, however, is after all a *comparison* with the *foot*, taken as a unity of measure,) or it may be *by comparison*, thus, "much less than the ordinary height of Europeans."

1312. Or we may have the question of quantity as to the comprehensiveness of the sphere of the conception. Thus in describing a class, we say it is a "large" or a "small" one. Or possibly we give the precise number of individuals included in it, especially if the number be small. Or again, we may give an idea of the quantity by comparison with another class, calling it larger or smaller than some other whose comprehensiveness is known.

Quantity of the Comprehensiveness of the Sphere.

1313. There are many objects which we do not conceive of as Cause or as Effect. Thus in speaking of a Geometrical Figure, we should not be likely to conceive of it as an effect whose cause is important to our knowledge; nor yet should we think of it as a cause whose effects it could be important to investigate. Still, however, the conception of a triangle for example is an effect. It is the creation of mind, and it is a cause; for it has stirred up all that mental activity which has produced the Sciences of Geometry and Trigonometry.

Cause and Effect not always required.

1314. We come, therefore, to the Essentia and the Differentia as that which is always necessary to a distinct and definite conception of any subject; and which, therefore, must be Logically first in all Methods of Instruction,* as well as in all constructions of systems and sciences. Without them there can be no conception of the subject, whether general, special, or individual.

Essentia and Differentia always necessary.

* It is often advisable, for rhetorical reasons, not only to state the Differentia in such positive terms as connote the subject, but also to increase the distinctness of the outline of our conception, by contrasting it with its coördinates speaking of their Differentia, thus fixing the attention upon them, and thus affirming that they do *not* belong to the class of objects of which we are speaking. This is sometimes called defining a subject by negatives, or negatively—that is, distinctly saying what it is not.

1315. By the Essentia we get a *distinct* conception—the mind is assured of a reality, a substance, since it has its Constitutive or Material Properties. But the conception becomes *definite* only by means of the Differentia. The Differentia distinguish it from others, consequently *defines* it, or fixes the limits within which it is a reality.

Distinct and Definite Conceptions by Essentia and Differentia.

We may, therefore, perhaps sum up the principles of Order in the Method of Instruction as follows:

Principles of Order.

1316. (1) State first the general subject by its Essentia and Differentia; referring always to the natural classifications, even when we have occasion to use a scientific one.*

First Principle.

1317. (2) Divide it into coördinate parts or species, on the simplest principle at your command, and then subdivide as far as the case may require, giving to each coördinate and subordinate part its Differentia, as we proceed to treat each of the parts in the order and degree of their subordination.

Second Principle.

1318. (3) Whatever subject we teach, whether the general or either of the subordinate parts, define it first by Essentia and Differentia, that so the learner may know distinctly and definitely what we are treating of.

Third Principle.

1319. (4) The order in which the other topics, as Accidents, Quantity or Comparison, and Cause and Effect ought to follow, will depend upon the End we have in view. It is possible that Quantity is all that is desired. It other cases it will be wholly unimportant, and therefore deserving to

Fourth Principle.

* We are to remember that not all the *Peculiar* Properties of any class are to be regarded as its Differentia. The Differentia are only those peculiar properties which are most obvious and conspicuous. At least this is always so in the Natural Classifications. And much is added to the perspicuity and vividness with which instruction is communicated, by a successful tact in characterizing the subjects by those properties which, while they are peculiar and so determinate of species, are also conspicuous to the observation.

be omitted as surplusage. Again, the Cause or the Effect, either or both, may be the only thing demanded, or they may be a matter in which no interest is taken, and must be given or omitted accordingly. And so among the Accidental Properties—those must be selected which the object in view requires, remembering here as every where, that whatever is not conducive to the End, is to be rejected (764). This is one of the most fundamental principles of Method.

1320. The mind is always impatient of any matter that is irrelevant to the End in view, and even of the intrusion of any piece of matter which is relevant, provided it be out of place and comes in before something else that is necessary to its proper progress. Take the following example:—"The Coquallin was sent from America, by the name of the *Orange-colored Squirrel.* It is, however, not a squirrel. It is a beautiful animal, and very remarkable for its color, its belly being of a fine yellow, and its head as well as body varied with white, black, brown, and orange; it covers its back with its tail, like the squirrel, but has not, like that animal, small brushes of hair at the tips of the ears: it never climbs up any trees, but dwells in the hollows and under the roots of trees, like the garden squirrel."

The mind impatient of impertinent matter.

1321. Now here after the assertion, "it is not a squirrel," the mind was expecting the Differentia between it and the squirrel, whereas the author gives a series of propositions, which so far from being Differentia of natural species, may as well be applicable to the Squirrel as to the Coquallin.

1322. Every body has observed the difference in the degree of ease with which they remember the writings and instructions of different teachers. This is owing in a great measure to the perfection of the Method of the Teacher. He has what is always necessary to successful teaching, a clear conception in his own mind of the subject and of the special end for which the instruction

Ease of remembering depends upon Method in Teaching.

is at that time sought, and upon which therefore the interest in the subject itself depends. He, therefore, by the natural laws which govern the operation of his own mind, mentions the subject, referring it to a well known Proximate Genus, and then giving the most marked and distinguishing Differentia of its species. He carefully excludes all matter that is not pertinent and conducive to the end for which he is communicating the instruction,* and finally selects and arranges whatever he is to predicate of his subject with reference to that end.

First awaken an interest in the subject.

1323. *Rhetorically* one of the first things for a teacher to do is to awaken an interest in his subject, by fixing in the mind some End to be gained by the instruction. Although this is a violation of the principles of Logical Method, it is nevertheless so important to the rhetoric of instruction, that it may well be placed in the rank of the highest importance.

Nature of the End.

1324. The End must of course be sufficiently important to awaken an interest in the subject itself, and to excite that interest to such a degree of intensity as to raise the mind to a high state of activity, and do away with the sense of tediousness which attends upon all aimless exertion.

Necessity for omission of Matter.

1325. If the mind were sufficiently capacious to comprehend all things—all the properties and bearings of any one subject even—there would be many cases in which there could be no need of such a principle of selection and omission as we have referred to. But the mind is not of sufficient comprehension to receive and retain all that we can learn or may desire to know. This fact is not perhaps very flattering. But it is well to have it distinctly understood and admitted. It may humble our pride

* Quidquid præcipies, esto brevis: ut citò dicta
Percipiant animi dociles, teneantque fideles.
Omne supervacuum pleno de pectore manat.
HOR. De Ars Poet. 335.

somewhat, but it will make us wiser and teach us at an early day the necessity of economizing time and labor, and saving ourselves a vast amount of labor and toil, which would otherwise have been spent in vain.

1326. It is no part of Logic to ascertain the various Ends for which instruction may be sought, and from which we may derive our interest in any subject. The End may be merely and purely the love of truth. It may be some immediate practical application which we wish to make of the knowledge we are seeking. But without such an End in view, but little will be sought and still less, effectually obtained.

SECTION VII.

Method of Logical Criticism.

1327. Hitherto in our discussion of Formulæ and Methods, we have supposed ourselves occupying a point of time anterior to construction; and discussing the Formula and Principles by which to be guided in our work. But in experience it is quite as often that we occupy a different position, and have to perform the part of the judge or the critic of that which has already been produced or constructed, or at least imagined for construction. We wish to criticise our own arguments and investigations, theories and systems, before they go out to the world. And every where in Literature and Science we meet with the like productions of other minds which need to be thus examined and criticised, as a part of the process by which they can become our own or in any way profitable to us.

The point of view occupied by the Critic.

Necessity for Criticism.

1328. It is obvious that the Formulæ and Principles must be precisely the same for Criticism as for Construction. And so far as the Method of Criticism is determined by the Idea of the True, nothing further need be said than is contained in the preceding pages. It is immaterial in what way or

Principles of Criticism the same as those of Construction.

order we apply these principles, if so be that we apply them and find the conformity or want of conformity to them in what comes under our notice. What we shall

Its Methods.

have to say further of the Method of Criticisms, therefore, will be determined by the Idea of the Useful, as giving the readiest and quickest way of accomplishing the result.

Idea of the Whole the starting-point.

1329. In order to a successful and scientific Criticism, the first and indispensable step is to get an adequate idea or conception of the work to be criticised, *as a whole*, its structure and its aim. For in most cases we cannot get at the parts to form any conception of them, and criticise them without first analyzing the whole, that we may thereby discover what are its parts. But more than this an adequate conception of a part can never be formed without considering its relation to the whole

The necessity for it.

as a constituent part of it. Considered as a whole and *absolutely*, many a subject of our criticisms may be faultless, while yet it has no value or adaptation if considered *relatively* to its whole; and *vice versa*, parts that are faultless in reference to their comprehending wholes, are without comeliness and meaning, considered by themselves.

The Whole not a mere general Conception.

1330. Wholes are never a mere accumulation or generalization of the parts. They are rather collective than general. Many things may be predicated of them which cannot be predicated of any one of the contained or comprehended parts. Much, for example, can be said of man as a living whole, which could not be predicated of any of the parts into which Anatomy, Chemistry, or even Metaphysical Analysis can resolve him. It is so of all wholes, and hence the necessity of examining and criticising them *as* wholes over and above any examination or criticism which we may give to their component parts.

1331. This fault of judging of parts *as* wholes and not as parts merely, or in their relation to the whole,

Whately has referred to the Fallacy of Division and Composition. It is, however, no Fallacy in Form. It is a Fault of Method originating in a want of comprehensiveness of views. I have already quoted Whately's language in regard to it (749). To take his example: "The spendthrift compares his income with each particular item as a whole, and finds it small compared with what he has to expend—five dollars for an evening's amusement out of an income of a thousand! It is certainly inconsiderable. Such a sum cannot ruin any body. It is mere niggardliness not to afford it." But considered as a part of the annual expenditure it may, after all, be found to be just the sum and the item which will leave one in arrears at the end of his financial year. The same fault is often committed by persons in making their estimate of their own character and abilities. Not considering that one or two acts are sufficient in some cases to determine the character, they form quite a different estimate of themselves from that which their neighbors have formed. One or two acts of fraud, of intemperance, of intentional deception, destroy entirely one's character for honesty, temperance, and veracity. So, too, although it be true that "the best fail sometimes," yet frequent failures to meet our engagements, or to perform the duties required or expected of us from our position, is ruinous to one's character for capacity or competency to the duties and responsibilities of his position.*

The Spendthrift's Fault.

* It is often a successful trick of Sophistry to criticise what are called "the Points" of an Argument, as if they were wholes; that is, Arguments each complete in itself, obstinately and artfully keeping out of view and out of consideration the fact that they are but parts of a cumulative whole. In this way the force of any Argument from circumstantial testimony or cumulative Argument of any kind, may be shown to have little or no force. The Method is no less absurd than would be the attempt to estimate the strength of an arch by ascertaining how much each stone taken separately would sustain, and then taking the aggregate as indicative of the strength of the whole arch; when in fact more than one-half of the stones, perhaps, not only would not sustain any thing in their position, but need to be supported by those below them to keep them from falling.

1332. What are to be regarded as wholes and what as parts, is determined by the choice of the mind from which they emanate; and the same thing may be regarded as a part or as a whole, just as in the use which has been made of it in the case under consideration it was designed for a whole in itself, or to serve as a part to a larger whole and a means to an end not contained in itself. Thus a Treatise on the Evidences of Christianity may be planned and executed as a whole, to be complete in itself; or it may be planned and written with reference to a particular end, to serve, for instance, as an introduction to a Treatise on Christian Ethics, or as a part of a system of Theology. A volume on Algebra may be designed to be complete as a whole, or only to serve as a part of a series on Mathematics; and it will be modified in its plan and in its execution, according as it is to be a whole or a part, and will of course require to be criticised and judged by different rules, as it is to be regarded from the one or the other of these points of view.

Wholes by what determined.

The same thing sometimes a Whole & sometimes a Part.

1333. Wholes are to be criticised chiefly with a view to the Principles of Method, the Methods by which they are constructed. We may, of course, have them as Investigations or Inquiries as they are sometimes called, as Arguments, or as Scientific Systems. And in con sidering the Methods the points to which our attention is to be chiefly directed, are (1) the End or Aim to be accomplished; (2) the compatibility of the End with the Matter in which it is to be accomplished; and (3) the adaptation of the Method to the Matter and the End. For example, we cannot produce the absolute certainty of demonstration in Moral Matter, or by means of Testimony. Nor would it be in accordance with the Principles of Method to prove a proposition in Geometry by an induction of facts, or a doctrine of Revelation by means of the opinions of uninspired men.

Parts to be considered in the Criticism of Wholes.

1334. We are not to suppose that the whole of any book or treatise designed to convince or persuade, can be reduced to any Logical Formula, or will fulfil the conditions of any Method of Proof or Refutation. Much is often thrown in for embellishment addressed to the Fancy, and much is designed merely to make *an impression* upon the sensibilities and feelings either in favor of or against the main conclusion; and some whole books have no other object than to please or amuse, or to make an impression upon the feelings without convincing the reason. Even books designed to convey instruction do not necessarily contain much or even any argument. They may be occupied with stating facts alone, from which no conclusion is designed to be drawn.

Not all of books included in the province of Logical Criticism.

1335. An *impression* made by a description, a narrative, a sarcasm, or a jeer, may often be a more efficient motive of action than a conviction of the understanding produced by facts and reasoning. But these impressions, unless under the control of the Conscience and Reason, are always in danger of misleading us. They are not, however, Fallacies. We cannot reduce them to Logical Formulæ. We can meet them for the most part by arguments addressed to the Reason, designed to show that the course to which the impression would lead us is wrong. Yet it is probable that the largest part of mankind are governed and guided more by their impressions than by their convictions. Convictions alone, however, belong to the sphere of Logic and of Reasoning—Impressions and Persuasion to Rhetoric.

An impression upon the sensibilities more effective than Arguments.

1336. It is the right and privilege of the framer of an argument to introduce whatever terms, and to put them in whatever relation to each other he may choose. We may introduce no new ones in completing the Formula, and if he has not given us material enough to complete the Formula, the responsibility of the failure must be his.

No new matter may be introduced in Praxis.

His language must be regarded as mere declamation, unfounded assertion, *vox et præterea nihil.*

1337. And here, I take it, is the distinction between argument and mere assertion. The former contains all that is necessary to complete the Formula under the rules already given, so as to satisfy the mind completely what are the grounds upon which the speaker or writer would rest his conclusions. But from mere assertion no form of a complete argument can be made out without introducing new matter; and this would throw the responsibility for the Argument upon the critic who completes it, rather than upon the author who should have given it already completed.

Distinction between Argument and Assertion.

1338. But besides all that is addressed merely to the fancy and the feelings, all that is intended as mere instruction to be received on authority of the teacher, and all that is mere declamation, there are also the artifices or tricks to be separated from what properly comes within the sphere of Logic. These tricks have already been defined (753), and discriminated from Faults or Fallacies. They have not been enumerated; for no diligence could collect, classify, and describe all the artifices of this kind which carelessness may let fall or cunning devise.* Sagacity and constant watchfulness alone can guard one against falling into them himself, or being entrapped by them when dealing with the unscrupulous and designing.

Between Arguments and mere Artifices.

1339. The first step, therefore, towards a Logical Analysis of any work is to discriminate the Thought from the Rhetoric, to select all that belongs to the province of reasoning and intelligence, from that which is mere Trick or Artifice—gaseous declamation, or mere didactic development of Premises.

1340. In criticising the Terms it will be necessary to consider whether they are properly used or not, and

* "Quas aut incuria fudit
Aut humana parùm cavit natura."—HOR.

whether a word may not be improperly used to express a cognition, which is after all just the one which is required. And if the Term be complex we are to consider whether the Modals and the Term are not incompatible; as for example, "triangular ellipse." Or to give some illustrations from a book that is before me, the author speaks of "the substantiality of motion," "absolute relativity," "abstractly extended subsistence." It is impossible to form any conception of what is meant (if any thing is really meant) by such terms. This Fault of Terms has been called a *Contradictio in adjectis.*

Criticism of Terms.

Contradictio in adjectis.

1341. In the criticism of Arguments, it will be necessary to identify in the first place the Conclusion aimed at, since this determines the whole with reference to which all the parts, as Terms, Premises, &c., are to be criticised, and in the next place to identify the subject of the Conclusion as that which determines the unity of the Formula. By means of the Subject and Predicate of the Conclusion as Minor and Major Terms, we are to identify the other parts of the Formula. In doing this we shall, of course, find all of the principles and statements of the preceding work called into requisition. And I trust that it will be found that nothing is required which is not contained more or less explicitly and fully in these pages. If any thing more is required, the fact will serve to show how far this Treatise is from being complete.

Parts and Wholes of Arguments determined by the Conclusion.

1342. In the Methods of Investigation and of Instruction the unity of the End or Object will determine for us what are to be regarded as Wholes, and of course by the same means what are to be regarded as subordinate Parts. The means to any End are always the parts of any Method to that End. The End of an Investigation is the attainment of the Predicate which we are investigating. The End of a Construction is to put our thoughts

Wholes and Parts in Investigation and Construction determined by the End in view.

into such form and order as to be communicable to others. To this End, division of the Subject, order in arranging, definition and description, and each part of the division—the order, the definitions, descriptions, comparisons, and whatever else we may have occasion to use, are Parts, and should be judged as Parts, subordinate and conducive, according to the rules and principles already discussed; and whether faultless or faulty in themselves, they are each to be approved or condemned, according as they shall be found conducive to that End or not; always remembering that whatever does not conduce to the End which is most prominently before the mind, and help on towards its attainment, is a fault, a hindrance, and an annoyance.

APPENDIX.

EXAMPLES FOR ANALYSIS AND CRITICISM.

§ 1. *Of the order in criticising Arguments.*

In analyzing and criticising the following Examples, which have been selected with a special view to illustrate the Principles and Formulæ of the foregoing Treatise, we shall find the following order useful as expediting the process.

In the first place, in each unity or totality of an Argument we must ascertain what is the point to be proved—the Conclusion of the Argument as a Whole. This is necessary at this stage. For by this only can we identify the Minor and Major Terms—the Subject of the Argument, and what is proved of it. And it is only by this process of identifying the Subject and Predicate of the Argument that we can identify the Premises, and ascertain their character and position.

Having identified the Minor, Middle, and Major Terms by means of the Subject and Predicate of the Conclusion, we can next identify the Premises, and arrange the Matter of the Argument into its appropriate Formula, and complete the Formula if it should require completing.

And as soon as we have done this, we shall find an advantage in disconnecting the Matter from the Form, by substituting in the Formula some one of the Letters of the Alphabet. We derive the same advantage in Logical Analysis as in Algebra, from using the symbolical letters for the sums and quantities which they represent. It facilitates the process, and errors are less likely to be made, and are more easily detected if they are.

In the next place we are to consider if there is any Fault or Fallacy in the general form or argument. It will always be best to look for them in the following order:

(1) An Ignoratio Elenchi.
(2) Any Fault in Form or in Method.
(3) Any Fallacy in Matter or in Diction.

If either of these defects is found, the work, whatever other excellencies and attractions it may have, is worthless as an Argument, or effort to sustain the truth of its Conclusion.

The next step, after having selected and arranged the parts of the main Argument, is to separate each of the subordinate parts into logical wholes or unities; remembering always that the unity of the Argument or Formula consists in the unity of its Subject.

Having thus divided the work up into its smallest parts that can be regarded as wholes at all, we are to proceed to reduce them to the Formulæ.*

The first thing here is to identify the Conclusion, and from the Conclusion the Terms, Minor and Major, which are given in it. We are also to notice whether it be simple, complex, or compound; and what is the complicity of the judgment of which it is compounded, with reference to its including any thing illicit, by this means.

We may here consider whether there be any Ignoratio Elenchi, or Fault in Method in this part of the main argument, or not; for if there is, we need go no farther in our analysis of this part, since though it should be otherwise faultless, it is nothing to the purpose.

We are next to identify the Premises by means of the Terms which we have found in the Conclusion; note their Relation, as whether Categorical, Conditional, or Disjunctive. Then put the elements thus given into the Formal position, and complete the Formula if it be not complete.

* Most of the Scholastic Writers on Logic whose works I have seen, speak of two kinds of Syllogisms, Formal and Material; the Material Syllogisms are those which contain all the Matter of a Syllogism, but not stated in any recognized Formula. A Formal Syllogism is an argument stated in a recognized Formula. The business of Praxis is, therefore, to reduce Material to Formal Syllogisms.

In the course of this completion, we are not only to find the supposed or assumed Premises in Enthymemes of the various forms, but also the Sequence in Conditionals, the Excluded Middle in Disjunctives, and the identity of kind in things compared.*

Having completed the Formula, we are next to consider it in relation to the Faults and Fallacies in the order above given.

If we find the part of the main argument which is under examination inconclusive for any reason, we are next to consider how important it is as a part of the main argument. And whether a failure or not, we are carefully to estimate its value and its force, if it has any, as a means of establishing the main Conclusion. We shall find the Conclusion either a Premise in the main Argument, or the assertion of a fact which is used by way of Induction, Analogy, Example, or Circumstance, &c., to prove a Conclusion which is used as such a Premise.

In this way we are to analyze each subordinate part of the main Argument, taking as an ultimate part or unity of argument only those which have but *one* subject, and which therefore, *as arguments*, can be resolved no farther.

§ 2. *Examples in Categorical Syllogisms.*

1. Every effect must have had an adequate cause—the creation of the world is an effect; therefore the creation of the world must have had a cause.

2. He that is always in fear cannot be happy. But those that are conscious of guilt are always in fear; therefore those that are conscious of guilt cannot be happy.

3. Satire is a legitimate mode of exposing the failings of others. But the calling others by ill-names is not satire; therefore it is no legitimate mode of exposing their failings.

* As it is convenient to have a name for this fault, of passing from one species to another improperly (for it is one of frequent occurrence), we may call it *Metabasis*. This, if I understand him rightly, is what Aristotle means when he speaks of "passing over into another species:" Μετάβασις εἰς τὸ ἄλλο γένος.

4. Tyranny is an unnecessary restraint upon human liberty. The English government imposes no unnecessary restraint upon the liberty of its subjects; therefore the English government is no tyranny.

5. No one is free who is enslaved by his appetites. The sensualist is enslaved by his appetites; therefore no sensualist is free.

6. All accountable beings are free agents. Men are accountable; therefore they are free agents.

7. Sensualists wish to enjoy perpetual gratification without satiety. But this is impossible; therefore the sensualist desires what can never be attained.

8. That which has no reality of being cannot, as cause, produce or be the ground of existence to any thing. Chance has no reality of being; therefore nothing can be properly ascribed to chance by way of accounting for its origin.

9. Liberality is a means of making others happy. But it is not a means of making one's self rich; therefore making one's self rich does not always make others happy.

10. Murderers never escape punishment. Yet even murderers hope to elude the laws of their country; therefore some who hope to elude the laws of their country do not escape punishment.

11. All amiable men merit the esteem and respect of their fellow men. And certainly all who aim only to do good to their fellow men, deserve to be esteemed and respected on that account. Hence all who are striving to do good to others are amiable men.

12. Some effectual check to the progress of seditious publications is absolutely essential to the safety of our country. The total abolition of the art of printing would prove such a check; therefore the art of printing should be totally abolished.

13. No one is rich who has not enough. No miser has enough; therefore no miser is rich.

14. The things that cannot be enumerated do not exist. Innate ideas cannot be be enumerated; therefore there are no innate ideas.

15. Some poisons are vegetable. But no poisons are useful drugs; therefore some useful drugs are not vegetable.

16. Some recreations are necessary to the preservation of health and spirits. All recreations, however, are liable to be carried to excess and be abused; so that some things liable to abuse are nevertheless necessary for man.

17. No tale-bearer is worthy of confidence. But all talebearers are great talkers; therefore great talkers are never worthy of confidence.

18. That one who has been accustomed to liberty can never be happy in the condition of a slave is indeed true. But the negroes on our Southern plantations have never been accustomed to liberty. Hence they are content and happy in their present condition.

19. "He that is of God heareth my words; ye therefore hear them not, because ye are not of God."

20. All the most bitter persecutions have been religious persecutions. Among the most bitter persecutions were those which occurred in France during the French Revolution. Consequently they must have been religious persecutions.

21. That man is independent of the caprices of Fortune who places his chief happiness in moral and intellectual excellence. A true philosopher is independent of the caprices of Fortune; therefore a true philosopher is one who places his chief happiness in moral and intellectual excellence.

22. Of two evils the less is to be preferred; therefore since occasional turbulence is a less evil than a rigid despotism, it is to be preferred.

23. Some objects of great beauty answer no other perceptible purpose but to gratify the sight: many flowers have great beauty; and many of them accordingly answer no other purpose but to gratify the sight.

24. A man who deliberately devotes himself to a life of sensuality is deserving of strong reprobation; but those do not deliberately devote themselves to a life of sensuality who are hurried into excess by the impulse of the passions: such therefore as are hurried into excess by the impulse of the passions are not deserving of strong reprobation.

25. It is a difficult task to restrain all inordinate desires: to conform to the precepts of Scripture implies a restraint of all inordinate desires; therefore it is a difficult task to conform to the precepts of Scripture.

26. Any one who is candid will refrain from condemning a book without reading it: some Reviewers do not refrain from this; therefore some Reviewers are not candid.

27. My hand touches the pen, the pen touches the paper; therefore my hand touches the paper.

28. Lias lies above red sandstone, red sandstone lies above coal; therefore lias lies above coal.

29. A true prophecy coincides precisely with all the circumstances of such events as could not be conjectured by natural reason. This is the case with the prophecies concerning the Messiah in the Old Testament; hence these prophecies are true.

30. All that glitters is not gold: tinsel glitters; therefore it is not gold.

31. No trifling business will enrich those that engage in it. A speculation is no trifling business; therefore speculation will enrich all who are engaged in it.

§ 3. *Examples in the Hypothetical Formulæ.*

32. If some fishes have no teeth, some animals without teeth are fishes.

33. If some who are very sentimental are nevertheless not benevolent, then some who are not benevolent are sentimental.

34. If fire may be separated from a flint, a property may be separated from its subject: but fire cannot be separated from the flint; therefore a property cannot be separated from its subject.

35. If hatred and malice are contrary to the Divine law, they ought to be avoided: that they are so no one can deny; therefore they should be avoided.

36. If the penal laws against the Papists were enforced, they would be oppressed and wronged. But those laws are

not enforced, and therefore they have nothing to complain of in the way of oppression or persecution.

37. If testimony to miracles is to be admitted, the miracles claimed for Mahomet are to be admitted. But as the narrative of those miracles cannot be admitted, no testimony to miracles is to be admitted.

38. If the exercise of war in defence of one's country were sinful, it would have been forbidden in the Scripture, either expressly or by implication. But it is not so forbidden; therefore we may safely infer that defensive wars are not sinful.

39. If the fourth commandment is obligatory, we are indeed bound to set apart one day in seven. But no one supposes now that that commandment is obligatory. Hence there is no obligation to keep one day any more sacred than another.

40. Romanism is that form of religion which has the most forms: and if forms are necessary to religion, then that religion which has the most forms is the best, and we ought all to turn Romanists.

41. The adoration of images is forbidden to Christians if the Mosaic law was designed, not for Israelites alone, but for all men. It was, however, designed for Israelites alone; hence the adoration of images is not forbidden to Christians.

42. A wise lawgiver must either recognize the rewards and punishments of a future state, or he must be able to appeal to a Providence dispensing them in this life. Moses did not do the former, and therefore he must have done the latter.

43. The virtues are either passions, faculties, or habits. But they are not passions: for passions do not depend on previous determination. And they are not faculties: for faculties are possessed by nature. The virtues, therefore, are habits acquired by voluntary exertion and effort.

44. The early assignment of the Epistle to the Hebrews to St. Paul as its author, must have been either from its being really his, or from its professing to be his and containing his name. But it makes no claim to being his. Consequently, nothing but a knowledge of the fact that he wrote it could have led the early Christians to attribute it to him.

45. If the everlasting favor of God is not bestowed at random, and on no principle at all, it must be bestowed either with respect to men's persons, or with respect to their conduct: but "God is no respecter of persons;" therefore his favor must be bestowed with respect to men's conduct.

46. If every objection that can be urged would justify a change of established laws, no laws could reasonably be maintained. But some laws can be reasonably maintained; therefore no objection that can be urged will justify a change in established laws.

47. If any complete theory could be framed to explain the establishment of Christianity by human causes, such a theory would have been propounded before this time. But no such theory has been proposed; therefore we may conclude that no such theory can be devised.

48. If a man is ignorant he should consult others as a means of making up his deficiency in knowledge. If he is wise, yet two heads for counsel are better than one; therefore in all important matters one should take counsel with others.

49. If one is superior to others he should be polite and gentle in his manners towards them, as a matter of Christian compassion and magnanimous condescension. If he is among equals he should be civil and courteous, since such a demeanor is as much their right from him and his right from them. And if he is among his superiors, he should show himself courteous and civil, as being due to those having authority over us for the good of the whole. In any case, therefore, we are bound by the most sacred obligations to be civil and considerate of the feelings of others.

50. If the Government provides for these debts by imposition, it will become odious to the people and perish. If it does not provide for them, it will be overthrown by the most dangerous of all parties, I mean extensive discontent of the moneyed interest.

51. If I am under the chastening hand of God, and if there is no unrighteousness in Him, it must be that I am punished for my iniquity.

52. If virtue is voluntary, vice is voluntary. But virtue is voluntary; therefore so is vice.

53. If expiatory sacrifices were divinely appointed before the Mosaic law, they must have been expiatory not of ceremonial sin (for there could be none then), but of moral sin. If so, the Levitical sacrifices must have had no less efficacy. In that case the atonements under the Mosaic law would have 'made the comers thereunto perfect, as pertaining to the conscience.' But this they could not accomplish. Hence we infer that expiatory sacrifices could not have been appointed before the Mosaic law.

54. If transportation is not felt as a severe punishment, it is in itself ill-suited to the prevention of crime: if it is so felt, much of its severity is wasted, from its taking place at too great a distance to affect the feelings, or even come to the knowledge, of most of those whom it is designed to deter; but one or the other of these must be the case: therefore transportation is not calculated to answer the purpose of preventing crime.

55. Fontenelle on seeing a criminal led to punishment said, "There is a man who has calculated badly;" whence it follows that if he could have escaped punishment, his conduct would have been laudable.

56. If the prophecies of the Old Testament had been written without knowledge of the events of the time of Christ, they could not correspond with them exactly; and if they had been forged by Christians, they would not be preserved and acknowledged by the Jews: they are preserved and acknowledged by the Jews, and they correspond exactly with the events of the time of Christ; therefore they were neither written without knowledge of those events, nor were forged by Christians.

57. Now "if Christ be preached that He rose from the dead, how say some among you that there is no resurrection from the dead? But if there be no resurrection of the dead then is Christ not risen; and if Christ is not risen then is our preaching vain, and your faith is also vain. Yea, and we are found false witnesses against God, because we have testified of God that He raised up Christ whom he raised not up, if so be that the dead rise not. For if the dead rise not, then is not Christ raised; and if Christ be not raised your faith is vain, ye are yet in your sins. Then they also which are fallen alseep in Christ are perished."

58. If the bishops of England, before the Reformation, when they were nominated by the Pope, were true and valid bishops, then the bishops since the Reformation, when they have been nominated by the Crown, are not true and valid bishops. But if the bishops since the Reformation, which have been nominated by the Crown are true and valid, then these before the Reformation are not so. In either case the claim of Apostolic succession and authority for the English bishops is absurd.

§ 4. *Incomplete and Compound Formulæ.*

59. The study of Mathematics is essential to a complete education, because it produces a habit of close and constant reasoning.

60. Familiarity is productive of contempt, inasmuch as it occasions a needless exposure of private failings.

61. Man needs the restraints of law, since he is naturally selfish; and is, moreover, subject to desires and passions which have no limits or power of restraint in themselves.

62. Sin is hateful, because it is opposed to the Divine Will.

63. A good face is a letter of recommendation, for it prepossesses the beholder in favor of its possessor.

64. A wise man is never surprised because he is never disappointed; and he is never disappointed, because he forms no expectations that are not placed upon the most certain basis.

65. Discord is a greater vice than intemperance, since discord always implicates more than one person in its guilt.

66. Jupiter was the son of Saturn; therefore the son of Jupiter was the grandson of Saturn.

67. They who are not conscious of guilt are not subject to fear: hence while conscious hypocrites are always shy and timid, the innocent are unsuspecting and self-possessed.

68. A negro is a man; whoever, therefore, kills a negro wantonly or maliciously, is guilty of murdering a fellow man.

69. I think; therefore I am.

70. Discord is not so great an evil as intemperance, for that generally arises from the impulse of anger; while the latter almost invariably proceeds from an uncontrollable appetite, or an inveterate habit.

71. Americans enjoy a greater degree of political liberty than any other civilized people, and therefore they can have no excuse for sedition.

72. Hard substances are elastic; for ivory is both hard and elastic.

73. Meanness is never useful since it is always base; and because it is always honorable to be honest, it is always useful.

74. "Whosoever shall keep the whole law, and yet offend in one point, is guilty of the whole; *for* He that said, Do not commit adultery, said also, Do not kill."

75. The care of the poor ought to be the object of all laws, for the plain reason that the rich can take care of themselves.

76. Wilkes was a favorite with the populace: he who is a favorite with the populace must understand how to manage them: he who understands how to manage them, must be well acquainted with their character: he who is well acquainted with their character, must hold them in contempt: therefore Wilkes must have held the populace in contempt.

77. The child of Themistocles governed his mother: she governed her husband; he governed Athens; Athens, Greece; and Greece, the world: therefore the child of Themistocles governed the world.

78. The Scriptures are the standard of truth: and it is admitted that the Church of England is in accordance with the Scriptures. Hoadley was in the English Church. But Hoadley denied the divine institution of Episcopacy, and the authority of the Church in matters of Faith. Hence no member of the English Church can condemn those doctrines as unscriptural or heretical.

79. None but whites are civilized: the Hindoos are not white; therefore the Hindoos are not civilized.

80. None but whites are civilized: the ancient Germans were whites; therefore they were civilized. [See 332–339, and 587.]

81. None but civilized people are white; the Gauls were white, therefore they were civilized. [See 587.]

82. Popular commotions, though commencing on a small scale, are so liable to ripen into systematic sedition, that they ought to be speedily and decisively suppressed.

83. Every duty is accompanied with a certain propriety and decorum; whatever, therefore, is not accompanied with propriety and decorum cannot be a duty.

84. The Earth has been repeatedly circumnavigated; we need, therefore, no other proof that it is not an interminable plane, as the ancients supposed.

85. Whatever subjects fall under one and the same general definition are of one and the same kind; consequently those things which do not fall under that definition, must differ in kind from each other and from all that do.

86. Those only who understand other languages are competent to teach correctly the principles of their own; since such a competency requires that philosophic view of language which can be acquired only by the comparison of several with each other.

87. Not a man of all the antediluvians escaped except those that were in the Ark with Noah. Hence after the flood there were none who had not proceeded from him as their progenitor, and been acquainted with what he knew of divine things.

88. Will often combats desire as it often also yields to it: will is not therefore desire.

89. If Paley's system is to be received, one who has no knowledge of a future state has no means of distinguishing virtue and vice: now one who has no means of distinguishing virtue and vice can commit no sin: therefore, if Paley's system is to be received, one who has no knowledge of a future state can commit no sin.

90. When the observance of the first day of the week, as a religious festival in commemoration of Christ's resurrection, was first introduced, it must have been a novelty: when it was a novelty, it must have attracted notice: when it attracted

notice, it would lead to inquiry respecting the truth of the resurrection: when it led to this inquiry, it must have exposed the story as an imposture, supposing it not attested by living witnesses: therefore when the observance of the first day of the week, &c. was first introduced, it must have exposed as an imposture the story of the resurrection, supposing it not attested by living witnesses.

91. A system of government which extends to those actions that are performed secretly, must be one which refers either to a regular Divine Providence in this life, or to the rewards and punishments of another world: every perfect system of government must extend to those actions which are performed secretly: no system of government therefore can be perfect, which does not refer either to a regular Divine Providence in this life, or to the rewards and punishments of another world.

§ 5. *Miscellaneous Examples of Formulæ and Fallacies.*

92. The end of a true soldier's life is the welfare of his country: but death is the end of a soldier's life: therefore his death is requisite to the safety and welfare of his country.

93. The fish inclosed in the net were an indiscriminate mixture of all kinds: those that were set aside and saved as valuable, were fish that had been inclosed in the net: therefore fish of all kinds were set aside and saved as valuable.

94. No man can possess the power to perform an impossibility. But a miracle is an impossibility; therefore no man can work a miracle. [See 75.]

95. Few scientific treatises communicate truth in a clear and conspicuous manner, without any admixture of error. Although a treatise which should so convey truth would be exceedingly valuable, yet it must be admitted that there are but few treatises comparatively which are very valuable.

96. All the miracles of Jesus would fill more books than the world could contain; the things related by the Evangelists are the miracles of Jesus: therefore the things related by the Evangelists would fill more books than the world could contain.

97. If a man say, I love God, and hateth his brother, he is a liar; for he that loveth not his brother, whom he hath seen, how can he love God whom he hath not seen?

98. If the Romish doctrine of Transubstantiation be true, in receiving the Eucharist, the Romanists are guilty of cannibalism. But if they are not guilty of cannibalism their doctrine is false. [See 221.]

99. The principles of justice are variable; the appointments of nature are invariable: therefore the principles of justice are no appointment of nature.

100. A story is not to be believed, the reporters of which give contradictory accounts of it; the story of the life and exploits of Bonaparte is of this description: therefore it is not to be believed.

101. It is certain that in the moral government of God, virtue will produce happiness and vice will produce misery. We may therefore say, that whatever will produce happiness is virtue, and define virtue to be the pursuit of happiness in accordance with the will of God.

102. It is evident that drunkenness is a sin most odious in the sight of God. It is equally certain that the use of alcohol is destructive to the moral and physical energies of man. I claim, therefore, not only that it is the duty of every man to abstain totally from the use of alcoholic drinks, but as a good citizen and a philanthropist, to exert all his influence to obtain and enforce a law which shall totally prevent the sale of intoxicating drinks of any kind.

103. Nothing which is of less frequent occurrence than the falsity of testimony can be fairly established by testimony; any extraordinary and unusual fact is a thing of less frequent occurrence than the falsity of testimony (that being very common): therefore no extraordinary and unusual fact can be fairly established by testimony.

104. Testimony is a kind of evidence which is very likely to be false; the evidence on which most men believe that there are pyramids in Egypt is testimony: therefore the evidence on which most men believe that there are pyramids in Egypt is very likely to be false.

105. He who cannot possibly act otherwise than he does, has neither merit nor demerit in his action. A liberal and benevolent man in relieving the sufferings of the poor cannot do otherwise than relieve them: therefore there is no merit in his actions.

106. Slavery is an outrage upon the inalienable rights of man. It operates, wherever it exists, as a means of corruption and degeneracy to the social and political condition of mankind. Hence, as citizens, as Christians, and as philanthropists, we are called upon to labor for the promotion of its immediate abolition.

107. It is generally held that St. Paul wrote the Epistle to the Romans. But the Epistle itself expressly declares that Tertius wrote it (xvi. 22). Therefore St. Paul cannot properly be regarded as its author.

108. The publication of a libel is criminal: but the act of putting a libel into the post, is an act of publication (for the moment a man passes the libel from his hand his control over it is gone); that act, therefore, must be pronounced criminal.

109. True wisdom cannot be too dearly purchased. Humility always accompanies true wisdom: therefore humility cannot be too dearly purchased.

110. No man could bind him, no not with chains; because that he had been often bound with fetters and chains, and the chains had been broken asunder by him, and the fetters broken in pieces. [See 425.]

111. That which is greater than faith and hope must be the highest Christian grace. Charity, therefore, which is but another name for almsgiving, is greater than faith and hope, and must therefore be more important than any degree of accuracy or orthodoxy in the faith.

112. It is sufficient to show the fallacy of the Protestant dogma, "the Bible, and the Bible alone is the religion of the Protestants," to state the fact, that many parts of the Bible are wanting, as for example, the Book of the Wars of the Lord, the Book of Jasher, and of the New Testament, the Epistle to the Laodiceans, to mention no more. If, therefore, the *whole* Bible would be a sufficient rule of faith to the

Protestant if he possessed it, yet since he has not the whole, what he has can be no sufficient rule.

113. The New Testament as a distinct book, was never heard of until the Council of Laodicea, which at the earliest was 314 years after the commencement of the Christian era. It is, threfore, absurd to pretend that it was written by the Apostles, who were all dead more than a century before this date.

114. A collection of rules, designed to enable us to understand the principles of any subject, is a science; but if those rules are designed to assist us in the application of these principles to a specific end, they constitute an art. Now Logic collects and states the rules with a view to the comprehension of the rules themselves; but Rhetoric with a view to their application to the specific end of conviction and persuasion: therefore Logic is a science, and Rhetoric is an art.

115. Russia knows full well that she is engaged in a contest with two nations that were never yet overcome by valor of arms, nor circumvented by fraud or cunning in diplomacy. But Russia is contending against France and England: therefore neither France nor England was ever overcome by valor, or circumvented by cunning or fraud.

116. If the forgiveness of sins was imparted at one's conversion, Ananias could not have said to St. Paul three days after his conversion, "Arise, be baptised, and wash away thy sins." But such was precisely the message which he was commissioned by the Holy Ghost to deliver to him; therefore remission of sins takes place in Baptism.

117. An unholy minister is the greatest of all sinners; for either he is a person of more than ordinary knowledge or he is not. If he is not, he sinned greatly in undertaking that office, for which so great knowledge is required. If he be, his knowledge will doubtless increase his guilt.

118. The works of creation imply far more of design and of wisdom than the Iliad of Homer or the Geometry of Euclid. But no one ever supposed that the Iliad, or the Geometry of Euclid were composed without an intelligent author; therefore the works of creation must have had an Intelligent Creator.

119. The Jesuit cites Ruffinus in proof of the infallibility

of his church. But if Ruffinus is right the church is not infallible, since it does not agree with Ruffinus. If, however, Ruffinus is wrong, his testimony is worthless.

120. The doctrine which holds to an omnipresent divine power and agency in the operations of Nature, is as contrary to the Scriptures as it is to sound philosophy; for the Scriptures say expressly, "the earth bringeth forth fruit *of herself*" (St. Mark iv. 28).

121. Nature is either the author of Nature, or it is the order of things established by a Supreme Intelligence. But nothing can be the author of itself; therefore, Nature can be only the order of things established by a Supreme Intelligence.

122. The cause of evil is itself an evil. But that Christianity has caused much evil in the shape of wars, oppression, imposture, fanaticism, and persecution, cannot be denied.

123. Our Lord said, "If a man keep my saying he shall never taste of death. Then said the Jews unto Him, Now we know that thou hast a devil. Abraham is dead, and the Prophets. Art thou greater than our father Abraham? whom makest thou thyself?"

124. "The argument of the atheist assumes that it is possible to create an intelligent moral agent, and place it beyond all liability to sin. But this is a mistake. Almighty Power itself cannot create such a being, and place it beyond the possibility of sinning, as we shall prove," &c.

125. He who has a confirmed habit of any kind of action, exercises no self-denial in the practice of that action; a good man has a confirmed habit of virtue; therefore he who exercises self-denial in the practice of virtue is not a good man.

126. He is the greatest lover of any one who seeks that person's greatest good; a virtuous man seeks the greatest good for himself; therefore a virtuous man is the greatest lover of himself.

127. Whatever is real is limited [by that which it is not]. But whatever is limited is not infinite; therefore if God is real, and not a mere fiction of the imagination, He is not an infinite being.

128. Theft is a crime: theft was encouraged by the laws of Sparta; therefore the laws of Sparta encouraged crime.

129. Every hen comes from an egg: every egg comes from a hen: therefore every egg comes from an egg.

130. Nothing is heavier than platina: feathers are heavier than nothing: therefore feathers are heavier than platina.

131. Meat and drink are necessaries of life: the revenues of Vitellius were spent on meat and drink; therefore the revenues of Vitellius were spent on the necessaries of life.

132. No evil should be allowed that good may come of it. But all punishment is an evil; therefore no punishment should be allowed.

133. Repentance is a good thing. But no persons have so much repentance as the wicked; therefore none have so much good as the wicked.

134. He who bears arms at the command of the magistrate does what is lawful for a Christian. The Swiss in the French service, and the British in the American service bore arms at the command of the magistrate; therefore they were doing only what was lawful for a Christian to do.

135. He who calls you a man speaks the truth; but he that calls you a knave calls you a man; therefore he who calls you a knave speaks the truth.

[This Minor Premise may be pronounced a *non vera*. But I should prefer to refer the Formula to the Fallacy of Accidents (750, 1057–8). In this view we must regard as accidental, that which is not in the Conception when used as a Predicate (195), however essential it may be to the existence of any individual in that genus among the realities of being.]

136. A monopoly of the sugar-refining business is beneficial to sugar-refiners; and of the corn-trade to corn-growers; and of the silk-manufacture to silk-weavers, &c., &c.; and thus each class of men are benefited by some restrictions. Now all these classes of men make up the whole community; therefore a system of restrictions is beneficial to the community. [See 58–60, 748.]

137. "We have seen in a preceding chapter, that *naturally* no man has any authority over another—his pursuits, his possessions, his life or his liberty, except what arises from the pri-

mary law of nature, self-defence. Now as a State is made up of men, the State can have no authority which each man in the State did not possess before he entered into the body politic. And from this it follows, not only that capital punishment, banishment, and such like punishments are unauthorized and wrong, but that all attempts on the part of the State to promote education, impose oaths, or to encourage religion in any form, or to regulate the institution of marriage in any way, is a tyrannical assumption of rights over man, which power may indeed enable it to enforce," &c., but nothing can justify. [58.]

138. If the difference in the various races of men has not been produced by climatic causes, they must each of them have had a separate proto-plastic pair for their progenitors. But these differences cannot have been produced by climatic causes; therefore the races cannot have sprung from the same parents originally. [See 400 and 412.]

139. Opium is a poison; but physicians advise some of their patients to take Opium; therefore physicians advise some of their patients to take poison.

140. Animal food may be entirely dispensed with (as is shown by the practice of the Brahmins and of some monks): and vegetable food may be entirely dispensed with (as is plain from the example of the Esquimaux and others): but all food consists of animal food and vegetable food; therefore all food may be dispensed with.

141. I have shown, gentlemen, that it is the natural right of all God's creatures to be free. I have shown that a people having the same tongue, historic recollections and associations, conveniently situated, and existing in sufficient numbers for the purpose, are entitled to a distinct national existence; and I claim, therefore, not only the sympathy of Americans for my poor and oppressed Hungary, which I know that I shall have, but also their intervention as a nation, and their generous liberality in furnishing the material aid necessary to enable us to carry on our struggle, and secure our independence of Austrian rule and despotism.

142. Whilst all other sorts and orders of men conversed with our Lord, never do we hear of any interview between Him and the Essenes. Suppose one Evangelist to have

overlooked such a scene, another would not. One Evangelist was impressed with one scene and a second by another. And thus it must have happened that, amongst the four, at least one would have noticed the Essenes. But no one of the four Gospels alludes to them. The Acts of the Apostles is a fifth body of recollections, but this does not notice them. The Apocalypse of St. John says not one word about them. St. Peter and St. James in their Epistles entirely overlook them. St. Paul gives no sign that he had ever heard of them. Wherefore we must conclude that there was no sect known by that name, except in the delusions conjured up by his own ignorant heart (Josephus).

§ 6. *Examples presenting Questions of Method.*

143. All the facts of man's mental activity may be referred to two classes, Spontaneity and Reflection. But of the two classes, the spontaneous must be first in point of time. For reflection implies volition, and volition implies that the thing chosen is already in the mind, as an object of conscious thought before the choice. Hence it could not have been given in reflection, and must therefore have been given in spontaneity.

144. "With God nothing is impossible." But God cannot make the three angles of a triangle more than two right angles; therefore some things are impossible with God. [See 423, 424.]

145. The religion of the ancient Greeks and Romans was a tissue of extravagant fables and groundless superstitions, credited by the vulgar and the weak, and maintained by the more enlightened, from selfish or political views: the same was clearly the case with the religion of the Egyptians: the same may be said of the Brahminical worship of India, and the religion of Fo professed by the Chinese: the same of the romantic mythological system of the Peruvians, of the stern and bloody rites of the Mexicans, and those of the Britons and of the Saxons: hence we may conclude that all systems of religion, however varied in circumstances, agree in being superstitions kept up among the vulgar, from interested or political views in the more enlightened classes.

146. A feeble Executive implies a feeble execution of the Government. A feeble execution is but another name for a bad execution; and a government ill executed, whatever it may be in theory must be in practice a bad government. Hence with a feeble or inefficient executive, a government will always be bad, whatever may be its form or its theory.

147. In the Scriptures it is written concerning the Church, and we see that the Church exists. There it is written concerning idols that they shall cease, and we see that they are not. There it is written that the Jews were to lose the kingdom, and we see that the fact is so. There it is written concerning heretics that they should exist, and we see that it is so. There it is written also concerning the Day of Judgment. There it is written concerning the rewards of the good and the punishment of the wicked. In all things we have found God faithful. Will He fail and deceive us in the last?

148. I maintain that the Fugitive Slave Law is unconstitutional, or at least a law not required by the Constitution. "*Slaves*" are not mentioned in the clause requiring the rendition of persons held to service in one State escaping into another. The gentlemen [of the South] say indeed that slaves are included in the scope and intent of the law. But I answer so are undoubtedly the Negroes, who have been admitted to citizenship in the Northern States, included in that clause of the Constitution which declares that the "citizens of each State are entitled to the privileges and immunities of citizens in any of the other States into which they may go to reside." And they exclude Negro citizens of the Northern States from citizenship in their States, if they choose to go into their borders.

149. St. Paul says, "Whom God did foreknow He also did predestinate to be conformed to the image of his Son. Moreover whom He did predestinate them He also called, and whom He called them He also justified, and whom he justified He also glorified." But Christians, so long as they are living in the body are not glorified; therefore they are not among those of whom St. Paul was speaking as predestinated by God to be conformed to the image of His Son.

150. If these acts are valid, the old corporation is abolished and a new one created. The first act does, in fact, if it

can have any effect, *create a new corporation*, and transfer to it all the property and franchises of the old. The two corporations are not the same in any thing which essentially belongs to the existence of a corporation. They have different names and different powers, rights and duties. Their organization is wholly different. The powers of the corporation are not vested in the same or similar hands; and the act itself provides for the first meeting and organization of the new corporation. It expressly provides that the new corporation shall have and hold all the property of the old; a provision which would be quite unnecessary upon any other ground than that the old corporation was dissolved.

151. It has been noticed that when we see a good act performed, we approve the act and feel a sympathy with the agent. It has hence been laid down as a fundamental principle in Ethics, that those actions are good which thus elicit our sympathy and approbation. But this is a false criterion. It implies a judgment concerning the act, "it is good," and a feeling or emotion, and holds that the judgment is based upon the emotion. But the judgment precedes and is the cause of the emotion, for the emotion will always remain the same so long as our estimate of the act remains unchanged. But let us hear something concerning the act which changes our estimate of its character, and the emotion or feeling towards the person who performed it changes also.

152. If a paste be made of wheat flour, boiled in water, and allowed to stand for a few days, there will be in it not only small plants or vegetables, but also small animalculæ. Now the boiling would of itself have destroyed all the *seeds* of vegetables, as well as the ova of any animal existence, so that we are led inevitably to the conclusion that inorganic matter will produce both vegetable and animal life, without the seeds or ova of preceding plants or animals of the same species; and if so, the theory of creation, and a personal Creator, is shown to be unnecessary to philosophy, and even unphilosophical.

153. It is said that at death all appearance of life becomes extinct, and every indication of a total cessation of existence is presented.

But in the first place we see that parts of the body, as

hands, feet, &c., may die and decay, and the soul remain entirely unimpaired.

Again, it is a principle which prevails every where in Nature, that nothing once in existence can be lost. The wood that is consumed in the fire is resolved thereby into its elements, but every particle of it exists somewhere. So with the body at death. But the soul being immaterial is not capable of dissolution, or resolution into constituent elements.

Again, we have frequent cases of change of the form of existence, without a cessation of the existence of that whose form is changed. Such changes we have in the fœtus in passing from its state before birth to its mode of life after; in the chick emerging from the shell, and especially in the case of all the metabolians which appear as worms: these go into a state of apparent death, and after a while emerge as insects with wings.

In all these cases that which is once in being, continues to exist notwithstanding the changes in its form or state of existence. Hence we may conclude that the human soul will do so likewise at death.

154. Some years since there appeared in the West a disease, which was called the *milk-sickness.* The following hypotheses were suggested as accounting for it; namely, that (1) it proceeded from some miasma *in the air;* (2) from some peculiarity *in the water;* (3) from arsenic, cobalt, and other minerals *in the soil;* and finally, (4) that it was owing to *some disease in the vegetable productions.*

As facts it was found: (1) that its appearance was confined within narrow limits; (2) that when it makes its appearance among men, there has been preceding it a disease among the animals, called the *Slows* or *Trembles.* It is also ascertained (3) that the flesh, the milk, the butter, and the cheese made from animals having the Slows, causes the milk-sickness in men [hence its name]; (4) the disease appears in pastures where there is no water; and (5) the flesh of animals diseased imparts none of its poisonous properties to the water in which it is boiled; (6) the disease affects those animals which graze at night, and especially in the woods; (7) carnivorous animals never have the disease until they have taken it by eating animals already affected; and (8) females during lactation, cows, sluts, &c., often escape the disease themselves after having eaten the poison, but communicate it to their offspring. And (9) in those cases in which the flesh of diseased animals had been swallowed and vomited up soon afterwards, there was either no disease or only very little following. [To be treated as a case of Elimination.]

155. The various systems of pagan idolatry correspond so closely, that they cannot have been struck out independently in the several countries where they have been established, and must therefore have originated from a common source. But if they had a common source, then either one nation must have communicated its peculiar theology to every other people in the way of peaceful and voluntary imitation, or through the medium of conquest and violence; or all nations must have been assembled together in a single community, and then agreed to adopt the theology in question as a new and recent invention; or, having received it from the past, and believing it on whatever grounds to be true, they must have carried it with them as from that common centre to all parts of the globe. The first and second are impossible in the nature of things; therefore all these various systems must have had a common origin.

But the third position is nearly as incredible as either the first or the second; namely, that they should have all agreed in one stupendous system of imposture, professing to believe as divine that which they knew that they had of themselves but recently invented.

Idolatry, therefore, must have arisen before the dispersion of mankind, and be a corruption of a tradition that was believed true at an age so near to the origin of the race (or its restoration after the flood), that its foundation must have been in the truths which were either observed by man, or supernaturally communicated to him at the time of his creation.

156. The fundamental doctrines and institutions of Christianity are not to be held as mere opinions, with regard to which men may innocently differ, and be entitled in their diversities to that consideration and respect to which they are entitled in matters of mere indifference or uncertainty. For otherwise no persons could be allowed to affirm the truth with that confidence and certainty which its proper influence requires. It follows, moreover, from the wisdom and justice of God, that the evidence of the truth of those doctrines and institutions is

such that they cannot be innocently rejected. If God is infinitely wise he knew what was sufficient evidence, and if He is just He would never require belief and obedience without giving such evidence as would throw the guilt of unbelief upon the unbeliever. And in all other cases, in all departments of thought, we hold to certain fundamental principles with regard to which we allow of no differences of opinion, which we acknowledge to be entitled to respect. In Geometry, in Astronomy, in Mechanics, every where in fact, we expect the assent of all intelligent and well-disposed men to certain fundamental principles. We do not treat the man who pretends to science, and yet denies that the earth revolves on its axis around the sun, instead of the sun's moving around the earth as entitled to argument. We regard him as either a fool or a madman. In like manner the Articles of Faith contained in the Apostles' Creed, the Ministry, the Worship, and the Sacraments of the Church, have been held in all ages of the Church as too fundamental in their character, and too fully and obviously revealed in the Scriptures, to be properly regarded as mere subjects of opinion and preference, in regard to which unbelief could be innocent or properlv entitled to favor.

§ 7. *Abstract of* LESLIE'S *Short and Easy Method.*

"What you ask and I undertake to accomplish, is to furnish some one topic of reason which shall demonstrate the truth of the Christian Religion, and at the same time distinguish it from the impostures of Mahomet and whole pagan world."

"If the *matters of fact* which are recorded in the Gospels be true, the truth of *doctrine* of CHRIST will be sufficiently evinced; for if His miracles be true they do vouch the truth of what He delivered."

"The same is to be said as to Moses and the Old Testament."

I shall then *first* lay down such rules as to the truth of matters of fact in general, that where they all meet, such matters of fact cannot be false. And then, *secondly*, I shall show that all these rules do meet in the matters of fact of Moses and of Christ; and that they do not meet in the matters of fact of Mahomet and the Heathen deities, nor can possibly meet in any imposture whatever.

I. The Rules are:

1st. That the matters of fact be such as that men's outward senses, their eyes and ears may be judges of it.

2d. That it be done publicly in the face of the world.

3d. That not only public monuments be kept up in memory of it, but some outward actions to be performed.

4th. That such monuments, and such actions or observances be instituted, and do commence from the time that the matter of fact was done.

The two first rules make it impossible for any such matter of fact to be imposed upon men at the time when such matter of fact was said to be done.

The only alternative, therefore, is that such matter of fact might be invented some time after.

But against this the two last rules (3d and 4th) secure us, as much as the two first rules in the former case.

II. The matters of fact of Moses and of Christ have all these rules or marks before mentioned, and that neither the matters of fact of Mahomet, nor what is reported of the Heathen deities have the like, and that no imposture can have them all.

As to Moses. He persuaded the Israelites that he had brought 600,000 of them from Egypt and through the Red Sea, that he fed them forty years without bread by a miraculous manna. But he could not have persuaded them of these facts if they had not been true, since every man's senses that were then alive must have contradicted it. So that here are the *first* and *second* of the above-mentioned four marks.

For the same reason it would have been impossible for him to persuade them to receive his five Books (the Pentateuch) as truth, unless they were so; since in those books he constantly appeals to them as eye and ear witnesses of those things.

The utmost that we can suppose then is, that these Books were written in some age after Moses and put out in his name.

But in that case it is impossible that the Books should have been received, for they speak of themselves as delivered by Moses, and kept in the Ark from his time, and likewise a copy with the King.

Now in whatever age we may suppose the imposture to have been attempted, it was impossible that it should be received as truth, since no such copy would have been in existence in the Ark or in the King's possession, as the Book itself claims.

But besides this the Book speaks of laws and ordinances, and of the time and circumstances of their origin, and claims that they had been observed from the time of their origin, as of the Passover, the institution of the Levites, the budding of Aaron's rod, which was still kept in the Ark, the pot of manna, the brazen serpent, and the Feast of Pentecost. Then there was also the Sabbath, the daily sacrifices, the yearly expiation, the new moons, and other monthly, weekly, and daily remembrances and recognitions of these things. Here then the *third* and *fourth* marks mentioned above are found.

But suppose that these things had been practised before the Books of Moses were forged; that these Books imposed upon the people only in making them believe that they had kept these observances in memory of what had never occurred.

Now this supposes that the Jews kept these observances either in memory of nothing, or without knowing what they commemorated.

But the observances themselves express the ground and reason of their being kept.

Again, suppose the Jews did not know any reason why they kept these observances, and that they were persuaded that they had been keeping them as observances of that of which they had never heard before.

Does any Deist think it possible that such a cheat could pass?

Secondly, all these four marks do meet in the matters of fact which are recorded in the Gospel, of our Saviour. For the *two* first: the miracle of feeding three thousand at one time; five thousand were converted at one time by what they had seen—miracles that were done publicly and before their own eyes. Then for the *two last:* Baptism, the Lord's Supper, were instituted as memorials of what was then done; and the institution of the Ministry, which has continued by a regular succession to this day, in all which respects the matters of fact of the Gospel narrative as completely fulfil the four rules as those that are related of Moses.

III. The matters of fact of Mahomet and the fabled deities, do all want these four marks.

First, Mahomet did not claim in his day to have performed any miracles.

Secondly, those that are told of him want the first two rules; they were not performed in the presence of any one, and we have only his word for them.

The same is to be said of the fables of the Heathen gods.

It is true that the Heathen deities had their priests. They had also feasts and games, and other institutions in memory of them. But all these want the fourth mark, they were not instituted at the time of the occurrence of the events which they claim to commemorate; and their priests were not appointed by the gods, but only by others in honor of them. And therefore these orders of priests are no evidence to the truth of the matters of fact which are reported of their gods.

IV. Now to apply what has been said. You may challenge all the Deists in the world to show any action that is fabulous, which has all the four rules or marks before mentioned. No, it is impossible. And (to resume a little what has been spoken of before) the histories of Exodus, and the Gospel, never could have been received, if they had not been true; because the institution of the Priesthood of Levi, and of CHRIST; of the Sabbath, of the Passover, and of Circumcision; of Baptism, and of the Lord's Supper, &c., are there related as descending all the way down from those times, without interruption. And it is full as impossible to persuade men that they had been circumcised or baptized—had circumcised or baptized their children—had celebrated passovers, sabbaths, sacraments, &c., under the government and administration of a certain order of priests, if they had done none of these things, as to make them believe that they had gone through seas upon dry land, seen the dead raised, &c. And without believing these, it was impossible that either the Law or the Gospel could have been received.

§ 8. *Mr.* WEBSTER'S *Argument in the Girard Will Case.*

This Will devises a certain sum of money to be appropriated to the erection and support of a College (10).*

The first question is whether this devise can be sustained

* These numbers in parentheses refer to the page in the printed speech, from which the statements preceding them are taken.

otherwise than as a charity. If the devise be a good limitation at law, if it require no exercise of the favor which is bestowed upon privileged testaments, there is already an end to the question—this point is conceded.

The devise is void according to the general rules of law, on account of its not mentioning the persons to whom the bequest is made.

The bequest must stand then, if it stand at all, on the peculiar rules which equitable jurisprudence applies to charities.

But I maintain that neither by judicial decisions, nor by correct reasoning on general principles, can this devise or bequest be regarded as a charity; (11) because,

It is derogatory to the Christian Religion.

It tends to weaken men's reverence for that Religion, and their conviction of its authority and importance; and, therefore, it tends in its general character to mischievous and not to useful ends.

The College is founded to promote infidelity, and a gift or devise for such objects is not a charity (12).

The object of this bequest is against the public policy of the State; therefore the devise ought not to be allowed to take effect.

These are the two propositions which it is my purpose to maintain on this part of the case (12).

> The Will excludes all Ministers of the Gospel from the College (13).
>
> There is no Christian charity that excludes the Ministry (16).
>
> It has so been understood from the time of Constantine down to our own (16).
>
> The opening counsel admitted that there is no charity without Christianity (19), and I maintain that wherever the authority of God is disowned, the duties of Christianity derided, and its Ministers shut out, there can be no charity (19, 20).

He who rejects the ordinary means of accomplishing an end means to defeat that end itself, or else he has no meaning; this is true even if the means be but of human appointment, although the end rested on divine authority. But if the means be of divine authority also, then the rejection of them is direct rejection of that authority (30).

But nothing is more certain in Christianity, than that the Author of the Christian Religion Himself did appoint a Christian Ministry.

He who does not believe this cannot believe the rest (31).

This Ministry have continued to our day, and gone over the whole world performing their work. Nowhere has any part of the globe been Christianized without the Ministry. It is therefore idle mockery to pretend that that man has any respect for the Christian Religion who derides and rejects its Ministers (32).

In the next place this scheme of education is derogatory to Christianity, because it proceeds upon the presumption that Christianity is not the only true foundation, or any necessary foundation of morals.

So the world has not thought.

The Word of God declares otherwise in the Decalogue (34).

Christ taught otherwise (35).

Reason and human nature teach otherwise (35, 36).

Again, the Will excludes the observance of the Christian Sabbath.

But the Christian Sabbath is a part of Christianity. This is admitted by all Christians (37), and the Will excludes the means for observing the Sabbath (37, 38).

And where the Christian Sabbath is not observed, there is no public worship of God.

But the reasons assigned for the exclusion of Christianity from the College, are still more derogatory to Christianity.

They are that the evils resulting from the diversity of opinions and sects, is greater than the good which Christianity itself produces; whence he infers that we should cut up Christianity by the roots (42).

But this mode of reasoning, if it were allowed, would destroy men's social relations and all human institutions (46, 47).

But there is a settled policy of the State of Pennsylvania; this is not denied; and Christianity is a part of that policy.

Any school or system of education which is contrary to that policy, cannot be sustained by the State (65).

The Courts of Pennsylvania have declared that a charitable

bequest which counteracts the public policy of the State cannot be sustained (67). [The case of Methodist Church *vs.* Remington and the 8th of Johnson, p. 291.]

§ 9. *Mr.* DANA'S *Argument in the Ellsworth School Case.*

This was a suit brought by Laurence and Bridget Donahoe against Richards and others, Superintending Committee of Schools, claiming damages of the Committee for having excluded the Plaintiffs from the benefit of the common schools, by making the reading of the Bible, in the common English Version, obligatory upon all the pupils. The Plaintiffs being Roman Catholics could not comply, on grounds of conscientious scruples.

This is a novel suit; there is no one like it in the Reports.

The general principle of law is, "that a public officer exercising a discretion, judicial in its character, cast upon him by the law, is not liable to private actions for damages, unless he acts in bad faith or from malice."

But in this case it is not pretended that there was malice or bad faith (6).

By the constitution and laws of Maine it is the duty of the Committee, "to direct the general course of instruction, and what books shall be used in the respective schools." In the exercise of this authority, the Committee continued the use of the Bible in the common English Version (7).

By authority of the State also they have power to expel from any school, any pupils who shall not comply with the regulations which they have made (7).

Now the point whether the Defendants in this suit are liable has never been decided.

But in the case of Wheeler *vs.* Patterson, 1 N. H. 88, it was decided that Selectmen of a town, were not liable for refusing a man his privilege of voting, even though they were wrong in their act, "so long as their motives are pure and untainted with fraud and malice."

In the case of Griffin *vs.* Rising, 11 Met. 339, it was held that Assessors were not liable for refusing to tax a man, although he lost his vote thereby, on the ground that they "are exempted from liability for damages when acting with integrity."

In Allen *vs.* Blunt, 3 Story 141, it was held that, "where a particular duty is confided to a public officer, to be exercised by him at his discretion, upon an examination of facts, of which he is made the appropriate judge, his decision is conclusive."

In 7 Howard 89, and 12 Howard 390, it was held that the commander of a ship was not responsible for the punishment of a marine, though he were innocent, so long as he did it not from malice, and that he was not responsible for error of law, or in his judgment of facts if he acted in good faith.

All these cases are analogous to the one before the Court. The only exception is the case of Lincoln *vs.* Hapgood. This decision, however, has been overruled.

But not only are the defendants not liable for damages in this suit. The continuance of the use of the Bible is a reasonable exercise of their discretionary power.

It has always been used in the schools of Maine.

The Defendants are obliged by law to see that the principles of morality and all the virtues shall be taught in the schools. But how can principles of morality be taught except on the basis of religion? A system of morality not founded on religion is not morality, but only a system of self-interest.

The objection however is not, they say, to the Bible, but to our English Version of it.

But "great portions of the translation were made by men in the bosom of the General Church before the Reformation." Testimony to its accuracy has been borne by learned men of the Roman Church.

As a fountain of pure idiomatic English it has no equal in the world. From it we derive our household words. Hence as a preparation for life, an acquaintance with the common English Bible is indispensable, while the Romish Version is un-English.

But the effect of this objection is to exclude the Bible altogether. Each denomination has a translation, or at least prejudices and peculiar views of its own. If one is to insist on his version, others will; and all will be excluded. The question, therefore, is whether the Bible shall be read at all or not.

It only remains to consider the constitutional objections against the law under which the Committee acted.

The power to regulate schools and determine what studies shall be pursued, and what books read, must be lodged somewhere. The Constitution of Maine gives the Legislature power "to make and establish all reasonable laws and regulations for the defence and benefit of the people, not repugnant to the Constitution of Maine, or to that of the United States." And if this power to select books, and suspend or refuse children for disobedience, were not expressly given in the Constitution, it would be implied in the necessity of the case (Sherman *vs.* Charlestown, 8 Cush. 161; and Spear *vs.* Cummings, 22 Pick. 223).

It is said that the schools are public, and that all resident tax-payers have a vested right in them.

But this right must be enjoyed subject to restrictions and limitations, necessary for the good and rights of others. This does not subject one denomination to another, but the choice of a few to the good of the many.

The only constitutional question worthy of attention, is that which arises from the clause which declares that "no one shall be hurt, molested, or restrained in his person, liberty, or estate for his religious opinions."

This clause was intended to guard against persecution, directed against person or property. But there is no such persecution in this case; whatever inconvenience may have been suffered, is the incidental and indirect consequence of the opinions which the Plaintiffs choose to hold.

But if they were "hurt or molested," in the sense of the Constitution, still the act of the Committee is not unconstitutional.

It is a constitutional provision, for instance, that no man's property shall be taken for public uses without compensation. And yet the Legislature has full power to regulate the manner in which men shall use and enjoy their property, so as to preserve the rights of the public. In this exercise of legislative power, a man's property may sometimes be much diminished, or even destroyed, and he have no remedy.

In the Warren Bridge case it was established that the State may impair or destroy the value of an existing franchise for the public good, and that no compensation need be made, if it be not confiscated or abolished. The daily making of highways, railroads, and canals for the public good, is constantly impairing the value of some private property, and in some cases totally destroying it, and yet no compensation is made.

In the case of Tewksbury it was held (11 Met. 55) that the State might prohibit Mr. T. from taking sand from his own beach. So in Alger's case (7 Cush. 53), burials in cities may be prohibited without compensating the owners of vaults for their loss, however costly or valuable they may have become. The Sunday laws also are held to be constitutional, although the Jews, by reason of their religious profession, lose one sixth of their working life, and are "hurt and restrained in their liberty and estate," and put to an inequality with Christians.

The Constitution prohibits religious tests as qualifications to office. Yet all judicial officers are required to administer oaths, although the Quakers regard the taking of oaths as unlawful.

Hence we must conclude that the power of the Committee is not rendered unconstitutional, by the mere fact that it incidentally operates to the disadvantage of an individual who, by his opinions or preferences, has put himself in opposition to the laws of the land and the acts of its legitimate authorities.

INDEX

OF SUBJECTS AND OF THE TECHNICAL TERMS OCCURRING IN THE WORK.

THE END.

FIRST LESSONS IN ENGLISH COMPOSITION.

BY G. P. QUACKENBOS, A. M.

12mo. Price 45 Cents

These "First Lessons" are intended for beginners in Grammar and Composition, and should be placed in their hands at whatever age it may be deemed best for them to commence these branches—say from nine to twelve years. In the first fifty pages, by means of lessons on the inductive system, and copious exercises under each, the pupil is made familiar with the nature and *use* of the different parts of speech, so as to be able to recognize them at once. He is then led to consider the different kinds of clauses and sentences, and is thus prepared for Punctuation, on which subject he is furnished with well considered rules, arranged on a new and simple plan. Directions for the use of capital letters follow. Next come rules, explanations and examples, for the purpose of enabling the pupil to form and spell correctly such derivative words as *having*, *debarring*, *pinning*, and the like, which are not to be found in ordinary dictionaries, and regarding which the pupil is apt to be led astray by the fact that a change is made in the primitive word before the addition of the suffix. This done, the scholar is prepared to express thoughts in his own language, and is now required to write sentences of every kind, a word being given to suggest an idea for each; he is taught to vary them by means of different arrangements and modes of expression; to analyze compound sentences into simple ones, and to combine simple ones into compound. Several lessons are then devoted to Style. The essential properties, purity, propriety, precision, clearness, strength, harmony, and unity, are next treated, examples for correction being presented under each. The different kinds of composition follow; and, specimens having been first given, the pupil is required to compose successively letters, descriptions, narrations, biographical sketches, essays, and argumentative discourses. After this, the principal figures receive attention; and the work closes with a list of subjects carefully selected, arranged under their proper heads, and in such a way that the increase in difficulty is very gradual. The work has received the universal approval of Teachers and the Press throughout the Union.

QUACKENBOS'

ADVANCED LESSONS IN COMPOSITION AND RHETORIC.

(NEARLY READY.)

A DIGEST OF ENGLISH GRAMMAR.

BY L. T. COVELL.

12mo. Price 50 Cents.

This work, which is just published, is designed as a Text-Book for the use of Schools and Academies; it is the result of long experience, of an eminently successful Teacher, and will be found to possess many peculiar merits.

At a regular meeting of the Board of Education of Rochester, held June 13, 1853, the following resolution was unanimously adopted:

"*Resolved*, That Covell's Digest of English Grammar be substituted for Wells' Grammar, as a Text-Book in the public schools of this city, to take effect at the commencement of the next school year."

Extract from the Minutes of a Regular Meeting of the Board of Education of Troy, May 31st, 1853.

"Mr. Jones, from Committee on text-books, and school librarias, moved, that Bullion's English Grammar be stricken from the list of text-books, and Covell's be substituted.—Passed."

From forty-four Teachers of Public Schools, Pittsburg, Pa.

"The undersigned have examined 'Covell's Digest of English Grammar,' and are of opinion that in the justness of its general views, the excellence of its style, the brevity, accuracy, and perspicuity of its definitions and rules, the numerous examples and illustrations, the adaption of its synthetical exercises, the simplicity of its method of analysis, and in the plan of its arrangement, this work surpasses any other grammar now before the public; and that in all respects it is most admirably adapted to the use of schools and academies."

From all the Teachers of Public Schools of the City of Alleghany, Pa.

"We, the undersigned, Teachers of Alleghany city, having carefully examined Mr. Covell's Digest of English Grammar,' and impartially compared it with other grammars now in use, are fully satisfied that, while it is in no respect inferior to others, it is in very many respects much superior. While it possesses all that is necessary for the advanced student, and much that is not found in other grammars, it is so simplified as to adapt it to the capacity of the youngest learner. We are confident that much time and labor will be saved, and greater improvement secured to our pupils in the study of this science, by its introduction into our schools; hence we earnestly recommend to the Boards of Directors of this city, its adoption as a uniform text-book upon this science in the schools under their direction."

From JOHN J. WOLCOTT, A. M., *Pr. and Supt. 9th Ward School, Pittsburg, Pa.*

"'Covell's Digest of English Grammar' not only evinces the most unceasing labor, the most extensive research, the most unrelaxing effort, and the most devoted self-sacrificing study of its author, but it is the most complete, the most perfect, and, to me, the most satisfactory exposition of English Grammar that has come to my notice. It appears to me that every youth aspiring to become master of the English language, from the rudimental principles to the full, round, beautiful, faultless, perfect period, will make this volume his 'vade mecum.'"

EXPOSITION OF THE GRAMMATICAL STRUCTURE OF THE ENGLISH LANGUAGE.

BY JOHN MULLIGAN, A M.

Large 12mo. 574 pages. $1 50

This work is a comprehensive and complete system o English Grammar, embracing not only all that has been developed by the later philologists, but also the results of years of study and research on the part of its author. One great advantage of this book is its admirable arrangement. Instead of proceeding at once to the dry details which are distasteful and discouraging to the pupil, Mr. M. commences by viewing the sentence as a whole, analyzing it into its proper parts, and exhibiting their connection; and, after having thus parsed the sentence logically, proceeds to consider the individual words that compose it, in all their grammatical relations. This is the natural order; and experience proves that the arrangement here followed not only imparts additional interest to the subject, but gives the pupil a much clearer insight into it, and greatly facilitates his progress.

From DR. JAMES W. ALEXANDER.

"I thank you for the opportunity of perusing your work on the structure of the English language. It strikes me as being one of the most valuable contributions to this important branch of literature. The mode of investigation is so unlike what appears in our ordinary compilations, the reasoning is so sound, and the results are so satisfactory and so conformable to the genius and great authorities of our mother tongue, that I propose to recur to it again and again."

Extract from a letter from E. C. BENEDICT, Esq., *President of the Board of Education of the City of New York.*

"I have often thought our language needed some work in which the principles of grammatical science and of the structure of the language, philosophically considered, were developed and applied to influence and control the *usus* and *consuedo* of Horace and Quintilian, which seem to me to have been too often the principal source of solecisms, irregularity and corruption. In this point of view, I consider your work a valuable and appropriate addition to the works on the language."

From WM. HORACE WEBSTER, *President of the Free Academy, New York.*

"The exposition of the grammatical structure of the English language by Professor Mulligan, of this city, is a work, in my opinion, of great merit, and well calculated to impart a thorough and critical knowledge of the grammar of the English language.

"No earnest English student can fail to profit by the study of this treatise, yet it is designed more particulary for minds somewhat maturer, and for pupils who are capable and have a desire, to comprehend the principles and learn the philosophy of their own tongue."

DICTIONARY OF THE ENGLISH LANGUAGE

BY ALEXANDER REID, A. M.

12mo. 572 pages. Price $1 00.

This work, which is designed for schools, contains the PRONUNCIATION and Explanation of all English words authorized by eminent writers.

A Vocabulary of the roots of English words.

An Accented List of GREEK, LATIN, and SCRIPTURE proper names.

An Appendix, showing the pronunciation of nearly 3,000 of the most important GEOGRAPHICAL names.

It is printed on fine paper, in clear type, strongly bound.

And is unquestionably one of the best dictionaries for the school-room extant.

From C. S. HENRY, *Professor of Philosophy, History, and Belles-Lettres, in the University of the City of New York.*

"Reid's Dictionary of the English Language is an admirable book for the use of schools. Its plan combines a greater number of desirable conditions for such a work, than any with which I am acquainted; and it seems to me to be executed in general with great judgment, fidelity, and accuracy."

From HENRY REED, *Professor of English Literature in the University of Pennsylvania.*

"Reid's Dictionary of the English Language appears to have been compiled upon sound principles, and with judgment and accuracy. It has the merit, too, of combining much more than is usually looked for in dictionaries of small size, and will, I believe, be found excellent as a convenient manual for general reference, and also for various purposes of education."

GRAHAM'S ENGLISH SYNONYMS,

CLASSIFIED AND EXPLAINED;

WITH PRACTICAL EXERCISES. DESIGNED FOR SCHOOLS AND PRIVATE TUITION WITH AN INTRODUCTION AND ILLUSTRATIVE AUTHORITIES.

BY HENRY REED, LL. D.

1 Vol. 12mo. Price $1 00.

This is one of the best books published in the department of language, and will do much to arrest the evil of making too common use of inappropriate words. The work is well arranged for classes, and can be made a branch of common school study.

It is admirably arranged. The Synonyms are treated with reference to their character, as generic and specific; as active and passive; as positive and negative; and as miscellaneous synonyms.

HAND-BOOK OF THE ENGLISH LANGUAGE

BY G. R. LATHAM, M. D., F. R. S.

12mo. 400 pages. Price $1 25.

This work is designed for the use of students in the University and High Schools.

"His work is rigidly scientific, and hence possesses a rare value. With the wide-spreading growth of the Anglo-Saxon dialect, the immense present and prospective power of those with whom this is their 'mother tongue,' such a treatise must be counted alike interesting and useful."—*Watchman and Reflector.*

"A work of great research, much learning, and to every thinking scholar it will be a book of study. The Germanic origin of the English language, the affinities of the Eng lish with other languages, a sketch of the alphabet, a minute investigation of the etymology of the language, &c., of great value to every philologist."—*Observer.*

HISTORY OF ENGLISH LITERATURE.

BY WILLIAM SPALDING, A. M.

PROFESSOR OF LOGIC, RHETORIC, AND METAPHYSICS, IN THE UNIVERSITY OF ST. ANDREWS

12mo. 413 pages. Price $1 00.

The above work, which is just published, is offered as a Text-book for the use of advanced Schools and Academies. It traces the literary progress of the nation from its dawn in Anglo-Saxon times, down to the present day. Commencing at this early period, it is so constructed as to introduce the reader gradually and easily to studies of this kind. Comparatively little speculation is presented, and those literary monuments of the earlier dates, which were thought most worthy of attention, are described with considerable fulness and in an attractive manner. In the subsequent pages, more frequent and sustained efforts are made to arouse reflection, both by occasional remarks on the relations between intellectual culture and the other elements of society, and by hints as to the theoretical laws on which criticism should be founded. The characteristics of the most celebrated modern works are analyzed at considerable length.

The manner of the author is remarkably plain and interesting, almost compelling the reader to linger over his pages with unwearied attention.